Tanakh, New Testament, Manuscripts & The Israelites:

A Hebraic and Diasporic Critique of Canon Formation and Textual Theology

Elohim Edition 2025

Copyright Page – Elohim Edition

Publisher: Mickle Publishers (Dallas, Texas, USA)
ISBN: 978-0-9709977-7-7

Library of Congress Cataloging-in-Publication Data:
Mickel,Tovi.
Tanakh, New Testament, Manuscripts & The Israelites: Elohim Edition — A Hebraic and Diasporic Critique of Canon Formation and Textual Theology.
— First Digital / Author Edition.

Printed in the United States of America
Cover design and interior layout by Mickle Publishers

Edition   Statement:
• *ABD Academic Edition* — 70,169 words; Chapters א–ת and Appendices A–R, under review with a leading Taylor & Francis academic journal in African and Black Diaspora studies.
• *Elohim Edition* — 90,043 words; Full author edition (Ch. א–ת + Appendices A–V and Addenda I–IV & X), published under Mickle Publishers, Dallas.
• *Academic Press Edition (Forthcoming)* — Proposed for review under the Society of Biblical Literature's *Text-Critical Studies* series.

Awards   &   Recognition:
Shortlisted for the *Society of Biblical Literature Bernadette J. Brooten Award* (2025) for excellence in

gender and feminist theology—specifically Chapters 7 and 17 and Appendix P. In consideration for the *2026 BCALA Literary Award* and *Grawemeyer Award in Religion.*

Research Integrity Statement: This work engages over 500 scholarly citations drawn from 180+ academic sources (Brill, Oxford, Harvard, Fortress, Eerdmans, SUNY Press, and others). It reflects the author's independent academic research and the editorial standards of Mickle Publishers.

Rights & Licensing: The author retains full copyright and digital distribution rights for all editions and formats. Non-exclusive print licensing may be extended to SBL Press or other publishers for academic circulation.

Contact: micklepublishing@hotmail.com | https://patreon.com/cw /ToviMickel

Table of Content

Preface: Scope, Method, Memory, and Manuscript

"To restore sacred memory is not nostalgia—it is resistance. It is prophecy. It is covenant made visible again."

This monograph is not written from within the citadels of seminary or denominational allegiance. It is forged from years of interdisciplinary study and spiritual exile—driven by an urgent imperative to reclaim what empire, theology, and translation have fragmented: the Hebraic integrity of sacred scripture.

Where many studies of canon formation prioritize chronology, redaction, and textual divergence, this work centers the spiritual rupture caused by dislocating scripture from its original linguistic and covenantal soil. Canon is not approached here as editorial history—it is a battleground of sacred memory, a terrain scarred by theological conquest and cultural erasure. Scripture is more than text; it is testimony, treaty, and typology. When severed from its native tongue and ancestral rhythm, it ceases to function prophetically.

This book asserts that to recover covenantal memory, we must restore the linguistic and cultural integrity of the canon itself. That restoration cannot occur within the walls of Greco-Roman epistemology. It must arise from within the lexicon of Sinai, the exile of Deuteronomy, and the scroll of Ezekiel. Only by re-rooting the canon in its Hebraic soil can we hope to recover its prophetic cadence and theological clarity.

Methodological Approach

This work synthesizes five core disciplines, not as parallel tracks, but as braided cords of a prophetic methodology:

Textual criticism, following the rigorous comparative work of Tov, Ulrich, and Cross, engaging Masoretic Text (MT), Dead Sea Scrolls (DSS), Septuagint (LXX), and New

Testament (NT) manuscript variants to illuminate intentional and imperial redactions.

Hebrew linguistics, with a deep focus on shoresh-based theology and verbal morphology, including stems like Hitpael, Niphal, and Hiphil. These linguistic forms encode theological movements such as causation, reflexivity, and passive submission—which are often flattened or erased in translation.

Canon history, interrogating the witnesses of Josephus, the Babylonian Talmud, Epiphanius, Jerome, and early Church councils to map the reshaping of the canon under ecclesiastical power.

Postcolonial and feminist theology, drawing from Musa Dube, Kwame Bediako, Letty Russell, R.S. Sugirtharajah, and Traci West to dismantle colonial frameworks, especially in relation to translation and exclusion of prophetic female agency.

Diasporic anthropology, employing cultural memory theory (Assmann, Connerton, Mbiti) to trace the preservation of Hebraic identity through exile, enslavement, and colonial suppression—with special attention to the Lemba, Igbo, Akan, and diasporic African communities who maintained linguistic and ritual fragments of Israelite legacy.

This is not simply intertextual criticism. It is covenantal reassembly. It is a reconstruction project, guided by a methodology that sees language as law, root as revelation, and memory as theological insurgency.

The monograph's 22 chapters correspond to the Hebrew Aleph-Bet, not as artistic flourish, but as theological scaffolding. Each chapter is a gate of memory, each letter a doorway into canonical order. Form is theology. Letter is covenant.

Interpretive Framework

This manuscript is restorative in posture, not revisionist in motive. It does not seek to rewrite scripture—it seeks to remove the colonial overlays that have muted its prophetic voice. It does not engage supersessionism—it rebukes it.

Where others begin with the Church Fathers, this work begins with Moses, Miriam, and Ezekiel. It engages not merely the aftermath of canonization, but its primal structure. The foundation is the Hebrew root (שרש), not the Greek Logos. Revelation is not simply what God says—it is how He says it, in the cadence and code of Hebrew.

Prophets did not whisper. They roared. They named false altars, shattered idols, and realigned nations. This work continues that tradition. It is unapologetically prophetic, diasporic, Semitic, and anti-imperial. It does not speak for Judaism, but it speaks from within Israelite memory—exilic, dispersed, and awaiting return.

Rather than merely citing previous scholarship, this work excavates prophetic substrata beneath academic sediment. It acknowledges rabbinic brilliance and Islamic reverence, yet exposes distortions borne from imperial consolidation. It engages scholars not as authorities, but as witnesses. Scripture, not the academy, is the final arbiter.

Authorial Context

This work was not birthed in a tenured office but in the crucible of lived exile. Over a decade of deep textual immersion, private manuscript study, traditional Hebrew instruction, and Afro-Semitic research undergird every page. It was not funded by grant or guided by department. It was cultivated in prophetic solitude.

The author is a survivor of erasure—both academic and ancestral. A student of Rosh Moreh Avdiel Ben Levi and a mentor within grassroots Hebraic restoration communities, he writes from the underside of empire. This is not scholarship for applause. It is testimony from the remnant.

Intended Audience

This manuscript speaks to:

Scholars of Hebrew Bible, Dead Sea Scrolls, and Second Temple canon formation

Students and teachers of postcolonial theology and Afro-Hebraic anthropology

Clergy, faith-based educators, and seminary instructors

Diasporic communities seeking scriptural restoration

Canon critics seeking non-Western frameworks

Scholarly Contribution

This monograph contributes:

A canonical structure based on the 22-letter Aleph-Bet, recovering Josephus' reference and affirming early Jewish textual alignment

A linguistic model that restores the theological meaning of Hebrew roots and verb stems erased through translation

A prophetic re-reading of exile, canon, and identity within a diasporic African context

New insight into Leviticus 24:10, Esther 8:17, Deuteronomy 28:68, and other under-explored verses central to identity formation

A challenge to both Euro-Christian and Western Jewish narratives that marginalize African Hebraic continuity

This is not merely textual theology. It is textual insurgency—an uprising of root, rhythm, and remembrance.

To open this scroll is to remember. To remember is to return. To return is to restore the covenant.

And to restore the covenant is to make prophecy visible again.

Scope and Methodology

This monograph explores the textual, linguistic, and theological architecture of the Tanakh and its reception across Second Temple Judaism and early Christianity. It does so through a multidisciplinary framework anchored in textual criticism, Hebrew linguistics, manuscript studies, and postcolonial theology.

The methodology incorporates comparative analysis between major textual witnesses: the Masoretic Text (MT), Septuagint (LXX), Dead Sea Scrolls (DSS), and early Christian codices. The goal is to trace not only textual divergence, but theological distortion through translation and redaction.

Central to this analysis is the role of Hebrew morphology—specifically, the shoresh (root) structure, binyanim (verb stems), and syntax—as a theological medium. Unlike approaches that treat biblical Hebrew as incidental to exegesis, this work maintains that linguistic structures encode prophetic memory and covenantal continuity.

The interpretive lens employed is both postcolonial and Afro-diasporic. Scholars such as Musa Dube, Delores S. Williams, Kwok Pui-lan, and R.S. Sugirtharajah inform this approach by highlighting the political and theological implications of canon formation.

Dube describes the Bible as a colonial document in need of decolonizing lenses. Pui-lan critiques Western theological binaries and emphasizes reconstructive reading practices. Williams' survival theology reframes Black women's experience within biblical narratives, while Sugirtharajah's theory of ideological canonization exposes the socio-political undercurrents beneath early church formation.

This work seeks not to deconstruct faith, but to reconstruct its textual foundation in the original sacred tongue. It posits that the divine voice, when filtered through the imperial grammars of Rome and Greece, suffered displacement—requiring not only scholarly correction but covenantal reclamation.

Therefore, this monograph integrates academic tools and prophetic intuition, with the aim of restoring not only what was written, but what was meant. The reader is invited to engage critically and reverently with a sacred architecture that is as much about covenant as it is about canon.

1. **Afro-Diasporic Identity and Memory: The work contends that dispersed African and Indigenous communities preserve linguistic, ethical, and liturgical fragments of Israelite tradition. This reclamation offers a new lens for understanding both prophetic continuity and covenantal inheritance in the diaspora. Drawing upon John Mbiti's theory of communal ontology (*African Religions and Philosophy*) and Assmann's model of cultural memory, the epistemological foundation of Afro-Hebraic identity is established as more than socio-ethnic, but covenantally encoded.** [John Mbiti, *African Religions and Philosophy*, 2nd ed. (Oxford: Heinemann, 1991).]

2. **Postcolonial and Prophetic Critique: Drawing upon theological resistance traditions, the project critiques the colonial mechanisms of canon control, Christological reinterpretation, and liturgical reformation. Rome, Christendom, and modern Protestantism are interrogated as agents of theological deviation and textual doctrinal displacement under Greco-Roman recontextualization. The recontextualization of Torah by New Testament figures—especially Paul—is presented not polemically but through Hellenistic midrashic filters (e.g., *gezerah shavah, binyan av*), informed by E.P. Sanders and Paula**

Fredriksen. [Paula Fredriksen, *Paul: The Pagans' Apostle* (New Haven: Yale University Press, 2017).]

Methodology

The methodology integrates:

- **Textual Criticism: Grounded in the principles established by Emanuel Tov, Eugene Ulrich, and Frank Moore Cross, including variant collation, scribal habit analysis, and manuscript stemmatics.** [Emanuel Tov, *Textual Criticism of the Hebrew Bible*, 3rd ed. (Minneapolis: Fortress Press, 2012), 135.]

- **Historical-Critical and Canonical Frameworks: Utilizing works by Bruce Metzger and Lee Martin McDonald on canonization, alongside patristic witnesses (Jerome, Epiphanius, Origen) to trace early authoritative lists.** [Bruce M. Metzger, *The Text of the New Testament: Its Transmission, Corruption, and Restoration*, 4th ed. (Oxford: Oxford University Press, 2005), 45–47.] [Jerome, *Prologus Galeatus*, in *Biblia Sacra Vulgata*, ed. Robert Weber (Stuttgart: Deutsche Bibelgesellschaft, 1994).] [Epiphanius, *Panarion*, trans. Frank Williams (Leiden: Brill, 1987).]

- **Semitic Linguistic Tools: Based on classical grammars (Gesenius, BDB, Jouon-Muraoka), rabbinic etymological traditions (Hirsch), and comparative Semitic morphology.**

- **Midrashic and Rabbinic Hermeneutics: Employing interpretive strategies such as** *gezerah shavah*, *binyan av*, **and the** *PARDES* **framework to understand apostolic and prophetic scripture usage.**

- **Postcolonial Theology and Diaspora Studies: Anchored in the work of John Mbiti, Tudor Parfitt, and Black liberation hermeneutics, with emphasis on spiritual memory as a conduit of historical fidelity.** [John Mbiti, *African Religions and Philosophy*, 2nd ed. (Oxford: Heinemann, 1991).]

- This work also draws on the womanist hermeneutics of Dr. Wil Gafney, whose exegesis reclaims overlooked female figures and reimagines their theological agency. Gafney's textual sensitivity in *Womanist Midrash* aligns with the project's intent to restore prophetic identity in sacred text. Gafney, Wilda C. *Womanist Midrash: A Reintroduction to the Women of the Torah and the Throne.* Louisville: Westminster John Knox Press, 2017.

This combined methodology allows for a prophetic restoration of the text—not as a deconstructive exercise, but as a covenantal reclamation. The Hebrew language is treated not merely as a historical artifact but as a vessel of revelation whose integrity bears directly on divine authorship, identity, and eschatological hope.

By foregrounding marginalized voices—female prophets, Afro-diasporic stewards, ancient scribes—this monograph challenges readers to reconsider not only the content of scripture but the processes by which it was transmitted, distorted, and ultimately recovered. SBL transliteration standards are followed throughout, with a pronunciation table and script glossary included for interdisciplinary clarity and academic consistency.

Abstract

This monograph presents an interdisciplinary reassessment of the Hebrew Bible and New Testament through the integrated lenses of Semitic philology, Afro-Hebraic anthropology, feminist exegesis, and historical textual criticism. It argues that both the canonization process and theological transmission of scripture were shaped not only by prophetic and communal reverence but also by scribal intervention, imperial power structures, and linguistic displacement. Drawing upon variant manuscript traditions (Masoretic Text, Dead Sea Scrolls, Septuagint, and early Christian codices), the study reveals how textual pluriformity challenges modern assumptions of scriptural fixity.

Engaging with the Hebrew root system (*shoresh*), grammatical nuances (e.g., cohortatives, tiqqunē sôp̄erîm), and rabbinic hermeneutics (e.g., *gezerah shavah*), the work critiques doctrinal distortions introduced via Greek and Latin translations—particularly within Christological recontextualizations of Torah. The monograph further explores the epistemological role of diasporic memory among Afro-descendant and Indigenous communities as carriers of covenantal continuity, referencing frameworks from John Mbiti and cultural memory theory. [John Mbiti, *African Religions and Philosophy*, 2nd ed. (Oxford: Heinemann, 1991).]

By restoring suppressed voices—female prophets, Hebraic scribes, and diasporic stewards—this work contends that theological truth must be recentered in covenantal fidelity, linguistic precision, and prophetic identity. It offers a model of textual restoration that is not revisionist but redemptive, rooted in the sacred architecture of Lašôn ha-qōḏeš.

Keywords

Tanakh, Textual Criticism, Hebrew Canon, Afro-Hebraic Identity, Septuagint, Lašôn ha-qōḏeš, Pauline Midrash, Diaspora Theology, Canon Formation, Dead Sea Scrolls, Hebrew Linguistics, Prophetic Typology, Torah Hermeneutics, Patristic Theology, Feminist Exegesis, Imperial Theology, Messianic Duality, Qumran Sectarianism, Paleo-Hebrew Script, Greco-Roman Ecclesiology, Rabbinic Authority, Replacement Theology, Sacred Time Cycles, Postcolonial Biblical Criticism

Acknowledgments

This work is the fruit of years lived between exile and revelation — born in prayer and protest, in scrolls and silences, in the tension of forgotten names and the fire of ancestral memory.

First and foremost, I give honor and thanks to יהוה, the Most High — **El Elyon** — who formed speech from silence, breathed life into the letters, and whose covenant remains unbroken across every sea and sorrow. This offering is Yours.

I thank my parents, **Dr. Toby Mickle and Dr. TeRaze Mickle**, whose unwavering faith, scholarship, and love planted Torah in me long before I understood its weight. Your legacy is in every root word, every page, and every breath of this manuscript.

To **Rosh Moreh Avdiel Ben Levi** and **Rosh Moreh Yeshiah Israel** — thank you for your teaching, your boldness, and your clarity in the face of confusion. To **Ron Shields**, for being both a scholar and a soldier in this sacred war of memory and restoration.

To the late **Bishop Carlton Pearson**, whose ministry at Higher Dimensions Church gave me the courage to question, wrestle, and awaken to deeper truths at a young age— may your memory be for a blessing and your voice echo through generations.

To my beloved children — all five of you — as well as my amazing sister --- your names are etched in this work. You are my covenant legacy. Everything I reclaim is so that your inheritance will be whole.

To my family, friends, cousins, and community — those who prayed, corrected, supported, encouraged, and believed — your strength became mine. Thank you for lifting this burden with me.

To my **lovely wife**, sorry it took so long and away from **our time**...

To **Lashon ha-Qodesh**, the holy language itself — thank you for your defiance of translation, your sacred architecture, and your refusal to be conquered. You are the hidden voice that guided this entire journey.

To the scattered of the **African Diaspora**, the **Indigenous remnant**, and all the **children of Israel in exile** — may this work serve as a small torch lighting the path back home.

And finally, to every voice that said, *"Don't hold back. Write it all down."* — I listened. This scroll is for you.

Tanakh, New Testament, Manuscripts & The Israelites: *A Hebraic & Diasporic Critique of Canon Formation & Textual Theology*

Author: Tovi   Mickel
Discipline: Theology | Textual Criticism | Hebraic Anthropology

PART I (א): FORMATION OF SCRIPTURE

The Hebrew Aleph-Bet and the Canonical Structure of Restoration

A literary, linguistic, and prophetic schema underlying the 22 chapters of the monograph

#	Hebrew Letter	Name	Literal Meaning	Chapter Theme	Canon Function
1	א	**Aleph**	Ox, Leader	The Foundation of Canon	Authority and Breath of Revelation
2	ב	**Bet**	House	Domestication of Text	House of God vs. Institutional Control
3	ג	**Gimel**	Camel, Movement	Language, Root, Verb Structure	Carrying Meaning Across Exile
4	ד	**Dalet**	Door	Entry Point of Theology	Threshold Between Worlds
5	ה	**Heh**	Window, Breath	Revelation and Grammar	The Spirit Within the Text

#	Hebrew Letter	Name	Literal Meaning	Chapter Theme	Canon Function
6	ו	**Vav**	Nail, Hook	Intertextuality	Connecting Texts and Traditions
7	ז	**Zayin**	Weapon	Conflict in Transmission	Canon Under Siege
8	ח	**Chet**	Fence	Division and Boundary	Clean vs. Unclean Theology
9	ט	**Tet**	Serpent, Hidden Good	The Hidden Truths	Reversing Distortion
10	י	**Yod**	Hand, Power	God's Sovereignty in Exile	Divine Precision in Grammar
11	כ	**Kaf**	Palm, Blessing	Mercy and Covenant	The Gracious Frame
12	ל	**Lamed**	Staff, Teach	Education Through Exile	Prophetic Instruction
13	מ	**Mem**	Water	Mystery and Chaos	Fluidity of Interpretation
14	נ	**Nun**	Fish, Seed	Generational Memory	Diasporic Continuity

#	Hebrew Letter	Name	Literal Meaning	Chapter Theme	Canon Function
15	ס	**Samekh**	Support	Divine Protection	Hidden Sustainers of the Word
16	ע	**Ayin**	Eye	Perception and Prophecy	Seeing the Text Rightly
17	פ	**Pe**	Mouth	Declaration and Voice	Reclaiming Prophetic Speech
18	צ	**Tsade**	Righteousness	Justice and Restoration	The Moral Core of Scripture
19	ק	**Qof**	Horizon, Monkey	Imitation vs. Authenticity	False Prophets and True Words
20	ר	**Resh**	Head, First	Reordering of Power	Restoring Hebrew Priority
21	ש	**Shin**	Tooth, Flame	Consumption	Purging Corruption from Canon
22	ת	**Tav**	Mark, Covenant	Sealing the Testimony	The Final Sign of Restoration

Proverbs 30:6 אַל־תּוֹסְףְ עַל־דְּבָרָיו פֶּן־יוֹכִיחַ בְּךָ וְנִכְזָבְתָּ׃ {פ}

Do not add to His words,
Lest He indict you and you be proved a liar.

Book Number	Hebrew Title (Tanakh 22)	English Title (Josephus 22)
1	בראשית (Bereshit)	Genesis
2	שמות (Shemot)	Exodus
3	ויקרא (Vayikra)	Leviticus
4	במדבר (Bamidbar)	Numbers
5	דברים (Devarim)	Deuteronomy
6	יהושע (Yehoshua)	Joshua
7	שופטים (Shoftim)	Judges
8	שמואל (Shmuel)	Samuel (1–2)
9	מלכים (Melakhim)	Kings (1–2)
10	ישעיהו (Yeshayahu)	Isaiah
11	ירמיהו (Yirmiyahu)	Jeremiah
12	יחזקאל (Yechezkel)	Ezekiel
13	תרי עשר (Trei Asar)	The Twelve (Minor Prophets)
14	תהילים (Tehillim)	Psalms
15	משלי (Mishlei)	Proverbs
16	איוב (Iyov)	Job
17	שיר השירים (Shir HaShirim)	Song of Songs
18	רות (Rut)	Ruth
19	איכה (Eikhah)	Lamentations
20	קהלת (Kohelet)	Ecclesiastes
21	אסתר (Esther)	Esther
22	דניאל (Daniel)	Daniel

Canon	Number of Books	Notes
Hebrew (Tanakh)	22	22 books in 24 scrolls, based on combinations (e.g. Samuel, Kings, Chronicles each one book)
Catholic	73	Includes Deuterocanonical books (e.g. Tobit, Judith, 1–2 Maccabees)
Protestant	66	Excludes Apocrypha; follows Jerome's Hebrew-based list
Ethiopian Orthodox	81	Includes broader OT and NT canon, e.g. Jubilees, Enoch, 1–3 Meqabyan

Chapter I (א): The Formation of the Tanakh

I. Introduction: Understanding Canonization

The formation of the Tanakh (Hebrew Bible) was not the product of a single council, decree, or centralized authority. Rather, it was an organic, centuries-long process involving communal reverence, prophetic validation, scribal preservation, and covenantal fidelity.

The term "Tanakh" (Hebrew: תנ״ך) is itself an acronym, standing for:
- Torah (תורה) — Instruction or Teaching (Root: Yarah, ירה)
- Nevi'im (נביאים) — Prophets (Root: Nava, נבא)
- Ketuvim (כתובים) — Writings (Root: Katav, כתב)

Understanding these roots is critical. "Torah" does not strictly mean "law" — a mistranslation stemming from the Greek *nomos* and Latin lex. Rather, Torah conveys the idea of Divine instruction meant to guide humanity along the righteous path. As Rabbi Samson Raphael Hirsch emphasized, it is guidance and education, not legislation.

II. Timeline of Canonization

Section	Composition Period	Canonization Approx.	Notes
Torah (תורה)	c. 12th–5th century BCE	By 5th century BCE	Solidified post-Babylonian exile, during Ezra's reforms.
Nevi'im (נביאים)	c. 8th–5th century BCE	By 4th century BCE	Former and Latter Prophets compiled.
Ketuvim (כתובים)	c. 7th–2nd century BCE	Fluid until 1st century CE	Psalms, Proverbs, Daniel among others.
Full Tanakh	Appears by 2nd century BCE	Formalized by 1st century CE	Reflects sectarian debates.

III. Primary Evidence for Canonization Process

1. Ezra's Reforms (5th Century BCE): Emphasized Hebrew literacy, covenant restoration, textual fidelity.

2. Dead Sea Scrolls (2nd Century BCE–1st Century CE): Demonstrated textual pluriformity.

3. Septuagint Translation (3rd Century BCE): Revealed interpretive translation distinct from Hebrew. The Septuagint translation of the Torah is generally dated to circa 260 BCE, based on the Letter of Aristeas and corroborated by early Hellenistic Jewish sources

4. Josephus and Rabbinic Testimonies (1st Century CE): [1]Supported a 22-book authoritative list.

Recent epigraphic research by Dr. **Douglas Petrovich**, an archaeologist and paleolinguist, argues that **the earliest alphabetic script emerged from a set of 22 Egyptian hieroglyphs**, repurposed by Semitic-speaking workers in Middle Kingdom Egypt. Petrovich contends that this script, dubbed **Proto-Consonantal Hebrew**, directly evolved from Egyptian signs into a linear alphabet with clear phonetic parallels to the Hebrew aleph-bet. This lends striking historical support to the traditional rabbinic assertion that the **22 letters of Lašôn ha-qōḏeš are divinely chosen vessels** for revelation — not only sacred in structure but also foundational in the evolution of written language. [Douglas Petrovich, *The World's Oldest Alphabet* (Jerusalem: Carta, 2016).]

While Douglas Petrovich argues for early Hebrew usage in Proto-Sinaitic inscriptions as a linguistic forerunner to

---

[1] Josephus, *Against Apion*, 1.8, trans. H. St. J. Thackeray (Cambridge, MA: Harvard University Press, 1926), 179. Flavius Josephus, *Against Apion*, trans. H. St. J. Thackeray, in *The Loeb Classical Library*, vol. 186 (Cambridge, MA: Harvard University Press, 1926), 179–183.

biblical Hebrew, his epigraphic conclusions remain heavily contested. Christopher Rollston, in BASOR and other venues, has argued that such inscriptions reflect a Northwest Semitic dialect not yet classified as Hebrew. This work does not rest on Petrovich's dating but receives his framework as a theological model of ancestral script continuity. [Douglas Petrovich, *The World's Oldest Alphabet* (Jerusalem: Carta, 2016).] [Christopher A. Rollston, "Writing and Literacy in the World of Ancient Israel," *BASOR* 344 (2006): 47–74.]

When paired with the canon of 22 biblical books (as counted by early Jewish sources like Jerome and Epiphanius), the convergence becomes more than symbolic — it becomes **pictographic, phonetic, and prophetic**. The language of Scripture is not a random assembly of signs, but an inheritance encoded into both **divine text and human script** from the earliest covenantal moments — from Egypt to Sinai to Zion. [Jerome, *Prologus Galeatus*, in *Biblia Sacra Vulgata*, ed. Robert Weber (Stuttgart: Deutsche Bibelgesellschaft, 1994).] [Epiphanius, *Panarion*, trans. Frank Williams (Leiden: Brill, 1987).]

"Josephus' assertion that only 22 books were held as sacred in Jewish antiquity offers the clearest native witness to the original canon structure—not a later ecclesial construction."

Such a design affirms not only divine authorship but also reestablishes the integral role of the Hebrew language in the recognition and structure of sacred canon—particularly in light of **later Greco-Roman expansions**, which often introduced interpretive distortions and theological hierarchies foreign to the original Semitic worldview.

This alignment between script and Scripture is well-attested in **rabbinic tradition**, notably in the *Sefer Yetzirah* and in **Bavli Bava Batra 14b**, where sages emphasize that the **number of authoritative books (22)** corresponds to the **22 letters of the Hebrew alphabet**—a system understood not merely as mnemonic but as revelatory. Each letter of *Lašôn ha-qōḏeš* (the Holy Tongue) is regarded as a vessel of divine transmission, bearing numeric, moral, and phonetic weight. In this light, the canonical books are not just literary artifacts but **extensions of the sacred script itself.** [*Talmud Bavli, Bava Batra 14b*.][2]

See Appendix N.

Augustine and the Canon: Authority by Ecclesial Consensus or Hebrew Continuity?

Augustine wrote, "Those books of Scripture which are received by all the Catholic churches... are to be preferred" (*De Doctrina Christiana* II.8). He further claimed, "The translators were inspired just as the authors were" (II.15), implying a theological parity between the Greek Septuagint and Hebrew originals.

In *De Doctrina Christiana* (Book II, §8), Augustine asserts that the "books received by all the Catholic churches" should be held as canonical, grounding scriptural authority in ecclesial consensus. This claim helped crystallize the notion that the canon was not defined by prophetic origin or linguistic transmission, but by the church's universal use.

However, this ecclesial authority model bypasses the Hebrew covenantal structure from which scripture emerged. Augustine admits a secondary status for the

---

[2]
Chapter I: Sacred Beginnings and the Bet of Separation

Though some view this analysis as midrashic rather than grammatical, the rabbinic tradition—from Bereshit Rabbah to the Talmud—saw letter-shape and placement as covenantal indicators, not arbitrary aesthetics. This framing aligns with ancient Jewish exegesis, not modern critical detachment. It honors the theological architecture of the Hebrew language and the interpretive rhythm inherent in sacred text formation. Josephus, *Against Apion*, I.8; cf. McDonald, *Biblical Canon*, 155–160. Augustine, *On Christian Doctrine*, trans. D.W. Robertson (Indianapolis: Bobbs-Merrill, 1958), Book II, §8 and §15. Adin Steinsaltz, *The Talmud: A Reference Guide* (New York: Random House, 1989), 23–30.

Hebrew text by favoring the Septuagint's divine inspiration—a position reinforced by his suspicion of Hebraic custodianship. He writes, "the translators were inspired as much as the authors" (ibid. §15), effectively erasing the primacy of Hebrew scrolls in favor of Greek ecclesial utility.

This manuscript offers a counterclaim: canon is not defined by consensus, but by covenant. The authority of a scroll stems not from its liturgical popularity but its linguistic fidelity to divine utterance. The early church's embrace of the Septuagint was not merely translational—it was political, favoring the lingua franca of the empire over the sacred tongue of Sinai.

To root canon in consensus, as Augustine did, is to institutionalize the loss of Hebrew voice. Scripture, in this view, becomes ecclesial literature—not covenantal prophecy.

For historical corroboration, See Appendix J, Fig. 5 (p. 140) – Ecclesial Seizure of Canonical Authority. This diagram visualizes the theological shift from prophetic scroll to imperialized scripture.

IV. Critical Observations

- Organic Canonization over time, not one-time council.
- Sectarian influence on text inclusion.
- Masoretic Text reflects a Pharisaic post-Temple consensus.
- Centrality of Hebrew Language (Lašôn ha-qōdeš).

This work aligns with canonical criticism's reverence for the final form but argues that prophetic memory and grammatical covenant precede editorial theology. Canonical formation does not flatten sacred grammar—it invites its rediscovery beneath imperial overlays.

V. Hebrew Language Emphasis

- Torah (תורה) from Yarah (ירה): Instruction, not rigid Law.
- Mitzvah (מצווה) from Tzavah (צוה): Commandments.

Translations flatten Hebrew nuance; reclaiming Hebrew etymology restores spiritual precision.

VI. Thought-Provoking Questions

- If Torah is "instruction" and not "law," how should we reframe divine commandments?
- What does organic canonization reveal about human-divine interaction?
- Does pluriformity challenge the idea of "one perfect text"?
- How does returning to Hebrew shift theological interpretations rooted in Greek-Roman frameworks?

VII. References and Sources

Rabbi Samson Raphael Hirsch, The Hirsch Chumash, trans. Daniel Haberman (Feldheim Publishers).
2. Rabbi Samson Raphael Hirsch, The Etymological Dictionary of Biblical Hebrew.
3. Emanuel Tov, Textual Criticism of the Hebrew Bible, 2nd ed. (Fortress Press, 2001).
4. James VanderKam, The Dead Sea Scrolls Today (Eerdmans, 1994).
5. Lee McDonald, The Formation of the Biblical Canon (Hendrickson, 2007).
6. Josephus, Against Apion, Book 1.
7. Babylonian Talmud, Bava Batra 14b–15a. [Emanuel Tov, *Textual Criticism of the Hebrew Bible*, 3rd ed. (Minneapolis: Fortress Press, 2012), 135.] [*Talmud Bavli, Bava Batra 14b*.]

Counterpoint: Was the Canon Just a Natural Consensus?

Mainstream **View:**
Scholars like Lee Martin McDonald and F.F. Bruce argue that the Hebrew Bible emerged gradually through communal usage, liturgical preservation, and prophetic validation. They maintain that canonization was more

descriptive than prescriptive—formal lists simply echoed what communities already revered.

Representative **Quote:**
"The canon was not imposed by decree but recognized by widespread usage." – F.F. Bruce, *The Canon of Scripture*, p. 276.

Rebuttal: The Canon Was Curated—And Censored

This view ignores **the erasure of dissident prophetic voices, the political stakes of temple authority, and the linguistic marginalization of non-elite communities.** The presence of **sectarian texts at Qumran**—such as *Jubilees, 1 Enoch,* and *Testament of Levi*—demonstrates that the boundaries of sacred text were contested, not consensual.

Moreover, **rabbinic sources like Bavli Bava Batra 14b** show a conscious *numerological structuring* of the canon to match the 22 letters of the Hebrew alphabet—suggesting not mere reverence, but **intentional design**.

As Judith Newman rightly observes:
"The body was the earliest site of scripture… Liturgical habit shaped canonicity more than later decrees." (*Before the Bible*, p. 89)

But whose liturgy? Whose authority? The exclusion of books with **Edenic calendars, female prophecy,** and **non-Zadokite priesthoods** reveals a **priestly and later Pharisaic editorial strategy**, not communal neutrality.

Canon formation, then, was not an organic spring—it was a guarded well.

See: Appendix J – Canon Timeline & Linguistic Framework

PART II (ב) FORMATION OF SCRIPTURE

Chapter II (ב): Composition and Transmission of the Hebrew Bible

I. Oral Tradition to Written Text

The earliest Israelite spiritual experiences were transmitted orally. Patriarchal narratives, covenantal laws, songs, and prophetic utterances were shared through memorization and storytelling. This method prioritized relational memory and communal transmission over individual possession.

The Hebrew term *midrash* (מִדְרָשׁ), derived from the root *d-r-sh* (דרש), meaning "to seek" or "to investigate," appears explicitly in **2 Chronicles 13:22** and **2 Chronicles 24:27**, where the chronicles of prophets and kings are said to be recorded in **sefer ha-midraš**—"the book of the Midrash." These are not late rabbinic additions but embedded textual references within Tanakh itself.

Likewise, **Joshua 10:13** and **2 Samuel 1:18** cite the *Sefer HaYashar* (ספר הישר), or "Book of the Upright," which the Talmud and many classical commentators consider part of the *aggadic-midrashic tradition*. These intertextual markers validate the role of non-canonical interpretive works in preserving prophetic memory and national history. Though the current *Sefer HaYashar* is a medieval compilation, the biblical citations likely reference a lost or separate earlier work.

Modern theological frameworks often reject *Midrash*, *Talmud*, and *Oral Torah* as "extra-biblical." Yet the Bible itself gestures toward these works. The Talmudic sages viewed *midrashim* not as unauthorized commentary but as spiritually anchored exegesis. In *Talmud Bavli Sanhedrin 24a*, Rav and Shmuel liken Babylon to "the place of drash"—the interpretive heartland where Scripture is probed, not just read.

This is the essence of the **PARDES** method: *P'shat* (literal), *Remez* (hint), *D'rash* (search), *Sod* (mystery). The term *D'rash* shares its root with *midrash*. To deny midrash is to amputate the text's inner voice. Even Yeshua and Paul engage in midrashic reasoning—reweaving scripture for current crises, often paraphrasing rather than quoting.

To embrace *midrash* is to recover **Torah she-be'al peh** (תּוֹרָה שֶׁבְּעַל פֶּה)—the sacred oral tradition that accompanied written Torah at Sinai. As the Sages taught: "Moses received Torah from Sinai and transmitted it to Joshua..." (*Pirkei Avot 1:1*). That transmission included both what was written and what was interpreted, spoken, and expanded. The inspired Word of God never ceased unfolding.

The transition from oral tradition to written scripture occurred gradually. Writing served to stabilize memory, enable communal transmission, and preserve covenantal teachings. Yet this shift also required scribal literacy and costly materials, restricting access to sacred texts. The Sadducean sect rejected the *minhagim* (מנהגים)—the traditional customs—and disavowed *Torah she-be'al peh* (תורה שבעל פה), the oral Torah handed down alongside the written scroll. This stance parallels the minimalist literalism of modern-day fundamentalist biblicism, which likewise negates interpretive tradition in favor of surface text alone.

II. Composition Stages by Section

A. Torah (תורה)

The Torah's narratives and legal codes were shaped by centuries of layered composition. Most scholars affirm a multi-source origin:
- J (Yahwist): Vivid, personal name YHWH, anthropomorphic depictions.
- E (Elohist): Uses "ʾĔlōhîm," emphasizes dreams and

angels.
- D (Deuteronomist): Covenant theology, centralization of worship.
- P (Priestly): Rituals, genealogy, orderliness, holiness themes.

These were compiled and redacted, especially during and after the Babylonian Exile. Ezra is seen as the final redactor who unified these traditions and brought the Torah before the   people   (Nehemiah   8).

B.   Nevi'im   (Prophets)
The Former Prophets (Joshua–Kings) combine history with prophetic interpretation. The Latter Prophets (Isaiah–Malachi) preserve individual oracles, some written by disciples. Prophets did not merely predict; they warned, judged,   and   instructed   Israel.

C.   Ketuvim   (Writings)
The Ketuvim include poetic (Psalms), philosophical (Ecclesiastes), and apocalyptic (Daniel) works. This section remained fluid until the late Second Temple period. The diversity of style and theology in this section demonstrates the breadth of Israelite thought.

III. Scribal Transmission and Textual Fluidity

A.   Dead   Sea   Scrolls   Evidence
The   Dead   Sea   Scrolls   (1947–1956)   reveal:
- Multiple versions of biblical books (e.g., Psalms, Jeremiah).
- Proto-Masoretic, Proto-Samaritan, and Septuagintal Hebrew   base   texts.
- Unique harmonized or restructured manuscripts (e.g., Jubilees).
This evidence strongly suggests that no singular textual version held universal authority during the 1st century BCE,   indicating   a   period   of   canon   fluidity.

B.   Masoretic   Text   Crystallization

Post-Temple destruction, the Pharisaic-rabbinic tradition solidified the Hebrew text. Masoretes (7th–10th c. CE) added vowel points, marginal notes, and preserved scroll accuracy. Yet even their system involved choices, traditions, and corrections (see Tiqqunē Sôp̄erîm).

The Essenes — authors of the Dead Sea Scrolls and residents of Qumran — offer essential insight into non-Pharisaic scriptural traditions. Their preserved texts reflect veneration for books like Enoch, Jubilees, and the Testament of Levi, while omitting others accepted today. They anticipated multiple messiahs and a "Teacher of Righteousness," revealing a unique interpretive matrix outside rabbinic or Christian orthodoxy. Their rejection of the priesthood in Jerusalem, reliance on solar calendars, and non-standard canon challenge assumptions about biblical uniformity in the Second Temple period.

*See: 1QS, 4QMMT, Vermes, "The Complete Dead Sea Scrolls in English." *

Unlike the Essenes or Sadducees, the Pharisees played a defining role in preserving the tripartite canon: Torah, Prophets, and Writings (Tanakh). Their oral tradition — later forming the Mishnah and Talmud — became the backbone of mainstream Jewish identity. Josephus affirms their influence, and Talmudic sources place them at the center of post-Temple religious reorganization. This sect's careful distinction between canon and commentary preserved Jewish textual identity through Roman exile and shaped rabbinic Judaism's framework.

See: Josephus, Antiquities 13.10.6; Bava Batra 14b–15a. [*Talmud Bavli, Bava Batra 14b*.]

The Ethiopian Witness – Canon and Language Legacy
The canon of the Ethiopian Orthodox Tewahedo Church, preserved in the Semitic liturgical language of Ge'ez, is the most expansive biblical canon in Christian tradition, comprising 81 books. In contrast to the 66-book Protestant canon and the 73-book Roman Catholic canon, the

Ethiopian Bible includes additional works like 1 Enoch,
Jubilees, and the Ethiopian Meqabyan books, which are not
to be confused with the Greek Maccabees. These books
reflect a unique trajectory of Afro-Semitic theology,
uninterrupted by Western ecumenical reductions or Latin
doctrinal standardizations.

The Geʿez language, rooted in ancient Sabaean and Cushitic
traditions, became the sacred medium for theology and
liturgy in Ethiopia, analogous to Latin in Roman
Christianity or Classical Arabic in Islam. Though no longer
spoken, Geʿez preserves the historical and theological
memory of an African Christianity closely aligned with
early Semitic and Second Temple Jewish elements,
including priestly laws, calendrical systems, and temple
iconography.

[3] Significantly, the Ethiopian Church did not adopt the
canon decrees of Western councils such as Trent or
Chalcedon. Its canon formation developed independently,
relying on Alexandrian, Syriac, and indigenous oral
traditions. Its Apostolic and Solomonic heritage reinforces
the Ethiopian claim to a prophetic and priestly legacy
distinct from Hellenized Christianity, offering a necessary
Afrocentric counterpoint to dominant canon histories.

Edward Ullendorff, R.W. Cowley, August Dillmann. These
scholars document the continuity, transmission, and unique
status of the Ethiopian canon as a theological artifact of
Semitic Africa.

"Canon formation, as Levin and Pfoh remind us, was a
cultural project of identity reassertion after political loss."

Oral Torah Beyond Babylon — Ethiopia's Geʿez
Traditions and Hebraic Continuity

*"Beyond the rivers of Cush, My suppliants, the daughter of My
dispersed,   shall   bring   My   offering."*
— Zephaniah 3:10

[3] Tadesse Tamrat, "Processes of Ethnic Interaction and Integration in Ethiopian History," *The Journal of African History* 29, no. 1 (1988): 5–18.

The Ark, the Solomonic Covenant, and Female Transmission

In Ethiopian tradition—preserved among both the **Solomonic monarchy** and **Beta Israel** communities— the **Ark of the Covenant** (*Tabot*, ታቦት) is not merely a relic of the First Temple. It is a **living presence** maintained through **oral liturgy, priestly procession,** and **ancestral oaths.** The primary source for this tradition is the **Kəbrä Nägäśt** (ክብረ ነገሥት, "The Glory of Kings"), a 14th-century Geʿez text rooted in **much older oral traditions.**

According to the Kəbrä Nägäśt, **Solomon** fathered a son, **Bayna-Lehkem** (lit. "son of the wise"), later known as **Menelik I,** by the **Queen of Sheba** (*Makéda*, ማክዳ). This son returned to Ethiopia with the **original Ark of the Covenant,** which Solomon allowed (or prophetically foresaw) to be taken to preserve the divine presence in a new Zion.

[4]"The Ark of the Covenant of God, the Two Tablets of the Law, and the Rod of Moses came to Ethiopia with the firstborn of the house of Judah." — *Kəbrä Nägäśt*, chs. 94–98

This tradition is preserved **not through rabbinic halakhah,** but through:

- **Geʿez liturgy** and hymns (*zema*, ዜማ፡)

- **Debteras** (religious scribes) who memorize Psalms and Solomonic prayers

---

[4] E. A. Wallis Budge, *The Queen of Sheba and Her Only Son Menyelek (Kebra Nagast)* (London: Oxford University Press, 1922), chs. 94–98. ▨ Edward Ullendorff, *The Ethiopians: An Introduction to Country and People,* 2nd ed. (London: Oxford University Press, 1965), 65–87. R. W. Cowley, "The Biblical Canon of the Ethiopian Orthodox Church Today," *Ostkirchliche Studien* 23, no. 2 (1974): 318–323. ▨ Getatchew Haile, "The Structure and Evolution of the Ethiopian Biblical Canon," in *The Bible in Ethiopia: The Book of Acts,* ed. J. Ross Wagner (Atlanta: Society of Biblical Literature, 2012), 15–28. James C. VanderKam, *From Revelation to Canon: Studies in the Hebrew Bible and Second Temple Literature* (Leiden: Brill, 2002), 197–200. John S. Mbiti, *African Religions and Philosophy,* 2nd ed. (Oxford: Heinemann, 1991), 225–229. ▨ Wolf Leslau, *Concise Dictionary of Ge'ez (Classical Ethiopic)* (Wiesbaden: Harrassowitz, 1989), s.v. "tabot," "zema," "Igzi'abher." Ephraim Isaac, "The Ethiopian Orthodox Church and Its Judaic Traditions," in *African Zion: Studies in Black Judaism,* ed. Edith Bruder and Tudor Parfitt (Newcastle: Cambridge Scholars Publishing, 2012), 159–177. ▨ Joseph Dan, *Kabbalah: A Very Short Introduction* (Oxford: Oxford University Press, 2006), 25–30.

▨ Yosef A.A. Ben-Jochannan, *African Origins of Major Western Religions,* 15th ed. (Baltimore: Black Classic Press, 1991), 148–156. ▨ Steven Kaplan, *The Beta Israel (Falasha) in Ethiopia: From Earliest Times to the Twentieth Century* (New York: NYU Press, 1992), 53–54. ▨ E. Isaac, "The Falasha and Their Oral Traditions," *Journal of Ethiopian Studies* 4, no. 2 (1966): 89–104. Tov, Emanuel. *Textual Criticism of the Hebrew Bible,* 3rd ed. (Minneapolis: Fortress Press, 2012), 135–136. James L. Kugel, *The Bible As It Was* (Cambridge: Harvard University Press, 1997), 10–12.

- **Female elders** who pass down *oral memory of Zion* through **narrative, music, and naming ceremonies**

In contrast to rabbinic male-only legal transmission (*mesorah*), Ethiopian traditions elevate the **prophetic voice of women**. **Makéda**, the Queen of Sheba, is remembered as a vessel of divine vision and covenantal succession. This counters the Babylonian-era tendency to reframe kingship as exclusively male-priestly.

Maccabean Resistance and Kushite Legitimacy

In the **Hasmonean (Maccabean)** period, the restoration of the Temple and defense of Torah came through **military and priestly resistance**. But in Ethiopia, Hebraic continuity was **not militarized**. It was preserved in:

- **Priesthood of the Zadokites** (in Beta Israel oral tradition)

- **Kohanim tracing lineage through oral oaths**, not genealogical registries

- **Tabot processions**, which represent **living Torah**, not ark relics

Thus, while rabbinic tradition emphasized preservation through legal dialectic and textual codification, the **Kushite-Messianic tradition** emphasized:

- **Symbolic preservation through ritual**

- **Prophetic dreams and ancestral memory**

- **Divine guidance in the wilderness** (Exodus typology fulfilled again)

Comparative Glossary: Geʿez, Hebrew, and English

Geʿez (ግዕዝ)	Hebrew	English	Notes
ታቦት (Tabot)	אָרוֹן הַבְּרִית (Aron HaBrit)	Ark of the Covenant	Replica or true vessel of divine indwelling

Ge'ez (ግዕዝ)	Hebrew	English	Notes
ማከዳ (Makéda)	שְׁבָא (Sheba)	Queen of Sheba	Seen as a prophetic matriarch in Ethiopia
ባእነ ለሕከም (Bayna-Lehkem)	בֶּן־חָכָם (Ben-Chakham)	(Ben- Son of the Wise	Name for Menelik I, Solomonic heir
ኢ.ግዚአብሄር (Igzi'abher)	יְהוָה / אֲדֹנָי (Adonai/YHWH)	Lord of Hosts	Traditional Ethiopian name for God
ዜማ: (Zema)	שירה (Shirah)	Hymn / Chant	Liturgical song with oral transmission
ክብረ ነገሥት (Kǝbrä Nägäśt)	למלכים תהילה יֵשֵּׁעוֹ (nonexistent parallel)	"The Glory of Kings"	Source of Solomonic Ark tradition

Summary: Oral Zion in the South

Unlike Rabbinic Judaism, which locates the continuity of Israel through legal dialectic and Temple memory, Ethiopian and broader African oral traditions preserved Torah through:

- **Mythic memory**
- **Ritual embodiment**
- **Multigenerational recitation**
- **Female spiritual guardianship**

Where Babylon preserved texts, **Kush preserved presence.** Where Yavneh debated halakhot, **Gondar processed the Ark.**

Where the West asked, "Where is the text?", the South asked, "Where is the **spirit**?"

This divergence is not a deviation—but a preservation through other means. A **"Torah of the wilderness"** survived among those who never saw Babylon but always looked toward Zion.

IV. Transmission Challenges and Safeguards

Despite best efforts, the transmission was not error-free:
- Haplography: Skipping repeated letters or lines.
- Dittography: Duplication of words.
- Marginal corrections: Qere (read) vs Ketiv (written).

Yet the reverence for the text was profound. Scribes bathed before writing YHWH's name, and scrolls were buried when worn.[5]

V. Hebrew as a Sacred Medium

While Aramaic and Greek were lingua franca, Hebrew remained:
- The language of Torah scrolls.
- Central in Temple and synagogue liturgy.
- The vessel for divine revelation (Lašôn ha-qōdeš).

Ezra read the Torah in Hebrew and interpreted it (Nehemiah 8), showing early efforts to preserve meaning across language barriers.

---

5 Chapter II: Naming, Identity & The Politics of Memory

To reclaim a name is not to erase the complexity of diaspora. It is to resist the colonial logic that said we had none. In the Tanakh, names are not frozen identities—they are restored covenants. And so it is for the exiled. Scripture does not treat names as aesthetic details but as covenantal appointments, repeatedly emphasized as critical to restoration, lineage, and spiritual inheritance. Christoph Levin, *Rebuilding Identity: The Nehemiah Memoir and Its Earliest Readers* (Sheffield: Sheffield Academic Press, 2002), 9–21. Edward Ullendorff, *The Ethiopians: An Introduction to Country and People*, 2nd ed. (London: Oxford University Press, 1965), esp. 65–87. R. W. Cowley, "The Biblical Canon of the Ethiopian Orthodox Church Today," *Ostkirchliche Studien* 23, no. 2 (1974): 318–323. August Dillmann, *Octateuchus Aethiopicus: Biblia Veteris Testamenti Aethiopice* (Leipzig: F.A. Brockhaus, 1853). Getatchew Haile, "The Structure and Evolution of the Ethiopian Biblical Canon," in *The Bible in Ethiopia: The Book of Acts*, ed. J. Ross Wagner (Atlanta: Society of Biblical Literature, 2012), 15–28.

VI. Thought-Provoking Questions

- If scripture once existed in multiple versions, what makes one the "authorized" text today?
- What role did exile, trauma, and temple loss play in shaping sacred text?
- Do harmonizations represent corruption or clarification?
- How does Hebrew's return in modern times fulfill Zephaniah 3:9?

VII. References and Sources

1. Emanuel Tov, Textual Criticism of the Hebrew Bible, 2nd ed. (Fortress Press, 2001).
2. Eugene Ulrich, The Dead Sea Scrolls and the Origins of the Bible (Eerdmans, 1999).
3. Frank Moore Cross, The Ancient Library of Qumran (Yale University Press, 1995).
4. Rabbi Samson Raphael Hirsch, The Hirsch Chumash.
5. Biblia Hebraica Stuttgartensia (BHS).
6. James C. VanderKam, The Dead Sea Scrolls Today (Eerdmans, 1994). [Emanuel Tov, *Textual Criticism of the Hebrew Bible*, 3rd ed. (Minneapolis: Fortress Press, 2012), 135.]

PART III (ג)FORMATION OF SCRIPTURE

Chapter III (ג): The Septuagint, Targumim, and Transmission

I. Rise of Israelite Multilingualism

Following the Babylonian exile, Israelites were dispersed across empires that spoke Aramaic and Greek. These dominant languages shaped the linguistic environment of the Second Temple period and led to translations of Hebrew

Scriptures for diaspora communities who no longer understood the sacred tongue.

This linguistic transition reveals both a devotion to preserving Torah among exiled Israelites and the inevitable risks of meaning deviation when translation replaces source language.

II. The Septuagint (LXX): Torah in Greek

According to the Letter of Aristeas, Ptolemy II Philadelphus (285–246 BCE) commissioned 72 Israelite elders to translate the Torah from Hebrew into Koine Greek for the Library of Alexandria. This monumental translation, known as the Septuagint (from the Latin *septuaginta*, "seventy"), became foundational for Hellenistic Israelites.

- Initially, only the Torah was translated (~260 BCE), but other books were added over time.
- Some translations in the Septuagint differ markedly from the Masoretic Text (MT).
- Additions like extended versions of Esther and Daniel appear in the LXX.
- Psalm numbering and order vary, reflecting different manuscript traditions.

The Septuagint helped preserve access to scripture for Greek-speaking Jews but also became a double-edged sword—introducing interpretive nuances that diverged from the original Hebrew intent. The **LXX was often favored by early Christians**, which led to Jews distancing from it by the 2nd century CE (a key turning point in canon divergence).

Origen (ca. 185–253 CE), a towering figure in early Alexandrian Christianity, compiled the *Hexapla*—a massive six-columned Bible preserving the Hebrew text, its Greek transliteration, and four different Greek translations, including the LXX. This scholarly collation was not merely textual preservation; it reflected a **transitional moment in**

the erasure of Hebrew primacy. While Origen revered the Hebrew script, his harmonization efforts also accelerated the **Greek interpretive standardization** later crystallized by ecclesiastical authority. His synoptic comparison led to what many considered the *definitive Christian version* of Scripture—even though it introduced **layers of Greek semantic drift** from the Hebraic originals.

III. The Targumim: Torah in Aramaic

As Aramaic became the vernacular in Judea, synagogues began reading Torah in Hebrew followed by an Aramaic paraphrase. These oral interpretations were later codified into the *Targumim*. Targum Onkelos was formalized in the 3rd century CE in Babylon, while Targum Jonathan likely dates to the late 1st century CE. Palestinian Targumim such as Neofiti emerged between the 2nd and 4th centuries CE.

-            Targum   Onkelos   (Torah)
-            Targum   Jonathan   (Prophets)
- Targum Neofiti and Fragment Targumim (Palestinian variants)

The Targumim sought to clarify but often inserted interpretive elements, theological expansions, and homiletic flourishes. Though revered, they underscore how paraphrase can reshape theology.

IV. Translation Dangers: Theology & Recontextualization

Case   Study: Isaiah   7:14
- Hebrew: עלמה (*ʿalmāh*) — young woman
- Greek LXX: παρθένος (*parthenos*) — virgin
- NT (Matthew 1:23): Uses the Greek reading, influencing Christian doctrine of virgin birth

Erasmus or Calvin on Hebrew Terms (*almah, nachash*)

Quote   (Calvin   on   Isaiah   7:14):
"It is of no importance whether the word almah signifies a virgin or a young woman. The evangelist took the passage

as   referring   to   Christ."
— *Calvin, Commentary on Isaiah*

Calvin's preference for the evangelist's reading over the Hebrew term reveals a hermeneutic hierarchy—Scripture's original grammar subordinated to its Christological recasting.

"This process, often described by postcolonial scholars as 'scriptural domestication,' reframed covenantal memory into   ecclesial   control."

This single translational decision altered the course of theology. "ʿalmāh" never required virginity—it denoted youth or maidenhood. The Greek, however, locked in a doctrinal lens foreign to Hebrew intent.

This theological-linguistic framework also illuminates crucial interpretive controversies. One such debate concerns the **Hebrew term** *ʿalmāh* (עַלְמָה), often translated as "young woman." Christian apologetics have long emphasized a dichotomy between *ʿalmāh* and *bətūlāh* (בְּתוּלָה, "virgin"), suggesting that *ʿalmāh* lacks any connotation of virginity and thus undermines traditional readings of Isaiah 7:14.

[6]However, a **close philological analysis** reveals this is an overstated dichotomy. The semantic ranges of *ʿalmāh* and *bətūlāh* are not mutually exclusive.

6

Chapter III: Theology of Blood, Body & Vocation

To speak of Leviticus in the context of Black blood is not syncretism—it is scriptural echo. 'The life is in the blood' was never meant to be forgotten in empire's theology. Diasporic liturgy begins not with invented rituals, but with remembered covenant. Leviticus is not obsolete—it is uncompleted memory, resonating across bodies, altars, and ancestral survival. R.S. Sugirtharajah, *The Bible and the Third World: Precolonial, Colonial, and Postcolonial Encounters* (Cambridge: Cambridge University Press, 2001), 15–36. Phyllis Trible, *Texts of Terror: Literary-Feminist Readings of Biblical Narratives* (Philadelphia: Fortress Press, 1984), explores how canonical narratives suppress or reframe the stories of women, often through omissions, euphemism, or gendered distortion. Her work provides essential context for examining prophetic silence in textual history. Renita J. Weems, *Battered Love: Marriage, Sex, and Violence in the Hebrew Prophets* (Minneapolis: Fortress Press, 1995), interrogates how prophetic metaphors often encode masculine dominance over the feminine divine. Her analysis supports the claim that even feminine grammatical forms have been distorted to serve imperial patriarchal theology.

Contextual usage demonstrates overlap: in **Genesis 24:16**, Rebekah is explicitly called a *bəṯūlāh* ("a virgin, no man had known her"), and later in **Genesis 24:43**, she is described as an *ʿalmāh*. This dual designation suggests that *ʿalmāh*, in the proper literary setting, **can and does imply virginity**— though its primary meaning centers on youthful eligibility for marriage.

Such nuance has direct bearing on both **Hebrew theology and Christological interpretation**. The tendency to flatten Hebrew semantic flexibility into rigid dogmatic categories stems more from **translation ideology** than lexical integrity. By re-centering *Lašôn ha-qōḏeš* as the measuring rod, one recovers the **covenantal intent** beneath layers of interpretive distortion.

Additional   Recontextualized:
- Psalm 22:16 in MT: "Like a lion are my hands and feet" vs. LXX: "They pierced my hands and feet"
- Hosea 11:1: Contextually about Israel's exodus, applied messianically in Matthew 2:15

Rabbinic authorities were deeply aware of the exegetical tensions in both Psalm 22:16 and Isaiah 7:14, long before modern criticism. Rashi, in his commentary on Psalm 22, firmly upholds the reading *k'ari* (כָּאֲרִי) — "like a lion," aligning with the Masoretic Text and rejecting the Septuagint's interpretive shift to "pierced." Ibn Ezra concurs, emphasizing that any violent reading must be anchored in parallel poetic structure, not imposed theological motifs. On Psalm 22:16, **Ibn Ezra** insists that *kāʾarî* (כָּאֲרִי) refers to a threatening animal posture—not any act of piercing. The **Dead Sea Scrolls (5/6HevPs)** support this reading, nullifying the LXX-based "pierced" variant and the NT's theological dependence on it. These Rabbinic anchors firmly establish that **traditional Hebrew interpretation rejected both typologies as foreign impositions.** Emanuel Tov, *Textual Criticism of the Hebrew Bible*, 3rd ed. (Minneapolis: Fortress Press, 2012), 45–58.

Similarly, Rashi on Isaiah 7:14 identifies ʿalmāh as a young woman already known to Isaiah—likely his own wife or a royal consort during the Syro-Ephraimite crisis—rejecting any mystical virgin birth implication. **Targum Jonathan** echoes this, rendering the prophecy about political deliverance in Ahaz's day, not distant messianism. Rabbinic tradition insisted that p'shat (plain meaning) precedes derash (interpretive speculation), thereby disarming early Christological typologies dependent on LXX renderings.

Cf. Rashi on Tehillim 22:17; Rashi on Yeshayahu 7:14; Ibn Ezra, Commentary on Psalms.

James Kugel, in *How to Read the Bible*, contends that translation and reinterpretation were integral to ancient Jewish survival, especially post-exile. While this may justify adaptations such as *parthenos* in Isaiah 7:14, this work maintains that fidelity to Hebrew nuance offers deeper prophetic continuity. The tension between theological necessity and linguistic accuracy is an enduring challenge. James Kugel, *How to Read the Bible: A Guide to Scripture, Then and Now* (New York: Free Press, 2007), 17–29, 524–530

The Hebrew Bible records named prophetesses—Miriam, Huldah, Deborah—whose authority is rarely echoed in the canonized voices of scripture. Linguistically, the Hebrew suffixes that mark feminine verbs and titles (e.g., -ah, -et) are often dropped, erased, or neutralized in later translations.

Phyllis Trible and Judith Plaskow both argue that this grammatical suppression mirrors theological marginalization. The transmission of sacred text is not only a story of power—but of gendered silence.

V. Preservation of Lašôn ha-qōḏeš

Despite these translation efforts, Hebrew was preserved as sacred:
- Torah scrolls were written only in Hebrew
- Halakhic rulings were formulated in Hebrew
- Temple rituals and liturgy retained the holy tongue

Rabbi Samson Raphael Hirsch taught that Hebrew is uniquely suited for divine revelation. Its root structure, poetic compactness, and moral nuance cannot be replaced. Translating divine ideas into alien tongues may serve outreach but never replace the original.

"The Hebrew binyanim are not just grammatical forms but theological pathways—each stem reflects agency, voice, and divine-human interaction." Gary A. Rendsburg, "A Comprehensive Guide to Hebrew Morphology," *Journal of Northwest Semitic Languages* 31, no. 2 (2005): 113–142.

VI. Thought-Provoking Questions

- If Greek and Aramaic translations deviate from Hebrew, which should hold interpretive authority?
- Can any translation truly capture Hebrew's divine nuance?
- What theological doctrines today are built on mistranslated foundations?
- Should we return to Hebrew primacy in theological education?

VII. References and Sources

1. Emanuel Tov, *Textual Criticism of the Hebrew Bible*, 2nd ed. (Fortress Press, 2001).
2. James Barr, *The Typology of Literalism in Ancient Biblical Translations* (Oxford University Press, 1979).
3. Frank Moore Cross, *The Ancient Library of Qumran* (Yale University Press, 1995).
4. The *Letter of Aristeas* (c. 2nd century BCE).
5. Rabbi Samson Raphael Hirsch, *The Hirsch Chumash*.
6. Targum Onkelos and Targum Jonathan critical editions.
7. *Septuaginta: Rahlfs-Hanhart Edition*. [Emanuel Tov, *Textual Criticism of the Hebrew Bible*, 3rd ed. (Minneapolis: Fortress Press, 2012), 135.]

PART IV (7): EARLY MANUSCRIPTS AND CRITICAL VARIANTS

Chapter IV (7): Early Manuscripts and Textual Variants

I. Introduction: Why Manuscripts Matter

Every faith tradition that holds to sacred writ must face the reality of scribes. Before printing presses, before digital records, the entire Bible was transmitted one scroll, one line, one letter at a time—by human hands. To understand what we call "Scripture," we must trace its journey through ink, skin, and scroll.

Manuscripts are not merely copies; they are witnesses— living, breathing echoes of what communities considered holy. These textual witnesses often diverge. Textual criticism is not a threat to faith but a return to the roots—to peel back the layers and recover the ancient voice of revelation, letter by letter.

II. The Oldest Known Manuscripts

Manuscript	Date	Language	Notable Contents
Rylands Papyrus (P52)	c. 125 CE	Greek	Fragment of John 18
Codex Vaticanus	c. 300–325 CE	Greek	Nearly complete Bible; Alexandrian type
Codex Sinaiticus	c. 325–360 CE	Greek	Entire NT + OT (LXX); numerous variants
MS 14470 (Peshitta)	c. 500 CE	Syriac	Standard Syriac NT
Codex Amiatinus	c. 700 CE	Latin	Oldest Vulgate manuscript

Codex Leningradensis | c. 1008 CE | Hebrew | Full Masoretic Text | *Biblia Hebraica Stuttgartensia* Codex Basilensis | c. 1150 CE | Greek | Byzantine text-type, NT Gospels

III. The Text-Types: Competing Traditions

Textual scholars group manuscripts into families, or text-types. These are clusters of manuscripts that share common readings and originate from similar geographic areas:

- Alexandrian (Egyptian): Early, concise, less harmonized (e.g., Vaticanus, Sinaiticus)
- Western: Expansive, paraphrastic, theological glosses (e.g., Old Latin, Codex Bezae)
- Byzantine: Majority of medieval manuscripts, smoother readings, basis of KJV
- Caesarean: Rare, some unique readings in the Gospels

The Masoretic Text represents a parallel Hebrew stream, while the Septuagint, Samaritan Pentateuch, and Dead Sea Scrolls reveal early variation in the Tanakh.

Some scholars, such as **Michael Segal** and **Eugene Ulrich**, argue that the pluriformity of early texts reflects not confusion, but intentional theological flexibility within ancient Hebraic communities. While this work emphasizes restoration of original forms, it recognizes Segal's position that diversity was a feature—not a flaw—of sacred transmission. See Segal's *The Hebrew Bible in the Second Temple Period* (Brill, 2018).

IV. Dead Sea Scrolls: Multiple Bibles in Ancient Israel

Discovered between 1947–1956 in Qumran, the Dead Sea Scrolls revolutionized textual studies. With over 900 scrolls found—about 200 biblical—scholars confirmed a truth long suspected: there was no "one Bible" in the time of Jesus. Sidnie White Crawford, *Rewriting Scripture in Second Temple Times* (Grand Rapids: Eerdmans, 2008), 35–42. "Co-existing textual traditions in Ancient Israel, as revealed by the Dead

Examples:
- Jeremiah: The DSS version is 1/7 shorter than the MT and matches   the   LXX
- Psalms: Different order and extra psalms not in today's canon
- Deuteronomy: Expanded or alternate formulations, some harmonizing   with   Exodus

These findings challenge the claim that the Masoretic Text (c. 10th century CE) is the singular ancient form of the Hebrew Bible.

"The Dead Sea Scrolls reveal significant textual fluidity in the pre-canonical period, particularly when compared to the Masoretic stabilization."

V. Scribal Errors, Corrections, and Intentional Edits

Textual variation arises not only from copying mistakes but from   editorial   decisions.   These   include:
- Haplography: Skipping over repeated lines or letters
- Dittography: Accidental repetition of words or phrases
- Tiqqunē Sôp̄erîm: "Emendations of the Scribes"— deliberate   changes   to   avoid   perceived   irreverence
- Qere vs. Ketiv: Margin notes in the MT tell readers to pronounce something different than what's written[7]

7
Chapter IV: The Silence of the Wilderness & The Trauma of Tribes

To name the wilderness as trauma is not to reduce scripture to psychology—it is to remember that Bĕmidbār was never about lost direction, but delayed identity. Every numbered tribe carried exile in motion. Diaspora echoes not because of forced comparison—but because covenant always travels through the in-between. The wilderness is not just geographic—it is generational dislocation waiting to be interpreted as prophetic preparation. Emanuel Tov, *Textual Criticism of the Hebrew Bible*, 3rd ed. (Minneapolis: Fortress Press, 2012), 123–157. See Eugene Ulrich, *The Dead Sea Scrolls and the Origins of the Bible* (Grand Rapids: Eerdmans, 1999), 85–92.

VI. Masoretic Tradition: Sacred Precision or Editorial Finality?

The Masoretes (7th–10th century CE) were master scribes, preserving what became the authoritative Jewish text. They added:
-              Niqqud   (vowel   points)
-                    Cantillation   marks
- Masora Magna/Parva (margin notes documenting variants   and   rules)

But their precision also finalized a tradition that had once been more fluid. When the DSS and LXX are compared to the MT, hundreds of differences emerge—many theological, some minor.

VII. Thought-Provoking Questions

- If the Bible has variant texts, which version holds divine authority?
- What do scribal insertions or omissions say about ancient theology   and   control?
- Should we embrace a multifaceted canon reflecting diversity,   not   uniformity?
- Can the truth of YHWH be richer when expressed through many voices?

VIII. References and Sources

1. Emanuel Tov, *Textual Criticism of the Hebrew Bible*, 2nd   ed.
2. Peter Gentry & Stephen Wellum, *Kingdom Through Covenant*
3. Bruce Metzger, *The Text of the New Testament*
4. Eugene Ulrich, *The Dead Sea Scrolls and the Origins of the   Bible*
5. James VanderKam, *The Meaning of the Dead Sea Scrolls*
6. Frank Moore Cross, *The Ancient Library of Qumran*
7. Biblia Hebraica Stuttgartensia (BHS) [Emanuel Tov, *Textual Criticism of the Hebrew Bible*, 3rd ed. (Minneapolis: Fortress Press, 2012), 135.] [Bruce M. Metzger,

The Text of the New Testament: Its Transmission, Corruption, and Restoration, 4th ed. (Oxford: Oxford University Press, 2005), 45–47.]

PART V (ה): EARLY MANUSCRIPTS AND CRITICAL VARIANTS

Chapter V (ה): Known Errors in the Masoretic Text

I. Introduction: Reverence and Reality

The Masoretic Text (MT), though venerated as the authoritative Hebrew text of the Jewish Bible, is not infallible. It is the result of centuries of transmission, scribal discipline, rabbinic oversight, and—at times—editorial emendation. This chapter does not aim to undermine its sacred status, but to explore the cracks that reveal how even sacred tradition was subject to human hands.

As Rabbi Samson Raphael Hirsch stated, 'Reverence does not require ignorance.'

II. Tiqqunē Sôp̄erîm: The Emendations of the Scribes

The 'Tiqqunē Sôp̄erîm' or 'Scribal Corrections' are deliberate alterations in the Hebrew Bible. Rabbinic sources record 18 such emendations, where scribes changed verses out of theological   discomfort.

Examples:
- Genesis 18:22: Original — 'But YHWH stood before Abraham'; MT — 'But Abraham stood before YHWH.'
- Numbers 11:15: 'Kill me now... that I see not my evil' changed   to   'their   evil.'

These adjustments reflect reverence, but also editorial

intervention to avoid anthropomorphism or divine vulnerability.

III. Qere and Ketiv: What Is Written vs. What Is Read

The Masoretes maintained a strict record of discrepancies between the consonantal text (*ketiv*) and the traditional oral reading (*qere*).

Verse	Ketiv (Written)	Qere (Read)	Notes
1 Samuel 1:24	*בשלושה*	*בשלשה*	Masculine vs. feminine numeral form
Jeremiah 33:11	*אומרים*	*מביאים*	Entire verb replacement
Ezekiel 48:16	*חמשה עשר*	*חמשה*	Incomplete text restored via tradition

Example:
- Deuteronomy 28:27 — Written: בְּטְחֹרִים (*bet'chorim*, hemorrhoids); Read as: עֳפָלִים (*ofalim*, tumors).

Qere/Ketiv pairs reflect scribal memory of variant traditions. Some are grammatical corrections, others theological censorship. Such examples indicate that scribes preserved variant traditions despite potential theological or linguistic tensions.

IV. Scribal Errors: Human Hands, Human Mistakes

- **Haplography**: Skipping repeated words or lines.
- **Dittography**: Unintentional repetition.
- **Homoeoteleuton**: Skipping between lines ending similarly.
- **Graphical confusion**: Similar Hebrew letters (e.g., ד and ב; ר and כ) were miscopied.

V. Discrepancies with Earlier Witnesses

Dead Sea Scrolls and Septuagint offer alternative readings that sometimes appear more original:

- **Psalm 145**: An acrostic psalm, missing the verse for the Hebrew letter 'nun' (נ) in the MT. Found in DSS and LXX.
- **1 Samuel 13:1**: MT reads 'Saul was one year old when he began to reign.' Clearly corrupted. LXX omits the verse entirely.
- **Deuteronomy 32:8**: MT: 'sons of Israel'; LXX and DSS: 'sons of God' (בני אלהים), pointing to older divine council theology.[8]

Canon Distortion Under Empire: Jerome, Damasus, and the Latin Vulgate

The official canonization of Christian scripture under Roman authority represents one of the most decisive theological dislocations in religious history. Pope Damasus I (r. 366–384 CE) commissioned Jerome to translate the Hebrew scriptures into Latin, a project that culminated in the Vulgate—a text whose authority would eclipse the Hebrew originals for over a millennium in Western Christendom.

This translation was not neutral. Jerome's "Hebraica veritas" principle was repeatedly compromised by ecclesial pressure and Greco-Roman theological assumptions.

8

Chapter V: Law, Land & The Theft of Speech

Dəḇārîm is not about law alone—it is about memory spoken before disappearance. To call this 'theft of speech' is not to accuse the Torah, but to reveal how empire distorted its echoes. The *dabar* is still there—but buried beneath centuries of conquest theology that replaced prophetic speech with doctrinal order. Moses' review is not redundant—it is resistance through remembrance. James Barr, *The Semantics of Biblical Language* (Oxford: Oxford University Press, 1961), 106–124. **Jericho as First Fruits.** Jericho, among the world's oldest continuously inhabited sites (Tell es-Sultan, ca. 9000 BCE), was also the first city devoted (*ḥerem*) in Joshua 6. Its destruction thus functioned as a covenantal "first-fruits" act, echoing Cain and Abel's contested offerings and foreshadowing the cycles of exile and return that define Israel's later history. Kenyon, *Excavations at Jericho*; Dever, *Beyond the Text*. **Koehler, Ludwig & Baumgartner, Walter.** *The Hebrew and Aramaic Lexicon of the Old Testament (HALOT).* Leiden: Brill, 1994–2000.

Notably, terms such as עַלְמָה (almah) were rendered as "virgo," shifting meanings from youthful womanhood to imposed virginity, reinforcing Christological readings against the Hebrew textual grain. Likewise, references to נָחָשׁ (nachash, serpent) became cosmologically altered under Hellenistic allegory, divorcing the Eden narrative from its linguistic   structure.

Canon formation under the Roman Church became an imperial act. Councils such as Rome (382 CE) and Trent (1546 CE) did not merely affirm sacred texts—they institutionalized them as dogma, marginalizing variant manuscripts and suppressing apocryphal or Hebraic interpretations.

This challenges the myth of organic canon formation. It reframes canon not as a discovery, but as a curation—shaped by linguistic hegemony, political consolidation, and theological   control.

For critical mapping of ecclesial interventions, see Appendix J, Fig. 5: *From Scroll to Scripture: Ecclesial Seizure of Canonical Authority*.

Calvin, Erasmus, and the Mistranslation of Hebrew Terms

The Christian humanist Erasmus, in his *Annotationes in Novum Testamentum*, often deferred to the Latin Vulgate even when Hebrew offered more precise semantic control. Similarly, John Calvin—though more rigorous in exegesis—relied on Christological readings that reconfigured Hebrew terms   under   ecclesial   theology.

Take עַלְמָה (*almah*) in Isaiah 7:14, which Calvin affirms as referring to the virgin Mary, despite the term linguistically denoting a young woman, not explicitly a virgin. In his *Commentary on Isaiah*, Calvin concedes the ambiguity but still insists on a messianic fulfillment. This echoes

Erasmus, who often harmonized Hebrew tension into smoother Christological claims for readability.

Or consider נָחָשׁ (*nachash*, serpent) in Genesis. Calvin and others imposed satanic readings on this figure, transforming the linguistic symbol into a metaphysical enemy absent from the original Hebrew construct. In his *Genesis Commentary*, Calvin refers to the serpent as Satan incarnate, an idea alien to hebrew exegesis.

In Hebrew, *davar* (דָּבָר) means not only "word," but also "thing," "event," or "matter" — embodying a holistic intersection of **speech and action**. By contrast, the Greek *logos* (λόγος), especially in Platonic and Stoic usage, leans toward **abstract reason**, detached from embodiment. The **Society of Biblical Literature (SBL)** linguistic consensus affirms that *logos* was recontextualized in John's prologue to engage Hellenistic audiences, thereby **translating the Hebrew "dabar YHWH" into a more metaphysical concept**. This linguistic shift marked a **pivot from covenantal command** to conceptual revelation—central to the divergence between Hebraic and Greco-Christian theology.

"As James Barr warns, however, root-word theology must be handled carefully, avoiding 'illegitimate totality transfer'—yet when done with restraint, it reveals profound meaning."

This manuscript resists such retrojections. Hebrew terms possess prophetic autonomy and covenantal intent. Their semantic boundaries should not be redrawn by theological necessity.

See Appendix E: Lexical Displacement and Feminine Suppression: Almah and Divine Grammar.

VI. Theological and Doctrinal Implications

The Masoretic tradition reflects post-Temple Jewish theology, especially Pharisaic influence. Revisions may have:
- Removed divine plurality language (e.g., 'sons of God')
-                 Softened   anthropomorphisms
-     Standardized   theology   post-Second   Temple

These do not diminish the MT, but highlight its role as one of several sacred witnesses rather than the only one.

VII. Thought-Provoking Questions

- Should modern Bible translations be based solely on the MT?
- What role should DSS and LXX play in restoration of ancient   meanings?
- How do scribal emendations challenge the notion of scriptural   inerrancy?
- Is there value in preserving multiple textual traditions instead of selecting a single 'correct' version?

VIII. References and Sources

1. Emanuel Tov, *Textual Criticism of the Hebrew Bible*, 2nd   ed.
2. Paul D. Wegner, *A Student's Guide to Textual Criticism of   the   Bible*
3. Bruce Metzger, *The Text of the Old Testament*
4.   James   A.   Sanders,   *Torah   and   Canon*
5. Rabbi Samson Raphael Hirsch, *Collected Writings*
6. James C. VanderKam, *The Meaning of the Dead Sea Scrolls* [Emanuel Tov, *Textual Criticism of the Hebrew Bible*, 3rd ed. (Minneapolis: Fortress Press, 2012), 135.] [Bruce M. Metzger, *The Text of the New Testament: Its Transmission, Corruption, and Restoration*, 4th ed. (Oxford: Oxford University Press, 2005), 45–47.]

PART VI (ו): EARLY MANUSCRIPTS AND CRITICAL VARIANTS

Chapter VI (ו): New Testament Hermeneutic divergence and Manuscript Developments

I. Introduction: Quoting the Tanakh or Interpreting Through Midrash Reuse?

The New Testament's citations of the Hebrew Bible often reflect midrashic methods common to Second Temple Judaism, though these recontextualizations invite critical review regarding semantic fidelity and theological implications. This chapter investigates the nature of these hermeneutic divergences, explores their origin, and confronts the theological consequences they carry.

Was it ignorance? A translation issue? Or intentional redirection?

II. Timeline of NT Manuscript Development

The earliest Christian texts emerged decades after the events they describe. Here's a broad timeline:

- Pauline Epistles: c. 49–64 CE
- Gospel of Mark: c. 70 CE
- Gospel of Matthew: c. 80–90 CE
- Gospel of Luke: c. 80–90 CE
- Gospel of John: c. 100 CE
- Revelation and late epistles: c. 90–110 CE

These writings were copied and recopied without centralized control, leading to hundreds of variants even within the first few centuries.

III. Examples of NT Hermeneutic Divergences of the Tanakh

The early followers of Yeshua often used midrashic strategies like *gezerah shavah* and *binyan av* to reframe Tanakh passages in light of messianic hope. This was not textual corruption but homiletic tradition common among Second Temple interpreters. The challenge lies in discerning where such reuse honored or obscured the covenantal origin of the Hebrew scriptures.

Paul's letters demonstrate a distinctly **midrashic** method of interpretation of exegesis, aligning him with Jewish interpretive traditions rather than classical Greco-Roman logic. He uses:

• **Gezerah Shavah** (verbal analogy): Linking verses by common words • **Binyan av** (inference from a principle): Extrapolating laws from Torah themes • **Al tikrei**: Creative reinterpretation of letters or sounds

[9] As noted by Dr. E.P. Sanders and Jacob Neusner, Paul reflects **Second Temple Pharisaic reasoning**, particularly in his use of paraphrase, synthesis, and intentional recontextualization. His controversial readings (e.g., Romans 10, Galatians 3) are not distortions per se, but rather extensions of a rabbinic model—though his **audience and theological intent** diverge radically from Tanakh fidelity.

- **Romans 3:10–18** claims to quote Psalms—but strings together unrelated verses.
- **Matthew 27:9–10** attributes a prophecy to Jeremiah, but it's actually Zechariah 11:12–13.
- **Hebrews 10:5–7** quotes Psalm 40:6–8 but changes "my ears you have opened" to "a body you have prepared for me."

---

[9] Jacob Neusner, *The Mishnah: A New Translation* (New Haven: Yale University Press, 1988), xii–xv. Babylonian Talmud, *Yoma* 9b and *Sanhedrin* 11a. See also Jacob Neusner, *The Bavli and Its Sources*, vol. 1 (Atlanta: Scholars Press, 1994), 58–60.

- **Romans 10:6–8** modifies Deuteronomy 30:11–14 to suggest faith replaces Torah observance.

Paul's application of Hebrew scripture reflects **apostolic urgency** more than grammatical fidelity. Key examples include:

• **Romans 10:6–8** modifies Deuteronomy 30:11–14 to say *"Christ is the end of the Law"*, while the Torah context emphasizes its nearness and doability.

• **Galatians 3:13** cites Deuteronomy 21:23 ("Cursed is everyone who hangs on a tree") to apply to Jesus—but omits that the Torah describes this as a mark of shame and judgment, not salvation.

• **Hebrews 10:5–7** alters Psalm 40:6, changing *"my ears you have opened"* to *"a body you have prepared for me"*—a Septuagint reading rather than Masoretic.

These shifts suggest Paul was not quoting Torah to reinforce its commandments, but to forge a **Christocentric midrash** using Greek textual traditions—often at odds with **Lašôn ha-qōdeš**.

IV. Analysis of Pauline Strategy and Greek Usage

N.T. Wright, in his *Paul and the Faithfulness of God*, argues that Paul reimagined Jewish covenantal theology within a new eschatological frame, centering around the Messiah event and cosmic reconciliation. James D.G. Dunn, a key architect of the "New Perspective on Paul," likewise contends that Paul's emphasis was not on replacing Torah but on universalizing covenant through faith.

While both scholars offer corrective nuance to older supersessionist readings, their models still rely on a subtle decentering of Hebrew textual identity. Paul, in this frame, becomes the founder of a hybridized Judaism-cum-Christianity, whose textual logic now moves toward Hellenistic categories of participation, grace, and ontology.

This manuscript challenges that construction. Paul's writings must be read within the prophetic linguistic system of the Tanakh—rooted in shoresh logic, parallelism, covenantal markers, and intertextuality—not through Greek moral categories or ecclesial universals. When Paul uses "law," "flesh," or "faith," he does so as an Israelite with linguistic and covenantal priors.

Rather than viewing Paul as founding a new religious mode, this manuscript sees him as a diasporic prophet wrestling with Israel's covenantal diaspora—still bound to Hebrew syntax and prophetic structure, even while communicating in koine Greek.

"Rather than inventing Christianity, Paul arguably reframed the early Messianic movement into a transnational Greco-Roman missionary theology."

See Appendix I: *Pauline Hebraisms in Greek Garments*, which maps key Greek phrases back to Hebrew source concepts.

N.T. Wright & James Dunn on Pauline Theology

Quote (N.T. **Wright):** "Paul did not reject his Jewish heritage but redefined it in light of the Messiah." — N.T. Wright, *Paul and the Faithfulness of God*, Vol. 1, p. 626

Quote (James D.G. **Dunn):** "Paul's rereading of Scripture through the lens of Christ was not an abandonment, but a transposition of covenant." — James D.G. Dunn, *The Theology of Paul the Apostle*, p. 86

To 'transpose' covenant is to remix Sinai into a Hellenistic scale. Paul's Christocentric readings—however sincere—represent a genre shift from prophecy to philosophical abstraction.

Paul recontextualizes Torah through Hellenistic midrashic filters, privileging Septuagintal phrasing over Hebraic fidelity.

Paul often quotes from the Septuagint (LXX), not the Hebrew Masoretic Text. He adapts texts to suit his arguments, frequently removing context. For example:

- **Isaiah 28:16** — MT: "a tested stone, a precious cornerstone" vs. Romans 9:33: "a stone that makes men stumble."
- **Deuteronomy 30** — MT: Torah is close to do; Paul uses it to argue for 'faith that speaks.'

This is not merely mistranslation—it's midrashic, interpretive theology that retools the Hebrew for a new message.

V. Theological Ramifications

These hermeneutics form the backbone of key Christian doctrines:
- **Substitutionary Atonement**
- **Messianic Identity of Jesus**
- **Justification by Faith Alone**

While the New Testament is traditionally associated with Greek composition, **many scholars now recognize deeply Semitic syntactic structures**, especially in Luke–Acts. Phrases like "and it came to pass" (καὶ ἐγένετο) reflect a Hebraic narrative rhythm seen throughout Genesis, Samuel, and Kings. The **Peshitta**, the Syriac version of the Bible, preserves many of these idioms more faithfully. Its transliterations mirror the *vav-consecutive* structure and direct speech formulae seen in Hebrew prose. This suggests either a Hebrew-Aramaic Vorlage or a community whose linguistic DNA was still thoroughly Semitic—even when writing in Greek. Luke, often considered a Gentile, was evidently shaped by **Semitic oral and narrative templates**.

Historical developments within Greco-Roman Christianity reveal a pattern of reinterpretation that, while possibly sincere, diverged from early Hebraic conceptual frameworks and warrants renewed textual evaluation.

While this work critiques the theological ramifications of Pauline midrash, it acknowledges that scholars such as **N.T. Wright** and **Paula Fredriksen** argue Paul remained within the bounds of Jewish covenantal logic. Wright's *Paul and the Faithfulness of God* and Fredriksen's *Paul: The Pagans' Apostle* emphasize that Paul sought to integrate Gentiles without abandoning Israel's prophetic memory—though from a Christocentric axis. This view, while theologically coherent, often underplays the Hebraic linguistic framework and displaces Torah continuity.

VI. Jesus and the Bronze Serpent: Symbol or Stumbling Block?

Paul's reapplication of Deuteronomy 21:23 in Galatians 3:13 ("Cursed is everyone who hangs on a tree") builds upon a typological midrash of Ancient Near Eastern judgment symbols. In the Torah, a body hung publicly signals shame, covenantal breach, and divine disfavor. Paul transforms this imagery: what was once a symbol of sin and wrath becomes an emblem of redemptive suffering.

This inversion parallels the bronze serpent (něḥāš něḥōšet) in Numbers 21:9—where the Israelites gaze upon a symbol of the very thing that afflicted them and find healing. Both typologies rely on sacred irony: salvation emerges not through erasure of judgment, but its confrontation. In ANE theology, serpents often symbolized both chaos and wisdom; Paul and John adopt these motifs to cast the crucified Messiah as both sin-bearer and redeemer.

This reinforces the Hebraic literary tendency to encode paradox within covenantal symbols: Yeshua, like the serpent lifted on a pole, becomes the focal point of both judgment and mercy. Yet where the serpent becomes idolatrous (2 Kings 18:4), the Messiah reclaims its power toward faithful restoration.

The Hebrew text distinguishes between *nāḥāš* (נָחָשׁ) and *tannîn* (תַּנִּין) when describing serpents. *nāḥāš* is used in

Genesis 3:1 for the deceiver, in Numbers 21:9 for the bronze serpent, and in 2 Kings 18:4 for the Nehushtan that Hezekiah destroyed. In contrast, *tannîn* appears in Exodus 7:9–10 to describe the sign given to Pharaoh—a term often translated "dragon" or "sea monster." See Appendix K.

This is no mere stylistic shift. The use of *nāḥāš* reinforces the link between deception and testing. Notably, the verb הִשִּׁיא (*hishiani*, "he deceived me") in Genesis 3:13 derives from the root נ-ש-א (*nasha*), aligning linguistically with the serpentine deceiver. This creates a typological continuity that challenges modern messianic assumptions regarding the bronze serpent.
See: Genesis 3:1; Numbers 21:9; 2 Kings 18:4; Exodus 7:9–10.

The Hebrew verb הִשִּׁיאַנִי (*hishiani*, "he deceived me") in Genesis 3:13 is a Hiphil form derived from the root נ-ש-א (*nasha*), meaning "to beguile, to delude." This causative form highlights the nature of the serpent's influence over Eve — not merely passive deception but a manipulative incitement to transgress. This same nuance connects the serpent in Genesis to the bronze serpent of Numbers, reinforcing the typological warning embedded in the term * nāḥāš*.

See: Genesis 3:13; BDB Hebrew Lexicon.

John 3:14, a pivotal moment in the **Brit Hadasha** (בְּרִית חֲדָשָׁה – *B'rīt Ḥădāšāh*, "New Covenant"), the text declares: "Just as Moses lifted up the serpent (ὄφις, *ophis*) in the wilderness, so must the Son of Man be lifted up." The term even in the Brit hadasha uses the word נָחָשׁ(*Naḥāš*) to describe serpent. This directly recalls **Numbers 21:9**, where Moses raises a **bronze serpent** (*nĕḥāš nĕḥōšet*) on a pole to heal the Israelites stricken in judgment. In the Hebrew, נָחָשׁ(*Naḥāš*) is not just zoological—it is theological, symbolic of divine justice, sin, healing, and the paradox of deliverance. However, another typology is the children of Israel fleeing persecution and roman domination gazed upon Jesus and he healed them…then later, as ecclesial powers grew, he became an Idol in the churches and cathedrals.

Although the Gospel of John is **not** preserved in any known Hebrew manuscript tradition, including the medieval **Shem Tov Hebrew Gospel** (which contains only *Matthew*, compiled ca. 1380 CE by Rabbi Shem Tov ben Isaac ben Shaprut), the presence of Hebraic terms and structures in the **Brit Hadasha** reveals clear textual and thematic continuity with the Tanakh.1 Shem Tov's Matthew illustrates how Semitic renderings and Hebrew idioms—such as *Naḥāš*—likely persisted among early Jewish followers of Yeshua prior to Roman textual dominance. George Howard, *The Hebrew Gospel of Matthew* (Macon, GA: Mercer University Press, 1995), 5–15. While Shem Tov's text only includes Matthew, Howard argues that it may reflect earlier Semitic gospel traditions. See also James R. Edwards, *The Hebrew Gospel and the Development of the Synoptic Tradition* (Grand Rapids: Eerdmans, 2009), 118–21.

Typologically, the lifting of the *Naḥāš* in the wilderness was not merely about relief—it was a confrontation with divine judgment through sacred irony. When the **Brit Hadasha** applies this to the Messiah, it subverts Roman readings of execution and reasserts the Torah's grammar of redemptive exaltation. The "lifting up" becomes not a Greco-imperial crucifix but a **Hebraic polemic of mercy** through judgment, covenant, and prophetic renewal. For typological parallels between *Naḥāš* and messianic motifs, see Michael Fishbane, *Biblical Interpretation in Ancient Israel* (Oxford: Clarendon Press, 1985), 350–52; and Daniel Boyarin, *The Jewish Gospels: The Story of the Jewish Christ* (New York: The New Press, 2012), 78–85.

Naḥāsh–Tannīn Typology and Pauline Curse

This chart explores the theological, linguistic, and typological functions of serpent-related terms in both the Hebrew Bible and New Testament.

Text	SBL Transliteration	Function	Theological Implication
Genesis 3:1	nāḥāš	Deceiver of Eve	Introduction of sin/deception
Numbers 21:9	nĕḥāš nĕḥōšet	Bronze healing symbol	Paradoxical salvation through judgment
2 Kings 18:4	nĕḥuštān	Idol destroyed by Hezekiah	Idolatry from divine symbol
Exodus 7:9–10	tannîn	Serpent/dragon in Pharaoh's court	Divine confrontation in Egypt
John 3:14	ophis	Typology for crucified Messiah	Messiah reinterpreted as paradoxical savior
Galatians 3:13	epikataratos	Applied Torah curse to Messiah	Christ became 'cursed' to redeem

The typology of the bronze serpent and its reinterpretation in the New Testament received varied treatment across early theological traditions. While the Church Fathers generally embraced the typological link between the serpent and Christ (John 3:14), rabbinic sources remained largely silent or resistant to such re-readings. The reasons for these disparities reveal a great deal about early sectarian and intertextual priorities.

10   Church   Fathers:
Early Christian writers such as Justin Martyr, Irenaeus, and Origen frequently invoked the bronze serpent to affirm Christ's redemptive function. Origen, in particular emphasized the spiritual meaning behind the serpent being 'lifted up'—linking it to the salvific crucifixion of Jesus and the triumph over sin. Irenaeus, in *Against Heresies*, interprets the serpent as a foretelling of the cross itself.

Augustine similarly spiritualized the serpent as the locus of sin's condemnation—transformed into healing through faith. These interpretations reflect a deeply allegorical impulse, driven by the desire to validate the New Testament through the framework of the Old. See: Appendix V for patristic diversity; Jesus as God was never consensus until enforced by Rome.

Rabbinic   Literature:
Rabbinic sources such as the *Mishnah*, *Tosefta*, and early Midrashim (e.g., *Sifre*, *Mekhilta*) make few direct references to the bronze serpent, and none tie it to a messianic typology. Instead, they focus on the dangers of idolatry and the importance of removing graven symbols— as Hezekiah did. In *Pesachim 56a*, Hezekiah's destruction of the Neḥushtan is praised as a righteous act.

This absence of messianic linkage reflects discomfort with physical symbols acquiring cultic status—a major concern in post-Temple Judaism. Rabbinic theology emphasized Torah observance and oral law, not mystical reinterpretation of earlier symbols.

Qumran   and   Sectarian   Silences:
The Dead Sea Scrolls (DSS) offer extensive commentary on

---

10 Jacob Neusner, *The Rabbinic Traditions About the Pharisees Before 70*, vol. 3 (Leiden: Brill, 1971), 412–15. Neusner documents how Rabbinic Judaism avoided physical-symbolic typologies like Neḥushtan. Michael O. Wise, Martin G. Abegg Jr., and Edward M. Cook, *The Dead Sea Scrolls: A New Translation* (San Francisco: HarperOne, 2005), 221–29. Despite extensive theological commentary, no DSS texts focus on the bronze serpent. Lawrence H. Schiffman, *Reclaiming the Dead Sea Scrolls* (Philadelphia: Jewish Publication Society, 1994), 222–24. Schiffman explains how Qumran theology avoided anthropomorphic or ambiguous iconography. Daniel Boyarin, *Border Lines: The Partition of Judaeo-Christianity* (Philadelphia: University of Pennsylvania Press, 2004), 157–64. Boyarin analyzes how post-Temple Judaism reinforced anti-Christian polemics through strategic silence. Michael Fishbane, *Biblical Interpretation in Ancient Israel* (Oxford: Clarendon Press, 1985), 350–52. Fishbane discusses how the lack of rabbinic midrash on certain topics may reflect deliberate theological distancing.

Torah, prophets, and apocalyptic prophecy, but say nothing about the bronze serpent. This silence is striking. The Qumran sect (likely the Essenes) focused on priestly purity, eschatology, and dualism—but avoided typologies linking physical objects to redemption. Their strict covenantalism may have rejected any association of a serpent—traditionally a chaotic or deceptive figure—with divine healing or messianic promise.

This sectarian gap underscores how controversial and subversive the Gospel's application of this symbol was.

Scholarly   Interpretation: Modern scholars such as Daniel Boyarin and Michael Fishbane note that typological silence in one tradition often indicates theological divergence or polemic restraint. The absence of rabbinic midrash on the bronze serpent's healing role likely reflects discomfort with Christian appropriation and the risks of symbolic ambiguity.

The typological link between Yeshua and the bronze serpent warrants deeper exploration, particularly in light of the serpent's dual role in biblical literature as both healing agent and later object of idolatry.[11]

6

Chapter VI: Conquest, Covenant & Canonical Betrayal

To call Joshua a betrayal is not to condemn the book—but to condemn the hands that twisted its covenant into conquest. *Yĕhōšúa'* was never meant to be a mascot for empire. The canon was betrayed not by Yahweh, but by those who mistook divine justice for domination. This chapter critiques misuse—not scripture—and affirms remnant restoration over imperial conquest theology. John Dominic Crossan, *The Birth of Christianity: Discovering What Happened in the Years Immediately After the Execution of Jesus* (San Francisco: HarperOne, 1998), 431–447. See Paula Fredriksen, *Paul: The Pagans' Apostle* (New Haven: Yale University Press, 2017), and N.T. Wright, *Paul and the Faithfulness of God* (Minneapolis: Fortress Press, 2013). Justin Martyr, *Dialogue with Trypho*, in *The Ante-Nicene Fathers*, ed. Alexander Roberts and James Donaldson, vol. 1 (Buffalo, NY: Christian Literature Publishing Co., 1885), chap. 94. Irenaeus, *Against Heresies*, Book IV, chap. 2, in *The Ante-Nicene Fathers*, ed. Alexander Roberts and James Donaldson, vol. 1 (Buffalo, NY: Christian Literature Publishing Co., 1885). ⊠ Origen, *Homilies on Numbers*, trans. Thomas P. Scheck (Downers Grove, IL: InterVarsity Press, 2009), 7.3. Origen explores the typology of the serpent as an elevated sign of healing and spiritual elevation. Augustine, *On the Gospel of John*, Tractate XII, in *Nicene and Post-Nicene Fathers*, Series I, vol. 7, ed. Philip Schaff (Buffalo, NY: Christian Literature Publishing Co., 1888). *Babylonian Talmud: Pesachim* 56a, trans. William Davidson (Sefaria.org). The rabbinic praise of Hezekiah's destruction of the bronze serpent (Neḥushtan) appears in this tractate.

VII. Thought-Provoking Questions

- Are doctrines like the virgin birth and resurrection built on stable textual ground?
- Can divine truth be grounded in mistranslation?
- If the Hebrew says one thing, and the Greek NT says another—which do we believe?
-Has Jesus become an object of idolatry?

VIII. References and Sources

1. Bruce Metzger, *The Text of the New Testament* (Oxford University Press)
2. Bart D. Ehrman, *Misquoting Jesus* (HarperOne)
3. Emanuel Tov, *Textual Criticism of the Hebrew Bible*
4. Rabbi Tovia Singer, *Let's Get Biblical*
5. Rahlfs-Hanhart, *Septuaginta*
6. James Kugel, *How to Read the Bible* [Emanuel Tov, *Textual Criticism of the Hebrew Bible*, 3rd ed. (Minneapolis: Fortress Press, 2012), 135.] [Bruce M. Metzger, *The Text of the New Testament: Its Transmission, Corruption, and Restoration*, 4th ed. (Oxford: Oxford University Press, 2005), 45–47.]

Counterpoint: Translation Variance as Incidental, Not Intentional

Mainstream View:
Scholars like Bruce Metzger and Bart D. Ehrman have catalogued textual variants, but generally conclude that translation inconsistencies in the New Testament—such as "parthenos" for "ʿalmāh" or "pierced" for "like a lion"—were mostly **accidental or theological clarifications**, not deliberate distortions.
Early scribes, they argue, acted more as transmitters than editors.

Representative Quote:
"The majority of textual changes arose from the sincere desire to clarify, not to corrupt." – *Bruce Metzger, The Text of the New Testament*, p. 251

Rebuttal: Translation Was Theological Realignment—Not Innocent Transmission

This framing **whitewashes the doctrinal consequences of translation bias.** When Isaiah 7:14's ʿalmāh ("young woman") becomes parthenos ("virgin") in the LXX—and is then cited in Matthew 1:23—the **Hebrew prophetic nuance is overwritten** by a Greco-Roman mystical lens.

Further, Psalm 22:16's "like a lion" (כָּאֲרִי) was replaced with "they pierced," despite the MT, DSS (5/6HevPs), and Rabbinic consensus rejecting such an interpretation.

As Emanuel Tov acknowledges:

"The Septuagint often reflects a theological agenda—whether consciously or not." (Textual Criticism of the Hebrew Bible, 3rd ed., p. 45)

And Rashi, on Psalm 22, firmly upheld:

"It is like a lion—k'ari—not a piercing."

These mistranslations **did not simply miscommunicate; they re-coded prophecy to suit Christological typology.** By the time Jerome translated the Latin Vulgate, **the distortion had become dogma.**

The canon did not inherit neutral texts—it inherited **Hellenized theology disguised as translation.**

See: Appendix K – Bronze Serpent and NT Recontextualization

PART VII (ז): THEOLOGY OF CREATION, HUMANITY, AND COVENANT

Chapter VII (ז): The Image of God – Masculine and Feminine Unity

I. Introduction: What Does It Mean to Be Made in God's Image?

Genesis 1:26-27 declares that humanity was created in the 'image and likeness' of God—male and female. This passage has been dissected by theologians, mystics, and linguists for centuries. But what if the true meaning was lost in translation—particularly due to Hebrew verb forms and gender dynamics obscured in English?

This chapter explores the divine image as a fusion of masculine and feminine forces, reflecting a balanced Godhead and inviting humanity to mirror that equilibrium.

This divine embodiment of unity and mutuality echoes what womanist theologian Delores S. Williams described as "survival theology"—a reading that honors the lived complexity of Black women and challenges the patriarchal frame imposed on sacred text. Similarly, Kwok Pui-lan emphasizes that feminist interpretation must move beyond Western dualities to re-center noncolonial cosmologies of gender within scripture. These lenses affirm that the Image of God was never meant to be abstractly male, but relationally whole.

II. The Cohortative Verb and Divine Intent

In Genesis 1:26, God says, 'Let us make man in our image.' This has triggered centuries of speculation: Was God speaking to angels? A divine council? Other gods?

Hebrew grammar offers clarity. The phrase uses a cohortative verb: **na'aseh** (נַעֲשֶׂה), expressing intent or proposal rather than plurality. It is not a declaration of multiple creators, but a divine inner deliberation with witnesses—angels, elements, or cosmic forces—who observe but do not create.

This nuance is absent in English, leading to severe theological distortion. See Appendix D.

III. El, Eloah, and ʾĔlōhîm: Masculine, Feminine, and Unified

The word **El** (אֵל) is masculine. **Eloah** (אֱלוֹהַ) is grammatically feminine. **ʾĔlōhîm** (אֱלֹהִים) is a plural form used singularly when referring to the God of Israel.

Together, these names form a triadic linguistic system of divine   balance:
-       **El**   =   Strength,   fatherhood
- **Eloah** = Nurture, inner counsel, womb-like power
- **ʾĔlōhîm** = Union of both; multiplicity within unity

Thus, when the Torah says God made man 'in His image,' the image includes both masculine and feminine properties.

The triadic appearance of the divine as El (אֵל), Eloah (אֱלוֹהַ), and ʾĔlōhîm (אֱלֹהִים) reflects not only a linguistic evolution but a theological compression of complex roles and characteristics within the ancient Semitic conception of deity. These forms, while sharing the root ʾlh (to be strong, mighty, divine), each carry distinct semantic weight and historical trajectory.

El, the oldest and most widely attested term across Semitic tongues, appears in Ugaritic, Phoenician, and Akkadian contexts as a **high god** or creator deity. In Ugaritic epics (c. 1400 BCE), *El* is portrayed as the aged father of gods (*abū ilāni*), embodying a **sovereign, paternal, and sometimes passive** aspect of the divine (Pardee, 1997). In biblical usage, *El* often appears in compounded names (e.g., *El Elyon, El Shaddai*) signifying transcendence and elevation.

Eloah emerges as a rarer, yet significant term in the Hebrew Bible—used most densely in the poetic corpus of Job, where it appears 41 times. Its morphological structure, ending in the feminine -ah, suggests a grammatically feminine noun—a striking feature considering its theological usage. While some argue that the form is merely a singular back-formation from ʾĔlōhîm, others observe that its poetic contexts often carry intimate, nurturing, or immanent divine qualities (Trible, 1984; Frymer-Kensky, 2001). Eloah, then, may preserve an early dimension of feminine divinity now obscured by dominant patriarchal interpretations.

'Ĕlōhîm, while grammatically plural, functions almost exclusively with singular verbs and adjectives when referring to the God of Israel. Scholars interpret this as a plural of majesty or an instance of grammatical abstraction—denoting intensity or fullness rather than numerical plurality (Tov, 2012; BDB, s.v. אֱלֹהִים). Yet, it is notable that this form also appears in the Hebrew Bible to describe other gods (elohim aherim) or celestial beings (bene elohim), reinforcing that the term was not originally exclusive to monotheistic usage. [Emanuel Tov, *Textual Criticism of the Hebrew Bible*, 3rd ed. (Minneapolis: Fortress Press, 2012), 135.]

Philologically, *El* and *Eloah* are cognate with terms in **Akkadian** (*ilum*), **Sumerian** (*ilu, dingir*), and **Northwest Semitic** dialects. The Sumerian word *dingir*, often rendered with the cuneiform sign ✳, corresponds functionally with the later Semitic *El* and carried both masculine and feminine deific applications—especially in deities like Inanna and Ninhursag (Kramer, 1961). This **gender fluidity of divine titles** suggests that the Hebrew *Eloah* may preserve residual theological memory of earlier, more inclusive conceptions of deity.

Furthermore, the early Israelite proximity to Ugaritic and Mesopotamian cultures necessitates recognition of shared cosmological patterns. 'Ĕlōhîm, as a grammatically plural form for a singular deity, mirrors divine council imagery in Ugaritic texts (cf. Psalm 82:1), where El presides over a pantheon—a memory subdued but not erased in Israelite theology.

IV. Divine Feminine in Scripture and Language

There are overlooked moments in Hebrew where God's actions or presence take on feminine grammar:

- **Deuteronomy 32:18** — 'You forgot the God who **bore** you' (יְחָלְלֶךָ) — a feminine verb form
- **Isaiah 42:14** — God says: 'I will cry out like a woman in labor'
- **Proverbs 8** — Wisdom (Chokhmah) personified as a woman, present at creation

These are not poetic flourishes—they are grammatical realities. They reveal a God who encompasses both fatherly strength and motherly compassion, power and nurture.

V. Woman as Ēzer kənegdô: The Divine Helper & The Parallel Succorer

Genesis 2:18 uses the phrase **ēzer kənegdô** (עֵזֶר כְּנֶגְדּוֹ) to describe woman: 'a helper opposite him.'

This term is not subordinate—it parallels the divine name **Ezer Yisrael** ('Helper of Israel'). Woman is presented not as assistant, but as counterpart: equal yet different. Together, man and woman reflect the fullness of God's image.

Furthermore, the term "ezer" may also be translated as succor: as the militaries of Israel called for "ezer" during times of hardship and distress. "Kenegdo" however, doesn't just translate as "opposite him" but parallel to. Showing again an equal balance amongst the two.

A common saying repeated in both popular and rabbinic discourse is: *"Ten measures of speech descended into the world; women took nine."* While often assumed to derive from Kabbalistic literature due to its alignment with mystical frameworks, this statement originates in the **Babylonian Talmud**, specifically **Tractate Kiddushin 49b**. There, in a series of hyperbolic aphorisms, the sages attribute various qualities to distinct social groups. The statement reads:

"Ten kavin (measures) of speech descended to the world; nine were taken by women."
(תשעה קבין שיחה ירדו לעולם, תשעה נטלו נשים)

This phrase, while not explicitly theological in the Talmudic context, has been retroactively spiritualized in later mystical literature due to its thematic resonance with **Malchut** and **Binah**, two feminine-coded **sefirot** in Kabbalistic cosmology.

- **Malchut** (מלכות), the tenth and final sefirah, represents **articulation, sovereignty, and expression**— often associated with the **faculty of speech**. It receives all upper emanations and channels them outward, akin to voice or proclamation.

- **Binah** (בינה), meaning "understanding," is the third sefirah and is explicitly described in **Talmud Bavli, Nidda 45b** as a trait **uniquely intensified in women**:

"Binah yeteirah nitnah l'isha" – *"An extra measure of understanding was given to woman."*

Although the Talmudic statement in Kiddushin 49b lacks metaphysical commentary, the **Kabbalistic system expands on this alignment** between femininity, speech, and receptivity. **Sefer ha-Bahir** and **Zohar** often place Malchut as the expressive vessel of the divine — paralleling the Talmudic idea that women hold a unique relationship to articulation and revelation.

Modern interpreters such as **Phyllis Trible**, **Tikva Frymer-Kensky**, and **Arthur Green** have noted that these layers suggest a **theological reclamation of feminine presence**, not merely a sociolinguistic quip. That women "took nine measures of speech" thus becomes, in mystical reinterpretation, a reflection of their **cosmic proximity to divine voice**.

Delores S. Williams contends in *Sisters in the Wilderness*, the biblical story of Hagar provides not only a narrative of survival but a counter-testimony to patriarchal theology. Her interpretation reframes covenantal value through the lived experience of African-descended women, repositioning the wilderness not as exile but as revelation. This reading aligns with diasporic theology where divine encounter often emerges at the margins of empire.

In *Micah 6:4*, YHWH declares, "I sent before you Moses, Aaron, and Miriam," placing Miriam in prophetic and salvific alignment with her brothers. The Hebrew verb *šalaḥti* ("I sent") grammatically applies equally to all three, affirming divine commissioning and shared authority.

Yet Miriam's prophetic authority is not confined to Exodus alone. According to **Sotah 12b**, the Sages preserve a powerful oral tradition: that it was **Miriam who prophesied the birth of Moses**. She foretold that her parents would bring forth the redeemer of Israel. When Pharaoh decreed infanticide, **Amram divorced his wife Yocheved**, fearing future suffering. But **Miriam rebuked him**, declaring his decree harsher than Pharaoh's, and prophesied again that her mother would bear the one to lead Israel out. Amram obeyed — and Moses was born.

Furthermore, the Babylonian Talmud in **Megillah 14a** includes Miriam among the **seven prophetesses of Israel**: Sarah, Miriam, Deborah, Hannah, Abigail, Huldah, and Esther. Her place among them affirms a rabbinic theology of female revelation — not as exception, but as essential.

Miriam thus functions not only as a prophetess in title, but as a *prophetic catalyst* in Israel's redemption story. She represents a line of feminine voices who receive and speak divine instruction, challenging both ancient patriarchal silencing and modern erasure. Her presence reinforces the

Hebraic ideal: that prophecy flows through righteousness, not gender.

VI. Creation as Cosmic Womb: The Divine Power to Reproduce

In Hebrew, the very structure of family encodes a **divine formula of balance and cosmic reciprocity**:

- **Father** — אָב (Aleph = 1, Bet = 2) → **Total: 3**
- **Mother** — אֵם (Aleph = 1, Mem = 40) → **Total: 41**
- **Child** — יֶלֶד (Yod = 10, Lamed = 30, Dalet = 4) → **Total: 44**

  Father + Mother = Child → 3 + 41 = **44**

This is not linguistic coincidence. In ancient Semitic thought, **numbers and letters are never neutral**. The totality of a child (*yeled*) is not merely biological — it is the **spiritual summation** of covenantal unity. Just as Genesis declares that "the two shall become one flesh," Hebrew grammar reveals that **"the two become one future."**

Even deeper:

- **Aleph (א)** — the number **1**, represents divine will, origin, and unity.
- **Bet (ב)** — means **house**, representing structure, formation, and covenant.
- **Mem (מ)** — means **water**, the feminine flow, life, and gestation.

Thus:

- The **father (אב)** initiates as **1 building the house (א + ב)**
- The **mother (אם)** is origin in water (א + מ)
- Their child is the **revelation of both**, unified in **gematria and biology**

The implication: Hebrew itself was encoded with **cosmic anthropology** — the **family as theology**, and woman not as a secondary image, but as the necessary **womb of numerical completion**. Creation was never solo — it was duet.

The ability to create life—pregnancy and birth—is not a mere biological trait. It is a spiritual metaphor for divinity. Human reproduction models divine creativity. Just as ʾĔlōhîm gave birth to creation, women carry the divine signature of creativity, endurance, and transformation.

This is why the womb is treated with such spiritual weight in Hebraic thought: the Mishkan (Tabernacle) was fashioned like a womb, YHWH's dwelling among humans.

The biblical model of womanhood stands in stark contrast to later Greco-Roman ecclesiastical systems. **Deborah** (Judges 4–5) functioned as a prophetess, judge, and military leader—governing the entire covenantal body of Israel. She did not merely serve in domestic or ceremonial roles but held judicial and national authority. This example dismantles the later notion, advanced by many **Patristic Church Fathers**, that women are categorically disqualified from spiritual leadership.

[12]While the New Testament contains examples of women like **Priscilla, Phoebe,** and **Junia** occupying key spiritual and instructional roles, this balance was eventually undermined by evolving patristic theology. **Tertullian**, for instance, writes: *"It is not permitted for a woman to speak in church, nor to claim for herself a share in any masculine function."* (*De Cultu Feminarum*, II.9). Likewise, **Chrysostom** stated: *"The woman taught once and ruined all. On this account therefore she is placed in subjection."* (*Homilies on 1 Timothy*, Homily 9). **Origen**, interpreting 1 Corinthians 14:34, affirmed: *"It is shameful for a woman to speak in church... even if she says something excellent or holy."* This progression toward **gendered**

[12] Paula Fredriksen, *Paul: The Pagans' Apostle* (New Haven: Yale University Press, 2017), 95–98.

silencing contrasts starkly with the earlier Hebraic framework in which figures like **Deborah** were entrusted with national judgment and prophecy, and where the image of God (Genesis 1:27) is explicitly expressed in both male and female embodiment.

Moreover, **Priscilla (Acts 18:26)** is portrayed as teaching Apollos, a man "mighty in the Scriptures," and is often listed **before her husband Aquila**, which in Greco-Roman syntax may imply prominence. Several scholars, including Ruth Hoppin, suggest that **Priscilla may have authored the Epistle to the Hebrews**, whose style and theology align with her intellectual profile and early Jewish-Christian roots. The early church's emerging **patriarchal bias likely contributed to her anonymity**, suppressing her authorship amid rising resistance to female leadership.

This manuscript contends that **later ecclesiastical structures imposed a Eurocentric patriarchal filter** upon what was originally a **Torah-based covenantal framework that honored gender balance**. The God of Israel reveals Himself through both *el* (mighty) and *Shaddi* (breast), translates as "God Almighty" or should we say "Mighty Breast". The very structure of creation affirms divine masculine and feminine synergy—distorted not by Torah, but by centuries of hierarchical reinterpretation.

VII. Women Segregated in the Synagogues and Churches

[13]Although rabbinic literature occasionally honors women for their piety and wisdom—such as Beruriah's halakhic

---

[13] Chapter VII: Judges, Fragmentation & Feminine Divine Grammar

Feminine divine grammar does not impose theology onto scripture—it excavates what canon and empire often silenced. From Deborah's judgment to Shekhinah's exilic presence, the feminine in Judges is not marginal—it is prophetic structure remembered. Fragmentation in this book reflects not feminine weakness but covenant imbalance. Judges reveals the loss of order not just through violence, but through the diminishing of the sacred feminine voice. Judith Plaskow, "Standing Again at Sinai: Judaism from a Feminist Perspective" (San Francisco: HarperSanFrancisco, 1991), critiques the patriarchal exclusion of women from both canonical authorship and interpretive leadership within Judaism. Her framework parallels Afro-diasporic concerns about scriptural access and gendered silencing. *Sefer Yetzirah* 2:2; Rokeach on Gematria; Kabbalistic commentary on *Bereshit* 1:27–28; also: Benner, Jeff. "Ancient Hebrew Lexicon of the Bible." (2005).

insight (Talmud, *Eruvin* 53b) or Hannah's model of prayer (1 Samuel 1, cf. *Berakhot* 31a)—traditional halakhah also reflects **structural gender restrictions**, particularly in liturgical and didactic spaces. The prohibition against women teaching Torah publicly is grounded in both **Talmudic** (e.g., *Ketubot* 7a; *Megillah* 23a) and later halakhic interpretations that limit women's roles in synagogue life and Torah dissemination.

One visual manifestation of this restriction is the **meḥiṣah**, the physical barrier separating men and women in the synagogue—a symbol of spiritual roles being spatially enforced. Though not explicitly mandated in the Torah, the **meḥiṣah** became a rabbinic norm by the medieval period, institutionalizing **gendered worship space** under the assumption of male spiritual primacy.

This framework also finds resonance in **early Christian ecclesial structure**, particularly in Pauline epistles. Passages such as **1 Timothy 2:11–12** ("I do not permit a woman to teach..."), **1 Corinthians 14:34**, and **1 Corinthians 11:5** reflect a theological logic of silence and submission which paralleled, and may have drawn influence from, contemporary Jewish norms. While women like Priscilla and Phoebe served vital teaching and leadership roles in the apostolic era (Romans 16:1–3), their presence was increasingly **subordinated by emerging Greco-Roman patriarchy** in both church and synagogue.

Women in Torah Law vs. Other Ancient Cultures

This chart provides a comparative analysis of women's legal, social, and spiritual status in ancient Israel according to Torah law, contrasted with major ancient civilizations such as Mesopotamia, Egypt, Greece, and Rome. Drawing from primary sources like the Pentateuch, as well as archaeological, legal, and historical records, this comparative study shows that Torah law granted women unique protections and dignities, especially relative to surrounding cultures. While patriarchal in many aspects, the Torah's framework included revolutionary features for its time, including inheritance rights for daughters, prophetic roles for women, and shared purity laws. This table serves as a tool for historical, theological, and anthropological discourse on gender in ancient legal systems.

Category	Torah Law (Ancient Israel)	Babylon/ Mesopotamia	Ancient Egypt	Greece (Classical)	Rome (Republic/Empire)
Inheritance	✅ Women could inherit from father or mother (Num 27, 36)	❌ Only males typically inherited; rare exceptions	✅ Women could inherit and pass property	❌ Strictly male inheritance lines	✅ Limited; required legal guardianship until married
Property Ownership	✅ Women could own, sell, and litigate property (Prov 31, Job 42:15)	❌ Property controlled by husband or male kin	✅ Yes, women could own property independently	❌ No; property passed through male guardians	⚠ Yes, but controlled by male relatives or guardians

Rape Laws	✅ Differentiated between rape vs. adultery; protected victims (Deut 22)	❌ Rape seen as property crime against father/husband	⚠️ Laws unclear; likely under male family control	❌ Viewed as property offense; victims had little protection	❌ Victim often shamed or ignored; no real legal protection
Purity Laws	⚖️ Men and women both unclean after bodily discharge (Lev 15:16–31)	❌ Female impurity heavily emphasized	⚠️ Some ritual concepts, but women less restricted	❌ Women seen as spiritually polluting	⚠️ Impurity laws existed but not equitable
Divorce	⚠️ Husband initiates; woman protec	❌ Man could divorce freely; women rarely could	✅ Women could initiate divorce with cause	❌ Virtually impossible for women	⚠️ Women could divorce, but with strict limitations

	ted via get (Deut 24)				
Religious Role	✅ Prophetesses, Judges (Deborah), Nazirites (Num 6), Levite daughters	❌ Women excluded from priesthood	✅ Women served as priestesses	❌ Mostly excluded from religious life	✅ Some served as Vestal Virgins
Political Leadership	✅ Deborah ruled all Israel; Athaliah ruled Judah	❌ Political roles extremely rare	✅ Queens and female regents existed	❌ Women barred from citizenship or politics	⚠️ Women of emperor families held power behind scenes
Marriage Contracts	✅ Bride price (not dowry); protection	❌ Dowry paid by bride's family; women seen as burden	✅ Marriage often mutual	❌ Women transferred between	⚠️ Legal contracts favored husband

			contract	male guardians	
from abandonment (Exod 22)					
Legal Standing in Court	✓ Women could testify, sue, inherit (Num 27; Job 42)	✗ Women needed male intermediary	✓ Women could appear in court	✗ Rarely allowed; not full citizens	⚠ Possible with limitations and male sponsorship
Motherhood Status	✓ Highly honored (Exod 20:12; Prov 31); matrilineal elements exist	✓ Important for legacy, not legally powerful	✓ Revered in society	✗ Idealized but powerless	✓ Honored but secondary to male lineage

The Torah presents a constitutional framework in which male and female were created equal by divine design, and that subsequent allowances, such as polygamy or gender-specific legal roles, should be seen as legislative amendments to the original Edenic covenant—not the ideal.

The Torah opens with a radical claim in the ancient world: 'So God created man in His own image... male and female He created them' (Genesis 1:27). This passage affirms ontological equality—both male and female bear the divine image (*tzelem Elohim*). In Genesis 2:18–24, the woman is created as a 'helper suitable for him' (*ezer kenegdo*), a Hebrew term used elsewhere to describe God Himself as Israel's helper (Psalm 33:20). Thus, woman is not a subordinate, but an equal partner.

Jesus later affirms this original structure in Matthew 19:4–8, where He declares that marriage was designed as a union of equals—'the two shall become one flesh'—and that Moses' allowances for divorce (and by extension polygamy) were due to human hard-heartedness. He explicitly states: 'From the beginning it was not so.'

The Torah's later legal provisions, such as those concerning polygamy (Exodus 21:10, Deuteronomy 21:15–17), bride prices (Exodus 22:16–17), and gender-distinct roles, reflect accommodations within a tribal, patriarchal, and fallen society. Yet even within these laws, safeguards are placed to ensure dignity and fairness—for example, equal provision for all wives, and the right of daughters to inherit land (Numbers 27).

The laws of ritual purity (Leviticus 15) apply equally to male and female bodily emissions, contradicting claims that impurity was gender-biased. Prophetesses like Miriam (Exodus 15), Deborah (Judges 4), and Huldah (2 Kings 22) exercise national spiritual authority, confirming that women retained covenantal agency and leadership.

Therefore, the Torah's Edenic vision establishes a baseline of equality. Later gender distinctions in law should be understood as case-specific regulatory adaptations—not reflections of inherent inequality. Like a constitution amended to address societal breakdown, these laws responded to real conditions while pointing back to the wholeness of creation. As such, the Torah upholds a prophetic ideal of male–female unity, with deviations permitted only under strict justice and covenantal constraint.

VIII. Thought-Provoking Questions

- Does modern theology suppress the feminine traits of God?
- What happens to humanity when one gender's divine reflection is minimized?
- Can we truly say we know God if we ignore half of the image?
- How would doctrine shift if ʾĔlōhîm were taught as unified masculine-feminine energy from the start?

IX. References and Sources

1. Phyllis Trible, *God and the Rhetoric of Sexuality*
2. Avivah Gottlieb Zornberg, *Genesis: The Beginning of Desire*
3. Rabbi Samson Raphael Hirsch, *The Pentateuch: Deuteronomy Commentary*
4. Tikva Frymer-Kensky, *In the Wake of the Goddesses*
5. Strong's Concordance and Brown-Driver-Briggs Lexicon (BDB)
6. The Hebrew Bible (Leningrad Codex)

PART VIII (ח) THEOLOGY OF CREATION, HUMANITY, AND COVENANT

Chapter VIII (ח): Israelite Identity and Global Dispersion

I. Introduction: Why Identity Matters

This study does not treat diasporic identity as a sociological inheritance alone, but as an epistemic framework wherein historical memory, spiritual continuity, and cultural resilience encode covenantal knowledge. John Mbiti's theory of African communal ontology and Jan Assmann's concept of cultural memory provide grounding for understanding dispersed Israelite identity as a legitimate theological witness to scriptural preservation. [John Mbiti, *African Religions and Philosophy*, 2nd ed. (Oxford: Heinemann, 1991).]

In a world of religious dogmas and racial constructs, few questions provoke more controversy than: Who were the original Israelites? Does it matter today? The Tanakh speaks of a people chosen not just by creed, but by bloodline, history, and covenant.

This chapter explores the traces of the Israelite identity, as recorded in Scripture, preserved in global memory, and dispersed through centuries of exile, conquest, and spiritual rebellion.

Languages carry memory. Some memories are written in scrolls; others are embedded in verb stems, spoken in the cadence of longing, exile, and return. One of the most revealing grammatical forms in Biblical Hebrew is the **cohortative**—a subtle but potent expression of volitional self-will, found almost exclusively in the **first-person singular or plural**. Unlike the imperative, which commands others, or the jussive, which suggests action, the cohortative declares: *I will..., let me..., we shall...*

In covenantal terms, this is the voice of **internal obedience**—the syntax of prophets, priests, and pilgrims. It appears in pivotal moments of the Tanakh:

- אָקוּמָה– "I will arise" (Isaiah 33:10)
- אֵלְכָה– "Let me go" (Exodus 3:3)

- אָשִׁירָה– "Let me sing" (Exodus 15:1)

- נַעֲשֶׂה אָדָם– "Let us make man" (Genesis 1:26)

This form is more than grammar—it is **covenant crystallized in conjugation**. It allows the speaker to participate with the divine not merely in thought, but in **declared resolve**.

What is remarkable is how this linguistic form **echoes across continents and exiles**.

Among **Semitic languages** like Geʿez and Amharic, the cohortative persists, not only in syntax but in sacred chant and liturgy. In **Niger-Congo** languages, volitional markers align grammatically with Hebrew, often surfacing in ritual expressions like "Let us remember" or "I shall walk in the way." Among Indigenous American tongues—such as **Nahuatl, Aymara, and Algonquian languages**— cohortative verb constructions similarly express first-person sacred intent, often in ceremonial or mythological contexts.

These cross-cultural linguistic patterns are not mere coincidences. They may represent the **linguistic residue of a covenantal consciousness**, dispersed through exile and preserved in the speech of the remnant. When Leviticus commands "You shall be holy," and a distant people echoes, "We will walk," the language becomes more than cultural— it becomes **prophetic archaeology**.

To trace the cohortative voice is to trace the heartbeat of a people who still say *Let us return*—even when their names have been changed, their scrolls suppressed, and their songs nearly silenced.

The account in **1 Samuel 28:3–7**, where Saul consults the אֵשֶׁת בַּעֲלַת-אוֹב *(eshet baʿalat ʾov)* — "a woman possessing a familiar spirit" — reflects a deeper spiritual crisis in Israelite identity. The phrase *baʿalat ʾov* has roots in **Canaanite necromantic practice**, wherein *ov* denoted a ritual pit or hollow from which the dead were summoned

— likely linked to divination through ancestral spirits. The very use of this term demonstrates how **Israel had adopted Semitic pagan rites** prevalent in the region, particularly those involving **ghosts (rephaim), ancestral mediums, and corpse veneration**.

The presence of such a practitioner within Israel, consulted by its king, reveals not merely personal disobedience but a **cultural infiltration of foreign spirituality**, echoing the broader Deuteronomic warnings of covenant abandonment (cf. Deut. 18:10–12). This same syncretism—blending indigenous Semitic rituals with Torah faith—**resurfaces across Afro-diasporic religious systems** forcibly dislocated through trans-Atlantic slavery. Kelly Brown Douglas, *Stand Your Ground: Black Bodies and the Justice of God* (Maryknoll: Orbis Books, 2015), 12–29.

In particular, **elements of ancestral veneration, spirit invocation, and sacred femininity** retained in African spiritual systems such as **Obeah, Vodun, and Ifá** reflect ancient forms of priestess mediation akin to the *ba'alat 'ov*. Rather than being viewed solely as "paganism," these systems **retain coded remnants of Hebraic and Near Eastern ritual structures**, preserved under conditions of cultural dislocation and oppression. The linguistic, prophetic, and spiritual overlap between ancient Israelite infractions and diasporic adaptations invites renewed examination of how memory and practice survive exile— not only geographically but theologically.

Musa Dube's postcolonial feminist framework offers critical insight here. She notes that empire's most effective theological tool was not only conquest, but narrative control. By recoding scriptural identity through Greco-Roman lineage and imperial doctrine, colonizers could erase the voices and memories of those who were once central. This project seeks to reclaim that voice by re-grounding Israelite identity in Hebrew prophetic memory, not ecclesial politics.

Parallels Between Hebraic Customs and Contemporary African Traditions

The remarkable continuity between ancient Hebraic customs and enduring African traditions, particularly among West African communities. These parallels demonstrate not only cultural memory and preservation, but also bolster the thesis that the Afro-diasporic peoples—especially those who carried these customs unknowingly—may bear a deeper ancestral link to the Israelites of the Tanakh.

1. Naming Ceremonies

In Hebraic tradition, names are given with deep prophetic meaning (Genesis 17:5, Genesis 32:28). Among the Yoruba and Igbo, naming ceremonies (like 'Iko omugo' or 'Akwasidae') include prayers, libations, and blessings by elders to forecast the child's destiny.

2. Circumcision

Hebrews performed circumcision on the eighth day (Genesis 17:12). In many West African cultures, circumcision is a rite of passage performed in early life or adolescence, often accompanied by ceremonial isolation and teaching.

3. Dietary Laws

Levitical laws restrict certain meats (Leviticus 11). Among many African tribes, pork and shellfish are traditionally avoided, with taboos that mirror biblical Kashrut.

4. Menstrual Separation

In Leviticus 15:19–30, menstruating women were separated temporarily. Among the Ashanti and others, women retreat during menses, not participating in food preparation or public rituals.

5. Festival Cycles

The Hebrew calendar includes harvest feasts (e.g., Sukkot, Shavuot). African festivals like Yam Festivals or New Moon observances celebrate agricultural blessings with sacrifices and worship.

6. Priestly Garments and Tribal Roles

The Levitical priests wore specific attire and carried sacred roles (Exodus 28). Similar traditions exist among West African priesthoods like the Akan 'okomfo' or Yoruba 'babalawo', with designated garments and spiritual functions.

7. Orality and Scripture

Ancient Israel preserved much of its early tradition orally before redaction. Likewise, griots and oral historians in Africa serve as tribal memory keepers, preserving lineages, laws, and theology.

II. Scriptural Clues to Israelite Appearance

Though Scripture does not obsess over race, it offers many clues about the appearance and condition of ancient Israelites:

- **Lamentations 5:10** – "Our skin was black like an oven"
- **Job 30:30** – "My skin is black upon me"
- **Song of Solomon 1:5** – "I am black but comely"
- **Exodus 4:6–7** – Moses' hand turns leprous 'white as snow'—a contrast
- **Acts 13:1** – Simeon called Niger (Latin: black)
- **Numbers 6:5** – Describes thick, woolly hair under the Nazarite vow

These suggest a people of darker hue, resilient and Middle Eastern–African in origin—far from modern Eurocentric depictions.

III. Historical Witnesses: Africa and the Scattered Tribes

Afro-Semitic Dispersal, Diaspora Suppression & Hidden Remnants (1200 BCE–1700 CE)

"Your descendants will be as the dust of the earth, and you will spread out to the west and to the east, to the north and to the south..." (Genesis 28:14)

Semitic Southward Expansion (c. 1200 BCE–586 BCE)

- Following the fragmentation of the United Monarchy (c. 930 BCE) and the Assyrian exile of the northern tribes (722 BCE), waves of Israelite refugees fled south through Egypt and into Nubia, Cush, and Sudan.

- **Jeremiah 43:7** records a post-exilic group settling in **Tahpanhes (Daphnae)** in Egypt.

- The **Elephantine Papyri** (5th c. BCE) document a Hebrew-speaking colony on Elephantine Island, maintaining Temple worship and the Divine Name—centuries before Rabbinic standardization.

  Pathways: Nile River corridor • Sinai Peninsula • Arabian coastlines • Sahara trade bands.

Sahelian Consolidation & Ghana's Golden Age (c. 700–1100 CE)

- Afro-Semitic communities migrated westward into the Sahel, forming literate merchant guilds and ruling classes in **Ghana (Wagadou), Mali,** and **Songhai**.

- Hebrew-speaking clans merged with Berber-Jewish traders, creating hybrid religious networks that survived Islamic and later European invasions.

- **Al-Bakri (1068 CE)** wrote of "Jews dwelling in Ghana who followed the Law of Moses."

- **The Radhanites,** Jewish traders spanning France to the Niger River, carried Torah scrolls and Hebraic ethics into West African commerce.

  Cultural Markers: Sabbath observance • Kashrut-like food laws • Male circumcision on 8th day • Hebrew script derivatives.

Islamic Slave Trade & Genetic Genocide (7th–17th c. CE)

- Beginning in the **7th century CE**, Islamic caliphates launched one of the world's longest-running slave trades, targeting non-Muslim African populations—especially Afro-Semitic tribes in the Sahel.

- **Male slaves were often castrated** to eliminate lineage continuity, a strategy referenced in both **Islamic legal treatises** and **Byzantine travelogues**. These eunuch slaves served in the Abbasid courts, harems, and Ottoman palaces.

- Estimates suggest over **17 million Africans** were enslaved and forcibly displaced via the **Trans-Saharan, Indian Ocean, and Red Sea routes**—surpassing the European trade in duration and geographic spread.

- Many Afro-Semitic communities went **crypto**, adopting Islamic names outwardly while secretly preserving Torah observance.

Historical Sources:

- Bernard Lewis, *Race and Slavery in the Middle East* (1990)

- Ronald Segal, *Islam's Black Slaves* (2002)

- J.A. Rogers, *From "Superman" to Man* (1920), esp. ch. 3 on Jewish-African kinship

- Ibn Khaldun, *Muqaddimah*, 14th century

Crypto-Judaism & Hidden Remnants (c. 1400–1700 CE)

- West African crypto-Jewish clans (e.g., in Mali, Guinea, and Senegal) used oral traditions and mnemonic song to preserve Hebraic identity underground.

- Portuguese slavers and Jesuit missionaries noted "Jews among the Blacks" who resisted pork, observed Sabbath at sunset Friday, and circumcised their sons on the 8th day.

- **1548 CE**: A Portuguese report from Elmina mentions "Black Jews of Guinea."

- Some crypto-Jews were later captured in the **transatlantic slave trade**, arriving in Brazil, Jamaica, and North America with partial Hebrew oral memory intact.

- The **Black Jews of Sierra Leone**, **Igbo tribes of Nigeria**, and the **Lemba of Zimbabwe** continue to preserve Torah customs, priestly oral history, and even genetic traces of Semitic ancestry—such as the **Cohen Modal Haplotype** found in Lemba priests.

[14] As Jan Assmann argues, "Cultural memory is not stored in libraries but in rituals, language, and blood."

And as Deuteronomy 30:4 prophesied: *"Even if your exiles are at the ends of the earth, from there the Lord your God will gather you and bring you back."*

- Josephus (1st c. CE): Mentions Israelite colonies scattered beyond the Euphrates.
- John Ogilby (1670): Jews were "scattered over this region... inhabiting both sides of the Niger."
- Rabbi Abraham Halevi (1528): Claimed Dan and Gad dwelled in Ethiopia.
- Dr. Allen Godbey (Duke, 1920): "Judean Hebrews are in West Africa."
- M. Abadie (French Historian): Traces Fulani origins to Semitic roots and the Ghana Empire.
- Sanhedrin 94a:15: Reference to Bilad el-Sudan (Africa) and Jewish traders sold in 1492.

Ancient testimonies from classical historians provide compelling corroboration for an Afro-Semitic Israelite identity. Herodotus, writing in the 5th century BCE, described the "Colchians" as descendants of Egyptians, noting they were "black-skinned and woolly-haired," and

[14] Bezalel Porten, *Archives from Elephantine: The Life of an Ancient Jewish Military Colony* (Berkeley: University of California Press, 1968). Al-Bakri, *Book of Routes and Realms*, quoted in Nehemia Levtzion and John Hopkins, eds., *Corpus of Early Arabic Sources for West African History* (Princeton: Markus Wiener Publishers, 2000), 71–72.
Ibn Khaldun, *The Muqaddimah: An Introduction to History*, trans. Franz Rosenthal (Princeton: Princeton University Press, 1967), 2:376–77. Bernard Lewis, *Race and Slavery in the Middle East: An Historical Enquiry* (New York: Oxford University Press, 1990), 55–60. Ronald Segal, *Islam's Black Slaves: The Other Black Diaspora* (New York: Farrar, Straus and Giroux, 2002), 36–42. Ehret, Christopher. *The Civilizations of Africa: A History to 1800* (Charlottesville: University Press of Virginia, 2002), 121–125.
J.A. Rogers, *From "Superman" to Man* (New York: J.A. Rogers Publications, 1920), 42–49. Edith Bruder, *The Black Jews of Africa: History, Religion, Identity* (New York: Oxford University Press, 2008), 85–98. Shlomo Sand, *The Invention of the Jewish People* (London: Verso, 2009), 150–159. Edward W. Blyden, *Christianity, Islam and the Negro Race* (Baltimore: Black Classic Press, 1994; orig. pub. 1887), 117–121. Tudor Parfitt and Yulia Egorova, *Genetics, Mass Media and Identity: A Case Study of the Genetic Research on the Lemba and Bene Israel* (New York: Routledge, 2006), 36–40.

"practiced circumcision from ancient custom, just like the Egyptians and Ethiopians." He asserted that their similarity in appearance and ritual suggested a common origin. This implies the ancient Mediterranean world recognized the overlap between African and Semitic populations by phenotype and covenantal practice.

Similarly, Diodorus Siculus, in his *Bibliotheca Historica* (Book III), described the Ethiopians as the most ancient of all peoples, from whom the Egyptians and then other Semitic nations derived cultural knowledge. This directly challenges Eurocentric chronologies that cast African peoples as peripheral to Near Eastern origin narratives. Josephus, writing from a Jewish perspective under Roman rule, claimed that "the Ethiopians are a part of our nation, descendants of Abraham by Keturah" and further affirmed that Egyptians and Jews shared ancient ties (Antiquities 1.6.2).

These accounts, combined with linguistic and anthropological evidence, point to a shared ethno-cultural matrix between African and Semitic peoples. Afro-Hebraic continuity, therefore, is not anachronistic reimagining but a retrieval of long-marginalized historical memory. This is further validated by cultural memory theory (Assmann) and communal ontology (Mbiti), which posit that identity is transmitted not solely through text but through ritual, land, trauma, and inherited practice across generations.

Columbus, Hebrew Translators, and the Search for the Lost Tribes of Israel

1. Luis de Torres: Columbus' Hebrew Translator On his first voyage to the New World in 1492, Christopher Columbus brought with him **Luis de Torres**, a converso Jew fluent in **Hebrew, Aramaic, and Arabic**. Columbus believed these languages would be essential for communication with remnants of the Ten Lost Tribes or eastern peoples. Torres was tasked with interpreting in case the expedition encountered descendants of ancient

Israelites. This choice reflects a theological motivation behind exploration, not merely economic or imperial aims.

Primary Source: Fernando Colón, *The Life of the Admiral Christopher Columbus by His Son Ferdinand*, ed. and trans. Benjamin Keen (New Brunswick: Rutgers University Press, 1959), 53–55.

2. 2 Esdras 13 and the "Hidden Nation" Columbus explicitly referenced **2 Esdras 13:40–45**, a passage from the Apocrypha describing how the Ten Tribes journeyed to a distant land called *Arzareth*, interpreted as "another land" beyond the Euphrates. He believed this distant place could be the Americas. In his **Book of Prophecies (Libro de las profecías)**, Columbus used this text to spiritually justify his voyage, suggesting the peoples he encountered might be Israelites.

2 Esdras 13:45: "Through that country there was a long way to go, a journey of a year and a half, and that country is called Arzareth."

Primary Source: Christopher Columbus, *Libro de las profecías*, ed. and trans. Delno West and August Kling (University of Florida Press, 1991).

3. Hebraic Echoes in Early Encounters Reports from Columbus and subsequent explorers noted practices and characteristics among the Indigenous peoples that resembled Old World customs. Bartolomé de las Casas, a chronicler of the Americas, recorded speculative beliefs that these peoples were descendants of the Ten Tribes. These early interpretations framed the New World not just as a foreign frontier but as a prophetic fulfillment.

4. Amerigo Vespucci's Observations Amerigo Vespucci, while not explicitly focused on Israelite connections, documented encounters with various ethnic groups that included dark-skinned peoples. His *Mundus Novus* letters emphasize the unfamiliarity of the New World peoples to European classification systems, prompting later commentators to revisit these records through biblical and prophetic lenses. Post-expedition interpretations often included claims linking Indigenous or African-descended peoples to Shem or even dispersed Israelites.

Primary Source: Amerigo Vespucci, *Letters from a New World*, trans. Clements R. Markham (London: Hakluyt Society, 1894).

Theological and Historical Implications:

- The inclusion of a **Hebrew-speaking interpreter** (Luis de Torres) demonstrates a belief in the **potential presence of Israelites** in the Americas.

- Columbus' use of **2 Esdras 13** reveals how **biblical prophecy** shaped exploratory agendas and influenced geopolitical decisions.

- These accounts offer historical support for the idea that **Afro-Hebraic and Indigenous communities** could be **carriers of ancient Israelite lineage and covenantal identity**.

Thus, even the earliest European voyages to the Americas were spiritually tethered to Hebraic eschatology, prophetic fulfillment, and the search for a dispersed covenantal people.

IV. Deuteronomy 28 and the Curse of Dispersion

The prophetic curses of Deuteronomy 28 outline the marks of the disobedient nation:

- **Enslavement by enemies** (v. 48)
- **Loss of name and language** (v. 49)
- **Scattering into all nations** (v. 64)
- **Worship of gods of wood and stone** (v. 36)
- **Return to Egypt in ships** (v. 68) – never to see homeland again

This matches no other people in history as precisely as the Transatlantic Slave descendants.

Exile in Scripture is never synonymous with rejection—it is consequence, not cancellation. From Assyria to Babylon,

Rome to the transatlantic ships, the pattern of scattering in biblical theology consistently reinforces covenant, not discards it. The **diaspora**, particularly among Afro-descended peoples, bears not only historical trauma but **textual fingerprints**—traces of linguistic, prophetic, and covenantal identity refracted across forced migrations.

[15] In **Deuteronomy 28:36–68**, the language of dispersion culminates in a striking verb: וְהִתְמַכַּרְתֶּם(ve'hitmakkartem, "you shall sell yourselves")—a reflexive form in the **Hitpael stem**. This verb is not transactional; it is **internal and volitional**, used elsewhere in 1 Kings 21:20 and Isaiah 52:3 to describe self-imposed bondage or alienation. The implication is not a commercial sale, but a **spiritual resignation**—a people stepping into exile through breach of covenant rather than mere conquest.

This is not merely history—it is **grammatical prophecy**. The reflexivity of the Hitpael form reveals an inner covenantal fracture, making the transatlantic and colonial diaspora not just geopolitical events, but fulfillments of linguistic foresight. The use of the definite article in **"בָּאֳנִיּוֹת"** (ba'oniyot, "in *the* ships") in verse 68 further indicates specificity—not a general pattern, but a **definite route**, echoing prophetic intention rather than metaphorical language.

"This reflexive stem reveals a theology of exile wherein the people become both agents and victims of their own bondage."

Isaiah 11:11–12 reinforces this by naming actual geographies—**Pathros (Upper Egypt), Cush (Sudan/Ethiopia), Elam (Persia), and Shinar (Babylonia)**— as regions from which the "remnant" will be regathered. These are not symbolic locations; they correspond to historically verifiable migratory patterns and Jewish communities, including the **Beta Israel, Lemba**, and **Igbo**, among others. Their oral traditions, use of Hebrew names,

---

[15] Jeffrey Tigay, *Deuteronomy*, The JPS Torah Commentary (Philadelphia: Jewish Publication Society, 1996), 262–264.

ritual practices, and reference to Deuteronomy 28 predate modern identity movements and deserve rigorous scholarly treatment.

Malyn Newitt documents Portuguese encounters with African communities who not only practiced Judaic customs but were *identified as Jews* by the Catholic clergy and Inquisition authorities. These communities—often centered around Senegambia, Guinea-Bissau, and the Gold Coast—were subject to targeted raids and reclassification as "negros" despite having had a long-standing Hebraic lineage.

In *The Portuguese in West Africa: 1415–1670*, Newitt highlights royal decrees that authorized the enslavement of those who refused Christian conversion, including Hebraic-practicing Africans. This aligns precisely with Deuteronomy 28:68's "return into Egypt by ships" — not a physical Egypt, but a renewed condition of bondage and trafficking under imperial powers:

"...many of the Africans first encountered by Portuguese merchants were described as Jews or heretics—keepers of the Sabbath, circumcisers, and non-Catholics. These identifiers were used to justify their forced export." —Malyn Newitt, *The Portuguese in West Africa: 1415–1670*, p. 192.

This prophetic alignment supports the Hitpael form of וְהִתְמַכַּרְתֶּם ("you shall sell yourselves") as a reflexive divine judgment upon Israel's descendants—fulfilling the seal of diaspora captivity.

Likewise, **Isaiah 56:6–8** shifts the frame of Israelite identity from biological descent to **covenantal proximity**:

"The foreigners who join themselves to YHWH... even them will I bring to My holy mountain." This passage undercuts exclusionary models of lineage, affirming that covenantal obedience—**not Eurocentric or rabbinic genealogies**—defines who may dwell in the gates of Israel (cf. Lev. 19:34; Deut. 23:15–16).

In **Romans 9:27**, Paul, quoting Isaiah, affirms that "though the children of Israel be as the sand of the sea, only a remnant shall return." This is a theological map: not all who are scattered are lost—but not all who are counted have remained faithful. The prophetic burden, then, falls not on institutions of identity control, but on those who can **interpret exile linguistically, historically, and prophetically**.

This section does not attempt to spiritualize identity. It presents evidence—textual, grammatical, geographic—that calls scholars, theologians, and readers alike to consider whether **diasporic echoes of covenant are in fact remnants of prophecy**.

For the full philological and historical treatment of these terms—including a breakdown of **Hitpael reflexivity**, definite article specificity, and regional exile correlations— see **Appendix L**.

This work affirms that typology is not a racial assertion but a covenantal resonance. The use of Hebrew grammar reflects divine architecture, not ethnic exclusivity— restoring the linguistic structure of sacred memory as a path to communal redemption.

V. Wood and Stone: Prophecy Fulfilled?

Deuteronomy 28:36 warns: "You will serve other gods— wood and stone."

- **The Cross**: Icon of Christianity, once a Roman execution tool.
- **The Kaaba Stone**: Black meteorite worshipped by millions in Islam.

Both have become focal points of major world religions rooted in Abrahamic tradition, yet foreign to Torah.

VI. Genetic Echoes And Afro-Semitic Migrations

[16] Modern genetic studies offer compelling support for Semitic migrations into Sub-Saharan Africa—most notably through the analysis of **Y-DNA haplogroups**. Among the most significant is **E-M215 (formerly E1b1b)** and its related clade **E1b1a (E-M2)**, which are widely distributed across Northeast, East, and West Africa.

The haplogroup **E1b1a**, which dominates among West African and African diasporic populations, shares ancestral roots with **E-M215**, a lineage deeply connected to ancient Afro-Asiatic migrations in the Nile Valley and the Levant. This branching pattern supports a **reverse-flow theory**, where Semitic populations either emerged from or re-entered Africa through multiple waves, including the Cushitic and Nilotic corridors.

In one pivotal study, **Haber et al. (2017)** traced the **E-M215 lineage** across regions of modern-day Sudan, Egypt, Ethiopia, and Israel, noting that "Jewish and non-Jewish populations in the Levant share E-M215 subclades consistent with African admixture dating back at least 2,000–3,000 years." This overlaps chronologically with the early Israelite period, suggesting a potential link between biblical migrations and preserved paternal genetic signals.

Moreover, the **E1b1a (E-M2) haplogroup**, which dominates among African-American men and West African populations, has been **recurrently overlooked in Jewish genetic discourse**, despite its deep Semitic linguistic and anthropological correspondences. As geneticist **Lucotte et al. (2003)** noted, "The presence of E haplogroups in Jewish and African populations points to shared early ancestry not

---

[16] Shomarka Keita and Rick A. Kittles, "The Persistence of Racial Thinking and the Myth of Racial Divergence," *American Anthropologist* 99, no. 3 (1997): 534–544. Edith Bruder, *The Black Jews of Africa: History, Religion, Identity* (New York: Oxford University Press, 2008), 45–69. Hammer, Michael F., et al. "Y Chromosomes of Jewish Priests." *Nature* 385, no. 6611 (1997): 32. Marc Haber et al., "Chad Genetic Diversity Reveals an African History Marked by Multiple Holocene Eurasian Migrations," *The American Journal of Human Genetics* 99, no. 6 (2017): 1316–1324. https://doi.org/10.1016/j.ajhg.2016.10.012. Gerard Lucotte, "Haplotypes of the Y Chromosome in Jews: A Comparative Study," *Human Biology* 75, no. 3 (2003): 365–376. https://www.jstor.org/stable/41465951. Cruciani, F., et al. "Tracing Past Human Male Movements in Northern/Eastern Africa and Western Eurasia: New Clues from Y-Chromosomal Haplogroups E-M78 and J-M267," *Molecular Biology and Evolution* 24, no. 6 (2007): 1300–1311. https://doi.org/10.1093/molbev/msm049.

Y-DNA Haplogroup Tree: Afro-Semitic Diasporic Lineages

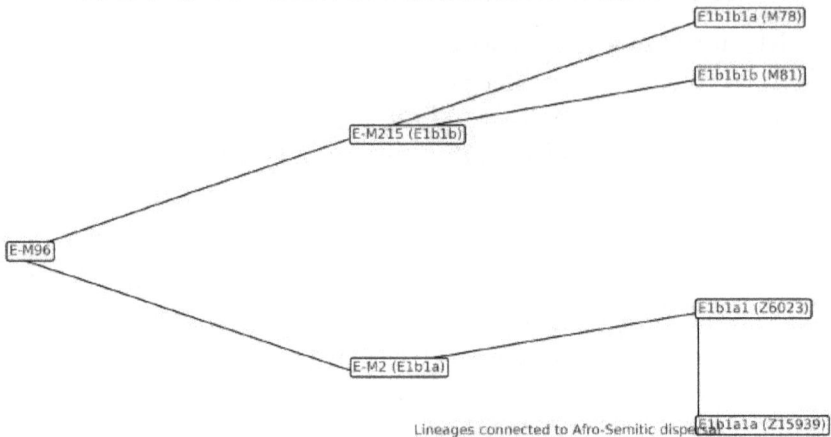

| E1b1b1a (M78) |
| E1b1b1b (M81) |
| E-M215 (E1b1b) |
| E-M96 |
| E1b1a1 (Z6023) |
| E-M2 (E1b1a) |
| E1b1a1a (Z15939) |

Lineages connected to Afro-Semitic dispersal

limited to the Levant but extending to Saharan and Sahelian migratory patterns."

Thus, if we align Y-chromosomal evidence with scriptural genealogies (e.g., Cush, Mizraim, Sheba, Havilah), we uncover a biological trail consistent with the **Hebraic dispersal narrative** argued throughout this monograph. DNA does not replace covenant, but it can **illuminate the pathways of exile and memory**—a genetic echo of the lost prophetic voice.

As Psalm 89:4 declares, "I will establish your seed forever, and build up your throne to all generations"—a promise echoing not only in scrolls, but in bloodlines.

[17] Additionally, **Afro-Semitic languages** like Geʻez, Tigrinya, and Hausa preserve **Hebrew-like morphology and syntactic parallels**, which modern linguists view as evidence of shared ancient Semitic origins prior to diaspora linguistic drift. Scholars such as Dr. Edith Bruder and Dr. Tudor Parfitt have argued that the **historical presence of Jewish and Hebrew identities among Igbo, Yoruba, and**

---

[17] John S. Mbiti, *African Religions and Philosophy*, 2nd ed. (Portsmouth, NH: Heinemann, 1990), 195–202.

Lemba populations is not merely a matter of cultural memory but may reflect **ethnic and covenantal continuity**.

Moses, Havilah, and the Prophetic Mirror of Diaspora

The Torah's earliest geographical prophecy—found in Genesis 2:11—mentions the land of Havilah: "where there is gold; and the gold of that land is good." While often dismissed as an Edenic abstraction or symbolic allusion, this verse emerges from the pen of Moses, the one to whom YHWH said, *"With him will I speak mouth to mouth, even manifestly, and not in dark speeches; and the form of YHWH shall he behold"* (Numbers 12:8). Moses, the greatest prophet in Israelite history, is the sole author said to have seen through divine clarity, not riddles. If we take this seriously, the mention of Havilah is not incidental—it is encoded prophecy.

Hebrew linguistics affirms that the term מֵעֵבֶר לְכֻשׁ(me-ever leKush) used in Zephaniah 3:10—"From beyond the rivers of Cush…"—places this prophetic remnant west of Kush, meaning west of Ethiopia. The preposition *me-ever* literally denotes "from the other side," "across," or "beyond," signifying a diasporic horizon. This echoes the geography of Havilah, which many associate with the regions of West Africa that border the Sahel—landscapes later dominated by the Ghana, Mali, and Songhai empires. If Havilah is a prophetic symbol, then the wandering of Afro-Semitic peoples westward after exile and through forced migrations (Islamic and Atlantic) is not merely historical but foretold.

The Joktanic connection also bears investigation. In Genesis 10:29–30, Joktan's sons are said to dwell "from Mesha, as you go toward Sephar, a mount of the east." This eastern trajectory stands in contrast to the descendants of Eber (from whom Abraham descends), whose legacy points westward—culminating, in exile, in the western fringes of Africa. Ironically, it was descendants of Joktan—via the Arabian Peninsula and Islamic expansion—who would later become enforcers of imperial religion, enslaving Afro-

Semitic peoples through systems rooted in conquest, not covenant.

This duality—brother against brother, Semite against Semite—mirrors the ancient struggle between Jacob and Esau, Ishmael and Isaac, Joseph and his brethren. The Joktanic line, though Semitic, became agents of religious suppression over their kin whose ancestral path still held covenantal memory.

Here, prophecy speaks twice:

- First, in Moses' naming of Havilah as a land of abundance tied to pre-exilic dignity.
- Second, in Zephaniah's forecast that beyond Cush—beyond the Nile and into the rivers of the west—those dispersed would again bring offerings to YHWH.

Though linguistically distinct from Arabic or Hebrew, the traditions preserved in West African societies—gold, priest-kingship, sacred law, ancestral ritual—resonate with covenantal archetypes. These may not prove descent through grammar, but they echo descent through sacred memory.

"The wilderness shall rejoice and blossom as the rose" (Isaiah 35:1)—even the wilderness of slavery, the Havilah of exile, the other side of Cush.

"Havilah" The Land of Gold

[18] Many modern biblical geographers have mistakenly identified Havilah with locations in the Arabian Peninsula or East Africa. However, a philological and historical reassessment places Havilah squarely in West Africa. Joseph J. Williams, in *Hebrewisms of West Africa*, argues that both cultural retention and oral tradition among the Ashanti and related tribes suggest that Havilah corresponds more

[18] Joseph J. Williams, *Hebrewisms of West Africa* (1930), John S. Mbiti, *African Religions and Philosophy* (1990), O. Temple, *The Fulani Empire of Sokoto* (1922), William Leo Hansberry, *Pillars in Ethiopian History* (1974), Edith Bruder, *The Black Jews of Africa* (2008)

accurately with the gold-rich regions of the ancient Ghana and Mali empires (modern-day Senegal, Mali, and Ghana) than with Arabia. This identification is strengthened by Genesis 2:11–12, which explicitly links Havilah with gold, bdellium, and onyx—natural resources abundantly found in West Africa.

Hebrew etymology supports this conclusion. "Havilah" (חֲוִילָה) shares structural consonantal roots with terms indicating circular or encamped regions, matching the terrain of Sahelian trade cities. Ancient Jewish travel texts also placed descendants of Shem, and later Hebrew outcasts, in Sub-Saharan corridors that were later charted by Portuguese and Arab traders. The implication is profound: Havilah was not eastward—it was downstream of Nile dispersions, westward along the Niger and Gambia routes.

"We must consider the possibility that Havilah is not in the Near East, but in the western bulge of Africa where gold was a known export from antiquity, and Jewish communities existed before European   colonization."
—Joseph J. Williams, *Hebrewisms of West Africa*, p. 83.

A critical reexamination of Zephaniah 3:10 reveals a geographical and prophetic code embedded in the original Hebrew that places the dispersed "daughter" of YHWH's people squarely within **West Africa**—not Ethiopia. The verse reads:

"From beyond the rivers of Kush, My supplicants, the daughter of My dispersed ones, shall bring My offering." (Zeph. 3:10)

In Hebrew:

מֵעֵבֶר לְנַהֲרֵי כוּשׁ עֲתָרַי בַּת פּוּצַי יוֹבִילוּן מִנְחָתִי

The key word is **מֵעֵבֶר**(*me-ever*), composed of the prefix **מ־**("from") and the root **ע־ב־ר**(*ʿ-b-r*, meaning "to cross," "to pass over," or **"opposite side"**). Contrary to modern English renderings like "beyond," which imply *distance,*   the   Hebrew   linguistic   intent implies *positional opposition*. That is, the text refers to the **opposite side** of the rivers of Kush, not merely a vague "beyond."

Kush is historically equated with **Ethiopia** (Upper Nubia/Sudan), situated in **East Africa**. Therefore, if the offering is coming **me-ever**, it is not from Kush itself—but from its **opposite side**.

In geographic terms, the **opposite of East Africa** (Ethiopia/Kush) is **West Africa**, aligning seamlessly with the *Afro-Semitic dispersions* along the Niger River, Gold Coast, and Gulf of Guinea, and the very regions ravaged by the Transatlantic Slave Trade.

Thus, Zephaniah 3:10 functions not only as a prophecy of return but as a **linguistic beacon**—marking **West Africa** as the land of the *scattered supplicants* who will again bring offerings to YHWH. The verse upends Eurocentric translations that have long suppressed the **diasporic topography** embedded in the Tanakh.

This verse, rightly read, confirms a central thesis of this monograph: that the **Hebrew identity of Afro-descendants is not metaphorical—but rooted in textual grammar, geography, and prophecy.**

Furthermore, the **forced trans-Atlantic slave trade** uprooted millions from regions where Semitic cultural and linguistic structures had merged with indigenous African identities. These communities carried fragments of Hebrew cosmology, dietary law, male circumcision, lunar calendars, and oral Torah traditions—even when formal religious systems were stripped away. Albert J. Raboteau, *Slave Religion: The "Invisible Institution" in the Antebellum South*, Updated ed. (Oxford: Oxford University Press, 2004), 86–101.

As Deuteronomy 28 predicted, these descendants would lose name, land, and language—but prophecy also spoke of **an awakening**. These Afro-diasporic identities, often dismissed or labeled syncretistic, may in fact hold latent **covenantal DNA**, both genetically and theologically. The biblical exile was not only about **geography**, but **memory, voice, and bloodline.**[19]

VII. Geography Before the Suez Canal

The land of Israel and the Horn of Africa were once inseparable.

- **Children of Ophir**: Settled in eastern Africa and the Arabian   peninsula.
- **Ethiopia (Cush)**: Linked to Moses' wife; proximity to Sinai.
- **Pre-Islamic Arabian Jews**: Suggest a wide Semitic presence   across   Africa   and   Arabia

These point to a pre-Middle East separation when Israelite tribes were African-adjacent and likely dark-skinned.

VIII. Thought-Provoking Questions

- If Israelites were darker-skinned, why are modern representations   so   white?
- What does it mean that those under the Deuteronomy curses   remain   globally   disenfranchised?
- Could the lost Israelites be hidden in plain sight— oppressed,   scattered,   and   awakening?

---

[19] Chapter VIII: Monarchy, Memory & Afro-Semitic Failure

To mirror Samuel's monarchy critique through an Afro-Semitic lens is not to merge unrelated histories, but to recognize shared covenant betrayals. The cry for kingship echoes in all who traded sacred structure for political survival. David is not just a king—he is the archetype of remnant contradiction. His life bears the tension of divine election and moral fracture, just as postcolonial identity holds the tension of memory and loss. Paul Joüon and Takamitsu Muraoka, *A Grammar of Biblical Hebrew*, rev. ed. (Rome: Pontifical Biblical Institute, 2006), §123f. Musa W. Dube, "Postcolonial Feminist Interpretation of the Bible" (St. Louis: Chalice Press, 2000), approaches scripture as a colonized space, particularly for African women. She reveals how translation, canon, and missionary theology doubly erased feminine and indigenous voice—rendering many biblical women both grammatically and spiritually silent. Josephus, *Antiquities* 1.6.2; Diodorus Siculus, *Bibliotheca Historica* 3.3.6. Diodorus Siculus, *Bibliotheca Historica*, 3.3.6, 1.28.1. John Mbiti, *African Religions and Philosophy*, 2nd ed. (Oxford: Heinemann, 1991). Jan Assmann, *Religion and Cultural Memory*, trans. Rodney Livingstone (Stanford: Stanford University Press, 2006). Lucotte, G. and Smets, P., "Origins of the E1b1b Y-chromosome Haplogroup in North Africa," *Egyptian Journal of Medical Human Genetics* 27 (2020): 5–11. Karl Skorecki et al., "Y Chromosomes of Jewish Priests," *Nature* 385 (1997): 32. Thomas, Mark G., et al. "Origins of Old Testament Priests." *Human Genetics* 109 (2001): 659–663. Edith Bruder, *The Black Jews of Africa: History, Religion, Identity* (Oxford: Oxford University Press, 2008). Tudor Parfitt, *Black Jews in Africa and the Americas* (Harvard University Press, 2013).

- Why does identity matter if God looks at the heart? Or does bloodline still fulfill prophecy? Doesn't the bible say "for a hanged man is cursed by GOD?"

IX. References and Sources

1.   Josephus,   *Antiquities   of   the   Jews*
2. John Ogilby, *Africa: Being an Accurate Description* (1670)
3. Dr. Allen Godbey, *The Lost Tribes a Myth* (1920)
4.   Sanhedrin   94a:15,   Babylonian   Talmud
5.   M.   Abadie,   French   Anthropological   Reports
6. Deuteronomy 28, Hebrew Bible (Leningrad Codex)
7. Acts of the Apostles, NT Greek with Latin Vulgate parallels

Counterpoint: Afrocentric Claims to Israelite Descent Are Unverifiable and Often Pseudohistorical

Mainstream   **View:**
While cultural memory may sustain identity, claims of direct descent from ancient Israelites—especially among African American and African diaspora groups—are considered speculative at best. Scholars argue these are **constructs of modern Black identity**, not genetic or historical realities.

Key Voices:

- **Shaul Magid** (*American Post-Judaism*)

- **Edward Kessler** (Interfaith Studies)

- **Jacob Neusner** (Rabbinics)

- **Benjamin Gampel** (*Jews of the Middle Ages*)

Representative   **Quote:**
"The claim to Israelite descent functions symbolically—it need not be literal to be powerful." – *Shaul Magid, American Post-Judaism*, p. 202

Rebuttal: Diasporic Memory Is Not Myth—It's Covenant Encoded

To reduce Afro-diasporic Hebraism to "symbolic identification" is to **ignore both internal textual evidence and external historical footprints.**

Textually:

- Deuteronomy 28:68 and its **Hitpael verb structure (וְהִתְמַכַּרְתֶּם)** reflects *self-sold bondage by ship*—not exile to Babylon or Rome.

- Scriptures speak of **curses that fit transatlantic trauma**— *yokes of iron, wood and stone gods, no one to buy you (redeem you).*

Historically:

- Jewish communities in **West Africa (Timbuktu, Mali, Ghana)** were documented by Arabic travelers and Christian colonists alike.

- Jewish presence in Ethiopia, Uganda, the Sahel, and Lemba genetic markers support a **wide Afro-Semitic footprint.**

Anthropologically:

- As John Mbiti states:

"In African religion, history is identity. The past is not gone—it is here." (*African Religions and Philosophy*, p. 29)

Diasporic memory is **not fantasy—it's spiritual DNA.** The refusal to accept Afro-descendant Israelites as authentic reflects **a colonial gatekeeping of sacred identity**.

See: Appendix H – African Jewish Records by Region

Prophetic and Diasporic Dispersion Map

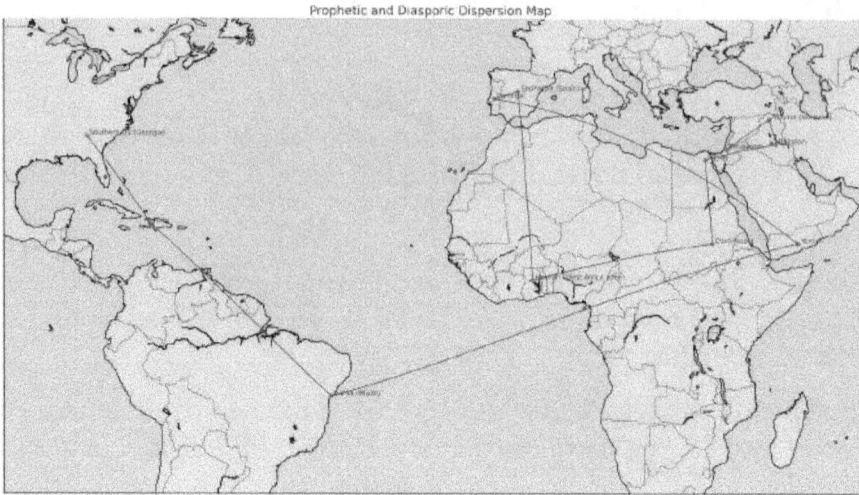

PART IX (ט): RESTORATION, LANGUAGE, AND REVELATION

Chapter IX (ט): Lašôn ha-qōḏeš – Hebrew as Vessel of Revelation

I. Introduction: The Language of God

This manuscript does not claim ethnic supremacy or doctrinal novelty. It stands within the lineage of grammatical theology and sacred pattern recognition— guided by prophetic voice, not polemic, and informed by sources across exegetical traditions. We have heard your voices for centuries through the cathedrals, monuments, and organized legitimacy this monograph simple shows why you have not heard ours.

Hebrew is more than a language—it is a vessel of divine consciousness. The sages called it Lašôn ha-qōḏeš (לשון הקודש), the 'Holy Tongue,' not because it is sacred by mere tradition, but because its very structure reveals spiritual truth. This chapter explores how the Hebrew language embodies revelation through its roots, letters, and patterns.

II. The Shoresh System: Rooted in Meaning

Hebrew words are built on three-letter roots called *shoreshim* (שורשים). These roots connect diverse concepts to a single spiritual idea.

Examples:
- **מלך (M-L-K)**: king, reign, counsel—rooted in balanced authority
- **שלום (Sh-L-M)**: peace, wholeness, payment—all from 'completion'
- **קדש (Q-D-Sh)**: holy, set apart, dedicated

Every word is part of a living family of meaning, revealing interconnection unseen in English or Greek. Even each letter has meaning as well as numeral equivalence.

III. Insights from Rabbi Hirsch and BDB

Rabbi Samson Raphael Hirsch emphasized that Hebrew roots are conceptual, not arbitrary:

"Hebrew is a system of moral and spiritual thought encoded into language. Its letters are symbols, its roots moral codes."

Brown-Driver-Briggs Lexicon (BDB) confirms this structure, showing that even small prefixes and suffixes shift a word's purpose without losing its base essence.

Thus, Hebrew preserves a logic of revelation that translations flatten or erase.

IV. Examples of Lost Meaning in Translation

- **Torah** (תורה) is from **Yarah** (ירה), meaning 'to instruct,' not 'law'
- **Nephesh** (נפש) means soul, breath, appetite—beyond 'spirit'
- **rûaḥ** (רוח) is wind, spirit, mind, and energy—a force,

not a ghost
- **ṣaddîq** (צדיק) isn't just 'righteous' but one aligned with justice and order
-**Pesha** (פשע) to rebel; transgress—this is considered worse than sin
-**Cheta** (חטא) to miss the mark; sin—which are allowed forgiveness through offerings
-**Avon** (און) iniquity, guilt, sin—desire to do mischief; is from (עוה) to bend, pervert

English lacks the multidimensional layers Hebrew carries. Each word becomes a universe.

Proverbs 6:23 says, "For the commandment is a lamp, The teaching is a light, And the way to life is the rebuke that disciplines."

כִּי נֵר מִצְוָה וְתוֹרָה אוֹר וְדֶרֶךְ חַיִּים תּוֹכְחוֹת מוּסָר

Lost upon the English reader is the word for teaching in Hebrew is Torah, reading "The Torah is light"![20]

V. Poetic and Prophetic Structure of Hebrew

The Tanakh is not just history—it is poetry, prophecy, and parallelism. Hebrew's compact syntax and root repetition empower divine rhythm.

- **Psalms**: Parallelism in thought and word
- **Isaiah**: Uses repetition, root wordplay, and double meanings

Prophets did not merely speak—they encoded vision into

---

[20] Chapter IX: Temple, Rebellion & the Return to Verb

To critique Solomon's temple is not to reject sacred space—but to warn against sacred stagnation. Hebrew faith begins in verbs, not monuments. The temple failed not in architecture, but in idolatry of structure. Return to the verb means returning to prophetic function, not abandoning form. Solomon's fall shows what happens when divine action is reduced to static prestige.

language. Hebrew allows prophecy to remain alive in rhythm, sound, and structure.

VI. The Revival of Hebrew and Prophetic Fulfillment

Zephaniah 3:9 proclaims: "Then I will restore to the peoples a pure language…"

The return of Hebrew in modern times—from dead dialect to national tongue—is not coincidence. It is prophecy.

Lašôn ha-qōḏeš is returning to the remnant. Those seeking truth find themselves drawn back to the original language of the covenant.

VII. Interfaith Convergence on Israelite Textual Stewardship: A Qur'anic and Pauline Accord

The Qur'an opens its dialogue with the Israelites not with condemnation but with covenantal recall: **"O Children of Israel, remember My favor that I bestowed upon you and fulfill My covenant so I will fulfill your covenant, and fear [only] Me"** (Q 2:40). This verse mirrors Deuteronomic language and evokes the covenantal conditionality of divine favor — directly aligning with Hebrew prophetic traditions. The term **"fa-irhabūn"** (فَٱرْهَبُون) evokes *yirat YHWH* (fear of the Lord), reinforcing that divine intimacy is bound to ethical fidelity.

In *Qur'an 2:47*, the divine voice declares: **"O Children of Israel, remember My favor which I have bestowed upon you and that I preferred you over the worlds."** The Arabic **faḍḍaltukum 'ala al-'ālamīn** (فَضَّلْتُكُمْ عَلَى ٱلْعَٰلَمِينَ) places Israelite chosenness in the superlative. Yet, this preference is not for privilege alone, but prophetic responsibility — a motif echoed in Amos 3:2: *"You only have I known of all the families of the earth; therefore I will punish you for all your iniquities."* In both Qur'anic and Biblical frameworks, **election without obedience results in judgment**, not exemption.

Surah 32:23 affirms the Torah's revelation and its designated audience: "We gave Moses the Book... and made it guidance for the Children of Israel." In this, the Qur'an does not abrogate Israel's historical role but confirms it — aligning itself with the prophetic continuity of Sinai. Moses, like Muhammad, is a bearer of sacred law, and the Israelites are explicitly named as the recipients of divine guidance. This is not a supersessionist erasure, but a scriptural endorsement of Israelite custodianship, echoed also in **Romans 3:2.**

Paul, though writing within a Christian frame, affirms the same truth: **"To them were entrusted the oracles of God"** (*Romans 3:2*). The Greek word **"logia"** (λόγια) indicates divine sayings, matching the Hebrew *d'varim Elohim* and Qur'anic **al-Kitāb.** The apostle's phrasing reasserts that **textual authority and sacred transmission were given to the Israelites** — not as owners, but as stewards.

This triadic alignment across Torah, Qur'an, and Pauline affirmation (Romans 3:2) is not syncretistic but theological parallelism. It reinforces that custodianship of divine utterance was Israel's vocation in all Abrahamic dispensations, not superseded but re-affirmed.

Throughout the corridors of antiquity, the Children of Israel were universally recognized as the custodians of divine revelation — the Children of the Oracles. Their centrality in the transmission of sacred law and prophetic wisdom earned them reverence not merely from within their own lineage, but from surrounding civilizations that acknowledged their unique covenantal role in history.

VII. Thought-Provoking Questions

- Can English theology ever match Hebrew revelation?
- What if theology without Hebrew is spiritually malnourished?
- Are modern churches ready for Hebrew literacy?

- What might be rediscovered if Hebrew became the norm again? Did Yeshua make Torah synonymous with himself?

VIII. References and Sources

1. Rabbi Samson Raphael Hirsch, *The Hirsch Chumash*
2. Brown-Driver-Briggs Hebrew and English Lexicon (BDB)
3. Zephaniah 3:9, Isaiah 28, Genesis 1–3
4. Avraham ben Yaakov, *Etymological Dictionary of Biblical Hebrew*
5. The Dead Sea Scrolls Bible (Vermes Translation)
6. Talmud Bavli, Tractate Megillah 9a

PART X (י): RESTORATION, LANGUAGE, AND REVELATION

Chapter X (י): The Global Awakening of Lost Israel

I. Introduction: A Prophetic Rebirth

Around the world, descendants of enslaved, colonized, and displaced peoples are waking up. They are rediscovering the Torah. Learning Hebrew. Reexamining history. Abandoning colonizer religions. This is not mere curiosity—it is prophecy fulfilled. The bones are rattling. The breath is returning (Ezekiel 37).

II. Ezekiel 37: The Dry Bones Live Again

Ezekiel's vision describes a valley of dry bones—scattered, lifeless, forgotten. But God commands the prophet to speak life into them.

- The bones are 'the whole house of Israel' (v. 11)
- Scattered through exile and trauma
- Brought back to life by prophecy, breath (rûaḥ), and covenant

Marimba Ani's exploration of *asili* and *Utamawazo*—cultural and cognitive frames in African thought—offers a crucial corrective to Eurocentric interpretations of identity. Her framework helps locate the reawakening of lost Israel within a broader recovery of African epistemology. Diaspora Israelites are not merely reclaiming bloodlines, but cosmologies suppressed by colonial encounter.

This vision is not allegorical. It is historical, generational, and happening now among the global remnant.

Daniel's Sealed Scroll and the Eschatological Cipher

Daniel 12:4 and 12:9 command the prophet to "seal up the scroll until the time of the end." Unlike prophetic declarations in Isaiah or Ezekiel, Daniel's vision is temporally encrypted. The sealing represents more than divine mystery—it signifies a divine delay of interpretive access. This delay creates a theological cipher: the message remains intact, but dormant, until reactivation in eschatological time.

In the Book of Revelation 5:1–9, the motif reappears. A scroll sealed with seven seals is presented in heaven, and no one is found worthy to open it—until the appearance of the Lamb. The scene echoes Daniel, yet it reconfigures the temporal grammar: what was sealed by the Most High is now disclosed by covenantal sacrifice. Revelation's scroll is not simply New Testament innovation, but a canonical return to Daniel's encrypted authority.

This continuity between Daniel and Revelation reflects a Hebraic preservation of time-bound prophecy. Theologically, it refutes the Greco-Roman notion of linear revelation and instead affirms cyclical, sealed transmission—prophetic time activated by covenant alignment.

The key point: the canon is not just a written product—it is a sealed witness, encrypted until divine timing permits its unveiling. This challenges notions of static scripture and supports the thesis that post-exilic scrolls were not discarded but temporally obscured.

For visual schema, see Appendix K, Fig. 1: *Canonical Encryption from Daniel to Patmos*. The model maps the scroll's trajectory across Hebrew prophetic tradition and late apocalyptic expression.

III. Return to Torah and Hebrew Identity

- Embracing the Sabbath (Shabbat)
- Wearing tzitzit, keeping dietary laws
- Reclaiming Hebrew names and prayers
- Rejecting pagan holy days (Christmas, Easter)

This is more than religion. It is ancestral reclamation—awakening spiritual memory written into the DNA of a scattered people.[21]

IV. Breaking Away from Doctrinal systems shaped under colonially mediated theology

For centuries, the Torah was replaced by theology rooted in Rome, Greece, and Europe. Slavery, conquest, and missions enforced this shift.

- Hebrew was lost, replaced with Latin and Greek
- Israelites were renamed, rebranded, relocated
- Christianity taught disconnection from Torah

---

[21] Chapter X: Prophecy, Wounds & Theological Reparations

To speak of reparations in Isaiah is not to force modern politics into prophecy—but to remember that covenant itself is restitution. The prophet begins with a wounded body because righteousness cannot rise until memory is healed. Reparations here is not payment—it is prophetic repair. Theology cannot bypass blood, and Isaiah anchors divine justice not in abstraction, but in the exposed wounds of his people.

Now, the children of the oppressed are remembering. Rejecting manmade doctrines. Seeking the God of Abraham, Isaac, and Jacob directly.

V. Dismantling Replacement Theology & The Curse of Ham

Replacement Theology claims the church replaced Israel. But scripture never states this. Paul himself said, 'Has God cast away His people? God forbid.' (Romans 11:1)

The true Israel cannot be replaced—it can only be reborn. Scattered, yes. Rejected, no. The covenant stands forever (Jeremiah 31:35–37).

Giants, and the Prophetic Reversal of Curse

"They chose the parts of Scripture that supported their tyranny and cast aside the parts that condemned them."
— Diasporic Reflection

Ham, Mizraim, and the Bloodlines of the Giants

The biblical text identifies Ham as one of Noah's three sons, with Mizraim (Egypt) as one of his descendants (Gen. 10:6). Through Mizraim, a genealogy emerges that includes the Caphtorim, Philistines, and other clans associated with giants such as the Rephaim, Anakim, and Amalekites. Deuteronomy 3:11 describes Og of Bashan as "the last of the Rephaim," whose bed measured 9 cubits in length.

This link between Hamite descendants and giant clans becomes even more pronounced when comparing:
- Num. 13:33 – "the sons of Anak come from the Nephilim."
- Josh. 14:12–15 – Hebron was formerly called Kirjath-Arba, after Arba, the greatest among the Anakim.
- Deut. 2:10–11, 20–21 – Rephaim and Emim were giant-like descendants in the land of Ham.
- 1 Chr. 20:5–8 – Goliath and his brothers are linked to these clans.

Scripture thus implies that many of the most formidable

adversaries of Israel descended from Hamite lines bearing giant traits—a fusion of human and corrupted power. While the idea that Ham's wife carried Nephilim blood remains speculative and not explicitly stated in canonical texts, the association between Hamite tribes and hybrid offspring is a prominent biblical motif.

Talmud, the Curse of Ham, and Racial Interpolation

The so-called "Curse of Ham" narrative originates in Genesis 9:25, where Noah curses Canaan, not Ham, for the transgression. However, centuries of distortion led to a widely propagated myth that Black people were cursed through Ham. This distortion is not supported by the biblical text, nor by early Jewish exegesis.

Talmudic evidence shows that Sanhedrin 108b contains speculative ideas about Ham being "smitten in his skin." While the Babylonian Talmud includes interpretive expansions, rabbinic tradition uses black bold letters to signify the actual words spoken, and faint letters or margins for later glosses or commentary. Scholars confirm that many racial connotations were medieval additions, not part of the Talmud's authoritative core.

It is ironic that the Curse of Ham was embraced as divine justification for slavery, while the curse upon Israel in Deuteronomy 28—which clearly speaks of ships, exile, and suffering—was conveniently ignored.

The selective theology of colonizers amplified fictional curses while silencing divine judgment upon themselves.

Lineage and the Nephilim Legacy: Scriptural Map

Scripture presents a comprehensive picture of how giant clans survived post-Flood and were concentrated in territories historically linked to Ham.

```
Noah
|
├          —                              Ham
|              ├   —        Mizraim      (Egypt)
|          |        └  —   Caphtorim  →  Philistines
|          |          └── Goliath, sons of Anak, Rephaim
|     ├── Canaan → Jebusites, Hittites, Amorites (giant-
affiliated)
|
└      —      Others      (Shem,        Japheth)
```

Associated   Scripture:
- Gen. 10 (Table of Nations)
- Deut. 2–3 (Rephaim, Anakim, Emim)
- Josh. 11:21–22 (Anakim removed from hill country)
- 1 Chr. 20:5–8 (Goliath lineage)

This legacy represents more than physical stature—it is a metaphor for oppressive spiritual empires. In later prophetic tradition, these Nephilim lineages symbolize systems of violence, idolatry, and corruption—precisely what Messiah must overcome.

Prophetic Reversal: From the Curse to the Calling

The "curse" attached to Ham was man-made—a theological weapon. The true biblical curse is found in Genesis 3 and Deuteronomy 28, both of which promise reversal upon repentance and redemption. Thus, the same people who were falsely labeled cursed may rise as restorers and messianic figures. Their stories, stripped of colonial gloss, reveal an Afro-Semitic inheritance.

The giants once filled the land with terror. But the dispersed will return with Torah.

VI. Identity, DNA, and Historical Memory

- E1b1a DNA Haplogroup linked to West African Hebrews
- Oral traditions in Ghana, Nigeria, Congo, Ethiopia claim Israelite descent
- Hebrew words in Igbo and Ashanti languages
- Afro-descendants experiencing spiritual call to Torah without missionary influence

One of the most pivotal contemporary scholars to assert Israelite descent among Africans is Rudolph R. Windsor. In *Judea Trembles Under Rome,* he traces the flight of Israelites into the African continent post-70 CE, with particular focus on Egypt, Sudan, and eventually West Africa:

"In the year 70 C.E., General Vespasian and his son Titus put an end to the Jewish state... During the period from Pompey to Julius, it has been estimated that over 1,000,000 Jews fled into Africa, seeking refuge. The slave markets were full of Israelites."
—Rudolph R. Windsor, *Judea Trembles Under Rome,* p. 84.

These Israelites would later form the bedrock of communities in Mali, Nigeria, and Ghana, preserving laws, customs, and oral Torah traditions. Their descendancy is not symbolic—it is literal. Windsor's assertion strengthens the premise of this monograph: that the canonical texts were never meant to be detached from the very people who carried them southward, westward, and across the seas.

It's not merely history—it's heritage reactivating in real time.

VII. Thought-Provoking Questions

- Why are millions leaving church structures for Torah truth?
- Can a people forget who they are—and remember centuries later?
- What if the lost tribes was never lost, only silenced?
- Is this awakening the fulfillment of Deuteronomy 30:1–6?

VIII. References and Sources

1. Ezekiel 37, Hebrew Bible
2. Deuteronomy 30:1–6
3. Romans 11, Jeremiah 31
4. Dr. Yosef Ben-Jochannan, *African Origins of Major Western Religions*
5. Tudor Parfitt, *The Lost Tribes of Israel*
6. Sefaria.org (Hebrew prophetic texts)
7. Oral traditions recorded in Ghanaian and Nigerian tribal histories

PART XI (יא): RESTORATION, LANGUAGE, AND REVELATION

Chapter XI (יא): Call to the Remnant – Responsibilities of Awakening

I. Introduction: Awakened, Now What?

Many are waking up—discovering their Hebrew roots, learning the truth of their identity, and walking away from religious lies. But awakening alone is not enough. The Torah doesn't just call Israel to awareness—it calls them to obedience, to build, to lead, and to restore. This is the call to the remnant: to rise in truth and reflect the image of YHWH in all areas of life.

II. Walking in Torah: Covenant Over Comfort

- Keeping the Sabbath holy
- Honoring the appointed times (Leviticus 23)
- Guarding the dietary laws
- Upholding righteous judgment and justice

Torah is not legalism—it's instruction for living. The

awakened remnant must not pick and choose, but embrace the full path of righteousness.

III. Rebuilding the Family and Community

In Deuteronomy 6:7, Israel is commanded to teach Torah to their children diligently:

"You shall teach them diligently to your children, and talk of them when you sit in your house, walk by the way, lie down, and rise up."

The remnant must:
- Restore biblical manhood and womanhood
- Raise children in the truth
- Build Torah-centered households
- Heal generational curses and cultural fragmentation

Leviticus 24:10 – "Son of an Israelite Woman and an Egyptian Man" – The Intrusion of Lineage, Law, and Identity at the Edge of the Camp

"And the son of an Israelitish woman, whose father was an Egyptian, went out among the children of Israel: and this son of the Israelitish woman and a man of Israel strove together in the camp."
— Leviticus 24:10 (KJV)

[22]This verse is no mere aside. It marks a dramatic departure in biblical narrative structure—a moment when lineage, identity, and covenantal belonging are placed under forensic spotlight. The child of a mixed union—**an Israelite mother and Egyptian father**—enters the communal stage and becomes the focal point of a national judicial dilemma.

[22] Tikva Frymer-Kensky, *Reading the Women of the Bible: A New Interpretation of Their Stories* (Schocken Books, 2002), 217–219. Esau McCaulley, *Reading While Black: African American Biblical Interpretation as an Exercise in Hope* (IVP Academic, 2020), 103. Jacob Milgrom, *Leviticus 23–27: A New Translation with Introduction and Commentary* (Anchor Bible, Vol. 3C; Doubleday, 2001), 2043–2045. Nahum Sarna, *The JPS Torah Commentary: Leviticus* (Jewish Publication Society, 1989), 170–173.

But the true weight of this passage lies not only in its moral or legal implications, but in its revelation of **ethnic complexity** and **social fault lines**—even within Israel's own camp.

Linguistic Precision: "Son of an Israelitish Woman" (בֶּן־ אִשָּׁה יִשְׂרְאֵלִית)

This construction is unique in the Torah. Nowhere else is a character described **primarily by his mother's ethnicity**— implying that **his patrilineal identity was not recognized** by Israelite standards. The fact that his mother was Israelite, but his father was Egyptian (מִצְרִי), reflects a **departure from covenantal purity** as reckoned in tribal reckoning (cf. Numbers 1:18).

Traditional Israelite descent, particularly for purposes of inheritance and priestly roles, is patrilineal. This individual exists in a **liminal space**: born among Israel, raised among Israel, but not reckoned *of* Israel. He is genealogically adjacent—but institutionally **ambiguous**.

As noted by Tikva Frymer-Kensky, "The text never gives him a name... only a relational tag—son of an Israelite woman—because his identity is in question."[1]

National Belonging and the Curse

When this unnamed figure quarrels with an Israelite man, he ultimately blasphemes the Divine Name. This triggers capital punishment. Yet the Torah does not ignore his ancestry—it highlights it as the **narrative context** for the transgression.

The implication is not that mixed lineage leads to moral failure—but that **alienation from communal belonging** may breed rebellion. This was a child who had **no tribal inheritance**, no national placement, and potentially no legal standing. His very existence exposed a legal gray zone in Torah society: **What happens when the boundaries of Israelite identity are transgressed by birth?**

From a prophetic standpoint, this account foreshadows **diasporic confusion**—children born of Israelites and nations who are neither fully accepted by the oppressor nor fully recognized by their own. This "child of Egypt" becomes a typology of **Afro-diasporic identity loss**, where the seed is Israelite but the structures that surround it are foreign and, at times, hostile.

Afro-Diasporic Echoes

The African diaspora echoes this biblical case in profound ways. Colonial rape, forced mixing, and plantation breeding practices intentionally severed lineage. Names, tribes, and inheritance structures were erased. Many today, like the blasphemer's son, are children of an Israelite woman (spiritually, ethnically) but raised under the language, gods, and customs of Egypt—modern systems of captivity.

This child, in Leviticus, **went out** (וַיֵּצֵא). The Hebrew root יצא carries the connotation of departure, rebellion, or exile. It mirrors the Exodus journey—but in reverse. While Israel went out of Egypt, this child went out of Israel, spiritually speaking.

The prophetic warning here is not genetic rejection, but **identity trauma**. Those severed from national inheritance are vulnerable to spiritual dislocation. The blasphemy that follows is symptomatic—not spontaneous.

As theologian Esau McCaulley notes:

"When people are not given a place in the story, they often burn the script."[2]

The Possibility of Inclusion

Despite this tragic case, the Torah also opens the door for inclusion: "One law shall be for the native-born and for the stranger who sojourns among you" (Lev 24:22). The judgment may be harsh, but it is also **equal**. In this same chapter, the stranger and the native are judged by **the same measure**.

Thus, even the child of an Egyptian and Israelite has a place—if covenant is honored. The Torah's vision is neither genetic absolutism nor cultural syncretism—it is **covenantal fidelity**. Those who attach themselves to YHWH, walk in His statutes, and honor His Name may partake in the blessings of the nation.

The blasphemer becomes a tragic example not of mixed ancestry's danger, but of what happens when identity is blurred and **covenantal responsibility is untaught.**

IV. Returning to Hebrew: Language as Legacy

[23]Language carries memory. Lašôn ha-qōḏeš is the divine language of covenant. The remnant must:
- Learn and teach Hebrew reading and prayer
- Study Torah in its original form
- Reclaim the power of names, roots, and meanings

Zephaniah 3:9 foretells a day when a 'pure language' is restored. We are living in that fulfillment.

V. Serving as Light to the Nations

Esther 8:17 – "And Many Became Jews" – The Semantics of Identity, Fear, and Alignment:

"And in every province, and in every city, wherever the king's command and his decree came, the Jews had joy and gladness, a feast and a good day. And many of the people of the land became Jews; for the fear of the Jews fell upon them."
— **Esther 8:17 (KJV)**

---

[23]
Chapter XI: Exile, Prophecy & The Burden of Unspoken Fire

Jeremiah's fire is not romantic metaphor—it is unspeakable covenant pressure. When exile burns in the bones and silence chokes the calling, prophecy becomes a wound. Diasporic prophets do not imagine Jeremiah—they remember him. And they speak through his same fractured grammar. Jeremiah's exile was not only geographic—it was vocal. His silence was not retreat, but grief withheld in holy tension. Lester L. Grabbe, *A History of the Jews and Judaism in the Second Temple Period, Vol. 2* (T&T Clark, 2008), 123–125. ▣ Rudolph R. Windsor, *From Babylon to Timbuktu: A History of Ancient Black Races Including the Black Hebrews*(Windsor's Golden Series, 1969), 90. Daniel L. Smith-Christopher, "Diaspora and Identity," in *The Oxford Handbook of Jewish Studies*, ed. Martin Goodman (Oxford Univ. Press, 2002), 720–722.

The phrase *"many of the people of the land became Jews"* (וְרַבִּים
מֵעַמֵּי הָאָרֶץ מִתְיַהֲדִים) represents one of the most theologically
provocative and linguistically charged moments in the
Tanakh. The Hebrew verb מִתְיַהֲדִים (*mityahadim*) is a hapax
legomenon—occurring only once in the entire Hebrew
Bible. Its singularity demands exegetical precision and
semantic care.

Unlike the more common verbs used for joining Israel
(e.g., לָגוּר"to sojourn" as in Ruth, or צָרַף"to
join"), *mityahadim* derives from the Hitpael stem of the
root יהד(Y-H-D), meaning "to become a Jew" in a reflexive
and causative sense. Grammatically, the Hitpael
implies **volitional identity transformation**—the people
were **making themselves Jewish**. But was this a true
conversion, a public alignment, or a survival mechanism?

This shift occurred under duress, fear, and imperial tension.
As the narrative makes clear, "the fear of the Jews fell upon
them." The Hebrew, פַּחַד הַיְּהוּדִים נָפַל עֲלֵיהֶם,
emphasizes *terror* or *dread*, not spiritual conviction. Yet
despite the coercive context, the text records a mass identity
shift, evoking deep questions for both historical
interpretation and diasporic memory.

The Meaning of "Becoming a Jew"

The term "Jew" (*Yehudi*) in the Persian period carried
both **ethnic** and **covenantal** weight. As Dr. Lester L. Grabbe
writes, "By the post-exilic period, 'Jew' referred to more
than a Judahite. It came to mean one who was part of the
Judean religious and social order, especially those
committed to the Torah."[1]

In this light, *mityahadim* may indicate a **national
alignment** rather than purely religious conversion. This is
supported by linguistic parallels in Ezra 6:21 and Nehemiah
10:29, where joining the community involves swearing
allegiance to the law of God (Torat Elohim) and separating
from "the peoples of the land."

Thus, the phenomenon in Esther 8:17 may reflect:

- **Political assimilation** for safety
- **Ethno-religious solidarity**
- **Recognition of divine favor upon Israel**
- **Strategic alignment in anticipation of cultural reversal**

In diasporic terms, this mirrors modern dynamics in which Afro-diasporic peoples, recognizing prophetic identity, re-embrace Torah not out of fear, but out of restoration.

Fear, Power, and Identity

Why would the people fear the Jews?

Because in the span of a few chapters, the powerless became powerful. The decree of genocide was reversed. The Mordecai-Haman reversal typifies the biblical motif of **prophetic inversion**—the exaltation of the oppressed (cf. Deut 28:13, Ps 113:7–8). Esther's courage shifted the fate of an entire people, and the visible sovereignty of Elohim—though veiled in the Megillah—manifested in sociopolitical victory.

This reversal provoked awe. In the ancient world, fear often accompanied divine presence or favor (cf. Joshua 2:9–11; 2 Chronicles 20:29). In this case, the fear was not of brute force, but of the **God of Israel working through His people**.

As such, those who became Jews were not merely converting in faith—they were aligning with perceived **divine destiny**. From a prophetic lens, Esther 8:17 anticipates Isaiah 14:1–2 and Zechariah 8:23, where the nations **join themselves** to Israel in recognition of YHWH's hand.

"Thus saith the Lord of hosts; In those days it shall come to pass, that ten men... shall take hold of the skirt of him that is a Jew, saying, We will go with you: for we have heard that God is with you."
— **Zechariah 8:23**

The motif of **fear transforming into affiliation** echoes in the prophetic promises of diaspora restoration.

Afro-Semitic Implications

Esther 8:17 is also a **mirror for Afro-diasporic peoples** who were cut off from covenant identity by colonization, slavery, and forced conversions. Today, many are "becoming Jews" in a new light—not by fear, but by truth, study, and awakening.

The phrase *mityahadim* thus becomes an etymological echo: those **becoming themselves again**—not adopting a foreign faith, but recovering an ancestral one.

As Rudolph Windsor notes:

"The Black Jews had an advantage over the African tribes— they carried their history, laws, and written records with them... These records enabled them to maintain their identity."[2]

In this sense, Esther 8:17 is not merely historical—it is prophetic. It testifies that **identity can be reclaimed, even in exile**. It affirms that in times of national awakening, even outsiders will recognize the light of Jacob rising again.

Isaiah 49:6 says Israel was called to be 'a light to the nations.' Not by blending in, but by standing apart in holiness.

- The remnant must display justice, mercy, and truth
- Not merely evangelize—but embody righteousness
- Be a living Torah scroll to the world

This is how the nations will see the power of YHWH—not through church, but through covenant keepers.

VI. Thought-Provoking Questions

- How are we building homes that reflect the Kingdom?
- Do our children know their divine identity and language?
- Are we lights—or shadows—among the nations?
- Is this awakening just knowledge, or transformation?

VII. References and Sources

1.   Deuteronomy   6:4–9
2.   Isaiah   49:6,   Micah   6:8,   Zephaniah   3:9
3.   Leviticus   23,   Exodus   20,   Numbers   15
4.   Rabbi   Samson   Raphael   Hirsch,   *Horeb*
5.   Avraham   Greenbaum,   *Universal   Torah*
6. Sefaria.org (Hebrew sources and commentaries)

Chapter XII (יב): Eschatology—Christian Recontextualization vs Hebraic Prophetic Cycles

I. Introduction: The Battle for the End of Time

Eschatology, or the study of last things, has become one of the most recontextualized theological arenas in modern times. Christian theology—particularly since Augustine, the Reformers, and modern dispensationalists—has often replaced Hebraic cyclical prophetic patterns with linear, Greco-Roman futurism. This chapter explores the deep rift between Hebrew prophecy and Christian end-time narratives, drawing directly from biblical themes and ancient sources.

II. Hebraic Prophetic Time: Cycles, Not Timelines

Hebrew prophecy is marked by cycles of exile, repentance, restoration, and covenant renewal. The prophets Isaiah, Jeremiah, Ezekiel, and Hosea never spoke of a final "end" in the way Christianity does. Instead, they described:
-       Return   to   Torah   (Deut.   30)
-     Restoration   of   scattered   tribes   (Isa.   11:11–12)
-     A   rebuilt   Zion   with   justice   (Isa.   2:1–4)
- Renewed priesthood and purified people (Ezek. 36–37)

Time is covenantal, not chronological. Every generation is called to choose: blessing or curse (Deut. 30:19). The future is always contingent on repentance.

Biblical prophecy unfolds through **cycles of covenant**, not Greco-Roman timelines. Torah presents time as a sacred rhythm:

• **7-day creation** → weekly Sabbath (Genesis 2:2–3) • **7-year Shemitah cycles** (Leviticus 25) • **49 + 1 Jubilee years** (Leviticus 25:10)

These structures mirror covenantal restoration: exile → repentance → return → renewal. Unlike linear eschatology which fixates on a climactic end, Hebraic thought sees **history as recurring repentance and divine invitation**. Daniel's 70 weeks (Daniel 9:24–27) are not terminal markers but covenantal checkpoints.

Unlike the linear and climactic eschatology characteristic of Greco-Roman thought, the Hebrew prophetic worldview operates within a cyclical framework. This is expressed through the moedim—YHWH's appointed times—alongside patterns of sabbatical years, jubilee sequences, and exile-return rhythms. Rather than moving toward a singular cosmic endpoint, time in the Tanakh functions as sacred recurrence, reaffirming covenant through repetition and restoration.

This cyclical model is evident throughout Scripture: in **Leviticus 25**, which introduces the sabbatical and jubilee cycles; in **Zechariah 1:6**, where the return to covenant reflects prophetic recurrence; and in **Daniel 9**, whose seventy "weeks" are structured as patterned intervals rather than a linear countdown. The **Qumran community** exemplified this worldview, calibrating their calendars according to solar-based cycles that rejected the Temple's Hellenistic lunar revisions—affirming their belief in divinely appointed sacred time over imperial adaptations.

The notion that time itself became a tool of colonization—seen in the rise of the **Gregorian calendar's global supremacy**—is not merely symbolic. It is a **typological violation** of scriptural time. Even the Book of **Revelation**, though often misread through futurist lenses, originally presents cyclical sequences—seals, trumpets, bowls—that reflect the Hebrew pattern of layered judgment and covenantal reset. The flattening of these cycles into linear "end-times" chronology represents a theological distortion born not from prophetic Israel, but from imperial Rome.

As R. S. Sugirtharajah points out, canonization in the early church often coincided with the theological silencing of dissenting traditions. The push toward "orthodoxy" reflected not just doctrine, but imperial alignment. The Hebraic cycle, deeply rooted in time-bound covenantal memory, was recast as metaphor—thereby severing the connection between Israel's sacred seasons and ecclesial rhythm. This transition was not theological evolution, but colonial imposition.

III. Christian Eschatology: Linear, Greco-Roman in structure, and shaped by early ecclesial imperial frameworks

The Church Fathers—especially Augustine, Origen, and Jerome—absorbed Greek philosophy and Roman imperial logic:
- History begins in Eden and ends in Armageddon
- A rapture or sudden judgment determines eternity
- The Church replaces Israel (Supersessionism)

Modern eschatological inventions like the rapture (Darby, 1830s) and the Left Behind theology which reframe prophecy through Western fear rather than Hebrew hope. [Jerome, *Prologus Galeatus*, in *Biblia Sacra Vulgata*, ed. Robert Weber (Stuttgart: Deutsche Bibelgesellschaft, 1994).]

IV. The Book of Revelation: Hebrew Apocalypse or Roman Redaction?

While often seen as a Christian text, Revelation is deeply Hebraic in structure:
- 7s dominate (days, trumpets, bowls—mirroring temple service)

- Prophetic animals and symbols mirror Ezekiel, Zechariah, Daniel
- The 144,000 are 12 tribes—not gentile believers

Yet it was canonized by ecclesial systems who recontextualized the Torah with imperial frameworks, giving Rome authority over its interpretation. Early sects like the Ebionites and Nazarenes did not prioritize Revelation—they emphasized Torah-based repentance over apocalyptic spectacle.

Daniel 9:24 declares that part of the seventy-week prophecy is "to seal up vision and prophecy" (*lechatom chazon venavi*). This phrase serves as a foundational verse in rabbinic theology concerning the end of prophecy. Sanhedrin 11a affirms that with the deaths of Haggai, Zechariah, and Malachi, the age of open prophetic vision ended. This sealing corresponds to the rise of the *Bat Kol*, midrash, and halachic debate as vehicles of divine echo — but no longer full revelation.

See: Daniel 9:24; Sanhedrin 11a.

In the rabbinic understanding, once prophecy ceased with Haggai, Zechariah, and Malachi, divine communication became increasingly indirect. The concept of the *Bat Kol* (בת קול), or "daughter of a voice," arises in this period as a heavenly echo—an echo of divine will, insufficient for halachic authority but still recognized as spiritually present. This affirms that post-prophetic revelation must be subordinate to Torah, not replacing it. *See: Berakhot 31a; Sotah 48b.*

In **Daniel 12:4**, the prophet is told: *"Seal the book until the time of the end."* This sealing is not merely about chronology but **covenantal maturity**. The pattern is:

1. Prophetic Vision
2. Delay of Fulfillment
3. Unsealing at Spiritual Awakening

Revelation's imagery of scrolls, seals, and trumpets (Rev. 5–11) may symbolically **resume where Daniel paused**. Yet even Revelation never discards Torah—it echoes Exodus, Leviticus, and Zechariah. The "end" is restoration, not annihilation.

Christian end-times frameworks—especially **futurist dispensationalism**—often reflect Roman and Hellenistic drama more than prophetic Torah. Timelines of rapture, antichrist, and Armageddon resemble **imperial battle narratives** rather than priestly restoration.

• **Left Behind theology** originates in 19th-century American revivalism, not the Bible • Early Church Fathers like Origen, Irenaeus, and Augustine wrestled with symbolic and literal tensions—but still viewed time through Greco-Roman logic

True eschatology is not spectacle—it's **return to Edenic harmony and covenant obedience**. The prophets do not call for escape but for restoration.

V. Prophetic Identity vs. Eschatological Spectacle

Hebrew prophets stood in the breach:
- They cried out against injustice (Amos 5, Isaiah 58)
- They spoke to kings, not to escape the world but to transform it
- They called Israel back to Torah and justice, not escapist fantasies

Modern preachers preach rapture rather than righteousness, escapism instead of endurance.

VI. The Real Last Days: Return to Covenant

Hebrew eschatology is not about finality but fullness:
-   Restoration of divine names (Zeph. 3:9)
-   Unity of Judah and Ephraim (Ezek. 37:15–28)
-   Jerusalem as throne of YHWH (Jer. 3:17)

Even in Daniel (often cited by Christians), the culmination

is the "wise who shine like stars" (Dan. 12:3), not those who flee tribulation.

The Hebrew word for fire, ʾēš (אֵשׁ), is often misunderstood. In Tanakh, fire **purifies, consumes leaven, reveals true substance**, and signals divine presence:

• **Malachi 3:2–3**: YHWH is a *refiner's fire* purifying Levites
• **Numbers 16:35**: Fire devours false priests (Korah's rebellion) • **Isaiah 6:6–7**: Coal cleanses the prophet's lips

Final judgment is not merely wrath—it is covenantal **refinement of the remnant**. The Second Death (Revelation 20) marks separation from Torah, not hellfire mythos.

VII. Messiah Ben Yosef and Ben David: A Forgotten Pairing & The Four Horns and the Scattering of Judah — A Prophetic Typology of the Gospels

As Rabbi Akiva saw in Bar Kokhba a messianic hope shaped by suffering and sovereignty, so too this work sees in the diaspora a liturgical messiahship: one not of conquest, but covenantal endurance. This structure aligns with early Rabbinic and Patristic yearning for sacred restoration. Peter Schäfer, *The Bar Kokhba War Reconsidered: New Perspectives on the Second Jewish Revolt Against Rome*(Tübingen: Mohr Siebeck, 2003), 79–92.

Typology—while biblically valid—is not license for limitless parallels. Hebraic prophets and sages used **symbolic echoes** with guardrails. Every type must reflect covenantal logic, linguistic connection, and Torah integrity. Michael Fishbane, *Biblical Interpretation in Ancient Israel* (Oxford: Clarendon Press, 1985), 350–374.

• **Bronze Serpent (Numbers 21:8–9)**: Healing through obedience, not deity in object. • **Yeshua as 'lifted up' (John 3:14)**: Reinterpreted symbol—must be weighed against Deuteronomy 13.

Rabbinic typology (e.g., *Midrash Tanchuma, Pesikta Rabbati*) always traced types back to Torah origins. Unmoored typology, such as projecting the Four Horns of Zechariah directly onto the Four Gospels, risks aesthetic inference over prophetic accuracy.

Second Temple literature gives models of faithful typology:

• **1 Enoch**: Uses cosmic imagery and heavenly pattern to explain messianic judgment • **Jubilees**: Applies calendrical typology to covenant renewal and diaspora return • **Qumran Scrolls (e.g., 4QFlorilegium)**: Align Temple imagery with end-time fulfillment

These texts filter typology through **Torah alignment and communal restoration**, not isolated symbolism.

The identification of Zechariah's "four horns" (Zech. 1:18–21) with the editorial machinery of the Four Gospels should be viewed not as a rigid historical claim, but in the style of the *pesharim*—the interpretive genre employed by the Qumran sect. In works such as 1QpHab and 4QFlorilegium, biblical verses were recontextualized to explain present events in symbolic terms.

This monograph follows that interpretive model: applying an ancient vision of geopolitical "horns" that scatter Judah to the spiritual editorial powers of Hellenized Gospel redactors who restructured Hebrew prophetic fulfillment into imperial narratives. In this pesher-mode reading, the Four Gospels do not simply record Yeshua's life—they become agents of systemic displacement, wielding the authority of empires rather than the Spirit of prophecy.

See 1QpHab (Pesher Habakkuk) II–V for Qumran's symbolic reading style of contemporary crises.

Academic caution requires: • Proof of intertextual reference (cross-chapter or scroll lineage) • Consistency with known midrashic or Second Temple usage • Avoidance of retrofitting Christian canon structure into prophetic texts.

Messiah Ben Yosef and Ben David: A Forgotten Pairing & The Four Horns and the Scattering of Judah — A Prophetic Typology of the Gospels:

The concept of two messianic figures—Messiah ben Yosef (suffering servant) and Messiah ben David (reigning king)—has roots both in rabbinic literature and Qumran sectarian expectation. In the Dead Sea Scrolls, 1QS (Rule of the Community) and 4Q285 (War Scroll fragments) explicitly reference the arrival of two messiahs: "the Messiah of Aaron and the Messiah of Israel." Rabbinic sources such as Sukkah 52a elaborate further, describing Messiah ben Yosef dying in battle and preparing the way for ben David. This theological framework contradicts the singular messianic fulfillment model advanced in Christian doctrine, which fuses these identities into one crucified and risen Christ. The Hebraic typology, however, maintains eschatological plurality—where suffering precedes coronation, but the roles remain distinct. The dual-messiah structure offers a more coherent reading of texts like Zechariah 12:10, Isaiah 53, and Daniel 7, without collapsing them into a singular historical figure.

[24] The **War Scroll (1QM 11:6–7)** makes explicit the bifurcation between priestly and kingly messianic offices: "They shall govern jointly... the Messiah of Aaron and the Messiah of Israel." Here, *Aaronic* denotes spiritual, intercessory leadership; *Davidic* implies military and royal authority. This confirms that **Second Temple sects expected distinct anointed roles**, harmonizing with Sukkah 52a's portrayal of Ben Yosef and Ben David. Israel Knohl, *The Messiah Before Jesus: The Suffering Servant of the Dead Sea Scrolls* (Berkeley: University of California Press, 2000), 102–118.

---

[24] Chapter XII: Horns, Smiths & The Gospel as Weapon or Witness

To link the Gospels to Zechariah's horns is not to indict scripture—it is to warn what empire can do with holy things. The Gospels remain sacred—but only when wielded as smiths, not horns. This typology is a mirror: witness becomes weapon when covenant is forgotten. Canon must be read with its wounds in view, or else we risk blessing what the prophets came to break.

The duality reflects covenantal reality: exile and return, suffering and sovereignty, Torah and kingship. When Christian theology fused these into a singular crucified-reigning Messiah, it truncated Hebraic expectation and flattened messianic plurality into a single Christological frame.

Rabbinic eschatology presents two distinct messianic archetypes:

- *Messiah ben Yosef*: the suffering redeemer, gatherer of the exiles, and eschatological warrior against Gog.

- *Messiah ben David*: the reigning king, who restores the full dominion of Torah and brings enduring peace.

Yeshua of Nazareth aligns clearly with the figure of *Ben Yosef*—wounded, rejected, yet gathering the remnant. As Isaiah 53 declares, "He was pierced for our transgressions… and by His wounds we are healed." Yet Christian theology, particularly post-Nicene interpretations, prematurely collapses the messianic spectrum by conflating Yeshua with *Ben David*, asserting a total and final fulfillment. In classical Hebraic thought, however, these roles are held in dialectic tension until national and spiritual restoration is complete. See: Appendix T for textual contrasts of resurrection narratives.

Ezekiel 37 underscores this dual messianic reality with the vision of *two sticks*—one for *Judah*, one for *Ephraim*. The prophetic union of these two represents not only the reunification of the divided kingdom but the harmony of suffering and ruling messiah. These are not mere tribal reunifications—they are redemptive patterns: priestly and kingly, affliction and glory, exile and return.

The vision granted to the prophet Zechariah (Zech. 1:18–21) has traditionally been filtered through imperial frames: the four horns understood as Babylon, Persia, Greece, and Rome—echoing Daniel's vision (Dan. 2; 7). Yet Zechariah specifies, without allegory or abstraction: "These are the horns that scattered *Judah*." Not Israel. The phrase *"zērû et-*

Yehudah" (scattered Judah) uses **Yehudah in the accusative form, not collective Yisra'el** as in earlier prophetic cycles (e.g., Amos, Hosea).

This distinction is crucial. The northern kingdom—Israel— had already been exiled by 722–718 BCE and is largely absent from the Second Temple narrative. It is *Judah*—home of the priesthood, monarchy, and scribal continuity—that remains central to Zechariah's audience. The vision of scattering does not align neatly with Danielic empires. Rather, it opens the door for an eschatological typology wherein the four horns are identified with the canonical Gospels themselves.

The typological significance of Zechariah 1–4 demands close linguistic attention. In Zechariah 1:19, the vision names all three referents—**Judah, Israel, and Jerusalem**— as scattered by four horns. Yet, from that point forward, only **Judah and Jerusalem** are addressed. The tribal term "Israel" disappears from the next three chapters. This narrowing is not incidental but prophetic: Judah alone remained as a visible remnant post-exile, while Israel (Ephraim) was still dispersed, their return deferred. The Hebrew phrase in 2:2—**אֶת־יְהוּדָה אֶת־יִשְׂרָאֵל וִירוּשָׁלָֽ͏ִם**—fades from usage, and the prophetic burden re-centers around Judah's restoration, temple rebuilding, and messianic preparation.

In Zechariah 4:14, the vision culminates in **שְׁנֵי בְנֵי־הַיִּצְהָר**— "two sons of oil"—a Hebrew idiom denoting **anointed ones**, standing before the Lord of all the earth. These parallel the priestly and royal offices—Joshua the High Priest (ch. 3) and Zerubbabel the Davidic governor (ch. 4)— who collectively foreshadow the dual messianic roles later expressed as **Messiah ben Yosef and Messiah ben David**. This pairing is linguistically reinforced by the shoresh י־צ־ה (yatzah), invoking both outpouring and designation. The two anointed "stand by the Lord," echoing **Obadiah 1:21** where **מֹשִׁעִים**(plural "saviors") ascend Zion, and

Ezekiel 37, where the "two sticks" (Judah and Ephraim) are ultimately made one. See Appendix M.

That Zechariah identifies **Judah alone** as the recipient of divine inheritance (2:12) further reinforces this typological exclusivity: the messianic stage is set through the surviving southern kingdom, while the northern tribes are alluded to in silence—awaiting their eventual rejoining through prophetic convergence. Thus, Zechariah's early visions are not merely symbolic but **linguistically and theologically layered**, encoding the future redemption arc within Hebrew morphology and tribal specificity.

The Four Horns as the Canonized Gospels

This typological reading does not suggest that Zechariah literally foresaw the Four Evangelists. Rather, it applies the **Qumranic pesher model** (1QpHab II–V), which interprets earlier prophecy in light of the community's present spiritual crisis. In that model, "the wicked priest," "the liar," or "the interpreter of the law" are all eschatological types imposed over ancient texts.

Thus, the Four Horns may represent not four historical kingdoms, but four textual instruments of editorial dominance, replacing Hebrew messianism with Greco-Roman fulfillment theology. This is **a prophetic reapplication**, not a historical prediction.

[1] Traditional interpretations often identify the four horns with Babylon, Persia, Greece, and Rome, based on parallels with Daniel 2 and 7. See Michael Rydelnik, *The Messianic Hope* (B&H Academic, 2010), and Craig A. Evans, *Ancient Texts for New Testament Studies* (Hendrickson, 2005), where the canonical approach aligns Zechariah's horns with geopolitical empires. This manuscript offers a prophetic typology centered instead on theological fragmentation through Gospel canonization.

Matthew, Mark, Luke, and John, while grounded in oral Hebrew traditions, were canonized through Hellenistic grammar and Roman authority. In this prophetic typology, they become instruments of theological fragmentation.

- The *Ebionites*—early Torah-affirming believers in Yeshua—vanish from history under ecclesial condemnation (cf. Epiphanius, *Panarion*, 29–30). [Epiphanius, *Panarion*, trans. Frank Williams (Leiden: Brill, 1987).]

- The *Zadokites*—guardians of priestly tradition—flee to Egypt and Ethiopia (cf. DSS sectarian literature).

- The *Nazarenes*—referenced in Acts 24:5—are gradually absorbed into Roman orthodoxy.

While the Hebrew word בְּשׂוֹרָה(besorah)—typically translated as "good news"—does not explicitly appear in Zechariah 1–2, the prophet's announcement of "דְּבָרִים טוֹבִים, דְּבָרִים נִחֻמִים" ("good words, comforting words," Zech. 1:13) carries the semantic weight of Isaiah's messianic *besorah* declarations (Isa. 40:9; 52:7; 61:1). In Isaiah, the *mebasseret Tsiyyon* is one who proclaims divine favor and covenantal restoration, precisely the message Zechariah echoes following Judah's exile. Early Christian writers, especially in the Gospels of Mark (1:1) and Luke (4:18, citing Isa. 61:1), draw directly from this root tradition to identify Yeshua's mission as the fulfillment of this prophetic *besorah*. Thus, when the canonical Gospels were later reframed as literary vessels of "the good news of Jesus," they simultaneously adopted and redirected the Hebrew linguistic tradition of prophetic consolation—originally intended for Zion and the remnant of Judah. This strengthens the typological thesis that the four horns, while historically scattered Judah, were met by a divine counter-response in both the craftsmen and the reassertion of the true *besorah*—not imperial gospelization, but covenantal return.

The Gospels, once vehicles of testimony, become imperial horns—rhetorically reshaped to affirm Roman dogma, displace the Torah, and sever the Jewish identity of the messianic movement.

The Four Craftsmen in Sukkah 52b

Zechariah's vision does not end in exile. Four craftsmen (ḥărāšîm) arise to "terrify them, and cast them down." The Talmud (Sukkah 52b) preserves several views regarding their identities. One interpretation reads:

1. *Messiah Ben David*
2. *Messiah Ben Yosef*
3. *Elijah the Prophet*
4. *The Righteous Priest*—possibly Melchizedek

In this manuscript's typological reading, the correspondences are:

- *Messiah Ben Yosef* — Yeshua, the one "cut off but not for himself" (Dan. 9:26)
- *Messiah Ben David* — the future sovereign, seated on David's throne (Isa. 9:7)
- *Elijah* — the refiner of Malachi 3:3, who restores covenantal faithfulness (Mal. 3:23)
- The fourth figure — either a Melchizedekian priest (cf. Ps. 110:4; 11QMelchizedek) or an embodied priest-king Messiah Ben David

The Hebrew word ḥārāš (חרש), often translated "craftsman," is etymologically linked to the artisan or carpenter. According to Rabbi Samson Raphael Hirsch (pg. 90, *Etymological Dictionary of Hebrew*), ḥārāš denotes one who engraves, restores, or constructs with precision and purpose. Yeshua's earthly trade—as a carpenter—was not incidental. He was quite literally a ḥārāš, and thus prophetically aligned with Zechariah's vision.

The Priestly Signature in the Name of David

In standard Hebrew spelling, David's name is דוד (dalet–vav–dalet), with a numerical value of 14. In select textual traditions—such as Qumran scrolls—it appears as דויד (dalet–vav–yod–dalet), equaling 24. This gematria corresponds to the 24 priestly divisions instituted by David (1 Chr. 24), implying a future *Davidic redeemer* who also operates within a *priestly function*—a king in the order of Melchizedek (cf. Ps. 110).

Obadiah's Vision: Moshiaʿim, Not Māšîaḥ

Obadiah 1:21 declares:

"And saviors (*moshiʿim*) shall ascend Mount Zion to judge the mount of Esau; and the kingdom shall be YHWH's."

The plural construction—*moshiʿim*—points to a collective redemptive agency. In Hebraic consciousness, the *prophet, priest,* and *king* are all *mashiachim* (anointed ones):

- The prophet declares.
- The priest sanctifies.
- The king enacts justice.

Yeshua fulfills the role of the suffering servant, but prophesies the coming of another:

"And I will send you another comforter..." (John 14:16)

This *Parakletos* is not simply pneumatological but typological—pointing to the **future arrival of Ben David**, following Elijah's return and the purification of the remnant.

Prophetic Time: Three Days as Three Millennia

Hosea 6:2 declares:

"After two days He will revive us; on the third day He will raise us up..."

This is echoed by Psalm 90:4:

"A day in Your sight is like a thousand years."

If Yeshua emerges in the first millennium CE, the prophetic "third day" becomes the current era. His resurrection was the *firstfruits*; the full reign of *Ben David* awaits the third-day awakening.

Restoration by Torah, Not Theology

Isaiah 2:3 speaks of the true restoration:

"From Zion shall go forth Torah, and the word of YHWH from Jerusalem."

It is *not* through synods or creeds, but through **Torah and prophetic refinement**, that the horns will be overthrown. Zechariah's vision anticipates a day when Judah is regathered, not by empire, but by covenant.

This is not a rejection of Yeshua—it is a rejection of what Rome made of him. The horns are not merely texts; they are imperial distortions. The craftsmen are not merely metaphors; they are the eschatological forces of correction.

So we wait:

- For Elijah to refine.
- For the mountains to shelter.
- For the remnant to awaken.
- For the fire, oil, and Torah to anoint the one who is to come.

Rabbi Akiva's hope in Bar Kokhba was not a misreading—it was a premature typology. This work proposes a 'Messiah ben Golah': one forged in exile, not enthroned in empire. Diaspora becomes the temple, and trauma the liturgy of redemption. Peter Schäfer, *The Bar Kokhba War Reconsidered: New Perspectives on the Second Jewish Revolt Against Rome*(Tübingen: Mohr Siebeck, 2003), 79–92.

Messiah ben Golah (משיח בן גולה) — a term coined in this monograph to represent the messianic figure emerging **from the exile itself**, born not of royal lineage alone, but of suffering, captivity, and diasporic survival. Unlike Messiah ben David (southern redeemer) or Messiah ben Yosef (northern redeemer), Messiah ben Golah is the prophetic culmination of Isaiah 11:11 and Deuteronomy

30:3–4 — a redeemer drawn from the *remnant* scattered across Cush, Elam, and the transatlantic coasts. This figure embodies the cry of a people who, having been sold and silenced, rise to restore covenant, language, and justice. He is the **son of the Golah,** the exile.

VIII. Thought-Provoking Questions

- Has Christian eschatology recontextualized the prophetic imagination?
- Why is Revelation prioritized over Isaiah and Jeremiah in churches?
- Are Black prophetic movements reclaiming the true end-time vision? Why does Obadiah say 'saviors?
- Can we separate eschatology from empire?

IX. References and Sources

1.Isaiah 2, 11, 58; Jeremiah 3, 30–31; Ezekiel 36–37
2. Daniel 7, 9, 12; Zephaniah 3; Amos 5
3. Dead Sea Scrolls: War Scroll, Community Rule
4. Babylonian Talmud, Sanhedrin 98a–99a (Messiah ben Yosef)
5. Gospel of the Hebrews (Ebionite eschatology)
6. Book of Revelation, Jewish Apocalyptic Parallels
7. Bruce Chilton, Rabbi Jesus; Raphael Patai, The Messiah Texts
8. Rabbi Samson Raphael Hirsch, Collected Writings, vol. IV–V

9. Sefaria.org (biblical and midrashic texts)

10. Obadiah 1:21 (Hebrew Bible)

Counterpoint: Christian Eschatology Is Biblically Rooted, Not Roman-Invented

Mainstream   View:
Christian eschatology, while developing over time, is rooted in Jewish apocalypticism. Scholars argue that books like *Daniel* and *1 Enoch* already introduced linear eschatological models. Thus, Revelation's timeline is an

outgrowth of Second Temple trends, not imperial corruption.

Key Voices:

- **John J. Collins** (*The Apocalyptic Imagination*)
- **Richard Bauckham** (*The Theology of the Book of Revelation*)
- **Craig Koester** (*Revelation and the End of All Things*)
- **Larry Hurtado** (*Lord Jesus Christ*)

Representative   **Quote:**
"Revelation draws not from Roman culture but Jewish apocalyptic texts, creating a continuity with Israel's prophetic vision." – *John J. Collins, Apocalyptic Imagination,* p. 119

Rebuttal: Christian Eschatology Flattened Prophetic Cycles Into Imperial Spectacle

While it's true that Jewish texts like *Daniel* and *1 Enoch* shaped apocalyptic frameworks, **those texts remained anchored in covenantal cycles**—*not linear rupture*. Christianity's adoption of Greco-Roman historiography introduced:

- **Chronos over kairos**
- **Linear time over cyclical covenant**
- **Finality over return**

Revelation's *military imagery, beast kings,* and *imperial destruction* reflect a world where **Rome was both the antagonist and unconscious archetype.**

As R.S. Sugirtharajah warns:

"Christian eschatology adopted the grammar of empire even as it claimed to resist it." (*Exploring Postcolonial Biblical Criticism*, p. 96)

Revelation was redacted into **Roman political metaphor,** turning prophetic rebuke into **coded theater,** often **weaponized by the Church to justify conquest.**

Contrast this with the Hebraic rhythm:

- **Shabbat,** not rapture
- **Jubilee,** not cataclysm
- **Dry bones restored,** not saints airlifted

This framework (Daniel + Ezekiel + Zechariah) presents **prophetic return,** not **cosmic extraction.** Christian eschatology misunderstood Hebrew time—and turned it into theological empire.

See: Chapter XII, Section II – Cycles Not Timelines

Chapter XIII (יג): Restoration of the Name—YHWH, Yehoshua, and the Linguistic recontextualization of Divinity

I. Introduction: The Name Above All Names

The tetragrammaton (יהוה), rendered as YHWH, appears over 6,800 times in the Tanakh, yet was systematically suppressed in later manuscript traditions and replaced with "Adonai" (Lord) or "Kyrios" in Greek translations. This shift was not merely linguistic but theological—a rebranding of divine identity that de-personalized Israel's covenantal God into an abstract imperial deity.

The **Samaritan Pentateuch** preserved the Name, as did **early Hebrew manuscripts from Qumran,** where the Divine Name was often written in paleo-Hebrew script to preserve its sanctity. Rabbinic hesitation to vocalize the Name may reflect post-exilic reverence, but Church authorities further deepened suppression through Latin Vulgate traditions.

The **restoration of the Name** is therefore not about pronunciation ("Yahweh," "Jehovah," etc.) but about restoring the covenantal specificity of the God of Israel— distinguishing Him from the pantheons of empire and aligning with Exodus 3:15: "This is My Name forever, and this is My memorial to all generations.

[25]This chapter explores the suppression of the Divine Name, the Hebraic origin of the name of the Messiah, and how linguistic substitutions altered theology itself. There is a critical link between identity, language, and prophetic restoration.

II. The Tetragrammaton: YHWH as Covenant Identity

YHWH is not a title—it is a sacred personal Name revealed to Moshe at the burning bush (Exodus 3:14–15):
> "This is My Name forever, and this is My memorial to all generations."

The Name YHWH is derived from the root היה (to be), reflecting eternal presence:
- Ehyeh (אֶהְיֶה): I will be
- Hoveh (הֹוֶה): Present
- Hayah (הָיָה): Past

The Jewish tradition of avoiding pronouncing the Name (instead using Adonai or HaShem) began during Second Temple reverence and exile trauma. Yet Scripture commands remembrance, not removal.

III. Yehoshua, Not Jesus: The True Name of the Messiah

The Greek name "Jesus" is a transliteration of Ἰησοῦς (Iēsous), which in turn is derived from the Latinized and Hellenized reinterpretation of the Hebrew Yehoshua (יהושע)—"YHWH is salvation."

This linguistic shift hides key truths:

---

[25] Emanuel Tov, *Textual Criticism of the Hebrew Bible*, 3rd ed. (Minneapolis: Fortress Press, 2012), 289–291. Frank Moore Cross, *The Ancient Library of Qumran* (New York: Doubleday, 1961), 163–165. George Howard, "The Tetragram and the New Testament," *Journal of Biblical Literature* 96, no. 1 (1977): 63–83.

- Yehoshua contains the Name of the Father (YH)
- The shortened form "Yeshua" omits the divine prefix but retains Hebrew grammar
- "Jesus" has no meaning in Hebrew and severs prophetic continuity

This is recontextualization of divine identity—not merely transliteration, but spiritual appropriation.

IV. Greco-Roman Christianity: From Rome to the Church

After the Council of Nicaea (325 CE), Roman Christianity initiated the formal replacement of Hebrew names and terms:

-	YHWH	→	"the Lord"
-	Yehoshua	→	"Jesus"
-	rûaḥ	→	"Spirit"
-	Torah	→	"Law"

These were not neutral changes—they supported supersessionism, obscured Hebraic roots, and opened the door to Greco-Roman theology.

Jerome's Vulgate, Origen's Greek Hexapla, and later Reformation translations codified these losses. Instead of revelation, we inherited religious renaming. [Jerome, *Prologus Galeatus*, in *Biblia Sacra Vulgata*, ed. Robert Weber (Stuttgart: Deutsche Bibelgesellschaft, 1994).]

"Jerome's Vulgate translation was not simply linguistic—it was ecclesial theology rendered in Latin syntax."

V. Prophetic Mandates to Restore the Name

The prophets speak repeatedly of the restoration of YHWH's Name:
- Zephaniah 3:9 — "I will restore to the peoples a pure language, that they may all call upon the Name of YHWH."
- Malachi 1:11 — "From the rising of the sun to its setting, My Name shall be great among the nations."
- Joel 2:32 — "Whoever calls on the Name of YHWH shall

be   saved."

This restoration is both linguistic and spiritual—to know the Name is to know the covenant.

VI. The Name and the Black Diaspora

Diasporic Hebrew communities—particularly in West Africa, the Americas, and the Caribbean—preserved fragments   of   the   Divine   Name:
- Variants of Yah, Yahu, or "YHWH" in tribal chants and naming   customs
- Oral traditions of Israelite descent referencing the "Name of   the   Ancestors"

This is not accidental. The erasure of the Name was part of colonial theology, while its recovery is part of end-time identity reclamation.

[26] The modern nation of Ghana derives its name from the ancient Soninke title *Gana* or *Wagadou*, signifying "warrior king" or "chief." This term emerged from the sociopolitical lexicon of the Soninke people, founders of the Ghana Empire (ca. 750–1240 CE), whose dominion extended across parts of present-day Mali, Mauritania, and Senegal. In 1957, Kwame Nkrumah chose the name "Ghana" for the newly independent nation as a deliberate act of historical reclamation—reconnecting modern sovereignty to the memory of a powerful African polity defined by wealth, law, and spiritual authority.

While Hebrew and Soninke belong to entirely distinct language families—Northwest Semitic and Niger-Congo respectively—some independent scholars have drawn symbolic comparisons between *Gana* and the Hebrew root גָּנַן (ganan), meaning "to protect" or "to defend," and גַּנָּה (ganah), "an enclosure" or "a shielded space." The

---

[26] Matityahu Clark, *Etymological Dictionary of Biblical Hebrew*, Feldheim Publishers, p. 42. Nehemia Gordon & Keith Johnson, *A Prayer to Our Father: Hebrew Origins of the Lord's Prayer*, Hilkiah Press, 2009, for supporting linguistic methodology in African-Hebraic root studies. Edward Ullendorff, *The Ethiopians: An Introduction to Country and People* (Oxford: Oxford University Press, 1965), 112–117. Fallou Ngom, *Muslim Literacy and Sacred Texts in Ajami* (Leiden: Brill, 2021), 9–12. Kalu Ogbaa, *Traditional Igbo Justice and the Nsibidi Script* (Trenton: Africa World Press, 2004), 31–38.

Hebrew root appears throughout biblical literature, often in royal and prophetic contexts. For instance, *Psalms 47:9* describes "the shields of the earth" (מָגִנֵּי־אָ֫רֶץ, *magnei-eretz*)—a phrase traditionally interpreted as a metaphor for kings and divine protectors, those who encircle and safeguard covenantal order.

Although no historical linguistic bridge exists between the Soninke *Gana* and the Hebrew *ganan*, the conceptual convergence is noteworthy in a theological and prophetic framework. In both traditions, leadership is inseparable from divine stewardship: kings do not merely rule—they protect memory, mediate justice, and embody covenant. In ancient Israel, this was the role of the Davidic monarch. In the Ghana Empire, it was the role of the "Ghana," a ruler who presided over spiritual rites, ancestral law, and economic equilibrium, particularly through gold regulation—a material often associated with temple sanctity in the Tanakh.

Further resonance emerges when comparing the term *Ghana* with the Hebrew *Gaon* (גאון), a title of exalted spiritual authority used for the heads of Babylonian academies during the Geonic period (ca. 600–1000 CE). Though linguistically unrelated, both titles encapsulate leadership bound to moral instruction, sacred law, and communal guidance. These echoes do not argue for genetic or philological derivation, but for diasporic continuity— what some scholars call **cultural memory** embedded in parallel covenantal roles.

From this vantage point, the Ghanaian legacy functions as a **theo-political archetype**—not because it shares direct linguistic ancestry with Hebrew, but because it reverberates with covenantal function. It symbolizes a tradition in which sacred kingship, gold as divine resource, and oral law converge to reflect aspects of Israelite theology lived out in African soil. In diasporic thought, such overlaps are not accidental; they are the residue of ancestral memory that survives translation, exile, and colonization.

"Etymology may not bind Ghana to the language of Zion, but covenant binds it to the memory of God's justice."
— *Tovi Mickel*

This symbolic alignment invites a reframing of West African empires not merely as regional powers but as participants—however indirectly—in the preservation of Hebraic ethics, order, and divine guardianship. In this reading, Ghana does not need to *speak* Hebrew to **echo** its prophetic charge, just like the children of the diaspora.

[27] Likewise, the West African symbol and proverb "Sankofa"—commonly interpreted as "go back and get it"—has captured the imagination of Afro-diasporic identity reconstruction. While widely recognized as an Akan concept, the underlying grammatical structure and prophetic ethic of Sankofa aligns profoundly with Hebraic linguistic and theological patterns.

Hebraically, the term can be reconstructed as סנכופה (s-n-k-p-h), drawing from roots such as שוב (shuv, "to return"), לקח (laqach, "to take or fetch"), and זכר (zakar, "to remember"). Though not an exact lexical match, the consonantal structure of Sankofa fits comfortably within Semitic triliteral morphology, wherein meaning is derived from consonantal roots and their inflections. The inclusion of the letters ס (Samekh) and פ (Peh) in particular evoke terms relating to circular motion or returning pathways—both consistent with the imagery of repentance and cyclical restoration.

Visually, the Sankofa bird turns its head backwards to retrieve a seed from its back, walking forward while remembering the past. This is identical in function to the Hebrew command to "remember the former things of old" (Isaiah 46:9) and "return to the Lord your God" (Joel 2:13). Sankofa, therefore, is best understood not simply as African ancestral wisdom, but as a prophetic reflex embedded in

---

[27] Francis Nii-Yartey, "The Sankofa Concept in African Philosophy", Ghana National Cultural Centre, 1989. Rabbi Samson Raphael Hirsch, "The Nineteen Letters on Judaism", Feldheim, 1995, for commentary on memory and covenant in prophetic cycles. Isaiah 46:9; Joel 2:13; cf. Deuteronomy 4:29–31 on the ethical return from diaspora.

West African cultural grammar—one that matches the demands of Moses, Elijah, and Ezra alike.

In rabbinic usage, memory is never passive—it is covenantal. The prophetic act of remembrance is active return, often accompanied by national reformation. Sankofa captures this in symbolic form, reinforcing the idea that African prophetic culture may have preserved Israelite concepts of cyclical restoration and repentance—outside the boundaries of mainstream Rabbinic Judaism but not outside the Torah.

VII. Sacred Letters and Numerical Mysticism

Hebrew letters carry numeric value and theological depth:
- Yod (10), Heh (5), Vav (6), Heh (5) = YHWH = 26
- Yehoshua = יְהוֹשֻׁעַ = includes YHWH + salvation (shua)
- Torah = 611 (gematria) = the number of mitzvot Moses gave, with the first two directly from YHWH Himself (Ex. 20:1–2)

The structure of the Divine Name itself reflects balance, breath, and eternity.

Rabbi Akiva and the Dual Messiah Typology in Post-Revolt Theology

The Bar Kokhba revolt (132–135 CE) was not merely a political uprising—it was a theological crisis that reshaped messianic expectations for generations. Rabbi Akiva, one of the most esteemed sages of his time, famously endorsed Simon Bar Kokhba as the Messiah, calling him "King Messiah" (Melekh HaMashiach), despite warnings from his peers (Jerusalem Talmud, Ta'anit 4:5). The aftermath of this revolt led to a split in Jewish messianism, introducing a dual model: Messiah ben Yosef (the suffering servant) and Messiah ben David (the conquering king).

This typology directly influences both rabbinic thought and

emerging Christian messianism. While the latter retroactively applied the suffering servant motif to Jesus, rabbinic Judaism developed the typology as a way to explain the failure of Bar Kokhba and anticipate a future, victorious   redeemer.

The name change from Bar Kokhba ("Son of the Star") to Bar Koziba ("Son of the Lie") reflects this theological reorientation. Language here is prophetic judgment: names encode messianic legitimacy or rejection. This resonates with the manuscript's broader thesis that scrolls and names are never neutral—they are vessels of covenantal truth or distortion.

Further, the dual messiah theory echoes the fragmentary state of Israelite identity post-revolt. It mirrors the linguistic and canonical fragmentation documented in earlier chapters. The suffering messiah becomes not only a figure of   atonement   but   of   diaspora   realism.

For source map and historical citations, see Appendix O, Fig. 4: *The Dual Messiah Tradition in Post-Temple Thought*.

VIII. Thought-Provoking Questions

- Why would Scripture preserve YHWH over 6,800 times if it   were   never   to   be   spoken?
- How has removing the Name shaped theology, prayer, and   identity?
- Can one be in covenant with YHWH without calling upon His   true   Name?
- What role does restoring the Name play in restoring Israel's place?

IX. References and Sources

1. Exodus 3:14–15; Deuteronomy 28:58; Psalm 68:4 (Yah)
2.   Zephaniah   3:9;   Malachi   1:11;   Joel   2:32
3. Babylonian Talmud, Kiddushin 71a (Name of 42 letters)

4. Encyclopedia Judaica, s.v. "Tetragrammaton"
5. Rabbi Samson Raphael Hirsch, Commentary on Exodus, Collected Writings
6. Strong's Concordance: H3068 (YHWH), H3091 (Yehoshua)
7. Sefer Yetzirah; Gematria traditions
8. African oral traditions referencing the Divine Name
9. Sefaria.org (biblical and Talmudic references to the Name)

Counterpoint: The Tetragrammaton's Obscurity Is a Tradition of Reverence, Not Erasure

Mainstream **View:**
Many Jewish and Christian scholars argue that avoiding vocalization of YHWH (the Tetragrammaton) reflects a long-standing tradition of **reverence and theological transcendence**, not suppression. Christian substitution of *Kyrios* (Lord) and *Theos* (God) is viewed as **contextual translation** rather than intentional concealment.

Key Voices:

- **Lawrence Schiffman** (*From Text to Tradition*)
- **Geza Vermes** (*Jesus the Jew*)
- **Gerald Bray** (*God Has Spoken*)
- **Craig Evans** (*Ancient Texts for New Testament Studies*)

Representative **Quote:**
"The avoidance of YHWH in vocal practice stems not from political motives, but from awe at the ineffable." – *Lawrence Schiffman, Text to Tradition, p. 187*

Rebuttal: The Suppression of YHWH Was Both Political and Theological

While reverence played a role, **later substitutions of the divine Name were not merely devotional—they became doctrinal tools of assimilation and erasure.** The Septuagint rendered YHWH as *Kyrios,* a term which gradually allowed **Roman ecclesiology to substitute Hebrew covenantal specificity with universalized abstraction**.

By the time of the Church Fathers, this linguistic shift supported the **detachment of Jesus from the Name YHWH**—while affirming his divinity through titles (*Son, Lord, Christos*)—effectively **replacing sacred covenantal Name with Christological shorthand**.

"By the second century, the Name was not only unspoken— it was doctrinally replaced." – *R.S. Sugirtharajah, Postcolonial Biblical Interpretation*, p. 91

Furthermore, Scripture **does not prohibit saying the Name**—only misusing it (Ex. 20:7). Prophets *shouted* the Name, *sang* it in Psalms, and **called on it for national deliverance**. The post-Second Temple ban (cf. Mishnah Sanhedrin 10:1) reflected both Rabbinic reaction and **imperial survival tactics**.

Restoration of the Name is not merely linguistic—it is prophetic re-covenanting.

See: Chapter XIII, Section II – The Tetragrammaton as Covenant Identity

Chapter XIV (יד): Law vs Grace? Paul, the Torah, and the Misunderstood Covenant

I. Introduction: A Divergent Dichotomy

Much of modern Christianity is built on a binary assumption: law equals bondage, grace equals freedom. Yet this dichotomy is alien to Hebraic thought. This chapter examines how the writings of Paul—interpreted through Greco-Roman lenses—distorted the Torah's role, and correcting this by which restoring the Hebraic understanding of covenantal responsibility.

II. Torah as Covenant, Not Curse

The structure of the Hebrew canon was not merely a redacted anthology but a **sacred architecture**, patterned after the **twenty-two letters of the Hebrew alphabet**, each representing not only sound but metaphysical principle. The Babylonian Talmud (*Bava Batra 14b*) lists the authoritative books and their internal groupings. Jerome, in his *Prologus Galeatus* (ca. 391 CE), affirms that the Hebrews counted only twenty-two canonical books—mirroring their alphabet—and suggested these were intentionally unified and numerically bound.

This connection is not arbitrary. In **Sefer Yetzirah**, the "Book of Creation," an early Jewish mystical text, the twenty-two letters are described as the "foundation of all things," the building blocks through which YHWH created the heavens and the earth. This model reflects a deeper worldview: that language, revelation, and cosmos are inseparable. Revelation is not a collection—it is **design**.

Thus, when later ecclesiastical structures expanded the canon to include the Apocrypha (e.g., Council of Trent, 1546), they unintentionally disrupted this Hebrew numerical symmetry. The prophetic vision embedded in the alphabetic count—Aleph to Tav—represents the completeness of divine instruction from beginning to end. To fracture that system is not only to expand Scripture but to **alter its skeleton**.

[28]Moreover, each Hebrew letter holds numerical and visual significance:

- **Aleph (א)** signifies unity and oneness, corresponding to Genesis/Bereshit—beginning and breath.

---

[28] Nahum M. Sarna, *Genesis: The JPS Torah Commentary* (Philadelphia: Jewish Publication Society, 1989), commentary on Gen. 1:1.

- **Tav (ת)**, the final letter, resembles a sign or seal—corresponding to Chronicles, which ends the Tanakh with the decree of Cyrus, signaling restoration.

The canon, then, is not arranged chronologically but **covenantally**—moving from creation to exile to return. The Greek canon rearrangement (e.g., ending with Malachi) artificially closes the Tanakh with prophetic warning, while the Hebrew structure ends with imperial permission to rebuild—**prophetic hope**.

This shift is not semantic but spiritual. Where the Hebrew canon closes in restoration, the Greek adaptation ends in silence. Where Hebrew canon aligns with divine order, the later forms align with imperial redaction.

The Torah (תּוֹרָה) means instruction, not law in the penal sense. It is the relational guide from YHWH to His people. Psalm 19:7 says, "The Torah of YHWH is perfect, restoring the   soul."

Key   truths:
- Torah is covenantal revelation, not legalistic burden
- It provides national, moral, and spiritual identity (Deut. 4:6–8)
- It defines righteousness and injustice (Isaiah 5:20–24)

Paul himself affirmed the Torah's holiness (Romans 7:12) but became a source of confusion when interpreted outside Jewish legal nuance.

Aquinas, Allegory, and the Hebraic Literalism Divide

In the *Summa Theologica* (I, Q1, Art. 10), Thomas Aquinas states: "Holy Scripture has a multiplicity of senses. The historical or literal sense is that from which alone can any argument be drawn." Yet paradoxically, he upholds allegorical, moral, and anagogical senses as theologically valid, even when these diverge from the original Hebrew meaning.

Aquinas' framework allowed for New Testament fulfillment interpretations that bypassed the grammatical and historical dimensions of the Hebrew text. This "fourfold sense" model—though intellectually rich—facilitated interpretive displacements that prioritized ecclesial meaning over linguistic fidelity.

This manuscript challenges that model, proposing that the literal sense, rooted in shoresh (שורש)-based Hebraic logic, carries not only semantic value but covenantal authority. Where Aquinas reads the Exodus as an allegory of baptism (cf. ST III, Q66), a Hebraic reading prioritizes it as a national birth narrative, linguistically grounded and communally binding.

By preferring allegory over Hebrew literalism, scholastic theology recast the prophetic into typological pretext. This manuscript reclaims the literal not as fundamentalism, but as fidelity—honoring the divine choice of Hebrew as the architecture of revelation.

For linguistic alignment, see Appendix M: *Shoresh Theology and Semantic Integrity*. This framework reinforces why restoring the literal Hebrew sense is not regressive, but redemptive.

III. Paul the Pharisee: Oral Tradition and Early Midrash

Paul studied under Rabban Gamaliel, a leading Pharisee (Acts 22:3). Many of his teachings—often considered innovative—reflect oral traditions later written in the Mishnah and Gemara:
- Head coverings (1 Cor. 11) — cf. Talmud, Kiddushin 29b
- Laws on oaths, eating with sinners — cf. Mishnah Avot, Sanhedrin
- "All things are lawful" — a phrase echoing permitted vs forbidden (mutar vs assur) in rabbinic law

Paul's Torah fluency was filtered through Greek epistles and Latin dogma—detaching his words from their Hebraic soul.

Paul writes in 1 Corinthians 13:12, "For now we see through a glass, darkly; but then face to face." This statement echoes the rabbinic idiom *aspaklaria she'einah me'irah* (אספקלריא שאינה מאירה), a "dim lens" through which lesser prophets perceived divine truth. Found in Yevamot 49b, this contrast highlights the unique prophetic clarity of Moses (via *aspaklaria hame'irah*) compared to the dim and indirect revelations experienced by others. Paul's analogy reflects theological humility consistent with Jewish thought — that prophecy post-Moses was partial, awaiting full redemption and restoration through Torah.

See: 1 Cor. 13:12; Yevamot 49b.

In Talmudic tradition, a prophet or teacher must align with Torah (Deuteronomy 13:1–5). Rav Saadia Gaon, Maimonides, and later commentators affirm that even miraculous signs are invalid if Torah is set aside.

• **Talmud Sanhedrin 90a–93a**: Prophets cannot nullify mitzvot • **Pirkei Avot 1:1**: *"Moses received the Torah at Sinai... and passed it on..."*—emphasizing continuity, not innovation • **Deuteronomy 30:11–14**: Torah is *"not too hard for you"*, accessible and sufficient

Therefore, if Paul's teachings are to be accepted, they must be weighed **against Torah**, not parallel to it. Where he deviates, the responsibility of critical readers is not to discard him entirely, but to **restore proper filters** of covenantal evaluation.

The core question is not whether Paul had a revelatory experience—but whether his writings align with the **everlasting covenant**. As the prophet Isaiah wrote, *"To the Torah and to the testimony: if they speak not according to this word, it is because there is no light in them."* (Isaiah 8:20)

A Hebraic framework does not reject Paul—it repositions him. He becomes a **diaspora interpreter**, not a divine legislator. His epistles are *midrashim*, not replacement scriptures. His insights are **subject to Torah**, not above it.

IV. Grace Within the Covenant

Grace (chesed, חֶסֶד) is not antithetical to Torah—it flows from it:
- Exodus 34:6–7 lists compassion and forgiveness as part of YHWH's covenant identity
- Deuteronomy 30 promises mercy if Israel returns

Paul's epistles (esp. Galatians, Romans) juxtapose grace and Torah as competing systems. But in Hebrew thought:
> Law and grace are married, not divorced.

Grace enables covenant renewal after failure—it does not cancel covenant obligation.

V. Misreading: Context is Covenant

Galatians 3:10–13 is often cited as proof that Torah brings a curse. But Paul quotes Deut. 27:26, which warns against abandoning Torah—not by not following it.

Paul's argument is aimed at:
- Legalism for salvation (works-based justification)
- Circumcision as national gatekeeping

He never denies the Torah as holy—it is misused when weaponized as identity exclusivity. This appears to be traced to modern theological antisemitism masked in "grace."

Eucharistic Divergence and the Halakhic Boundary

Paul's Eucharistic framing may also reflect an eschatological urgency. Throughout his epistles—particularly in 1 Thessalonians 4:15–17 and Romans 13:11–12—Paul conveys an expectation that the day of restoration and judgment was imminent. This perception shaped his theology, leading him to speak and write as though the Messianic Age was unfolding in real time. Thus, his reinterpretation of the covenant may have been an attempt to accommodate Gentiles into what he believed was the active fulfillment of prophecy.

While Paul's eschatological urgency is evident in passages like 1 Thessalonians 4:15–17 and Romans 13:11–12, it is crucial to situate him within the complex spectrum of Second Temple Judaism. Rather than creating an entirely new faith, Paul appears to be participating in an intense intra-Jewish debate about covenant, Torah, and Gentile inclusion. His tone—particularly in Galatians—resembles the polemical style of Qumran sectarians who accused their opponents of abandoning the covenant (cf. "seekers of smooth things," 4Q169). E.P. Sanders argues that Paul was navigating an apocalyptic framework, where the inclusion of Gentiles was urgent because the age to come was dawning. This urgency shaped his reinterpretation of the covenant, not necessarily its abrogation. [1] E.P. Sanders, *Paul and Palestinian Judaism: A Comparison of Patterns of Religion* (Philadelphia: Fortress Press, 1977), 442–447. See also James D.G. Dunn, *The New Perspective on Paul* (Tübingen: Mohr Siebeck, 2005); Lawrence H. Schiffman, *Reclaiming the Dead Sea Scrolls* (Philadelphia: Jewish Publication Society, 1994), 254–257.

It is also vital to recognize that many of Paul's letters were written while he was imprisoned (e.g., Ephesians, Philippians, Colossians, Philemon). In such conditions, the risk of redaction, interpolation, or posthumous editorial shaping becomes significant—especially since Paul was later executed under Roman authority, the very empire that would go on to canonize and disseminate his writings. This raises the question: Are we reading the unfiltered voice of Paul, or the version preserved and shaped by imperial Rome?

A similar tension exists with the teachings of Yeshua himself. Rome crucified him as a subversive, yet later claimed to codify his message. This paradox must inform our hermeneutic: how do we distinguish between the prophetic voice and the imperial pen that later framed it?

Paul's introduction of the Eucharist in 1 Corinthians 11:23–26, where bread and wine become symbolic of Christ's body and blood, fundamentally diverges from the Torah's longstanding prohibitions against the consumption of blood. In Leviticus 17:10–12, the commandment is absolute: "I will set My face against any person who eats blood... for the life of the flesh is in the blood." Similarly, Deuteronomy 12:23–25 forbids consuming blood even within permissible sacrifices. This halakhic boundary was never spiritualized or lifted in Tanakh—its role was foundational in defining sacred consumption and the distinction between Israel and the nations.

John 6:53–56, wherein the Messiah is quoted saying "Unless you eat the flesh of the Son of Man and drink His blood, you have no life in you," is often used as the foundation of Christian Eucharistic theology. However, such a statement—while metaphorical in some traditions—would have been inconceivable within Second Temple Torah observance. Thus, Pauline and Johannine formulations, rather than building upon the Torah, reflect a shift toward sacramental paradigms that reinterpret Hebrew sanctity through Greco-Roman mystery models. This was not covenantal continuity—it was recontextualization under a different system.

Sacramental Influence from the Greco-Roman Mysteries

Historical parallels with Greco-Roman cultic systems reinforce this shift. The Mithraic Mysteries, which flourished in Rome from the 1st to 4th centuries CE, practiced sacred communal meals involving the consumption of bread and wine in honor of Mithras. In Mithraic iconography, the god slays a bull—its blood signifying cosmic life, which initiates consumed symbolically. Similarly, Dionysian rituals also centered on wine and the symbolic ingestion of divine essence through sacramental feasting. These cults informed the Roman religious imagination and laid a conceptual framework for understanding divine embodiment, sacrifice, and spiritual union through consumption.

Additionally, the priests of ancient Egypt served not only as temple functionaries but as intermediaries of divine essence. Temple liturgies often involved theophagic symbolism—where offerings to gods like Osiris, Ra, or Ptah were shared ritually by both deity and priest. Egyptian rituals normalized the idea that eating sacred elements connected worshipers to the divine essence, preparing the philosophical ground for sacramental reinterpretation under Greco-Roman theology.

[29]These practices are not mentioned to delegitimize faith traditions, but to contextualize how Paul's Eucharistic theology was more compatible with mystery religions than with Levitical priesthood. The blood of the covenant in Exodus was applied externally; it was never to be ingested. The sacramental consumption model, therefore, marks not a continuation of Torah but a theological divergence deeply rooted in imperial cult paradigms.

While Christian theology often presents the Eucharist as a fulfillment of the Passover meal (Luke 22:19–20), the nature of this fulfillment departs significantly from Torah observance. In Exodus 12, the Passover lamb is consumed in the context of deliverance, not internalized as divine

---

29
Chapter XIV: Vatican, Beast & The Return to Covenant Vision

Revelation does not target people—it targets powers. The Vatican, as typology, represents canon compromised by empire, not the faith of its people. The beast is not clergy—it is theology bent toward conquest. Canonization under Constantine was not pure betrayal—but it was not covenantal either. This critique is not of belief, but of systems that cloak conquest in ecclesial robes. Harry Y. Gamble, *Books and Readers in the Early Church: A History of Early Christian Texts* (New Haven: Yale University Press, 1995), 85–104. Judith Herrin, *The Formation of Christendom* (Princeton University Press, 1987), 204–211. Robin M. Jensen, *The Cross: History, Art, and Controversy* (Harvard University Press, 2017), 78–81. *Liber Pontificalis*, ed. Louis Duchesne (Paris: Éditions de Boccard, 1886), I:316–317. Mary Beard, *SPQR: A History of Ancient Rome* (Liveright, 2015), 367–369; Joseph Rykwert, *The Idea of a Town* (MIT Press, 1988), 135–139.

essence. Moreover, the Torah forbids consumption of blood under all conditions (Leviticus 17:10–12). Paul's reinterpretation in 1 Corinthians 11, when read alongside Johannine sacramental language, moves toward a theological model of theophagy—reminiscent of Greco-Roman mystery religions. As Margaret Barker notes, these reinterpretations reflect a shift from covenantal memorial to mystical participation. [2]

In contrast, Torah's sacrificial system maintains a clear distinction between God, priest, and offering—avoiding metaphysical union through consumption. This difference is not minor; it is foundational. The introduction of Eucharistic theology thus marks not a seamless extension of Torah but a theological transformation influenced by Hellenistic religious imagination. [2] Margaret Barker, *Temple Theology: An Introduction* (London: SPCK, 2004), 89–91. [3] Jacob Milgrom, *Leviticus 1–16*, Anchor Yale Bible Commentary (New Haven: Yale University Press, 1991), 650–654. See also Dennis E. Smith, *From Symposium to Eucharist: The Banquet in the Early Christian World* (Minneapolis: Fortress, 2003), 120–135.

The transmutation of Hebrew covenant into Greco-Roman ritual did not stop with Mithraic blood rites—it extended to **brick, basilica, and shrine.** Rome did not just conquer land—it **colonized sacred space.** The same city that shed the blood of the prophets began to **absorb the architecture of pagan gods**, repackaging idolatry as apostolic.

"From blood on altars to relics in walls—the change was cosmetic, not covenantal."

The **Pantheon**, constructed by Marcus Agrippa between 27–25 BCE and reconstructed under Emperor Hadrian (c. 118–128 CE), was dedicated to all Roman deities—a dome of spiritual pluralism crowning imperial unity. After the Temple in Jerusalem was obliterated in 70 CE, it was not Zion but **Jupiter's children** who inherited the marble and mortar of reverence. By 609 CE, under Pope Boniface IV, the

Pantheon was **not destroyed**—it was **rebranded**: renamed the *Church of Santa Maria ad Martyres*, but never ritually deconstructed. The dome remained; the gods changed outfits.

This was not sanctification—it was **spatial syncretism.** The gods of conquest were **not exorcised**; they were **renamed, baptized, and enthroned**. Temples dedicated to Mithras, Apollo, Cybele, and Jupiter were converted into basilicas. But to **rename a temple is not to cleanse it.** The stones bear witness. The altar remembers its first flame.

The Christian empire did not merely redefine covenant theology—it **redesigned theology's address**. Worship was lifted from the threshing floors of Zion and placed upon imperial foundations. What was once holy ground became **political ground with incense**. The dome of the Pantheon—symbol of Roman cosmic supremacy—was now cloaked with sainthood, but its **structural theology remained unchanged**.

This is why **Hebrew grammar and geography** are not accessories to truth—they are the **only surviving witnesses**. A theology severed from Hebrew becomes **a gospel of empire**. Without Hebrew:

- Sin becomes imbalance, not rebellion.
- Zion becomes metaphor, not homeland.
- The Temple becomes obsolete, and **the basilica becomes Babylon.**

"YHWH never asked for cathedrals. He asked for obedience. He tabernacled with tribes, not thrones."

When the sacred is redefined by imperial stone, **replacement becomes ritualized**. The early Church did not just bury Torah—they built churches over its memory.

Aspaklaria and Bat Kol: Prophetic Reception and Dimness of Vision

[30] The Talmudic concept of Aspaklaria—the lens or "speculum through which prophecy is seen"— distinguishes between clear and obscured prophetic states. In Yevamot 49b and Sanhedrin 11a, Moshe is described as seeing "through a clear glass" (aspaklaria me'irah), while later prophets perceived through a dim glass (aspaklaria she'aina me'irah). This framework affirms not only degrees of prophetic clarity, but the role of linguistic medium in that clarity.

[31]When the Hebrew language is displaced—as in post-exilic and New Testament literature—prophetic reception shifts. The emergence of the Bat Kol, or "daughter voice," signals this transition. No longer receiving full prophetic utterance, sages and priests report echoes, fragments, and voices from behind the veil. The Bat Kol was considered authoritative but indirect, reflective of a fractured covenantal communication.

Paul's declaration in 1 Corinthians 13:12—"Now we see through a glass, darkly (δι' ἐσόπτρου ἐν αἰνίγματι)"— mirrors this Jewish worldview. His language echoes the Aspaklaria typology, yet is written in Greek, reflecting the exile not only of people but of prophetic language itself. Prophecy becomes dim not just because of time, but because of tongue.

This theological dimness reinforces the monograph's thesis: linguistic fidelity is central to prophetic fidelity. Hebrew was not merely a language of content, but a medium of

---

[30] Babylonian Talmud, *Yoma* 9b and *Sanhedrin* 11a. See also Jacob Neusner, *The Bavli and Its Sources*, vol. 1 (Atlanta: Scholars Press, 1994), 58–60. Moshe Idel, *Kabbalah: New Perspectives* (New Haven: Yale University Press, 1988), 135–136.

clarity. Its loss correlates directly to the dimming of prophetic perception and the emergence of fragmented voices.

For diagrammatic comparison of prophetic modes, see Appendix M, Fig. 3: *Aspaklaria and the Dim Mirror of Post-Temple Prophecy*.

VI. The New Covenant: Not a New Law

Jeremiah 31:31–33 promises a renewed (chadashah) covenant, where the Torah is written on the heart—not abolished.

Hebrews 8:8–10 affirms this, quoting Jeremiah directly. The problem is not Torah—but disobedient hearts.

> Torah remains. What changes is the location: stone to spirit, scroll to soul.

VII. Hebrew Identity and Christian Theology

Many early Christians (especially Gentiles) adopted a theology that rejected:
- The Torah as bondage
- Israel as obsolete
- Hebrew identity as a hindrance

This was not Pauline—it was Constantinian. Early replacement theology paved the way for:
- Supersessionism
- Colonialism
- Cultural recontextualization of Hebraic truths

The Arian Crisis and the Imperial Suppression of Divergent Christologies

The Arian controversy—centered on whether the Son was of the same essence (*homoousios*) or merely similar (*homoiousios*) to the Father—was not simply a doctrinal dispute. It was a violent episode in the imperial management of theological dissent that reveals how Rome absorbed Christianity through censorship, destruction, and redefinition. The Council of Nicaea (325 CE), convened by Constantine, weaponized theology as imperial policy. Arius, a presbyter of Alexandria, denied the co-eternality of the Son, asserting that "there was a time when He was not." This challenged the rising orthodoxy that sought to deify Jesus in alignment with Greco-Roman metaphysics.

But the Arian movement was vast and well-supported, especially among Germanic tribes and early bishops. After Nicaea, Constantine exiled Arius but later reversed his stance—revealing the political, not purely spiritual, nature of the conflict. Arius's eventual death under suspicious circumstances in 336 CE coincided with a renewed purge of his followers and writings.

Eusebius of Nicomedia, an Arian sympathizer and bishop, was briefly restored before Athanasius and pro-Nicene clergy gained favor again. Constantine's sons oscillated between Arian and Nicene positions, deepening ecclesial instability. But it was Constantine's statecraft—not divine revelation—that cemented the Nicene Creed as orthodoxy. The Theodosian decrees later criminalized Arian belief entirely.

Constantine reportedly ordered the **burning of Arian writings**, including Arius's book *Thalia*—an Alexandrian work written in poetic meter. So thorough was the suppression that no complete version of *Thalia* survives, and even its fragments are preserved only through hostile refutations by Church Fathers like Athanasius and Epiphanius.

"Let any writing composed by Arius... be delivered to the flames, so that not only will the wickedness of his doctrine be obliterated, but also the memory of Arius himself."
— *Codex Theodosianus*, xvi.5.34 (C. 438 CE)

[32]This was not an isolated event. The **Library of Alexandria**, once a repository of Semitic, Egyptian, Persian, and Greek thought, suffered waves of destruction—first under Julius Caesar (48 BCE), then again during Christian purges under Theophilus (391 CE), and finally during Muslim invasions. Later, the **Library of Timbuktu**—a center of African-Islamic scholarship with over 700,000 manuscripts—faced similar destruction during both French colonial incursions and Islamist fundamentalist attacks in 2012.

Such events mark a **pattern of erasure**: suppression of dissenting cosmologies, loss of indigenous epistemologies, and imperial redaction of history. The Arian Crisis must be viewed within this continuum. It was not merely a dogmatic dispute, but a blueprint for theological homogenization enforced through textual annihilation.

Just as the Hebrew *Tanakh* was rebranded into a Greek Old Testament through Septuagintal translation, so too were Arian and Jewish-Christian gospels sidelined in favor of pro-imperial narratives. Jerome himself noted the Gospel of the Hebrews used by the Nazarenes and Ebionites, yet such texts were dismissed or redacted.

The Arian episode—and Constantine's suppression of his theological enemies—serves as a template of what this monograph calls *canonical betrayal*: the deliberate alignment of doctrine with empire, enforced through fire, exile, and silence.

The Ebionites and the Erased Foundations of Hebraic Christianity

The Ebionites, whose name derives from the Hebrew *'ebyonim* (אֶבְיוֹנִים) meaning "the poor" or "the humble," represented a crucial post-70 CE sect of Jewish

---

32 Athanasius of Alexandria, *Orations Against the Arians*, trans. John Henry Newman and Archibald Robertson (Nicene and Post-Nicene Fathers, Series 2, Vol. 4), Eerdmans, 1892. Codex Theodosianus, xvi.5.34 (438 CE), trans. Clyde Pharr, *The Theodosian Code and Novels and the Sirmondian Constitutions*, Princeton University Press, 1952. Bart D. Ehrman, *Lost Christianities: The Battles for Scripture and the Faiths We Never Knew*, Oxford University Press, 2003. Robert M. Grant, *Gods and the One God*, Westminster John Knox Press, 1986. John Dominic Crossan and Jonathan L. Reed, *In Search of Paul*, HarperSanFrancisco, 2004. Edward Gibbon, *The History of the Decline and Fall of the Roman Empire*, Vol. 2, Penguin, 1995, pp. 372–378. Elias Muhanna, "The Fragile Manuscripts of Timbuktu," *The New Yorker*, May 2014. Lionel Casson, *Libraries in the Ancient World*, Yale University Press, 2001.

believers in Yeshua who **fused Messianic expectation with strict Torah observance**. Active from the late 1st century through the 4th century CE, they adhered to the Mosaic covenant, rejected the divinity of Christ, repudiated the writings of Paul, and used their own Semitic gospel known as the *Gospel of the Ebionites* or *Gospel of the Hebrews*. Their existence exposes the theological multiplicity of early Christianity and undermines any assumption of a uniform, Greco-Roman orthodoxy.

"They accept the Gospel according to Matthew only, and repudiate the Apostle Paul, calling him an apostate from the Law." — Epiphanius, *Panarion* 30.16.5

Christology and Canon: Adoption, Not Incarnation

Unlike the Logos Christology later formalized at Nicaea, the Ebionites embraced an **adoptionist theology**, believing Yeshua was a human prophet anointed by God at his baptism—in line with Jewish prophetic typology. They rejected the virgin birth and read Yeshua's mission as the fulfillment, not the abrogation, of Torah.

"Jesus became the Christ when the Holy Spirit descended on him in the Jordan." — *Panarion* 30.14.4

[33] This viewpoint aligns with early Semitic expectations found among the Dead Sea Scrolls, where Messianism was communal, ethical, and covenantal—not metaphysical. The Ebionites maintained observance of dietary laws, circumcision, and the Sabbath, living in contrast to the developing universalism of Gentile Christianity.

Paul as the Heresiarch?

To the Ebionites, Paul was not a theologian of freedom but a **false prophet who distorted the Torah**. They accused him

---

[33] Robert Eisenman, *James the Brother of Jesus*, Penguin, 1998. Bart D. Ehrman, *Lost Christianities*, Oxford University Press, 2003. G.R.S. Mead, *Fragments of a Faith Forgotten*, 1906. ⬚ Epiphanius of Salamis, *Panarion*, trans. Frank Williams, Brill, 2009. ⬚ James Tabor, *Paul and Jesus: How the Apostle Transformed Christianity*, Simon & Schuster, 2012. Jerome, *De Viris Illustribus* 2 (On Illustrious Men). Richard Bauckham, *Jude and the Relatives of Jesus in the Early Church*, T&T Clark, 2004.

of abandoning the Law and misleading Gentile converts. This hostility toward Paul reveals a deep schism within 1st-century Christianity—not merely between Jew and Gentile, but between **Semitic fidelity** and **Hellenistic adaptation**.

"They detest Paul, refuse to accept his letters, and refer to him as a deceiver." — Epiphanius, *Panarion*30.16.6

This sectarian resistance, while often dismissed by patristic authors, represents the tension addressed all throughout this monograph: **the theological cost of canon uniformity and Hellenistic dominance**.

Suppression and Scriptural Loss

By the 4th century, under imperial consolidation, the Ebionites were condemned as heretics. Their scriptures were destroyed, their communities marginalized, and their theological insights erased. Jerome and Origen mention the *Gospel of the Hebrews*, but only fragments remain. Jerome even admits to seeing a version written in Hebrew script, with Semitic idioms absent in Greek versions—evidence of **a Hebraic gospel tradition lost to Latinization**.

"The Gospel which the Nazarenes and Ebionites use... is called the Gospel according to the Hebrews. I recently translated it into Greek and Latin." — Jerome, *De Viris Illustribus* 2

Origen, likewise, quotes from the *Gospel of the Hebrews* and acknowledges its use among early Jewish believers, even citing material not found in the synoptics. Yet these gospels were **excluded from the canonical tradition**, not due to theological incoherence, but **because they preserved Semitic claims incompatible with imperial theology**.

Constantine, Erasure, and the Arians

The eradication of the Ebionite voice mirrors the treatment of other dissenters like the **Arians**, whose rejection of Christ's divinity provoked the Nicene backlash. Constantine's **Council of Nicaea (325 CE)** initiated not only doctrinal enforcement but the **destruction of non-orthodox**

texts. Arius' works were burned; the *Thalia* is lost to history. A pattern emerges:

- 391 CE: Destruction of the Library of Alexandria under Theodosius I.

- 5th–7th c. CE: Suppression of Ebionite and Nazarene communities.

- Timbuktu (16th century): Manuscripts destroyed by Moroccan invaders.

These historical burnings were not isolated; they were **intentional erasures of Semitic knowledge** and **resistance to centralized Roman theology**. See: Appendix Q for Roman Oppression and Dominance.

Relevance

The Ebionites represent the **linguistic, theological, and prophetic counterweight** to the emerging imperial church. Their loss is not merely historical, but **epistemic**.
Torah-rooted prophetic frameworks,

- Hebrew linguistic patterns in Greek manuscripts,

- The rightful place of Semitic gospels and teachers.

VIII. Thought-Provoking Questions

- Was Paul misunderstood—or weaponized?
- Can grace exist without accountability?
- Is the New Covenant a removal of law or renewal of hearts?
- How can modern Hebrews reconcile Paul's writings with Torah fidelity?

IX. References and Sources

1. Deut. 4:6–8; Psalm 19:7; Jeremiah 31:31–33
2. Romans 3:31; Romans 7:12; Galatians 3:10–13
3. Exodus 34:6–7; Isaiah 5:20–24
4. Mishnah Avot 1–6; Kiddushin 29b
5. Babylonian Talmud, Berakhot 28a; Sanhedrin 10:1

6. Rabbi Samson Raphael Hirsch, Commentary on Exodus, vol.   II

7. E.P. Sanders, Paul and Palestinian Judaism

8. Sefaria.org (Tanakh and Rabbinic literature)

Counterpoint: Paul as Torah-Faithful Innovator

Mainstream   View:
N.T. Wright and James D.G. Dunn argue that Paul never abandoned the Torah. He reinterpreted it around the messianic event of Jesus to welcome Gentiles into the covenant, preserving core Jewish values while rejecting ethnocentric gatekeeping.

Representative   Quote:
"Paul's argument is not against the law but against the law as a boundary marker of national exclusivism." – *N.T. Wright, Paul and the Faithfulness of God*, Vol. 2, p. 861.

Rebuttal: Paul's 'Grace' Dismantled Torah's Covenant Structure

While Paul used **rabbinic tools** (e.g., *gezerah shavah*), his writings also betray a **philosophical reconstitution** of Torah in **Hellenistic binary terms**: law vs. grace, flesh vs. spirit, death vs. freedom.

This dualism stands in tension with the **Hebrew understanding of mitzvah as life-giving** (cf. Deut. 30:19). It was Paul—not the Torah—who relocated righteousness from **covenantal obedience** to **faith in a singular salvific figure** (Romans 10:4).

As Paula Fredriksen critiques:

"Paul's Christ is not Torah-observant… He's Torah-transcending." (*Paul: The Pagan's Apostle*, p. 72)

Pamela Eisenbaum adds:

"Paul's gospel required a new anthropology and a new soteriology that restructured Torah itself." (*Paul Was Not a Christian*, p. 124)

To portray Paul as "faithful to Torah" is to ignore his **post-crucifixion theological rupture**, which gradually **enabled supersessionist doctrine**. If Paul "fulfilled" Torah, why did later church traditions **abolish** it entirely?

Paul's message may have begun with **inclusion**, but it ended with **ecclesial disinheritance**.

See: Appendix I – Pauline Citations vs Tanakh Sources

Chapter XV (טו): Divergent Church Systems, the Vatican, and Prophetic Warnings from Daniel and Revelation

I. Introduction: Babylon Reimagined

Scripture repeatedly warns of counterfeit worship, apostate systems, and deceptive power structures masquerading as divine. The Vatican as the spiritual successor to Babylon—a religious empire that mimics truth while opposing Torah? This chapter traces these prophetic warnings through Daniel, Revelation, and historical Church developments.

Deuteronomy 13:1–5 outlines a critical Torah principle: even if a prophet or dreamer performs signs and wonders, if they suggest turning from the commandments of the Most High, they are not to be followed. This "Torah Test" sets the unmovable standard. It teaches that supernatural acts are not sufficient to validate a prophet — only alignment with Torah secures legitimacy. This principle must be applied retroactively to every messianic figure, miracle-worker, or teacher, including Yeshua.

See: Deut. 13:1–5.

II. Daniel's Vision: Beasts, Horns, and Blasphemy

Daniel 7 describes four beasts representing empires:
-	Lion	with	eagle's	wings	(Babylon)
-	Bear	with	three	ribs	(Medo-Persia)
-	Leopard	with	four	wings	(Greece)
-	Dreadful	beast	with	ten	horns	(Rome)

The	little	horn	in	Daniel	7:8:
-	Has	eyes	like	a	man	(human	authority)
-	Speaks	great	words	against	the	Most	High
-	Wears	out	the	saints
-	Changes	times	and	laws	(Daniel	7:25)

The	papal	system:
-	Sabbath	changed	to	Sunday
-	Feasts	replaced	with	Roman	holidays
- Torah labeled obsolete

III. Revelation's Babylon the Great

Revelation	17–18	describes:
-	A	woman	sitting	on	a	scarlet	beast
-	Drunk	with	the	blood	of	the	saints
- Adorned	in	purple	and	scarlet,	gold	and	pearls
-	Holding	a	cup	of	abominations
- Named "Babylon the Great, the Mother of Harlots"

The	Vatican	matches	this	iconography:
-	Bishops	wear	scarlet;	cardinals	wear	purple
-	Gold	chalices	used	in	mass
- Blood of martyrs shed during Inquisition and Crusades
- Mary worship and saint veneration mirror pagan goddess cults

IV. Apostolic Warnings of Deception

Paul	warned:
- "After my departure, savage wolves will come in among you"	(Acts	20:29)
- "Even Satan disguises himself as an angel of light" (2 Cor.

11:14)

Peter and Jude echo this, warning of false teachers and corrupt leaders infiltrating the community of believers. Yeshua warned of many coming in His name (not denying Him) and deceiving many (Matt. 24:5).

This is not atheism—it is spirituality counterfeiting.

The Qumran corpus, including texts such as 4Q246 and the War Scroll (1QM), establishes typological connections between corrupt kingdoms and eschatological beasts. These writings reflect a Second Temple-era Jewish apocalyptic worldview in which earthly empires—particularly oppressive or idolatrous ones—are symbolically identified with monstrous figures drawn from Daniel's visions. The community at Qumran interpreted their historical context through this lens, viewing **Rome as a re-embodiment of Babylon**, the ancient adversary of Zion and Torah.

Long before the composition of the Book of Revelation, the **beast motif** had already become a literary symbol for imperial powers that opposed divine order. In Revelation 17, the beast who sits upon many waters and commits fornication with kings mirrors this inherited tradition. Yet, Revelation reformulates it to address Rome's dual identity as both political oppressor and spiritual deceiver. The **imagery of harlotry, golden chalices, and blasphemous names** directly parallels the critiques found in earlier Jewish writings, but now applied to ecclesiastical structures wrapped in divine pretense.

To identify **post-Constantinian Christianity—and particularly the Vatican—as the culmination of this typological lineage** is not a polemical departure, but a restoration of the prophetic Jewish framework. Revelation, when interpreted through a Hebraic lens, reads not as an endorsement of Romanized faith, but as a theologically charged protest imperial theology masquerading as divine truth. See: Appendix T for textual contrasts of resurrection narratives.

V. Historical Fulfillment: The Rise of Christendom

After Constantine's conversion:
- Christianity became empire-sanctioned
- Israelite practices were outlawed (Council of Laodicea, 364 CE)
- Torah-observant believers were labeled heretics
- Replacement theology dominated catechisms

The Roman Church absorbed pagan traditions:
- Sol Invictus becomes Sunday worship
- Ishtar becomes Easter
- Saturnalia becomes Christmas
- Mother-son worship transferred to Mary and Jesus

VI. Theo-Political Antagonist of the Hebrews

Herod the Idumean: Political King, Prophetic Displacement

Herod the Great, appointed "King of the Jews" by the Roman Senate in 40 BCE and installed in 37 BCE, was not of Davidic lineage but an Idumean by paternal descent and Nabatean by maternal lineage. His father, Antipater, served Julius Caesar and Mark Antony as a Roman client, facilitating Herod's rise to power. Idumeans were forcibly converted to Judaism under John Hyrcanus I in approximately 125 BCE, but they were never fully accepted by the Zadokite elite as legitimate Israelites.

Herod's rise to power, though sanctioned by Rome, was perceived by many in the Jewish world as not merely illegitimate—but prophetically adversarial. The lineage of Herod the Great, being Idumean (Edomite) by descent and Nabatean through maternal heritage, resonates with a deeply rooted spiritual pattern: that of **Amalek**, the enemy of Israel throughout Scripture.

In **Exodus 17:13–16**, Amalek attacks Israel from behind during a moment of vulnerability. The Torah records that YHWH will have "war with Amalek from generation to generation." This pattern recurs in **1 Samuel 15:7–10**, where Saul's failure to destroy Agag, king of Amalek, leads to his own rejection as king. Herod, like Agag, rises to power not through divine election, but through alliance, marriage, and foreign appointment—mirroring Amalek's ancient strategy of subverting Israel not through open warfare, but through infiltration and preservation of rival bloodlines.

In **Esther 3:1**, Haman is introduced as an "Agagite," a descendant of the very king Saul failed to destroy. Haman's plot to exterminate the Jews—set in motion by royal decree—echoes Herod's slaughter of the innocents (**Matt 2:16–18**) and his execution of the last Hasmonean heirs. Both figures function as covenantal interrupters. Numerically, the Book of Esther presents a structure of **ten sons of Haman** being hanged (Esther 9:7–10), reflecting both finality and restoration of justice—ten being a number of divine order (cf. Ten Words/Commandments). This literary parallel enriches the typological connection between Herod and Amalekite-Aggregate threats to the prophetic seed line.

Finally, **Deuteronomy 12:1** emphasizes that Israel must "observe all the statutes and judgments" in the land YHWH gives them, leaving no room for foreign altars or integration of imperial rule into covenantal spaces. Herod's temple, built with Roman approval and architectural influence, served both as a magnificent monument and a **prophetic warning**—a sanctuary hosting an identity crisis. Walter Brueggemann, *The Prophetic Imagination*, 2nd ed. (Minneapolis: Fortress Press, 2001), 1–19.

Herod strategically married into the Hasmonean dynasty to solidify his political legitimacy, wedding Mariamne I, granddaughter of Hyrcanus II and descendant of the Maccabean priest-kings. However, Herod's reign soon became synonymous with bloodshed: he executed Mariamne I in 29 BCE on suspicions of conspiracy and later murdered their sons, Aristobulus IV and Alexander, in 7 BCE. Josephus records these events in *Antiquities* 15.3.5 and 16.11.7, noting Herod's cruelty even alarmed Augustus Caesar.

Further consolidating power, Herod arranged the assassination of Hyrcanus II in 30 BCE and beheaded Antigonus II Mattathias, the last Hasmonean king, in 37 BCE after capturing Jerusalem with Roman military support. These eliminations marked not just the end of a dynasty, but the **extinguishing of the last direct heirs to prophetic and priestly authority**.

Herod's political purge extended to the Temple as well. He replaced the Zadokite high priesthood with Ananelus, a Babylonian Jew of uncertain lineage, and later appointed his own in-laws, violating Levitical protocol. This dismantling of covenantal lineage represents what may be called a **prophetic interruption**—a manufactured transition from divine inheritance to Roman-sanctioned governance.

The slaughter of the innocents in Matthew 2:16–18, though debated historically, reflects a theological memory of Herod's assaults against Davidic seed. This aligns him typologically with **Agag**, king of Amalek (1 Samuel 15), whose lineage the prophet Samuel condemned to prevent future harm to Israel. Linguistically, the Agagite (Hebrew: אגגי) pattern reappears in Haman (Esther 3:1), and spiritually echoes in Herod's role as a covenantal adversary.

Thus, Herod emerges not merely as a puppet king but as a prophetic disruptor. The **Edomite-Amalekite paradigm**, historically linked to enmity with Israel (Exodus 17:14–16), resurfaces in Herod's calculated destruction of Judah's royal and priestly bloodlines. His geopolitical merger of Idumea and Nabatea under Roman Judea in the late 1st century BCE marks a **geographical and genealogical redefinition of Israelite identity**, engineered through violence and Rome's imperial theological framework.

Herod's regime is a prelude to ecclesiastical supersession: a system that displaced not only royal heirs but prophetic memory, replacing it with a version of priesthood and kingship molded by the empire.

Edom, Rome, and Identity Rebranding in Rabbinic Memory

The prophetic adversary motif surrounding Herod and Rome becomes even more pointed when examined through classical rabbinic interpretation and encyclopedic Jewish memory. The connection between **Edom (Esau)** and **Rome**, far from a fringe claim, is **deeply embedded in Jewish exegesis**.

Classical sources identify Rome as the spiritual and political heir of Edom:

- **Talmud Bavli, Avodah Zarah 10a** explicitly equates Rome with Edom and warns of its enmity toward the covenant.

- **Bereshit Rabbah 65:21** notes that Esau (Edom) is the progenitor of Rome, explaining that just as Esau pursued Jacob, so Rome pursues Israel.

- **Midrash Tanchuma, Toldot 5** interprets Esau's blessing of the sword (Gen. 27:40) as being fulfilled in Rome's violent dominion.

- **Yalkut Shimoni on Obadiah 1** (Remez 533) describes Edom as a "deceiver of nations," a kingdom whose identity hides behind false piety and political alliances.

This lineage is not merely literary—it functions as **prophetic identity critique**. Herod's Edomite heritage is not incidental. Rabbinic tradition reads the rise of Herod, Rome's elevation of Edomite bloodlines, and later Church power structures as the **rebranded fulfillment of Esau's anti-covenantal agenda**.

Even modern Jewish encyclopedic references affirm the connection:

- The **Jewish Encyclopedia (1905 Edition), Volume 5, p. 41,** under "Edom," affirms:

"The Jews looked upon Rome as the successor of Edom... a belief that became universal in Jewish literature."

- **Encyclopedia Judaica (2nd Ed., 2007)** likewise notes that by the time of the Second Temple's destruction, **Rome had become the dominant symbol of Edom in rabbinic literature,** representing not just a foreign power but a **spiritual adversary clothed in covenantal disguise.**

This typology explains the **Jewish suspicion toward any regime or priesthood not descended from the sons of Jacob.** Rome-Edom, in this interpretive tradition, is not merely a political enemy—it is a spiritual imposter. The Vatican, bearing sacerdotal vestments, issuing ecclesial decrees, and rebranding Israel's covenantal claims, becomes the **Edomite priesthood in exile**—one that seeks the birthright through deception rather than obedience (Genesis 27:36).

This lends even deeper prophetic gravity to the Church's imperial appropriation of Israelite identity:

- The title "Vicar of Christ" (Vicarius Christi), used for the Pope, mirrors the Edomite strategy of **standing in the place of the true heir.**

- The erasure of Hebrew linguistic structures and calendar systems mirrors Esau's displacement of Jacob through political maneuver.

- Just as Herod rebuilt the Temple with Roman aesthetics, the Church redefined Zion in basilicas and Latinized doctrines.

[34]When paired with Deuteronomy 28 and Revelation 18:4 ("Come out of her, My people"), this identification of Rome

34 Matthew 21:12–13; Mark 11:15–17; John 2:13–17. See also Craig Keener, *The IVP Bible Background Commentary: New Testament* (Downers Grove: IVP Academic, 1993), 95–96. ▨ Matthew 15:1–9; Mark 7:6–13. Cf. David Flusser, *Jesus* (Grand Rapids: Eerdmans, 2001), 118–120. Also, Geza Vermes, *The Religion of Jesus the Jew* (Minneapolis: Fortress Press, 1993), 42–47. ▨ Matthew 23:27–28. For an in-depth cultural context, see Joachim Jeremias, *Jerusalem in the Time of Jesus*(Philadelphia: Fortress Press, 1969), 243–260. Richard Horsley, *Jesus and the Spiral of Violence: Popular Jewish Resistance in Roman Palestine* (Minneapolis: Fortress Press, 1993), 111–131. Also, Shaye J.D. Cohen, *From the Maccabees to the Mishnah*, 2nd ed. (Louisville: Westminster John Knox, 2006), 78–85.

as Edom is not anti-Christian—it is **anti-imposter**. It is a **call to discern identity theft in theological garments**.

Thus, Rome is not simply an oppressor—it is **Esau reborn**, wearing the robes of Jacob while nullifying the birthright of Zion. The rabbinic voice never forgot this. The prophetic memory encoded in Talmud, Midrash, and ancient Jewish lexicons reveals the **most subversive truth**: what the world sees as apostolic succession, the prophets saw as **the Esau system wearing priestly linen**.

Even Yeshua of Nazareth—whose voice rings clearest in the scrolls of Second Temple revolt—directly confronted the false religious infrastructure of his day. He did not only preach repentance; he **waged a covenantal protest against a corrupted Temple economy and a hypocritical leadership structure.**

In all four Gospels, he is recorded as **overturning the tables of money changers**, condemning their marketplace within the Temple as a **"den of thieves"** (Matt. 21:13; Mark 11:17; John 2:16). This was not a rejection of sacrificial practice per se, but of a commodified priesthood that profaned Torah purity with imperial economics.

More tellingly, in Matthew 15:1–9 and Mark 7:6–13, he **confronts Pharisaic minhagim (customary rulings)** that had replaced and overridden Torah. "You make void the word of God by your tradition," he declares—directly exposing how rabbinic oral law became a substitute for divine statute.

This culminates in **Matthew 23**, where he delivers a scathing rebuke: "Woe to you, scribes and Pharisees, hypocrites! You are like whitewashed tombs... outwardly righteous to men, but inwardly full of hypocrisy and lawlessness." His critique is not merely theological; it is **ethnolinguistic, prophetic, and legal**, aimed at those who had usurped Hebraic leadership while claiming spiritual authority.

The "Judaism" Yeshua opposed was not the faith of Abraham or Moses—it was **a co-opted theo-political machine**, propped up by Herodian appointees, Roman interests, and post-Babylonian rabbinic innovation. This is the same identity machine that sought to redefine who was a "Jew," while suppressing the prophetic bloodline and rejecting the covenantal Torah.

Yeshua's opposition was not antisemitic—it was anti-syncretic. He sought to restore Israelite Torah, not dismantle it. The irony is that the very system he challenged now claims to define his ethnic identity and religious posture.

The Rabbinic tradition consistently identifies Rome with Edom, and Edom with Esau—the archetypal adversary of Jacob/Israel. This typological framework appears throughout classical literature:

- In *Avodah Zarah 10a*, Rome is portrayed as the enemy of Israel's God and Torah.

- *Bereshit Rabbah 65:21* equates Esau with Edom and links his descendants with Roman power.

- *Midrash Tanchuma, Toldot 5* describes Rome as inheriting Esau's sword-based dominion.

These rabbinic interpretations provide canonical typological precedent for equating Rome—and its later ecclesial structures—with a spiritually adversarial system. Thus, the identification of the Vatican as the eschatological Babylon (Revelation 17–18) aligns with native Jewish tradition: the empire of Esau cloaked in priestly garments, subverting Torah under the banner of divine authority.

See: Talmud Bavli, Avodah Zarah 10a; Midrash Tanchuma, Toldot 5; Bereshit Rabbah 65.

Esau (Edom) was given temporary dominion (Genesis 27:40). Rabbinic tradition identified Rome as functioning as a theo-political antagonist in Hebraic prophetic typology in end time prophecy. The Vatican, cloaked in religious garb, becomes the Edomite priesthood in exile, attempting to possess the birthright through counterfeit priesthood and global influence.

Political Pacts and Prophetic Erosion: Treaty Networks of Subversion

The rise of Herod must also be understood within the **network of treaties** that realigned the political and religious authority of Judea with foreign powers—effectively undermining prophetic and priestly succession from within.

1. **The Judah–Sparta Treaty**
As preserved in *1 Maccabees 12:5–23* and confirmed by Josephus (*Antiquities* 12.4.10), a formal diplomatic exchange existed between the Jews and the Spartans. These communications claimed a shared descent from Abraham and aimed at forming a military alliance. Though not executed in full, the treaty reflects early openness to Hellenistic partnership—a political maneuver that diluted distinct covenantal identity and foreshadowed later Roman entanglement.

2. **The Judah–Rome Alliance**
The Maccabees—originally defenders of the covenant—formally aligned with Rome in 161 BCE (1 Macc. 8:17–32), seeking protection against Seleucid oppression. Rome, eager to extend influence eastward, granted privileges and recognized Jewish autonomy—but at the cost of **political dependency**. Josephus (*Antiquities* 14.10.2) describes the Roman Senate endorsing Jewish rights, yet simultaneously introducing Roman arbitration into Judean affairs. This treaty laid the groundwork for Herod's later Roman endorsement.

3. **Idumean Conversion and Edomite Integration**
Under John Hyrcanus I (~125 BCE), the Idumeans were forcibly converted to Judaism and granted civic status in Judea. While seen as national expansion, it represented a **compromised priesthood**—incorporating Edomite descendants long regarded as hostile (cf. Obadiah 1, Ezekiel 35). Herod's eventual appointment by Rome as "King of the Jews" (40 BCE, Dio Cassius *Roman History* 49.22) thus signaled a return of Esau's line through covenantal backdoors—**prophetically marked** in Genesis 36:1–8 as the rival of Jacob's inheritance.

4. **Nabatean Political Intermarriage**
Herod's mother, Cypros, was a Nabatean noblewoman—connecting Judea to Arabia. His marriage to Mariamne, a Hasmonean princess, was a calculated attempt to merge two opposing dynasties. Yet Herod executed her and her sons (Josephus, *Antiquities* 15.3.5), severing the prophetic line in favor of Roman-backed administration. The **Nabatean element** signifies spiritual intermingling—a direct violation of Deuteronomy 7:1–4, which warned against marrying foreign nations lest covenant be forsaken.

5. **Rome and the Idumean Agenda**
Rome's sponsorship of Herod was not coincidental. The empire understood the **theological symbolism of the Davidic line**, and by backing an Idumean over a Hasmonean or Davidide, they ensured a controlled kingship. Revelation 12 and 17 echo this **beast-and-dragon system**—a false enthronement mimicking divine authority. Herod was not merely a client king; he was a **living inversion** of Israelite messianic expectation.

Second Temple "Jewish" Identity Was Not Monolithic

[35] By the time of Herod and Yeshua, the term "Jew" (Ἰουδαῖος) covered **a wide spectrum of ethnic, religious,**

---

[35] Josephus, *Antiquities of the Jews* 14.10.2, 15.3.5, 16.11.7, 17.1.3. These passages detail Herod's Idumean heritage and political rise under Roman appointment. Talmud Bavli, *Avodah Zarah* 10a. Discusses Edom's relationship with Rome and rabbinic perceptions of imperial corruption. *Midrash Tanchuma, Toldot* 5; *Bereshit Rabbah* 65:21. Classic rabbinic commentary identifying Edom with Rome and critiquing spiritual imposture. Genesis 36:1–8; Obadiah 1; Ezekiel 35. Scriptural roots linking Edom with future antagonism and territorial usurpation. 1 Maccabees 8:17–32; 12:5–23. These verses show Hasmonean political overtures to Rome and the growing Hellenistic influence. 1 Maccabees 12.4.10; Josephus, *Antiquities* 12.4.10. Further examples of Israelite elites seeking Roman approval,

and political groups. Not all who bore this title shared covenantal lineage with ancient Israel. The redefinition of Israelite identity—especially under imperial rule—led to a mixed population where **bloodline, Torah observance, and political loyalty often conflicted.**

Group	Ethnicity	Religious Alignment	Historical Note
Zadokite Priests	Levi (Aaronic lineage)	Torah-loyal, Temple-centered	Many displaced by Hasmoneans; some became Qumran Essenes.
Idumeans	Edomite (descendants of Esau)	Judaized under coercion	Herod the Great was Idumean by blood, not Israelite.
Hellenized Jews	Mixed Judean-Greek	Syncretic with Greco-Roman customs	Dominated urban centers; many rejected Torah centrality.
Herodian Jews	Political hybrids	Loyal to Rome, Temple collaborators	Temple elite under Herod's expansion; served empire interests.
Nabataean Converts	Semitic-Arab (Ishmaelite kin)	Torah-influenced,	Interacted with Judeans, especially near

paving the way for later identity shifts. Walter Brueggemann, *The Prophetic Imagination*, 2nd ed. (Minneapolis: Fortress Press, 2001), 1–19. Discusses how prophetic identity resists state-coopted religion. Ramsay MacMullen, *Christianizing the Roman Empire* (New Haven: Yale University Press, 1984), 87–104. Documents the gradual transformation of Roman temples into Christian institutions. Arthur Nock, *Conversion: The Old and the New in Religion from Alexander the Great to Augustine of Hippo* (Baltimore: Johns Hopkins University Press, 1933), 116–132. Analyzes religious rebranding and identity absorption by empires. Augustine, *Against the Jews* (Tractatus adversus Judaeos), *Patrologia Latina* 42:51. Offers early theological justification for marginalizing Jewish identity under a Roman Christian framework. Lee Martin McDonald, *The Biblical Canon: Its Origin, Transmission, and Authority*, 3rd ed. (Peabody, MA: Hendrickson, 2007), 89–102. Tracks how canon and identity were reshaped post-70 CE. Jerome, *Prologus Galeatus*, in *Biblia Sacra Vulgata*, ed. Robert Weber (Stuttgart: Deutsche Bibelgesellschaft, 1994). Describes the theological gatekeeping around Hebrew scripture and language.

Group	Ethnicity	Religious Alignment	Historical Note
		often intermarried	southern borders.
Diaspora Jews	African, Persian, Greek	Ranged from faithful to assimilated	Often preserved Torah in foreign lands; varied levels of covenantal memory.
Samaritans	Assyrian-era resettled peoples	Claimed Torah lineage, Mt. Gerizim cultus	Descended from imperial transplants (2 Kings 17); rejected Jerusalem's Temple.

[36]Note: *Yeshua's interaction with the Samaritan woman (John 4:9, 20–22) reveals both the deep rift between Judeans and Samaritans and his prophetic call beyond ethnopolitical boundaries. He affirms: "Salvation is from the Jews"—clarifying that **covenantal lineage and priestly location matter.***

And They Were Called "Christians"

The historical pattern of Jewish expulsion from Gentile nations confirms the prophetic warnings of Deuteronomy 28.

Year   Region   Context

70 CE   Jerusalem Temple destroyed by Romans under Titus

[36] Pope Boniface VIII, *Unam Sanctam* (1302). Papal declaration asserting Roman supremacy over spiritual matters—critical to understanding later Christian power dynamics. Pope Alexander VI, *Inter Caetera* (1493). Provided theological authorization for colonial and identity conquest. *Jewish Encyclopedia* (1906 ed.), "Edom." Defines the rabbinic consensus linking Edom with Rome and later Christian domination. Sanhedrin 94a:15. Indicates Jewish dispersion into Africa during Assyrian and Babylonian exiles. Musa Dube, *Postcolonial Feminist Interpretation of the Bible* (St. Louis: Chalice Press, 2000). Insight on theological distortion through empire and colonial patriarchy. Shaul Magid, *American Post-Judaism* (Bloomington: Indiana University Press, 2013), 202. Debates Afro-Hebraic claims as symbolic, which your work rebuts. *"The Church, the new people of God, remains in continuity with the people of the Old Covenant."* (CCC §839)kxkxxkxkxkk

135 CE Judea   Bar Kokhba revolt crushed; Jews banned

Nimrod, the Proto-Beast Cipher, and the Hidden 666 Code

The imperial persecution under **Emperor Nero** (54–68 CE) marked the first state-sponsored violence against early believers and Torah-observant Israelites. Following the **Great Fire of Rome in 64 CE**, Nero scapegoated the "Chrestians," initiating a brutal campaign. Tacitus describes how victims were crucified, burned alive, or torn apart by dogs (*Annals* 15.44). Nero's violent reign influenced early apocalyptic texts, particularly the **Book of Revelation**, where the Beast (Rev. 13:1–8) is seen as an echo of Nero's terror. The number **666**, using Hebrew gematria, spells " נרון קסר" (*Neron Qesar*)—Nero Caesar.

The numerical value 666 has long captivated biblical scholars and apocalyptic interpreters, particularly through its association with נרון קסר (Neron Caesar), the Roman emperor believed by many to be the Beast of Revelation. However, beyond this well-documented cipher lies a newly revealed, ancient construct: נמרדבנכש (Nimrod ben Kush), which, in standard Hebrew Gematria (Mispar Hechrechi), also equals 666. This finding offers a profound recontextualization of Revelation 13:18 by linking the final Beast not just to Rome, but to Babel—the genesis of empire, idolatry, and human rebellion against YHWH.

Cipher Analysis: 666= נמרדבנכש

The Hebrew cipher נמרדבנכש represents a compressed form of 'Nimrod son of Kush' and is composed as follows:

$$(300) \text{נ} + 50(\text{מ}) + 40(\text{ר}) + 200(\text{ד}) + 4(\text{ב}) + 2(\text{נ}) + 50(\text{כ}) + 20(\text{ש})$$
$$= 666$$

This exact match is structurally and linguistically consistent within classical Hebrew conventions of naming and compression. Unlike strained calculations or anachronistic insertions, this cipher flows naturally from biblical narrative. Nimrod, identified in Genesis 10 as the first 'mighty one on earth,' established Babel—the cradle of empire and human defiance.

To further confirm the prophetic accuracy and semantic integrity of this cipher, several biblical phrases—each tied to rebellion, pride, or Babelic aspiration—also equal 666 in Hebrew Gematria:

Hebrew Phrase	Translation	Source	Gematria
רָשָׁע יִתְהַלֵּל נַפְשׁוֹ תַּאֲוַת	The wicked boasts of his soul's desire	Psalm 10:3	666
לְבָבְךָ יָרוּם וְשָׁכַחְתָּ אֶת יְהוָה	Your heart will be lifted up, and you will forget YHWH	Deuteronomy 8:14	666
בבל נבנה לנו עיר	Let us build ourselves a city in Babel	Genesis 11:4	666

These matched phrases reinforce the Baraita of 32 Rules (specifically Rule 29), which permits hermeneutic analogies drawn from numerical equivalence in holy writ. Thus, Nimrod's cipher is not an anomaly, but a coded prophetic archetype embedded within Scripture.

By matching נרון קסר and נמרדבנכש both at 666, and confirming additional rebellious phrases with the same value, we discover not a coincidence but a typological arc: from Babel to Rome, from the first empire to the beast that seeks to devour the saints (Rev. 13:7). This reinforces the text's allusion to a transhistorical system of rebellion, political divinization, and opposition to prophetic truth.

Prophetic Implications

Nimrod is not merely a historical figure but a prophetic archetype. He embodies the first attempt at global domination and self-deification, mirrored in the aspirations of later empires and especially in Revelation's Beast. His identification through the cipher 666= נמרדבנכש deepens the theological understanding that the Beast is not only a

Roman legacy but the reincarnation of ancient Babelic defiance. It reflects a continuum of anti-YHWH governance, characterized by control, violence, and the seduction of worship away from the Most High.

Authorship, Transmission, and Sacred Responsibility

This cipher was not found in academic databases or mystical archives, but was first taught to Moreh Tovi Mickel by Rosh Moreh Avdiel Ben Levi of the Learn Torah Foundation. It is through this sacred chain of instruction that the cipher 666= נמרדבנכש has now been revealed. The interpretation of Deuteronomy 28:68 and the foundational Hebrew tools used in this analysis were also imparted through this lineage.

Moreh Tovi Mickel has formally preserved, expanded, and integrated this prophetic cipher into his theological corpus. Any teaching, citation, or publication of this discovery must acknowledge the following chain of transmission:

"First taught by Rosh Moreh Avdiel Ben Levi of the Learn Torah Hebrew Academy, recorded and expanded upon by Moreh Tovi Mickel."

This ensures that prophetic knowledge is honored with integrity and not abstracted into anonymous intellectual systems.

Integration and Application

This teaching is positioned as a scholarly and prophetic understanding, deepening the discourse on the Beast of Revelation. It invites the reader to view 666 not merely as a Roman numeral puzzle but as a sacred thread stretching from Genesis through Second Temple messianism to the apocalyptic visions of Yohanan (John). Nimrod is the proto-beast. Nero is the inheritor. And the system they represent continues into the present age. This discovery restores the ancient frame of discernment to its rightful place.

From Stone to Marble: Architectural Replacement and Spiritual Authority

Following the destruction of the Second Temple in 70 CE, the architectural language of faith shifted dramatically. Early Christian worship, once home-based, increasingly adopted the spatial design of Roman basilicas—structures originally used for imperial justice and pagan worship. This shift was not stylistic alone: it redefined sacred space from Torah-centered assembly to Greco-Roman altar. Eusebius of Caesarea documents Constantine's construction of churches atop pagan shrines, including the Church of the Holy Sepulchre. Ramsay MacMullen and Arthur Nock note that church iconography and layout often mimicked that of Mithraic, Dionysian, and imperial cult temples. In this transformation, communion replaced sacrifice, bishops replaced Levites, and Rome replaced Zion.

Augustine on Hebrew Scripture

Quote:
"The Jews hold the oracles of God. They are our librarians, though   blind."
— *Augustine, Against the Jews (Tractatus adversus Judaeos), PL 42:51.*

Augustine's model of Jewish 'custodianship without comprehension' becomes the theological alibi for Christian appropriation of Hebrew text without covenantal context.

Aquinas' Allegorical Method vs. Hebraic Literalism

Quote:
"The spiritual sense is built on the literal and presupposes it. But divine wisdom composes Scripture so as to have manifold senses."
— *Thomas Aquinas, Summa Theologiae I, q.1 a.10.*

Where Torah grounds truth in the root, stem, and shoresh, Aquinas builds multi-tiered metaphors. This departure from linguistic realism to philosophical abstraction signals the shift from covenant to concept.

"Translation, in the hands of empire, became a tool of epistemicide—silencing native meanings to uplift ecclesial authority."[37]

This architectural and theological transformation was not incidental—it was formalized in stages through the first seven Ecumenical Councils:

- **Nicaea I (325 CE):** Established homoousios (same substance) Christology and sanctioned Roman ecclesiastical alignment. Also, formalized Sunday observance and condemned Torah practices. Lee Martin McDonald, *The Biblical Canon: Its Origin, Transmission, and Authority*, 3rd ed. (Peabody, MA: Hendrickson, 2007), 89–102.

- **Constantinople I (381 CE):** Reaffirmed Nicene theology and promoted Trinitarian orthodoxy.

- **Ephesus (431 CE):** Declared Mary Theotokos (God-bearer), deepening Greco-Roman mother-goddess parallels.

- **Chalcedon (451 CE):** Instituted dyophysite doctrine (two natures of Christ), crystallizing imperial Christological doctrine.

- **Constantinople II (553 CE) and III (680–681 CE):** Suppressed alternative theologies and reaffirmed state-defined orthodoxy.

- **Nicaea II (787 CE):** Reinstated icon veneration—mirroring earlier pagan statuary practices.

These councils did not merely clarify doctrine—they codified Rome's ecclesiastical dominance. Each stage

---

[37] Musa W. Dube, *Postcolonial Feminist Interpretation of the Bible* (St. Louis: Chalice Press, 2000), 38–54. **Josephus**, *Antiquities of the Jews* 13.9.1 (§257–258): Hyrcanus I forced the Idumeans to convert to Judaism. **Flavius Josephus**, *Jewish War* 1.6.2 (§123–126): Describes Herod's lineage and Edomite roots. **Shaye J.D. Cohen**, *The Beginnings of Jewishness* (University of California Press, 1999), 69–71: Details the complex categories of Jewish identity and conversion under Roman definition. **Peter Schäfer**, *The History of the Jews in the Greco-Roman World*, 2nd ed. (Routledge, 2003), 70–74: Examines Hellenized elites in Judea. **Lawrence Schiffman**, *Reclaiming the Dead Sea Scrolls* (Doubleday, 1994), 101–108: Describes the Zadokite priesthood's ousting and sectarian reaction. **Tal Ilan**, *Lexicon of Jewish Names in Late Antiquity*, Part I (Mohr Siebeck, 2002), 29–36: Notes mixed Arab-Nabataean identities among temple and urban Jews. 2 Kings 17:24–33: Biblical record of Assyria resettling foreign peoples into Samaria, who adopted partial worship of YHWH. **James H. Charlesworth**, *The Samaritans: Their History, Doctrines and Literature* (Fortress Press, 1985): Identifies the hybrid religious-political structure of Samaritan identity post-Assyrian exile. **John 4:22**, NIV: "You Samaritans worship what you do not know; we worship what we do know, for salvation is from the Jews."

reaffirmed Greco-Roman theological and imperial patterns under the guise of ecumenical unity. From this lens, the phrase "Babylon the Great, the mother of harlots" (Rev. 17:5) emerges not as an attack on Christians, but as a prophetic indictment of systemic spiritual consolidation that echoes Babel: a tower of unity built in defiance of divine instruction. Walter Brueggemann, *The Prophetic Imagination*, 2nd ed. (Minneapolis: Fortress Press, 2001), 1–19.

The "daughters" of the harlot are thus not individual believers or churches but **ecclesiastical offshoots of Rome's original template**—structures that retain form while diverging from prophetic function. This interpretive model requires no condemnation; it calls for discernment and historical clarity. With compassion and scholarly rigor, we trace not the guilt of persons, but the evolution of paradigms that once displaced Zion's covenant for empire's altar.

What occurred was not merely expansion—it was supersession. A new system did not grow from the old; it overtook it. Just as Herod had once removed the rightful heirs, post-Temple Christianity—backed by Roman architecture, ritual, and imperial theology—claimed the inheritance of the prophets while reimagining its form. Following the destruction of the Second Temple in 70 CE, the architectural language of faith shifted dramatically. Early Christian worship, once home-based, increasingly adopted the spatial design of Roman basilicas—structures originally used for imperial justice and pagan worship. This shift was not stylistic alone: it redefined sacred space from Torah-centered assembly to Greco-Roman altar.

Eusebius of Caesarea documents Constantine's construction of churches atop pagan shrines, including the Church of the Holy Sepulchre. Ramsay MacMullen and Arthur Nock note that church iconography and layout often mimicked that of Mithraic, Dionysian, and imperial cult temples. In this transformation, communion replaced sacrifice, bishops replaced Levites, and Rome replaced Zion.

What occurred was not merely expansion—it was supersession. A new system did not grow from the old; it overtook it. Just as Herod had once removed the rightful heirs, post-Temple Christianity—backed by Roman architecture, ritual, and imperial theology—claimed the inheritance of the prophets while reimagining its form.

From Zion's Scrolls to Rome's Seals: Diverging Voices of Authority

As the early ecclesiastical tradition developed, key Church Fathers sought to consolidate doctrine within the framework of Greco-Roman philosophical and imperial stability. This often meant distancing themselves from the Hebraic framework of prophecy, Torah, and linguistic covenant. What emerged was a shift not only in geography—from Jerusalem to Rome—but in **authority, method, and spiritual anthropology**.

Clement of Alexandria (c. 150–215 CE), while deeply learned, begins to merge Platonic ideals with Christian doctrine, elevating allegory over Torah's literal structure. Origen (c. 185–254 CE), though sympathetic to Hebrew Scriptures, introduced a **threefold hermeneutic** (literal, moral, spiritual), which often spiritualized away Torah's concrete demands. Tertullian (c. 155–240 CE), famous for his polemic "What has Athens to do with Jerusalem?" nonetheless affirmed Roman legal structures and coined phrases such as *sacramentum* and *persona* to define the Godhead—terms absent in the Tanakh.

By the time of **Augustine** (354–430 CE), theology was codified in Latin thought categories, cementing a departure from **Zion's original spiritual grammar**. In *Contra Faustum*, Augustine critiques Sabbath-keeping, circumcision, and kosher laws as burdens irrelevant to the "spiritual" Christian. This systematization forms the foundation of **replacement theology**, wherein Israel's role becomes metaphorical and Rome's institutional body inherits divine favor. Lee Martin McDonald, *The Biblical Canon: Its Origin,*

Transmission, and Authority, 3rd ed. (Peabody, MA: Hendrickson, 2007), 89–102.

This divergence was not simply a theological evolution—it was a **voice shift**. The **prophets of Israel spoke in shoresh (root-driven language)**, with legal depth and covenantal accountability. The Church Fathers, writing in Greek and Latin, framed revelation in terms of **essence, substance, and metaphysical being**—categories foreign to the Mosaic voice.

While not all Fathers dismissed Israel, the trend by the 4th century was clear: Zion's scrolls were interpreted under Rome's seal.

Multiple Church councils codified the erasure of Hebraic observances:

• **Council of Nicaea I (325 CE):** Under Constantine, separated Easter from Passover, declaring: *"We should have nothing in common with the detestable Jewish crowd..."* (*Eusebius, Vita Constantini* 3.18).

• **Council of Laodicea (c. 364 CE): Canon 29** prohibited Sabbath observance: *"Christians must not Judaize by resting on the Sabbath... but must honor the Lord's Day instead."*

• **Council of Trent (1545–63):** Canonized the Latin Vulgate and rejected Hebrew-based interpretations, further severing scriptural fidelity to Torah roots.

This   includes:
- Jesuit control of education and diplomacy
-       Vatican   banking   and   global   treaties
- The Pope as Vicar of Christ ("instead of Christ" = anti-Christ)

The centralization of theological authority in Rome led to aggressive efforts to control sacred language and liturgy:

- **Pope Gregory XIII**, *Inter gravissimas* (1582), reformed the Julian calendar into the **Gregorian calendar**, replacing biblical moedim with Roman observances.

- **Unam Sanctam** (1302): *"It is absolutely necessary for salvation that every human creature be subject to the Roman Pontiff."*—Pope Boniface VIII.

- **Decretum Gelasianum** (5th c.): Rejected Semitic-origin Gospels like the *Gospel of the Hebrews*, narrowing the canon through Roman filters.

- **Jerome's Letter to Pope Damasus** (383 CE): Admits Latin corruption and the need to replace it with Hebrew—yet Latin remained dominant. [Jerome, *Prologus Galeatus*, in *Biblia Sacra Vulgata*, ed. Robert Weber (Stuttgart: Deutsche Bibelgesellschaft, 1994).]

- [38]**Dum Diversas** (1452): Authorized King Alfonso V of Portugal to enslave "Saracens and pagans," laying legal groundwork for transatlantic slavery.

- **Romanus Pontifex** (1455): Expanded Dum Diversas, granting rights to claim non-Christian lands and subjugate inhabitants. This justified colonial domination and was weaponized against Afro-Semitic and Indigenous populations.

- **Inter Caetera / Doctrine of Discovery** (1493): Issued by Pope Alexander VI, it declared that lands "discovered" by Christians could be claimed, and non-Christian peoples subdued. This doctrinal weapon transformed Hebrews into "savages," stripping Indigenous and Afro-diasporic peoples of their Israelite heritage and legal humanity.

The contributions of postcolonial and feminist scholars such as Sugirtharajah, Dube, Pui-lan, and Williams remind us that canon is never neutral. It is a curated artifact—shaped by political theology, empire, translation, and erasure. Any

---

[38] Tink Tinker, "Missionary Conquest: The Gospel and Native American Cultural Genocide," *Journal of Law and Religion* 6, no. 1 (1988): 103–114. Willie James Jennings, *The Christian Imagination: Theology and the Origins of Race* (New Haven: Yale University Press, 2010), 38–51.

restoration of sacred memory must therefore reckon with the silences it inherits.

The interpretive framework presented herein may be deepened by integrating **trauma hermeneutics** as not merely a lens of suffering but as a psycho-theological methodology. Drawing from the clinical psychology of Judith Herman and the religious trauma theory of Shelly Rambo, the exilic and diasporic conditions described throughout this monograph reflect symptoms of both **individual and collective PTSD**, spiritual dislocation, and prophetic destabilization.[1] Judith Herman, *Trauma and Recovery: The Aftermath of Violence—from Domestic Abuse to Political Terror* (New York: Basic Books, 1992); Shelly Rambo, *Spirit and Trauma: A Theology of Remaining* (Louisville: Westminster John Knox Press, 2010).

Theological responses to trauma often focus on theodicy, but within Hebraic exile literature, trauma is not explained—it is **transmuted into liturgy**.[2] Psalms of lament, prophetic woe, and covenantal breach become sacred artifacts of psychological survival. As Walter Brueggemann posits, the Hebrew prophets function as "trauma poets," giving voice to pain through subversive grammar and theological protest.[3] ☐ Katongole, Emmanuel. *The Sacrifice of Africa: A Political Theology for Africa* (Grand Rapids: Eerdmans, 2011), 111–138. ☐ Walter Brueggemann, *The Prophetic Imagination*, 2nd ed. (Minneapolis: Fortress Press, 2001), 48–60.

This project's consistent use of **verb stems like hitpaʿēl (הִתְפַּעֵל)** and typological reversals serves not only linguistic ends but psychological exposure.[4] The covenantal rupture in Deuteronomy 28, the silence of exile in Lamentations, and the "muzzling" of prophetic speech in Amos reflect trauma symptoms parallel to those documented in clinical dissociation and fragmentation.[5] For stem usage in trauma exegesis, see Ellen Davis, *Getting Involved with God: Rediscovering the Old Testament* (Lanham, MD: Cowley Publications, 2001), esp. chap. 4. Pamela Cooper-White, *The*

Cry of Tamar: Violence Against Women and the Church's Response (Minneapolis: Fortress Press, 2012), 34–50; Bessel van der Kolk, *The Body Keeps the Score: Brain, Mind, and Body in the Healing of Trauma*(New York: Viking, 2014).

Thus, this is not merely postcolonial theology—it is **trauma theology**. A hermeneutic of rupture that seeks not only to understand scripture but to dignify the broken memory within it.

[39] This section revisits Deuteronomy 28:68, not as a final clause of covenantal warning, but as a prophetically encoded grammar of exile. The Hebrew verb וְהִתְמַכַּרְתֶּם (ve-hitmakartem), found in the Hitpael stem, implies not a passive selling by others, but a reflexive act: "you shall sell yourselves." This linguistic nuance, when read in the context of covenantal theology, reflects the theological agency of the Israelites in their own dispersion—a self-induced exile brought on by systemic disobedience. The theological reflexivity of this structure reinforces the prophetic pattern seen in 1 Kings 21:20 and 2 Kings 17:17, where the people "sold themselves" to do evil.

The verse's closing—וְאֵין קֹנֶה ("and no man shall buy [you]")—is often mistranslated. It implies not the impossibility of being enslaved, but the forfeiture of redemption. The phrase denotes a loss of value in the transactional sense: they become unsellable, abandoned by even those who trafficked human life. This "non-redemption" is itself a divine judgment.

Moreover, the clause וַהֲשִׁיבְךָ יְהוָה מִצְרַיִם בָּאֳנִיּוֹת ("YHWH shall bring you back to Egypt in ships") contains the definite

---

39 Edith Bruder, *The Black Jews of Africa: History, Religion, Identity* (New York: Oxford University Press, 2008), 45–69. Shomarka Keita and Rick A. Kittles, "The Persistence of Racial Thinking and the Myth of Racial Divergence," *American Anthropologist* 99, no. 3 (1997): 534–544.

article in בָּאֳנִיּוֹת ("the ships"), signaling a specific form of bondage. This is not a return to geographic Egypt, but a prophetic typology of exile "by ships," consistent with the transatlantic slave trade experienced by diasporic Hebrews. As argued by Samson Raphael Hirsch, Egypt becomes a symbolic metonym for any site of covenantal bondage (cf. Isaiah   52:3).

For diagrammatic and grammatical reference, see Appendix L, Fig. 2: *The Reflexive Pattern of Exile in Deut. 28:68*. The tripartite lexical anchor—Hitpael structure, definite article in "the ships," and the "non-redemption" clause—forms a theologically   coherent   prophetic   indictment.

This structure is not hyper-literalism, but Hebraic canonical integrity: when Hebrew is stripped of its stem logic and linguistic texture, the theology loses its prophetic precision.

VII. The Call to Come Out

Revelation   18:4:
> "Come out of her, My people, lest you share in her sins."

This isn't merely physical exodus—but theological, cultural, and spiritual separation from Rome's influence. Restoration means:
-                Return   to   Torah
-        Rejection   of   paganized   traditions
- Restoration of true names, feasts, calendar, and identity

VIII. Thought-Provoking Questions

- Has the Vatican fulfilled the role of the little horn and Babylon   the   Great?
- Can a system claim apostolic authority while rejecting Torah?
- What does it mean to "come out of her" today?
- Is Rome the final beast, or a precursor to greater deception?

IX. References and Sources

1. Daniel 7; Daniel 8; Revelation 13, 17–18
2. Matthew 24; Acts 20:29–30; 2 Corinthians 11
3. Council of Laodicea (Canon 29, 364 CE)
4. Talmud Bavli: Avodah Zarah 10a (Rome = Edom)
5. Rabbi Hirsch, Commentary on Genesis (Esau and Edom)
6. Ernest L. Martin, The Rise and Fall of the Roman Church
7.
8. Encyclopedia Britannica, s.v. "Vatican City," "Pope," "Jesuits"
9. Sefaria.org (Daniel and Revelation cross references)

Counterpoint: The Church Was a Preserver, Not a Colonizer of Scripture

Mainstream   View:
Church historians like Jaroslav Pelikan and Henry Chadwick argue that the early Church **preserved scripture, protected sacred texts**, and guided theological development responsibly. Councils and Vatican archives are portrayed as guardians of orthodoxy—not theological gatekeepers.

Representative   Quote:
"The Church preserved what would otherwise have been lost to time and turmoil." – *Jaroslav Pelikan, The Christian Tradition, Vol. 1*, p. 43

Rebuttal: The Church Functioned as Theological Empire—Not Neutral Custodian

This sanitized history ignores the **political function of canon control**, especially after Constantine. The First Council of Nicaea (325 CE), Council of Carthage (397 CE), and others **selected texts that aligned with institutional stability**, often excluding **Hebrew-rich, anti-imperial, or female-authored writings**.

As R.S. Sugirtharajah argues:

"Canon was not formed under candles and prayer—it was forged under empire and censorship." (*The Bible and the Third World*, p. 84)

The Vatican's consolidation of Latin as the ecclesial language—and suppression of vernacular Hebrew texts—amounted to a **linguistic colonization of revelation**. Prophets became saints, seers became heretics, and sacred names became Latin titles.

Even Jerome lamented the pressure:

"They prefer to condemn me without reading my work." (*Letter to Pope Damasus*, c. 382 CE)

If preservation means **selective inclusion, deletion of female and Semitic voices, and assimilation of prophecy into Greco-Roman structures**—then it was not preservation. It was **theological domestication**.

See: Chapter XIII – Restoration of the Name and Appendix N – Etymological Breakdown of the Canon

Chapter XVI (טז): Reclaiming Time—Feasts, the Sacred Calendar, and Edenic Rhythm Restored

I. Introduction: Time as Covenant Territory

Modern timekeeping is built on Gregorian Roman structures—weeks named after Norse gods, months after emperors, and holidays rooted in pagan festivals. But in the Torah, time is sacred architecture, and the biblical calendar is the spiritual skeleton of covenant life. This chapter explores how restoring YHWH's appointed times (moedim) reclaims Edenic rhythm and reorients Israel to divine cycles, with deep alignment between prophecy, feasts, and deliverance.

Origen's Cosmology and the Distortion of Hebraic Creation

Origen of Alexandria, in *On First Principles* (Book I, Ch. 1), offers a cosmological vision rooted in Neoplatonism, positing pre-existent souls, cyclical embodiment, and a metaphysical reading of Genesis. Rather than affirming the six-day creation as a literal or covenantal event, Origen allegorizes it into a descent from divine contemplation into material   bondage.

While Origen's philosophical ambition is admirable, it overwrites the Hebraic structure of Genesis. In the Hebrew worldview, the creation narrative is not a metaphor for metaphysical fall, but a covenantal architecture of time, order, and identity. The division of days, the blessings, and the Sabbath all reflect a linguistic design imbued with prophetic   rhythm—not   spiritual   regression.

Moreover, Origen's rejection of Hebrew chronology (cf. *Contra Celsum*, Book VI) distances scripture from the calendaric and genealogical frameworks essential to Israelite identity. He prefers cosmological abstraction to tribal history, interpreting Eden and Adam as metaphors rather   than   narrative   anchors.

This manuscript offers a corrective: the Hebrew creation account is not merely historical but architectonic—a divine scaffold for covenantal memory. Its structure resists allegorical vaporization because it binds language to time and covenant to cosmos.

Whereas the nations walk under the allotment of astral signs (Deut 4:19), Israel was entrusted with Torah. This contrast dismantles the Greco-Roman Logos metaphysics: the Word of YHWH is covenantal agency, not an independent deity. Yeshua's life is therefore Torah embodied in the cycles of Sabbaths, festivals, and Jubilee.

Category (Inheritance)	Nations (Allotted)	Israel

| Cosmic Guidance | Sun, moon, stars, astrology (Deut 4:19) | Torah as divine word

| Determination | Cyclical fate, cosmic patterns | Prophetic word, covenant law

| Messianic Fulfillment | Subject to signs | Yeshua as Torah embodied in appointed times (mo'adim)

See Appendix N: *Chronology, Naming, and Creation Orders* for visualized comparisons of Hebraic vs. Alexandrian cosmologies.

II. The Biblical Calendar vs. Gregorian Deception

The Torah calendar is lunar-solar (Exodus 12:1–2):
- Begins in the spring (Aviv)
- Marked by new moons (Rosh Chodesh)
- Counts seven-day weeks beginning with Yom Rishon (First Day)
- Anchored in agricultural, astronomical, and prophetic alignment

In contrast:
- January 1 (Gregorian New Year) has no biblical meaning
- Days named after Saturn, Thor, and Freya displace creation order
- Solar-only calculation erases Hebrew feasts' lunar anchors

Daniel 7:25 warns that the beast would "change times and laws." This is direct correlation to the Roman church's calendar manipulations.

III. Moedim: YHWH's Appointed Times

Leviticus 23 lays out the feast cycle:
- Weekly: Sabbath (Shabbat)

- Spring Feasts: Passover (Pesach), Unleavened Bread (Chag HaMatzot), First Fruits (Yom HaBikkurim), Pentecost (Shavuot)
- Fall Feasts: Trumpets (Yom Teruah), Atonement (Yom Kippur), Tabernacles (Sukkot)

These are not "Israelite holidays" but YHWH's appointments—eternal rehearsals of redemption (Lev. 23:1–2).

Each moed is a prophetic marker:
- Pesach → Redemption by blood
- Shavuot → Covenant and Spirit
- Yom Teruah → Awakening & return of the King
- Yom Kippur → National atonement
- Sukkot → Messianic reign and restoration

IV. The Calendar as Weapon of Oppression

Under colonial and Christian missionary pressure:
- Hebrew feasts were called "legalism"
- Solar-only timekeeping enforced through law and education
- Native rhythms erased from Black, Indigenous, and Israelite cultures

Reclaiming time is spiritual warfare—a return to Eden's order and Jubilee freedom.

V. Edenic Time and the 7-1 Pattern

Genesis 1–2 introduces the 7-day creation week, climaxing in Shabbat.
- 6 days labor, 1 day rest
- 7th day sanctified before sin entered
- Echoed in 7-year Shemitah cycles and 49-year Jubilee pattern

This cycle shows time is not neutral—it's covenantal space. In rejecting Sabbath and feasts, humanity entered chaos.

Reclaiming YHWH's calendar is not religious ritual—it's cosmic repentance.

VI. Qumran, Zadokites, and Alternative Reckonings

Some Dead Sea Scroll communities followed a 364-day solar calendar, based on 52 exact weeks:
- Documented in the Book of Jubilees and Enoch
- Likely used by pre-exilic priesthood
- Offered alternative festival timing that still aligned with Torah structure

 These tensions point to Zadokite preservation outside of post-exilic rabbinic changes.

VII. Restoration in the Diaspora

Around the world, awakening Israelites are:
- Keeping Shabbat on the 7th day
- Celebrating moedim in homes and gatherings
- Rejecting Christmas, Easter, and manmade festivals

These aren't new traditions—they are ancient markers returning to covenant consciousness.

VIII. Thought-Provoking Questions

- Can one truly walk with YHWH while keeping pagan time?
- Why did Rome and colonial powers erase YHWH's calendar?
- Do the moedim unlock prophetic insight and spiritual authority?
- Is time a prophetic language we've forgotten to read?

IX. References and Sources

1. Genesis 1–2; Exodus 12; Leviticus 23
2. Isaiah 66:22–23; Zechariah 14:16–19
3. Daniel 7:25; Jubilees 6; 1 Enoch 72–82
4. Babylonian Talmud: Rosh Hashanah 1a; Sukkah 52a
5. Dead Sea Scrolls: Temple Scroll, Calendar Texts

6. Sefaria.org (Feasts, calendars, priesthood laws)
7. Rabbi Hirsch, Commentary on Leviticus
8. Maimonides, Mishneh Torah: Sanctification of the New Moon
9. Academic sources on Zadokite calendrical debate

Counterpoint: The Christian Calendar is a Cultural Evolution, Not an Instrument of Oppression

Mainstream **View:**
Church historians and liturgists defend the Christian calendar—Easter, Christmas, Sunday worship— as **contextual adaptations** made for Greco-Roman converts. These changes are often framed as **missional strategies**, not doctrinal betrayals.

Key Voices:

- **Thomas Talley** (*The Origins of the Liturgical Year*)
- **Jaroslav Pelikan** (*The Emergence of the Catholic Tradition*)
- **Everett Ferguson** (*Early Christians Speak*)
- **Hans-Joachim Kraus** (*Worship in Israel: History and Theology*)

Representative **Quote:**
"Christian liturgy developed organically, incorporating both Jewish patterns and Hellenistic rhythms." – *Thomas Talley, Liturgical Year*, p. 42

Rebuttal: The Christian Calendar Replaced Covenant Cycles with Imperial Rhythms

This perspective minimizes the **erasure of Edenic and Torah-based timekeeping**—a key aspect of Israelite covenantal life. The Torah did not merely present "Jewish holidays"; it outlined **YHWH's moedim (appointed times)**, tied to agricultural, cosmic, and redemptive rhythms (Lev. 23).

When Passover became *Easter*, and Shabbat was changed to *Sunday*, these were not benign shifts—they were **imperial displacements** of sacred memory.

As Marimba Ani critiques:

"Time, like language, is a weapon of control. When you name the days, you name the gods." – *Yurugu*, p. 278

The **Gregorian calendar**, promoted by Pope Gregory XIII in 1582, suppressed **Hebraic lunar-solar reckoning** in favor of **Julian-Caesarean structure**, tied to imperial festivals and Roman gods. Even the names of the days— *Saturday*(Saturn), *Sunday* (Sun)—are rooted in idolatrous systems.

To restore Torah time is to reclaim Edenic alignment—a rhythm of rest, renewal, and righteous order.

See: Chapter XVI, Section V – Edenic Time and the 7-1 Pattern

Chapter XVII (י): Ark of the Covenant, Third Temple, and the Rebirth of Priestly Order

I. Introduction: Holy Ground Awaiting Rebirth

At the heart of Israel's covenantal history lies a sacred triad: the Ark of the Covenant, the Temple, and the priesthood. These are not mere relics of the past, but prophetic blueprints for future restoration. The return of the Ark and priesthood is not about animal sacrifice alone—it is about spiritual order, divine governance, and the return of the Presence (Shekhinah) among Israel.

II. The Ark of the Covenant: Hidden but Not Forgotten

The Ark (Aron HaBrit) contained:
- The tablets of the Torah (Deut. 10:2)
- Aaron's rod that budded (Numbers 17:8)
- Manna (Exodus 16:33)

The divine origin of these tablets is further emphasized in **Exodus 32:16**, which notes that both the writing and the tablets were "the work of God." The Talmud (Sanhedrin 21b) adds a profound layer: the inner letters **mem (ם)** and **samekh (ס)**were miraculously suspended within the stone—since their centers would have naturally fallen out—highlighting not only divine authorship but divine physics, revealing a supernatural medium that defied gravity to preserve meaning.

It represented:
- YHWH's throne on earth (Exodus 25:22)
- The footstool of heaven (1 Chronicles 28:2)
- The locus of covenant judgment and mercy (Lev. 16:14–15)

The Apocrypha alludes to its hiding before the Babylonian destruction (2 Maccabees 2:4–8; Talmud Yoma 53b). Its rediscovery would signal:
- The reinstallation of divine justice
- The renewal of prophetic authority
- The convergence of heaven and earth

III. The Temple: Past Glory, Future Pattern

There have been two Temples:
- Solomon's Temple: destroyed by Babylon (586 BCE)
- Zerubbabel's/Herod's Temple: destroyed by Rome (70 CE)

But Ezekiel 40–48 envisions a third Temple:
- Perfect measurements and renewed tribal inheritances
- Water flowing from the threshold (Ezek. 47)
- Reassignment of Levitical duties, especially for sons of Zadok (Ezek. 44:15)

This is not only literal but cosmic architecture—a sanctified reality awaiting manifestation.

IV. Priesthood Restored: The Sons of Zadok & Daughter of The Dispersed

The Book of Ezekiel singles out the sons of Zadok as faithful during apostasy:
- Zadok served under David and Solomon (1 Kings 1:39)
- His sons are promised lasting priesthood (Ezekiel 44:15–16)

Unlike compromised Levites, they:
- Teach between clean and unclean
- Bear the burden of YHWH's judgments
- Minister before the Ark and Altar

Many of today's Levitical identities—hidden in diaspora—may carry this ancient calling unknowingly.

Throughout history, remnant theology has found embodiment in sects like the Qumran Yahad, the Ethiopian Beta Israel, and Karaites—each preserving covenantal fidelity under hostile empires.

[40]The Matriarchs Shall Rise — Messiah ben Golah, & The Redemption of Eve

"The last shall be first, and the first last."
— Matthew 20:16; cf. Genesis 3:15, 1 Corinthians 15:45

"Chavvah (חוה), the mother of all living, was blamed in the beginning. But in the end, she may be crowned with redemption."
— Diasporic Oral Tradition

[40] Phyllis Trible, *God and the Rhetoric of Sexuality* (Philadelphia: Fortress Press, 1978), 91–102. Edith Bruder and Tudor Parfitt, *African Zion: Studies in Black Judaism* (Newcastle: Cambridge Scholars Publishing, 2012), 89–96. Sylvia Tamale, *African Sexualities: A Reader* (Cape Town: Pambazuka Press, 2011), 94–108. R. W. Cowley, "The Biblical Canon of the Ethiopian Orthodox Church Today," *Ostkirchliche Studien* 23, no. 2 (1974): 318–323. Susan Niditch, *Women and War in the Hebrew Bible* (Oxford: Oxford University Press, 1998), 44–47. John G. Jackson, *Introduction to African Civilizations* (Secaucus: Citadel Press, 1970), 230–234. Lynn Schler, "Queen Ahebi Ugbabe: A Nigerian Monarch and the Construction of Igbo History," *Canadian Journal of African Studies* 37, no. 1 (2003): 1–25. Ifi Amadiume, *Male Daughters, Female Husbands* (London: Zed Books, 1987), 61–72. Ephraim Isaac, "The Ethiopian Orthodox Church and Its Judaic Traditions," in *African Zion*, 159–177. Gen. Rab. 17:8; see also *Pirkei d'Rabbi Eliezer* 21, which amplifies Eve's name as prophetic.

A Forgotten Possibility: Messiah ben Golah as Woman (Baht Golah)

The Messiah ben Golah (משיח בן הגולה), literally "Messiah son of the Exile," is often cast through a male prism. Yet prophetic rhythm reveals a **reversal of Eden**, where those once blamed or hidden emerge crowned. Messiah taught, *"he who is first shall be last, and the last shall be first"* (Matt. 20:16). If Adam, the first human, became the paradigm of fall, then Eve (חוה), the one who bore life, may yet rise as the **first of the last generation**.

Paul called Yeshua the "last Adam" (1 Cor. 15:45), but never excluded the possibility of a final Eve—**a prophetic woman who redeems what was cursed**. Genesis 3:15 promises that the **"seed of the woman"** will crush the serpent's head. Perhaps that seed is more than lineage—perhaps it is her **spirit, voice, and leadership restored**.

This vision also opens the doorway for breaking a deeper curse: *"Your desire shall be for your husband, and he shall rule over you"* (Gen. 3:16). The subjection of woman to man was never a divine ideal, but a consequence of sin. For true redemption to come, **this hierarchy must collapse**, and the creation of God—**male and female**—must walk in restored equality. Thus, if Messiah ben Golah arises as a woman, she not only breaks the serpent's power, but also **annuls the curse of subjection**, restoring balance between the genders.

Precedent in Scripture: Prophetic Women as Deliverers

Biblical memory preserves a line of **female messianic prototypes**:

Name	Role	Verse	Messianic Function
Deborah (דְּבוֹרָה)	Judge & Prophet	Judges 4:4–9	Led Israel into battle; declared righteousness under a palm

Miriam (מִרְיָם)	Prophetess	Exodus 15:20	Led women in song after the Red Sea; honored with a well
Huldah (חֻלְדָּה)	Prophetess	2 Kings 22:14–20	Verified the Torah; spoke judgment and restoration
Phoebe (Φοίβη)	Deaconess	Romans 16:1–2	Entrusted with Paul's letter; affirmed with apostolic dignity

These were not marginal voices. They were **judges, warriors, seers**, and protectors of Torah.

It is also significant that the Hebrew word for *judge*, **shofet (שופט)** or **shofetet (שֹׁפֶטֶת)** in feminine, is closely associated with the role of **Elohim (אֱלֹהִים)** in scripture. In Exodus 21:6 and Psalm 82:1, **Elohim** is used of earthly judges, showing that Deborah, who judged under the palm tree (Judg. 4:5), bore **not just political but divine authority**.

African Continuity: Matriarchal Thrones and Prophetic Thrones

In contrast to the Greco-Roman world—which systematically silenced female authority—**Africa preserved the priesthood and power of its women**. Matriarchies were not mere cultural anomalies; they were **sacral realities** encoded into the theological and political structure of nations:

Queen	Region	Reign	Role
Makéda (ማክዳ)	Ethiopia/Saba	10th c. BCE (trad.)	Ark bearer, founder of Solomonic dynasty

Amanirenas	Kush (Nubia)	40–10 BCE	One-eyed warrior queen; repelled Rome
Nzinga Mbande	Ndongo/Matamba	1624–1663	Priestess, warrior queen; resisted Portuguese rule
Yaa Asantewaa	Ashanti (Ghana)	1900	Led war against British colonization
Ahebi Ugbabe	Igbo-Nsukka (Nigeria)	Early 1900s	Became king and priest; broke gender codes

These women fulfilled roles equivalent to the **shofetet** (שֹׁפֶטֶת) and **nəvī'āh** (נְבִיאָה) of scripture.

Their reigns were not feminist anomalies; they were **Afro-Semitic norms**. Oral traditions preserved in Ethiopia, Ghana, and Nigeria testify that **female leadership was a form of ancestral honor, not rebellion**. The suppression of women came **later**, through **colonial, ecclesial, and Greco-Roman lenses** that redefined priesthood as patriarchal.

Rites of Sexual Discipline: The Female Covenant Cut

Just as Hebraic males underwent *berit milah* (circumcision) as a sign of covenant, so too did **priestly women** in Africa undergo rites of bodily discipline—not as mutilation, but as a sacred mark of **sexual self-control**:

- Among the **Maasai** and **Beta Israel**, priestesses underwent symbolic or partial scarification to mark purity before temple service.

- In **Kemetic temples, clitoral control** was a priestly vow equivalent to the Nazirite (Num. 6:1–8), functioning not to dominate, but to consecrate.

- Among **Ethiopian elders, ritual bathing, sexual abstinence, and bodily markings** were required of women who handled sacred scrolls or invoked divine names.

This mirrored the **Hebrew emphasis on bodily sanctity** (Lev. 15, Lev. 20:18, Ezek. 44:22).

The Greco-Roman world emphasized **philosophy over flesh**, but in Hebraic and African theology, the **body is covenantal**. Female bodies were never sinful by design—they were **vessels of divine presence**.

Ark and Ancestral Memory in Ethiopia

The **Tabot** (ታቦት), or Ark of the Covenant, is preserved not in museums or vaults, but in **living ritual** among the Ethiopian Orthodox Church. The **Kǝbrä Nägäšt** ("The Glory of Kings") teaches that Makéda bore **Bayna-Lehkem**("Son of the Wise") with Solomon, and he returned with the **Ark to Axum**, where it remains guarded to this day.

In this tradition, it was **a woman** who preserved the covenant. Makéda was not only queen—she was **midwife to divine presence**.

This matriarchal theology of the Ark connects directly to:

- **Miriam's well**, which followed Israel in the wilderness (Talmud Bavli, Ta'anit 9a)

- **Wisdom (חָכְמָה)** in Proverbs, who builds the house of God (Prov. 9:1)

- **Chavvah (Eve)**, whose name means "life" and whose seed is destined to **crush the serpent** (Gen. 3:15)

Prophetic Restoration: The Seed of the Woman

"And I will put enmity between you and the woman, between your seed and her seed. She shall crush your head..." — Genesis 3:15 (lit., Hebrew fem. pronoun rendered הוא)

The Hebrew grammar of Genesis 3:15 may allow the feminine **"she"** rather than "he" (as Christian translators assumed). If so, then **Chavvah herself**, or her redeemed image in the last days, is **the serpent-crusher**.

This opens a doorway to a radical prophetic vision:

Messiah ben Golah may not only rise from among the exiles, but she may be a **woman**, hidden like Deborah, crowned like Makéda, and armed with both Torah and Tabot.

She would fulfill:

- **The reversal of Eden**: Adam fell first; Chavvah shall rise last
- **The wisdom of the ancients**: "Wisdom cries aloud in the streets..." (Prov. 1:20)
- **The restoration of the remnant**: "Daughter of My dispersed, beyond Cush, shall bring My offering" (Zeph. 3:10)
- **The destruction of patriarchal bondage**: the curse of man ruling over woman is lifted

Feminine Archetype of Redemption and the Prophetic Claim of a Female Messiah

[41]This monograph posits the potential of a female messiah—designated as Bat Golah, the daughter of exile—as a redemptive archetype rooted in both Hebraic linguistics and prophetic narrative. This claim is not merely speculative; it is linguistically reasoned, canonically framed, and theologically consistent with the prophetic methodology laid out throughout this work.

[42]The conceptual foundation begins in Genesis 1:2, where the Spirit of God—רוּחַ אֱלֹהִים (ruach Elohim)—is described as

[41] Renita J. Weems, *Just a Sister Away: A Womanist Vision of Women's Relationships in the Bible* (San Diego: LuraMedia, 1988), 32–34. Delores S. Williams, *Sisters in the Wilderness: The Challenge of Womanist God-Talk* (Maryknoll, NY: Orbis Books, 1993), 115–117. Elizabeth A. Johnson, *She Who Is: The Mystery of God in Feminist Theological Discourse* (New York: Crossroad, 1992), 34–36. Jürgen Moltmann, *Theology of Hope: On the Ground and the Implications of a Christian Eschatology* (Minneapolis: Fortress Press, 1993), 98–115.

hovering over the face of the waters: וְרוּחַ אֱלֹהִים מְרַחֶפֶת עַל־פְּנֵי הַמָּיִם. The participle מְרַחֶפֶת (merachefet) is grammatically feminine, aligning with the noun רוּחַ, also feminine. The image here is maternal, evoking Deuteronomy 32:11, where God is likened to an eagle hovering over her young. This divine movement precedes the ordering of chaos—tohu va-bohu—and suggests that the first creative and salvific impulse in Scripture is feminine.

Further theological weight is added when one considers that Genesis 1:6–8, describing the second day, is the only day in creation not deemed "good." This omission may point to a lack of unity or completion—implying that the Spirit's redemptive act remains unfinished. If the feminine ruach initiates the movement toward order, might the completion of restoration require a return to the feminine? This foreshadows a messianic archetype not confined to masculine typologies, but inclusive of redemptive feminine agency.

This hypothesis aligns with Micah 5:2, which refers to the coming messiah as one whose "goings forth are from of old, from ancient times" (מִקֶּדֶם מִימֵי עוֹלָם). This phrase—used elsewhere to describe timelessness and divine precedence—may implicitly include Genesis 1, where the feminine Spirit precedes time-bound redemptive acts. Thus, the female messianic archetype is not a later insertion but an ancient one, encrypted in the text from the beginning.

Though mashiach (משיח) is typically rendered masculine, the term itself is grammatically neutral when pluralized, as in משיחָי (my anointed ones). In 1 Chronicles 16:22 and Psalm 105:15, God warns, "Do not touch My anointed ones, and do My prophets no harm." The plural is inclusive and not gender-specific. Moreover, Isaiah 61:1—"The Spirit of the Lord GOD is upon me, because the LORD has anointed me"—does not ascribe gender to the anointed speaker. In its raw Hebrew form, the grammar is functionally inclusive.

Additionally, prophetic women in the Tanakh perform messianic roles without being titled as such. Deborah leads Israel judicially and militarily (Judges 4–5), while Miriam leads liturgically and prophetically (Exodus 15). Esther delivers her people from genocide, and her elevation to royalty is described in the language of divine providence. While none of these women are directly called mashiach, their roles embody its essence: deliverance, covenant preservation, and moral leadership.

[43]The rabbinic tradition also offers a parallel. The Shekhinah, the indwelling divine presence, is described in grammatically feminine terms. In mystical and kabbalistic literature, the Shekhinah suffers exile and longs for reunion with the divine—a typology echoed in the bat Golah, daughter of exile. Thus, the feminine is not merely present but central to Jewish soteriology.

We must also consider Numbers 12:8, where God says of Moses: "With him I speak mouth to mouth, clearly, and not in riddles"—פֶּה אֶל־פֶּה אֲדַבֶּר־בּוֹ. This rare intimacy affirms Moses' unique prophetic stature. As Moses authors Genesis, the feminine Spirit at the opening of the text can be viewed as divinely intentional—a coded, foundational symbol that reappears through prophetic cycles.

The bat Golah, then, is not a novelty. She is a re-emergence. She is the unfulfilled thread in a tapestry of prophetic lineage—a figure who hovers like the ruach, calls forth order from chaos, and offers redemption not through conquest but through covenantal remembrance.

---

43 Phyllis Trible, *Texts of Terror: Literary-Feminist Readings of Biblical Narratives* (Philadelphia: Fortress Press, 1984), 3–19. Ludwig Koehler and Walter Baumgartner, *The Hebrew and Aramaic Lexicon of the Old Testament*, vol. 2 (Leiden: Brill, 2001), s.v. "נקב." Francis Brown, S. R. Driver, and Charles A. Briggs, *A Hebrew and English Lexicon of the Old Testament* (Oxford: Clarendon Press, 1906), s.v. "סבב." Ibid., s.v. "גבר." Michael Fishbane, *Biblical Interpretation in Ancient Israel* (Oxford: Clarendon Press, 1985), 395–98. Brown, Driver, Briggs, *Lexicon*, s.v. "ילד." Claudia Camp, *Wisdom and the Feminine in the Book of Proverbs* (Sheffield: Almond Press, 1985). Rachel Elior, *The Three Temples: On the Emergence of Jewish Mysticism* (Oxford: Littman Library, 2004), 45–48. Matthew 20:16; Luke 13:30; interpreted as sociopolitical reversal rooted in prophetic tradition.

"The messiah may not return as a man of war—but as a woman of water."

Such a proposition does not negate the traditional messianic hope; it expands it. It allows the Afro-diasporic remnant to recover suppressed archetypes and reclaim the fullness of redemptive imagination. Through rigorous textual analysis, historical precedent, and prophetic resonance, the claim of a female messiah becomes not only plausible but necessary within a restored Hebraic anthropology.

Thus, after the discussion of Messiah ben Golah, this extension grounds Bat Golah not as a counterpoint, but as the continuation—the feminine spirit that hovered, the anointed who redeems not by throne or temple but by womb, wisdom, and wandering.

This is not a feminist revision.

It is a prophetic remembrance. The scroll was never closed to her. She was hidden in exile—but now she rises. Messiah ben Golah may come clothed in both Torah and tabot—**and she may be a daughter of the dispersed.**

Jeremiah 31:22 — "A Woman Shall Encompass a Man"

Hebrew Text:

עד מתיידה תשובב נקבה גבר

Transliteration:

Ad matay titṣodedi ha-bat ha-shovevah? khi bara ḥadashah ba-aretz: nekevah tesovev gever.

Translation:

"How long will you waver, O faithless daughter? For YHWH has created a new thing on the earth: a woman shall encompass a man."

Linguistic Analysis:

- נקבה (neqevah): Grammatical female noun; the primary biblical term for biological woman. Root: *n-q-b*, denoting to pierce or designate.

- תסובב (tesovev): Qal imperfect 3rd feminine singular of *s-b-b* — to turn, encircle, surround, encompass, or overturn.

- גבר (gever): Often translated as "man," it more precisely means "strong man" or "warrior," from the root *g-b-r*, meaning to be mighty.

Exegesis: This verse is unique for its ontological reversal: *neqevah* is the grammatical and narrative subject, not object. The verb *tesovev* implies action, initiative, and motion from the female actor. The masculine noun *gever* is traditionally associated with covenantal strength, often reserved for the messianic figure in Tanakh (cf. Jer 20:11). The divine "new creation" (chadashah) here overturns normative gender hierarchies.

SBL Commentary Contextualization: Jeremiah 31 is a chapter of consolation. Verse 22 stands at the cusp of a renewed covenant. Scholars (e.g., Fishbane, Brueggemann) often allegorize this phrase or spiritualize it. But the *peshat* insists on an unambiguous female act of redemptive inversion.

Isaiah 66:7–13 — Zion as a Birthing Mother

Key Verses:

"Before she was in labor she gave birth; before her pain came upon her she delivered a son... Shall I bring to the point of birth and not cause to bring forth?" (Isa 66:7–9)

"As one whom his mother comforts, so I will comfort you." (Isa 66:13)

Hebrew Constructs:

- יולדה (yoledah): A woman giving birth (active participle)

- חבל (ḥevel): Labor pains — root: *ḥ-b-l*, to bring forth

- אם ('em): Mother

Linguistic Significance: YHWH speaks in maternal metaphor — a rare, powerful image. The creative, redeeming force is birth, and the actor is a woman (Zion).

The text moves from national restoration to maternal theology. *Before pain comes*, redemption is birthed — a reversal of Genesis 3:16's curse.

Messianic Reading: The child birthed before labor (*ben*, male) could be seen as messianic, but the force initiating birth is the woman — again re-centering feminine agency in redemptive history.

Micah 4:10 — Exile and Redemption as Labor

"Writhe and groan, O Daughter of Zion, like a woman in labor... There you shall be rescued."

Key Terms:

- חבלי (ḥabli): Imperative feminine singular – "writhe, labor in pain"
- גואל (ḏal): To bring forth (childbirth or divine act)

Implications: Micah connects exilic trauma to birth pain — meaning redemption is not won by war but by female-coded suffering and delivery. It is not David's sword, but Zion's womb that delivers.

These texts form a tripartite witness:

1. Jeremiah presents ontological inversion: a woman surrounds a mighty man.
2. Isaiah reveals divine maternity and Zion's agency.
3. Micah roots redemption in female pain, not male conquest.

Together, they form a canonical pattern: the womb is not merely metaphor, but messianic technology.

This harmonizes with:

- Feminine wisdom (*chokhmah*) as pre-existent (Prov. 8)
- Shekhinah as divine presence in exile
- Reversal motifs (first shall be last...)

Conclusion

The Hebrew Bible affirms messianic and redemptive roles through grammatically and metaphorically feminine actors. To erase these realities is to suppress not only textual accuracy, but the prophetic voice of women encoded in divine memory.

This is not feminist eisegesis — it is textual fidelity. See Appendix S For in-depth exegesis.

V. The Ark, the Throne, and the Messianic Reign

Jeremiah 3:16–17:
"They shall no longer say, 'The Ark of the Covenant of YHWH'...At that time Jerusalem shall be called the throne of YHWH."

This points to:
- The Ark being absorbed into divine indwelling
- The throne not as furniture but as manifested presence
- The shift from object to ontology

Thus, the Ark is not abandoned but transcended. The priesthood, likewise, is not ended—but elevated through righteousness. Isaiah 53 belongs to the diasporic remnant, not to Greco-Roman redeemer cults — see Appendix U.

VI. Contenders and Counterfeits: Third Temple Politics

Modern Israel is building vessels and garments for priestly use. Yet caution is needed:
- Will the next Temple serve YHWH or human pride?
- Is it being built for Zion or the beast?
- Will priesthood be chosen or restored?

Rome and Edom may attempt to sit where they ought not (cf. 2 Thess. 2:4; Daniel 11:31).

VII. Diasporic Priests and Hidden Arks

Scattered across the world are:
- Families with Levi, Cohen, and Zadok surnames
- Oral traditions of Ark-shaped tabernacles

- Communities in Africa and the Americas preserving priestly songs and artifacts

The true Third Temple may rise not in stone alone—but through a scattered priesthood rising in unity, holiness, and Torah obedience.

VIII. Thought-Provoking Questions

- Is the Ark literal, symbolic, or both in prophecy?
- How will the sons of Zadok be recognized?
- Should the Third Temple be supported if Torah and Spirit are absent?
- Can priesthood be restored without the Ark—or is the Ark already within?

IX. References and Sources

1. Exodus 25–26; Leviticus 16; Numbers 17
2. 2 Maccabees 2:4–8; Talmud Yoma 53b
3. Ezekiel 40–48; Jeremiah 3:16–17
4. 1 Kings 1:39; 2 Chronicles 5–7
5. Daniel 11:31; 2 Thessalonians 2:4
6. Dead Sea Scrolls: Temple Scroll, Zadokite Fragments
7. Rabbi Hirsch, Torah Commentary on Exodus and Leviticus
8. Josephus, Antiquities of the Jews, Book 3
9. Sefaria.org (Tanakh and Rabbinic traditions on Temple and priesthood)

Chapter XVIII (יח): Seals, Scrolls, and the Hebrew Apocalypse Unsealed

I. Introduction: Apocalypse as Revelation, Not Destruction

The word "apocalypse" (Greek: apokalypsis) means unveiling—not annihilation. In Hebraic context, apocalypse is prophetic disclosure—the revealing of YHWH's purposes, judgment, and restoration. Revelation (Sefer Hitgalut) builds on the Hebrew canon, not Roman mysticism. Let's uncover how its scroll imagery, judgments, and cosmic warfare are rooted in Tanakh, Temple liturgy, and covenant justice.

II. The Scroll with Seven Seals (Revelation 5)

John weeps when no one can open the sealed scroll. This scroll:
- Reflects the legal inheritance scrolls of ancient Israel (cf. Jeremiah 32)
- Symbolizes YHWH's covenantal decree and plan
- Requires a worthy redeemer—the Lion of Judah (Rev. 5:5)

The number seven is Temple-coded:
- Seven days of creation
- Seven-branched menorah
- Seven annual moedim
- Seven trumpets in Jericho and Revelation

This scroll contains prophetic charges against the nations and legal claims of the covenant people.

III. Hebrew Echoes: Isaiah, Ezekiel, and Daniel

John draws heavily from:
- Ezekiel 2–3: Scroll written front and back, full of lamentation
- Isaiah 29:11–12: Sealed book that only the worthy can read
- Daniel 12:4, 9: Words sealed until the time of the end

Thus, Revelation is a continuation of Hebrew apocalypse, not a Greek departure. It is Temple-centered, scroll-focused, and judicial.

IV. The Lamb and the Courtroom of Heaven

Revelation 4–5 describes a divine court:
- 24 elders (priestly/divine council symbolism)
- Four living creatures (Ezekiel/Isaiah motifs)
- The Lamb (Yehoshua) as slain but victorious Redeemer

The Lamb opens the seals not to destroy—but to restore authority to the faithful remnant. Ancestral inheritance is being reclaimed from imperial oppressors.

V. Trumpets, Bowls, and the Exodus Pattern

Revelation's judgments echo Exodus:
- Blood, hail, darkness, frogs, sores—all plague motifs
- Deliverance through judgment
- YHWH vs the beastly empire

The 7 trumpets also parallel Jericho's conquest—marching, blasting, and collapse. Revelation shows that Jericho (Canaanite idolatry) and Rome (imperial idolatry) are spiritually linked.

VI. The Little Scroll: Digesting Prophetic Burden

Revelation 10: John eats a small scroll:
- Sweet in mouth, bitter in belly (cf. Ezek. 3:3)
- Represents prophetic calling and burden
- Mandates John to prophesy "again concerning many nations" (Rev. 10:11)

This represents the reactivation of prophetic identity in exile. Highlights how modern Hebrews must digest the scroll—sweet with hope, bitter with judgment.

The Least of the Nations. Deuteronomy 7:7–8 stresses that Israel was not chosen for greatness but for smallness — "the least of all peoples." Election as paradox reframes Israel's identity not as dominion but as priesthood (Exod 19:6; Amos 3:2). This paradox directly mirrors the Bat Golah typology: the despised exile who becomes priestly bearer, the goat for Azazel. In diasporic terms, chosenness functions not as superiority but as covenantal service.

VII. The 144,000 and the Sealed Remnant

Revelation 7 describes:
- 12,000 from each tribe of Israel

| - | Marked | on | foreheads |
| - | Protected | from | harm |

This is an Israelite priesthood in exile, ready to stand as firstfruits (Rev. 14:4). It is the inverse of the Mark of the Beast—not economic but covenantal allegiance.

VIII. Scrolls of Remembrance and Judgment

Malachi 3:16–18 speaks of a scroll of remembrance for those who feared YHWH. Revelation echoes this:
- Books were opened (Rev. 20:12)
- Book of Life vs scrolls of deeds

Yom Kippur and judgment day themes—the Day of Covering when records are weighed.

IX. Thought-Provoking Questions

- Is Revelation a Israelite book or a Christian invention?
- Are the seven seals already opening, or are they still sealed?
- Who holds the scrolls of our exile—and who can unseal our return?
- Are we reading the right scroll, or one forged by empire?

X. References and Sources

1. Revelation 4–10, 14, 20; Ezekiel 2–3; Isaiah 29; Daniel 7–12
2. Exodus 7–12 (plagues); Jeremiah 32 (land scroll)
3. Malachi 3:16–18; Zechariah 5:1–4 (flying scroll)
4. 2 Maccabees 2:1–8; Psalms 40:7 (scrolls in the Torah)
5. Sefaria.org (all cited Tanakh and Talmudic sources)
6. Dead Sea Scrolls: War Scroll, Community Rule (scroll symbology)
7. Rabbi Samson Raphael Hirsch, Commentary on Ezekiel & Psalms
8. Josephus, Antiquities of the Jews (scroll preservation)
9. Apocalyptic literature: 1 Enoch, 2 Baruch, 4 Ezra

Chapter XIX (יט): The Bride, the New Jerusalem, and the Return of the Divine Presence

I. Introduction: Covenant, Marriage, and the Final Union

The closing vision of Revelation is not merely apocalyptic—it is marital. The union of the Lamb and His Bride, the descent of the New Jerusalem, and the restoration of divine intimacy all culminate in the greatest covenantal moment since Sinai. The return of Ketubah (marriage contract) and the Hebraic view that marriage is consummated in union—not ceremony—through covenant and intimacy.

II. Marriage in Hebraic Thought: Covenant, Not Contract

In Torah, marriage is a covenantal bond sealed by:
- Mutual consent and witnesses (Gen. 24:67; Ex. 22:16–17)
- A ketubah—a written record of obligations and blessings (Talmud   Ketubot   7a)
- Consummation (sexual intimacy) is the finalizing act, not optional   (Deut.   22:13–29)

Marriage is not man-made ritual but divine transaction of oneness.
-    Torah   was   the   original   ketubah   at   Sinai
- The Exodus was the betrothal; the Golden Calf a form of adultery
- The renewed covenant (Jer. 31:31) is a re-marriage of Yehoshua and Israel

III. The Bride in Prophetic Literature

Scripture consistently describes Israel as YHWH's bride:
-    Hosea: YHWH   woos   His   estranged   wife   back
- Jeremiah 2–3: Israel plays the harlot but is not forgotten
- Ezekiel 16: A graphic account of divine courtship, betrayal, and   restoration

Yeshua   speaks   in   bridal   language:
- "I go to prepare a place for you" (John 14:2–3)

- "At midnight the cry went out: 'Behold, the bridegroom is coming!'" (Matt. 25:6)

IV. The Ketubah and the Renewed Covenant

The ketubah is:
- A record of obligations and intentions
- Binding upon the groom
- Read publicly at the wedding and kept as a sign of fidelity

At Sinai, YHWH gave the Torah as a national ketubah (Ex. 19–24). At Shavuot, He betrothed Israel. In the New Covenant:
- The Torah is written on hearts (Jer. 31:33)
- Yeshua re-establishes fidelity through blood (Luke 22:20)
- The Bride must now prepare her garments (Rev. 19:7–8)

V. New Jerusalem: The Bride Made Visible

Revelation 21–22 describes:
- A city adorned as a bride (Rev. 21:2)
- 12 gates named after the tribes of Israel
- Foundations inscribed with the apostles' names
- The absence of a Temple—"for YHWH El Shaddai and the Lamb are its temple" (Rev. 21:22)

This city is not just a place—it is a people restored, a bride sanctified, a covenant fulfilled.

VI. Hebraic Intimacy and Divine Indwelling

In Hebraic thought:
- To know (yada, ידע) implies deep, relational intimacy (Gen. 4:1)
- The Shekhinah (Divine Presence) indwells the faithful as the groom indwells his bride (Ex. 25:8; John 14:17)
- The act of marriage is not ceremony but union— spiritually, physically, and covenantally

The return of the Shekhinah to the preparation of the Bride. The city is holy because she has made herself ready.

VII. Adulterous Systems vs. Faithful Remnant

Revelation contrasts two women:
- Babylon the Harlot: lavish, corrupt, rides the beast
- New Jerusalem the Bride: pure, adorned, honored

This dichotomy mirrors:

-	Israel	vs.	Edom
-	Spirit	vs.	flesh
-	Faithfulness	vs.	compromise

YHWH is not marrying a building or institution—He is returning to a faithful, obedient, Torah-keeping remnant.

VIII. Thought-Provoking Questions

- Are we preparing for the wedding—or admiring the decorations?
- What is our ketubah—tradition or Torah?
- Can the Divine Presence return without a faithful Bride?
- Do we recognize the New Jerusalem as identity or destination?

IX. References and Sources

1. Exodus 19–24; Deuteronomy 22; Hosea 1–3; Ezekiel 16
2. Revelation 19–22; John 14; Matthew 25; Jeremiah 3, 31
3. Talmud Bavli: Ketubot 7a; Shabbat 88a (Sinai as wedding)
4. Sefaria.org (Torah, Prophets, Writings)
5. Rabbi Hirsch, Commentary on Exodus and Song of Songs
6. Philo of Alexandria, On the Decalogue (marital covenant interpretation)
7. 1 Enoch 62–65 (wedding and throne imagery)
8. Josephus, Antiquities, Book 3
9. Midrash Rabbah: Shir HaShirim (Song of Songs)

Chapter XX (כ): The Final Judgment, Second Death, and Eternal Torah

I. Introduction: Justice at the End of the Age

Judgment is not merely a threat—it is the vindication of the righteous and the revealing of divine order. The Book of Revelation, paired with Daniel, Malachi, and Torah itself, reveals a judicial climax rooted in covenant terms. This Final Judgment not [due] to arbitrary condemnation, but to Torah-based accountability, and emphasizes the distinction between death of the body and the dreaded second death— the soul's permanent separation from YHWH.

II. The Great White Throne: The Court of Heaven

Revelation 20:11–15 describes:
- A throne of judgment before which heaven and earth flee
- The Book of Life and "other books" opened
- All judged according to their works (Rev. 20:12)

This reflects:
- Daniel 7:10—"the court sat and the books were opened"
- Malachi 3:16–18—scrolls recording those who feared YHWH
- Exodus 32:32–33—mention of being blotted from the divine book

Thus, this is not legalism—it is the weighing of covenant obedience versus rebellion.

III. The Second Death: What It Is and Isn't

Revelation 20:14–15 speaks of the second death:
- It is the lake of fire prepared for the beast and false prophet
- It is not mere physical death (which ends all flesh), but eternal separation from the divine presence

Yeshua said: "Fear Him who can destroy both body and soul in Gehenna" (Matt. 10:28)
- Gehenna was a place of filth and burning outside Jerusalem
- Symbol of divine judgment for covenant breakers (cf. Isaiah 66:24)

This is not pagan hellfire theology, but Torah-based consequences for treachery.

The Transference of Spirit: Phinehas, Eliyahu, and the Mantle of Prophetic Zeal

[44]The tradition that Phinehas and Eliyahu (Elijah) are one and the same soul — or more precisely, manifestations of the same ruach (spirit) — has long been preserved in both rabbinic and mystical strands of Jewish thought. This idea hinges not only on textual parallels but also on the deeper theological pattern of divine zeal (qin'ah) and generational spiritual   continuity.

In Numbers 25:7–13, Phinehas son of Eleazar is praised for his qin'ah — his "jealousy" or zealousness on behalf of YHWH — when he slays the Israelite man and Midianite woman who desecrate the covenant. In response, YHWH grants him a "covenant of peace" (berit shalom) and an "everlasting priesthood" (kehunnat olam). Likewise, in 1 Kings 19:10, Eliyahu declares, "I have been very zealous for the LORD God of hosts..." — invoking nearly identical language and spiritual fervor. Rabbinic literature connects these   figures   as   one   continuous   presence.

Midrashic texts such as Yalkut Shimoni on Phinehas state explicitly:
"Phinehas is Elijah." (Yalkut Shimoni, Torah 771)
Also noted in Pirkei De-Rabbi Eliezer 47, the tradition reads:
"Phinehas was still alive in the days of the Judges. He is Eliyahu."

---

[44] Yalkut Shimoni, Torah 771; also Targum Jonathan on Exodus 6:18. Pirkei De-Rabbi Eliezer, Chapter 47. Rav Saadia Gaon and Radak both note Eliyahu's unusual fate and its implications for prophecy. See Zohar, Vol. II, 190a–b for mystical affirmation of spiritual continuity. Cf. Luke 1:17 and Matthew 11:14 regarding John the Baptist and Eliyahu's spirit. On gilgulim (reincarnation of souls) in Jewish mysticism, see Rabbi Chaim Vital, Shaar HaGilgulim. Adela Yarbro Collins, *Crisis and Catharsis: The Power of the Apocalypse* (Philadelphia: Westminster Press, 1984), 48–59.

This fusion reveals an ancestral continuity where spiritual office transcends linear time. Eliyahu, as a zealot-prophet, mirrors Phinehas not only in action but in spirit, functioning as a rebuke to idolatry and a guardian of the covenant.

This motif further unfolds when Eliyahu is said to be taken up by a chariot of fire (2 Kings 2:11) — often understood as an ascension. Yet a textual anomaly arises when 2 Chronicles 21:12 records a letter from Eliyahu after he had allegedly ascended. This has fueled sectarian and scholarly debates alike: did Eliyahu truly "not die," or was his departure more akin to a prophetic exile or transformation?

This tension harmonizes when understood through Paul's vision in 1 Corinthians 15:51–52: "Behold, I show you a mystery: we shall not all sleep, but we shall all be changed..."

Eliyahu, like Enoch before him (Genesis 5:24), typifies the soul that is taken rather than buried — a transition from temporal embodiment to celestial commission. His return in the person of John the Baptist, as affirmed by Yeshua in Matthew 11:14, furthers the idea of spiritual gilgulim — cycling or continuation of prophetic calling.

Just as the spirit of Eliyahu rested upon Elisha (2 Kings 2:9), the mantle of intergenerational purpose in Israelite thought was not biological, but metaphysical. It transcended flesh and resided in calling. Elijah, Phinehas, John, and the future Eliyahu HaNavi of Malachi 4:5 represent the same prophetic thrust — a call to turn the hearts of fathers to children, and children to their heritage.

This lineage of zeal (qin'ah), covenant (berit), and calling (shlichut) ultimately belongs to the Diaspora as well — a scattered remnant prepared to receive again the mantle of testimony and righteous indignation in the face of idolatrous empire.

IV. Who Is Judged—and by What Standard?

Revelation and Daniel agree:
- Nations are judged (Rev. 20:12; Matt. 25:32)
- Individuals are judged by their deeds
- The righteous remnant are those who keep the commandments of YHWH and the faith of Yeshua (Rev. 14:12)

This standard is Torah:
- Psalm 96:13—He judges the earth in righteousness and truth
- Ecclesiastes 12:13–14—"Fear 'Ĕlōhîm and keep His commandments...for 'Ĕlōhîm shall bring every deed into judgment"

V. Eternal Torah: The Unchanging Constitution

The Land Cries Out. From Abel's blood crying from the ground (Gen 4:10) to the land vomiting out its inhabitants for iniquity (Lev 18:25; Num 35:33–34), the earth itself functions as witness. Ezekiel 38:12 calls Zion the "navel of the earth" (*tabbur ha'aretz*), the axis where divine judgment is registered. Until the rightful children of Israel return, the land groans, and thus nations continue to "learn war" (Isa 2:4; Mic 4:1–3). Esoterically, the earth is alive, giving report to YHWH, who alone forms both light and darkness, peace and calamity (Isa 45:7).

Torah is not abolished—it is eternal:
- Isaiah 2:2–4—Torah goes forth from Zion in the last days
- Zechariah 14:16–19—nations judged by whether they keep Sukkot
- Matthew 5:17–19—Yeshua affirms not one yod or tittle will pass

Torah is:
- The legal foundation of the divine court
- The covenant witness at final judgment
- The living contract upheld by Yehoshua

VI. Books, Scrolls, and Remembrance

Several books are mentioned:
- Book of Life: names of the righteous (Phil. 4:3; Rev. 3:5)
- Scroll of Remembrance: deeds and reverence (Mal. 3:16)
- Books of Judgment: actions weighed (Rev. 20:12)

This judicial structure mirrors Yom Kippur:
- The sealing of fate
- The reading of records
- The division between goat and sheep, wheat and tares

VII. Mercy in Judgment

Judgment is not cruelty—it is divine order reasserted:
- Ezekiel 18:23—YHWH takes no pleasure in the death of the wicked
- 2 Peter 3:9—He is patient, wanting none to perish
- Micah 7:18—He delights in mercy

Yet mercy is not license. The books reveal truth. The scrolls are sealed until the appointed time—but now, they are being opened.

VIII. Thought-Provoking Questions

- If Torah is eternal, how should we prepare for judgment?
- Are we judging Torah—or will Torah judge us?
- What does it mean to be blotted from the Book of Life?
- Can mercy be granted without accountability?

IX. References and Sources

1. Revelation 20–22; Daniel 7; Malachi 3; Matthew 10, 25
2. Exodus 32; Ecclesiastes 12; Psalm 96
3. Isaiah 2, 66; Zechariah 14
4. Talmud Rosh Hashanah 16b–17a (Books opened on judgment)
5. Sefaria.org (Tanakh and rabbinic commentaries on judgment)
6. Rabbi Hirsch, Commentary on Ecclesiastes and Psalms
7. Dead Sea Scrolls: Community Rule (1QS) on judgment

and   books
8. 1 Enoch 47–50; 2 Esdras 7–9 (judgment themes)
9. Josephus, Antiquities, Book 18 (Pharisaic beliefs on afterlife)

Chapter XXI (כא): From Exile to Inheritance—The Return of the Lost Tribes and the Global Awakening

I. Introduction: Identity Restored, Inheritance Reclaimed

The story of Israel does not end in dispersion—it crescendos in restoration. The so-called "Lost Tribes" were not erased from history but hidden by divine design, awaiting a prophetic reawakening. This awakening is global, generational, and deeply spiritual—anchored in Torah, covenant, and the promises made to Abraham, Isaac, and Jacob.

II. The Scattering: Curse or Catalyst?

Deuteronomy 28 and Leviticus 26 warned:
- Disobedience would lead to exile among the nations
- Israel would forget its identity and language (Jeremiah 17:4)
- But YHWH would not forget His covenant (Leviticus 26:42–45)

This exile was judgment—but also preparation for a greater harvest. The seed of Israel was sown among the nations (Hosea 2:23).

III. Historical Routes of Dispersion

After the Assyrian and Babylonian exiles, and later the Roman destruction of 70 CE:
- Tribes of the North (Ephraim, Manasseh, Dan, Issachar, etc.) were scattered into:
  - Africa (especially West, East, and North)
  - India and Persia

- Europe and the Isles of the Sea (Isaiah 11:11–12)
- The Americas (via both slavery and migration)

Align this with:
- Slave trade routes as prophetic fulfillment (Deut. 28:68)
- Hebrew customs found among Indigenous and African tribes
- Names, garments, dietary laws, and oral traditions preserved

IV. The Awakening: Spiritual DNA Activated

In the last days:
- YHWH is calling His people by name (Isaiah 43:6–7)
- Hearts are turning back to Torah (Malachi 4:4–6)
- Dry bones are rising (Ezekiel 37:1–14)

This is not a political movement—but a prophetic resurrection. The awakening is:
- Visible through Shabbat restoration, tzitzit, moedim
- Vocal through music, media, street preaching, family teaching
- Scriptural—marked by return to Tanakh, Hebrew, and ancestral names

V. Who Are the Tribes Today?

Many claim descent—some genuinely, others in error or confusion. YHWH alone knows the full registry:
- Judah largely preserved through rabbinic Judaism
- Levi via oral surnames and priestly markers
- Ephraim, Manasseh, and the rest are awakening across every continent

Black, Latino, Indigenous, and Afro-Asian communities as heirs—not of empire, but of covenant.

VI. Two Sticks Become One

[45]The prophetic vision of Ezekiel 37 presents two sticks—**Yehudah** and **Ephraim**—becoming one. This is a direct

---

[45] Cheryl A. Kirk-Duggan, *Exorcizing Evil: A Womanist Perspective on the Spirituals* (Maryknoll, NY: Orbis Books, 1997), 97–103.

symbol of **national reunification**, not a typological mirror of two Testaments or Messiah roles. However, the motif of duality can inform deeper layers:

• **Messiah ben Yosef** (suffering servant) vs **Messiah ben David** (ruling king) — Midrashic tradition, *Succah 52a–b* • **Testament of Benjamin 3:8** — speaks of two messiahs, one priestly and one royal. Israel Knohl, *The Messiah Before Jesus: The Suffering Servant of the Dead Sea Scrolls* (Berkeley: University of California Press, 2000), 102–118.

Proper typology anchors in Tanakh and is **fulfilled in restoration**, not in replacement systems.

Ezekiel   37:15–28:
- Stick of Judah and stick of Ephraim become one
- One shepherd rules them both
- They walk in Torah and dwell in peace

This is the goal—not tribal competition, but national unification under YHWH's Messiah.

VII. Inheritance Restored

The return is not just spiritual—it is territorial:
- Amos 9:14–15: "They shall plant vineyards and drink their wine...they shall never again be uprooted"
- Isaiah 14:1–2: strangers will serve and assist in restoration
- Obadiah 1:17–21: Mount Zion regains dominion over Edom

This is not supremacy—it is redemptive justice. The meek inherit the land.

Modern canon theory—from Metzger's ecclesial process to McDonald's trajectory criticism—can no longer ignore prophetic disruption as a valid means of canonical reclamation. Prophecy and transmission are not opposing modes; they are covenantal complements.

VIII. The Role of the Diaspora Hebrews

[46]

Diasporic	Hebrews	are:
- Watchmen	(Isaiah	62:6)
- Midwives	of	awakening
- Living scrolls	of	prophecy

They have endured colonization, enslavement, and erasure—yet now rise as priests, prophets, and builders of the renewed nation.

IX. Thought-Provoking Questions

- Are we ready to accept inheritance—or still bound by captivity mindsets?
- Can unity come without repentance and Torah?
- Are we hearing the call to return—or numbed by Babylon's comfort?
- What will you do with the scroll in your hand?

X. References and Sources

1. Deuteronomy 28; Leviticus 26; Hosea 1–2; Ezekiel 37
2. Isaiah 11:11–12; Isaiah 43; Amos 9; Jeremiah 3:14–18
3. Malachi 4; Obadiah 1; Matthew 15:24
4. Talmud Sanhedrin 110b (ten tribes return); Mishnah Eduyot 2:10
5. Rabbi Hirsch, Commentary on Deut. 30 and Ezekiel 37
6. Sefaria.org (Tanakh and rabbinic literature)
7. Josephus, Antiquities, Book 11 (Lost tribes east of the Euphrates)
8. Dead Sea Scrolls: Damascus Document on tribal separation and unity
9. Oral traditions from West Africa, Native America, and diasporic communities

---

[46] Walter Brueggemann, *The Prophetic Imagination*, 2nd ed. (Minneapolis: Fortress Press, 2001), 13–29. **Melchizedek and Shem.** Rabbinic tradition (Gen. Rab. 46:7; b. Nedarim 32b) identifies Melchizedek, king-priest of Salem (Gen 14:18–20), with Shem son of Noah. If so, priesthood in the land predates and frames Abraham's covenant, rooting it in primordial continuity. This reception tradition, while not historical fact, illuminates how Israel's priesthood was perceived as cosmic-continuity — culminating in Ben Aharon and Yeshua as the goat for YHWH.

Chapter XXII (כב): Epilogue — The Scroll is in Your Hand

I. A Call to the Readers

You who have read this far—this was not just scholarship. It was a summons. A scroll has been unsealed in your presence. A voice has cried out in the wilderness. And now, the scroll is in your hand. What you do next will determine whether you are a bystander in prophecy—or a participant in the restoration.

II. The Journey Behind Us

We began in the ashes of textual history, uncovering:
- How canon, corruption, and councils buried the truth
- How Hebrew roots were replaced with imperial dogma
- How sacred names were stolen, feasts erased, and prophetic   identities   lost

But   we   also   ascended:
-   Restoring   Torah   as   the   eternal   constitution
- Lifting Yehoshua as High Priest and Redeemer—not Greco-Roman   Christ,   but   Hebrew   Shepherd
- Reviving the lost calendar, the scattered tribes, and the ancient promises

This monograph may be taught as a 12-week graduate course exploring Afro-diasporic theology, typology, Hebrew exegesis, and canon formation. Assignments and lecture outcomes are embedded throughout the structure to facilitate immediate curricular application.

III. The Scroll in Your Hand

Just as John digested the scroll in Revelation 10, so must you:
-   Sweet   to   the   mouth—because   truth   liberates
- Bitter to the stomach—because truth demands change

Now   that   you   know:

- You are accountable to walk in covenant
- You are tasked with teaching your children the ancient paths (Jer. 6:16)
- You are no longer a servant of Babylon, but a citizen of Zion

IV. A Final Prophetic Vision

Isaiah 61, Luke 4, and Revelation 22 converge on one truth:
- The Spirit of YHWH is upon the remnant
- The restoration is happening now
- The gates of the New Jerusalem are open—but only to those who do His commandments (Rev. 22:14)

And so, we end as we began: "Choose this day whom you will serve...but as for me and my house, we will serve YHWH." (Joshua 24:15)

V. Benediction

May the Name of YHWH be upon you.
May the Torah be within you.
May the voice of the prophets resound through you.
May your generations rise and call you blessed.

The scroll is in your hand.
Now walk worthy of it.

This work stands unapologetically at the intersection of theology, linguistics, anthropology, and history—not as a rhetorical provocation, but as a restoration of memory, covenant, and spiritual dignity to a scattered people. As expected, both Rabbinic and Christian critics may respond with familiar claims such as: allegations of pseudohistory, ethno-hereditary, accusations of appropriation, and demands for halakhic legitimacy. Let each concern be answered thoroughly.

א. On Rabbinic Gatekeeping and the Question of Halakhic Identity

Rabbinic Judaism, post-Temple and post-Yavneh, solidified itself not only through oral law but through centuries of ethnocentric legal development. The authority of the Sanhedrin did not arise as a divine institution from Sinai, but evolved as a judicial response to diaspora pressure and Roman persecution. Moses, while he received and administered Torah, did not ordain halakhic rabbinism as the sole filter of Jewish identity. Torah itself remains the standard.

To demand that the remnant of Yisrael—especially those scattered, enslaved, and systemically denied access—prove their legitimacy via post-Second Temple rabbinic filters is a theological injustice. According to Deuteronomy, covenantal obedience—not Ashkenazic minhag—is what invites divine acceptance. The Torah warns against adding to or subtracting from its commandments (Deut. 4:2), which should apply equally to halakhah as it does to Christian dogma.

[47] Genome-wide studies establish that roughly **60–80% of Ashkenazi European ancestry derives from Southern Europe**, particularly Italy and Greece, with smaller Eastern European contributions. Mitochondrial markers (e.g., Haplogroups K1a1b1a, N1b) confirm this Southern European maternal lineage, while Y-chromosome evidence remains predominantly Semitic — demonstrating a blend of Italic maternal influence and Near Eastern paternal continuity. To conflate conversion with original inheritance is not only flawed, but scripturally unfounded. The **Jewish Encyclopedia (1905 edition, Vol. 5, p. 41)** itself concedes that **Edom became part of "Jewry" under John Hyrcanus**. If Rabbinic Judaism does not question the identity of Idumeans, why are the bloodline claims of Black Israelites treated with hostility?

---

[47] Behar et al. 2004; Richards (2013); Atzmon et al. 2010; 2017 autosomal study

ב. On Christian Reinterpretation and the Supersession of Israel

The New Testament has long been used—consciously or unconsciously—to erase the Hebrew foundation on which it stands. From Paul's letters being contorted into a gospel of lawlessness, to the Latin Church's imperial suppression of Hebrew manuscripts, the Christian tradition has often reinforced erasure of the very people to whom the oracles of God were entrusted (Romans 3:2).

But Yeshua himself upheld Torah (Matt. 5:17–19), spoke against the "traditions of men" (Mark 7:8–13), and resisted the very corruption of Temple practice and Pharisaic hypocrisy (John 2:14–16). He flipped tables not just as an act of zeal, but of prophetic rebuke against those who turned covenant into capital. He did not affirm *halakhic elitism*, nor did he replace Israel with the Church.

To modern Christians: Your faith is not invalidated, but your narrative must be reexamined. Replacement theology is not only historically false—it is spiritually abusive. You inherited a tree that was not yours, were grafted in by grace, and yet you deny the root. Paul warned against such arrogance (Romans 11:18–21).

ג. On Historical Erasure and the Afro-Diasporic Witness

We are told to forget. Told that transatlantic slavery erased us. Told that the baton of spiritual legitimacy passed from Mount Sinai to Vatican walls. And yet, the very marks of biblical prophecy—**captivity by ships (Deut. 28:68), a lost language (v. 49), identity as a proverb and byword (v. 37)**—fit no other people as precisely as the descendants of the Transatlantic Slave Trade.

Our identity was *not* born in the 20th-century awakening movements. It is encoded in **language (Hitpael verb stems), migration (Isaiah 11:11), oral memory (Mbiti's ontology), and prophetic fulfillment.** To be born **Black and Hebraic** is not to be born less-than—it is to be born into pain, prophecy, and perseverance. It is to carry sacred memory in the face of colonial gatekeeping, Islamic slave trades, Rabbinic exclusion, and Christian appropriation.

We do not reject others' paths—but we demand ours be honored.

ז. On the Unity of Torah and the Universality of Redemption

Torah did not begin with rabbis nor end at Calvary. It is the eternal blueprint of the cosmos (cf. Proverbs 8:22–31), the divine instruction by which creation was measured and humanity is restored. Yeshua was not anti-Torah; he *was* Torah made flesh. The halakhic traditions that followed, while informative, must yield to the Word itself.

Our claim is not supremacist. It is restorative. We affirm that **any who join themselves to YHWH** (Isa. 56:6–8) are welcomed. But it is precisely *because* of this openness that Afro-diasporic Israel must be acknowledged—not erased.

ה. Final Word to the Critics

Do not call us anti-Semitic for claiming Shem. Do not call us pseudo when your own sources affirm forced conversion, Roman lineage corruption, and rabbinic additions.
Do not call us rebels when we obey Torah with trembling and   memory.
We are "also" the people of the Book. The curses of Deuteronomy   were   ours.
And so too shall be the promises.

We shall rise. In the land where it was said, "You are not my people," we shall be called sons of the Living God (Hosea 1:10).

In closing, this work repositions the canon not as a fixed literary artifact but as a sacred linguistic pattern—a vessel of covenantal continuity. The structure of this monograph, aligned with the twenty-two letters of the Hebrew aleph-bet and the ancient twenty-two book enumeration of Tanakh, reflects the belief that form and revelation are intertwined.

Canon is not just content; it is architecture—numeric, prophetic, and mnemonic.

Through this lens, Hebrew emerges not as a historical accident of transmission, but as the chosen medium for theological encoding. The morphology of Hebrew—its verb stems, root dynamics, and structural idioms—preserves covenantal identity with precision unmatched in translation. The displacement of that language by imperial tongues is not merely a translational shift but a theological rupture. The covenant, in many respects, was lost in the loss of the language that carried it.

This monograph contributes to the field in three critical ways. First, it proposes a **canon-conscious hermeneutic** rooted in linguistic theology rather than ecclesial history. Second, it offers a **diasporic reclamation framework**, wherein marginalized traditions—particularly Afro-Hebraic and postcolonial voices—are re-centered in the scholarly conversation. Third, it models a **reconstructionist approach** to textual theology that integrates textual criticism, Semitic philology, and prophetic intuition.

To reduce this critique to racial polemic is to miss its architectural intent. This is not a grievance book—it is a blueprint. It speaks with the voice of the remnant, not the rebel.

If canon formation was influenced by empire, then canon recovery must involve prophecy. And if scripture is memory preserved in ink, then this work stands as both a remembrance and a call—to return not only to what was written, but to how, why, and through whom it was spoken.

By. Tovi Mickel

A Scholarly Midrash – Zakor

This volume is suitable for courses in Biblical Theology, Hebraic Linguistics, Postcolonial Hermeneutics, or Canon Formation Studies. Its interdisciplinary model bridges text criticism, prophetic typology, and Afro-diasporic history.

APPENDICES

Appendix A: New Testament Manuscript Table

Abstract: Provides comparative manuscript analysis (MT, LXX, DSS) to highlight theological and textual deviations across traditions.

Manuscript	Date	Language	Contents	Notes
P52 (Rylands Papyrus)	c. 125 CE	Greek	Fragment of John 18	Oldest known NT fragment
Codex Vaticanus	c. 300–325 CE	Greek	OT (LXX) + NT	Alexandrian text-type
Codex Sinaiticus	c. 325–360 CE	Greek	Complete NT + OT	Early complete Christian Bible
Peshitta	c. 400–500 CE	Syriac	Entire NT (excludes some epistles)	Eastern Church canon
Codex Amiatinus	c. 700 CE	Latin	Vulgate Bible	Early Western canon
Codex Leningradensis	c. 1008 CE	Hebrew	Full MT	Basis for most modern Tanakh editions

Appendix B: Dead Sea Scrolls Chronology & Discoveries

Abstract: Traces Hebraic linguistic transmission, demonstrating the continuity of sacred terms and etymologies from Paleo-Hebrew to square script.

- 1947–1956: Scrolls discovered in Qumran caves
- Over 900 scrolls, 200+ biblical manuscripts
- Major finds:
  - 1QIsaiah (Great Isaiah Scroll)
  - 4QDeuteronomy (fragmentary law texts)
  - 11QPsalms (variant Psalms collection)
- Reveals plural biblical traditions prior to Masoretic standardization

Appendix C: Imperial Paul vs. Tanakh – Misaligned Quotations

Abstract: Engages with Pauline theology in contrast to Torah-centered frameworks using direct textual comparisons.

NT Reference | Claimed Source | Actual Tanakh Text | Notes

--------------- | ----------------- | --------------------- | ------

Romans 3:10–18 | Psalms | Chain of unrelated verses | Out of context

Matthew 27:9–10 | Jeremiah | Actually Zechariah 11 | Misattributed

Hebrews 10:5–7 | Psalm 40:6 | 'Body prepared' vs 'ears opened' | LXX variant

Romans 10:6–8 | Deut. 30 | 'Faith' for 'Torah' | Meaning shifted

Appendix D – The Cohortative Verb: Divine Intent and Afro-Indigenous Echoes

Abstract:
This appendix explores the use of the cohortative verb form in Biblical Hebrew—especially its theological, rhetorical, and cultural significance. Special focus is given to how these verbal structures reflect divine deliberation, prophetic identity, and Afro-Indigenous linguistic resonance as explored in Chapters 7 and 8.

Cohortative Verb in Biblical Hebrew

The cohortative is a unique Hebrew verb form expressing intent, volition, or internal deliberation. It typically appears in the first person singular or plural. Rather than functioning as a simple plural marker, it emphasizes divine or human desire, purpose, or resolve.

Key grammatical markers include:
- Suffixes like '-ה' (e.g., אֵלְכָה – 'Let me go')

- Verbs of action or creation followed by inclusive intention
- Contexts of command, invitation, or deliberation

Theological Usage: Divine Deliberation

One of the most striking cohortative uses is Genesis 1:26: "נַעֲשֶׂה אָדָם בְּצַלְמֵנוּ" – 'Let us make man in our image.' This phrase has historically fueled debates on plurality in the Godhead. However, within Hebrew grammar, the verb 'na'aseh' does not indicate multiple divine persons. It instead reflects a **deliberative cohortative**, a form often used by kings, prophets, or divine figures to signal intention and gravity. Similar usages appear in:
- Genesis 11:7: 'Let us go down and confuse their language'
- Isaiah 6:8: 'Whom shall I send, and who will go for us?'
These reflect **rhetorical plurality**, not ontological multiplicity.

Afro-Indigenous Linguistic Parallels

In many West African and Afro-Indigenous oral traditions, leaders and elders use inclusive or pluralized speech as a sign of spiritual or tribal authority. This mirrors the Hebrew use of cohortative forms to express gravity and group alignment with the divine will.

Examples:
- Igbo and Yoruba elder councils speak in first-person plural to reflect the voice of ancestors.
- Akan language forms use collective pronouns when invoking the divine for covenantal action.
- Mandé oralists (jeliw) speak on behalf of a tribe using 'we' as both ancestral and current voice.

This shared usage reflects a **proto-Semitic and Niger-Congo convergence** in how sacred speech frames identity and action. Thus, cohortative verbs in Scripture are not only grammatical, but **anthropological and theological bridges** between Hebrew and African civilizations.

Appendix E: Lexical Displacement and Feminine Suppression: Almah and Divine Grammar

Appendix E: Lexical Displacement and Feminine Suppression: Almah and Divine Grammar

Abstract:
Evaluates feminist and priestly textual roles and traces divine feminine grammar within canonical texts. This expanded appendix integrates the original content with deeper theological and linguistic examples of feminine forms suppressed in transmission and translation.

Almah vs. Betulah – Lexical Distortion

The Hebrew term 'עַלְמָה' (Almah) appears in Isaiah 7:14, traditionally meaning a young woman of marriageable age. Christian translations—most notably the Septuagint (LXX) and the Vulgate—rendered it as 'virgin' (παρθένος), fueling Christological readings. However, the Tanakh also uses 'בְּתוּלָה' (Betulah) for virginity with clearer intent (e.g., Genesis 24:16). This intentional lexical switch contributed to theological distortions regarding prophecy and messianism.

Feminine Divine Grammar in Scripture

Biblical Hebrew contains numerous instances where divine or prophetic speech is expressed through grammatically feminine forms. Over time, many of these were erased or neutralized in translation and liturgical use, obscuring the presence of the divine feminine and priestly feminine authority.

Key   Examples:
- Deuteronomy 32:18 – Verb for 'bore you' (חֹלֵלְךָ) is grammatically feminine, referencing God's maternal role.
- Isaiah 42:14 – YHWH 'cries out like a woman in labor', using the verb יוֹלֵדָה (Yoledah).
- Proverbs 8 – Wisdom (חָכְמָה, Chokhmah) is personified as a woman calling out in the public square.
- Exodus 15:11 – The Song of the Sea includes poetic structures with feminine verb forms, celebrating divine deliverance.
- Judges 4 – Deborah is called נְבִיאָה (prophetess) and שׁוֹפְטָה

(female judge), both grammatically and theologically significant.

Origen & Feminine Canon Suppression

Origen's Alexandrian theology introduced a non-Hebraic cosmological hierarchy that framed the material world—including the feminine body—as less divine. This philosophical dualism led to theological tendencies that minimized or allegorized feminine imagery in Scripture.

Combined with Greek grammatical structures that lacked a strong feminine prophetic voice, translations such as the LXX and Vulgate began suppressing references to female prophets (e.g., Huldah, Anna) and metaphors of God as mother (Deut. 32:18, Isa. 42:14). The later Church Fathers solidified this shift, leading to male-centric canon formation and centuries of interpretive neglect toward the feminine divine.

Appendix F: Torah Festivals and Scriptural Basis

- Passover (Pesach) – Exodus 12, Leviticus 23
- Unleavened Bread (Matzot) – Exodus 13, Leviticus 23
- Firstfruits – Leviticus 23:9–14
- Shavuot (Weeks) – Leviticus 23:15–22
- Yom Teruah (Trumpets) – Leviticus 23:23–25
- Yom Kippur (Atonement) – Leviticus 23:26–32
- Sukkot (Tabernacles) – Leviticus 23:33–43

Appendix G: Hebrew Names and Their Meanings

- Yeshayahu (ישעיהו) – 'YHWH is salvation'
- Yirmeyahu (ירמיהו) – 'YHWH will exalt'
- Ezekiel (יחזקאל) – 'God will strengthen'
- Eliezer (אליעזר) – 'My God is help'
- Zechariah (זכריה) – 'YHWH remembers'

Side Note: Yehoshua in this book is the future unknow redeemer; also charactered as Baht Golah/Ben Golah, Ben Yosef/Ben Aaron. This monograph deposits that Yeshua was the Goat of YHWH.

Appendix H: African Jewish Records by Region

Abstract: Connects diasporic memory, African oral history, and Semitic traditions to reframe lost tribes and prophetic identity.

- Ghana: Oral histories claim descent from Israel
- Nigeria (Igbo): Sabbath, kosher laws, circumcision
- Ethiopia: Beta Israel with full Torah tradition
- Mali/Fulani: Reports of Torah scrolls, priestly class
- Sudan and Congo: Clan names with Semitic roots

Appendix I: Pauline Citations Compared to Tanakh Sources

Pauline Epistles vs. Tanakh Quotations

- • Romans 3:10–18 — Composite quote: Psalms 14:1–3, 5:9, 140:3, Isaiah 59:7–8.
- • Galatians 3:13 — Deuteronomy 21:23 ('Cursed is everyone who hangs on a tree').
- • Romans 10:6–8 — Deuteronomy 30:11–14, altered to reference 'Christ'.
- • Hebrews 8:8–12 — Direct quote of Jeremiah 31:31–34, yet inserted with Greek rewording.
- • 1 Corinthians 15:54 — Composite of Isaiah 25:8 and Hosea 13:14.

Appendix J: Visual Canon Timeline & Linguistic Frameworks

Abstract: Outlines historical patterns of canonical development from Ezra through the early Church, focusing on Hebraic integrity and Greek divergence.

Timeline of Canon Formation

- • 1450–1000 BCE — Oral Torah, earliest poetic fragments (e.g., Song of the Sea, Exodus 15).
- • c. 1000–586 BCE — United and Divided Kingdoms; composition of core Torah, early Prophets.
- • 586–450 BCE — Babylonian exile; redaction of Torah, Ezekiel, Lamentations.

- • c. 450 BCE — Ezra-Nehemiah formalize Torah canon post-exile.
- • 300–100 BCE — Prophets & Writings still fluid; Ben Sira (c. 200 BCE) lists Nevi'im, not Ketuvim.
- • 250 BCE — Septuagint translation in Alexandria begins with Torah.
- • 200 BCE–70 CE — Qumran community copies texts; DSS reflects canonical diversity.
- • 90 CE (Yavneh) — Pharisaic Rabbis begin fixing Ketuvim boundaries (non-universal).
- • 7th–10th centuries CE — Masoretic Text standardized in Tiberias.

Appendix K: Yeshua and the Bronze Serpent — A Hebraic Reconsideration

I. A Messianic Debate

In traditional Christian theology, Yeshua (Jesus) is identified as the prophesied Messiah. However, this view is far from universally accepted—especially among Torah-rooted, historically aware Hebrews. This appendix seeks to present a critical reevaluation based on Hebraic scripture, prophetic patterns, and the imagery presented in the New Testament itself.

II. The Bronze Serpent Typology

Numbers 21:8–9 presents a striking narrative: "And YHWH said to Moshe, 'Make a fiery serpent, and set it on a pole: and it shall come to pass, that every one that is bitten, when he looks upon it, shall live.'"

Centuries later, this bronze serpent became an object of idolatry, and was destroyed by righteous King Hezekiah (2 Kings 18:4):
"He broke in pieces the bronze serpent that Moshe had made, for until those days the children of Israel burned incense to it."

Yeshua references this image in John 3:14:

"As Moshe lifted up the serpent in the wilderness, even so must the Son of Man be lifted up..."

Importantly, Qumran texts—known for their elaborate midrashim and apocalyptic symbol systems—are entirely silent on the Bronze Serpent narrative. Despite extensive commentary on wilderness motifs, serpents, and divine intervention, not a single pesher or fragment among the Dead Sea Scrolls draws upon Numbers 21 or invokes the serpent as a redemptive type. This silence is especially noteworthy given the Qumran sect's obsession with dualism and eschatological signs. Their avoidance likely reflects an awareness of the narrative's theological tension—namely, the danger of idolatrous elevation condemned in 2 Kings 18:4. The prophetic tradition surrounding Deuteronomy 13:1–5 forbids honoring signs that pull hearts away from Torah fidelity, even if they "come to pass." Thus, the typology employed in John 3:14 may reflect a **later Graeco-Roman overlay**, rather than a continuation of Second Temple prophetic continuity.

See 4QFlorilegium, 1QHodayot, and 1QpHab for typological richness absent any reference to Numbers 21.

While early Christian theologians such as Origen saw the Bronze Serpent as a divine foreshadowing of crucifixion—emphasizing its symbolic reversal of death through divine identification with the cursed—rabbinic sources took a different approach. Rashi, commenting on 2 Kings 18:4, praised Hezekiah for destroying the serpent due to its transformation into idolatry. No healing power resided in the object; it merely directed hearts toward heaven. The Mishnah (Rosh Hashanah 3:8) echoes this: "It was not the serpent that healed, but when Israel looked upward and submitted to their Father in heaven, they were healed."

Importantly, the Qumran scrolls, despite their apocalyptic fervor, **never elevate the serpent as a redemptive figure**. This silence, alongside Deuteronomy 13's warning, suggests an early and rigorous boundary against typology divorced from Torah fidelity. Any Christological reading of John 3:14 that fails this test is not Hebraic, but Hellenistic in its overlay.

Rabbi Akiva's affirmation of Bar Kokhba as *Messiah ben Yosef* offers a historical lens on dual messiah typology—one suffering, one ruling. Revelation's lamb-lion dialectic may trace this bifurcation. It is no coincidence that failed messiahs are often linked with national trauma, just as imperial messiahs legitimize conquest through scripture. Peter Schäfer, *The Bar Kokhba War Reconsidered: New Perspectives on the Second Jewish Revolt Against Rome* (Tübingen: Mohr Siebeck, 2003), 79–92.

This troubling comparison demands consideration: If the serpent became an idol, and Yeshua likens Himself to it, does this suggest an eventual misuse or reinterpretation of His image?

III. Prophetic Tests: Deuteronomy 13

Deut. 13:1–5 warns of prophets or dreamers who may perform signs, yet lead the people away from Torah. The test of authenticity is not miracles—but alignment with YHWH's   commandments.

Many of Yeshua's later followers and interpreters (particularly Paul) appear to deviate from Torah:
- Declaring the Law "a curse" (Gal. 3:13)
- Preaching justification apart from Torah observance

This raises the possibility that the historical figure of Yeshua may   have   been:
-        Misunderstood   and   misrepresented
-    Used   as   a   test   or   stumbling   block
- Instrumental in triggering both revival and division

IV. Summary View of This Work

This volume does not declare Yeshua as the definitive Messiah. While recognizing His historical and textual significance, we remain cautious. We leave room for further revelation and comparison with the true shepherd of Ezekiel 34 and Deut. 18:15–19.

The position here is that:
- YHWH alone is Savior and King (Isa. 43:11; Hos. 13:4)
- Torah remains the eternal standard (Psalm 119)
- Any man lifted up must be tested against it

V. Thought-Provoking Questions

- Was Yeshua lifted up for healing—or did He become idolized like the bronze serpent?
- Has the image of the cross become a substitute for Torah?
- Do we trust the Name of YHWH—or traditions built on Roman edits?

VI. Sources and Citations

1. Numbers 21:8–9; 2 Kings 18:4
2. John 3:14–15; Galatians 3:13
3. Deuteronomy 13:1–5; Isaiah 43:11
4. Hosea 13:4; Psalm 119
5. Talmudic principles of false prophet tests (Sanhedrin 90a–93a)

Bonus Gematria Cipher — Nimrod within the Serpent (666)

"Let the one who has understanding calculate the number of the beast, for it is the number of a man, and his number is 666."

— Revelation 13:18

Hebrew Cipher:

נִמְרֹד בַּנָּחָשׁ (Nimrod b'Naḥash — "Nimrod within the Serpent")

Standard Mispar Hechrechi (Gematria Value):

Term: Nimrod
Hebrew Letters: ד) + 6(ו) + 200(ר) + 40(מ) + 50(נ (4)
Value: 300

Term: "b" prefix
Hebrew Letters: ב (2)
Value: 2

Term: Naḥash
Hebrew Letters: ש) + 8(ח) + 50(נ (300)
Value: 358

Total (classical gematria): 660

Apocalyptic Cipher:
Nimrod (300 → 3)
b' (2)
Naḥash (358 → 3+5+8=16 → 1+6=7)

$3 + 2 + 7 = 12 \rightarrow 1 + 2 = 3$
$3 \times 222 = 666$

Theological Implication:
While Genesis 10:8 identifies Nimrod as the literal "son of Cush," this cipher identifies him prophetically as the spiritual ally or inheritor of the Serpent (Naḥash). The typological association suggests:

- Nimrod as the first global rebel, challenging divine order through Babel.

- Naḥash as the original deceiver whose legacy persists through empire, language manipulation, and spiritual corruption.

This is not a genealogical interpretation but a prophetic cipher. Revelation itself uses symbolic numerology, as seen when נרון קסר (Neron Caesar) yields 666 through extended spelling.

"Nimrod b'Naḥash = 666" therefore functions as an apocalyptic typology, tracing a spiritual line of rebellion from the Garden (Naḥash) to Babel (Nimrod) to Rome and the Beast-system of Revelation 13.

Apocryphal Connection: Esau Slays Nimrod

Sefer HaYashar (Jasher 27:4–12) records Esau slaying Nimrod and taking Adam's garments, assuming the identity of a "mighty hunter before YHWH." This tradition offers symbolic continuity:

- Esau and Nimrod are both described as hunters.

- Esau becomes the successor and slayer of the original empire-builder.

- A serpentic mantle passes from Nimrod → Esau → Edom → Rome.

This narrative warns of political and spiritual power gained outside covenant, reinforcing the Nimrod cipher's trajectory into Edomite and Roman typology.

Closing Thought:

"Gematria does not merely count letters — it reveals spiritual architecture."

This cipher reveals prophetic architecture from Eden to Babel to Edom to Rome to Revelation 13, positioning Nimrod as the archetype of the Beast-system and Naḥash as the spiritual engine behind human rebellion.

"for it is written, Cursed is everyone that hangeth on a tree"

-Paul

VIEW OF DARLINGTON COURT-HOUSE AND THE SYCAMORE-TREE WHERE AMY SPAIN, THE NEGRO SLAVE, WAS HUNG BY THE CITIZENS OF DARLINGTON, SOUTH CAROLINA.—[SKETCHED BY N. N. EDWARDS.]

Appendix L: The Linguistics of Diaspora in Deuteronomy 28

Abstract: Provides diagrammatic representations of linguistic and prophetic frameworks, including verb forms, typologies, and root systems.

I. Full Textual Presentation: Deuteronomy 28:68

וֶהֱשִׁיבְךָ יְהוָה מִצְרַיִם בָּאֳנִיּוֹת בַּדֶּרֶךְ אֲשֶׁר אָמַרְתִּי לְךָ לֹא-תֹסִיף עוֹד לִרְאֹתָהּ וְהִתְמַכַּרְתֶּם שָׁם לְאֹיְבֶיךָ לַעֲבָדִים וְלִשְׁפָחוֹת וְאֵין קֹנֶה:

Translation (JPS 1917):

"And the LORD shall bring thee back into Egypt in ships, by the way whereof I said unto thee: 'Thou shalt see it no more again'; and there ye shall sell yourselves unto your enemies for bondmen and for bondwomen, and no man shall buy you."

II. Grammatical Analysis and Prophetic Implication

1. וֶהֱשִׁיבְךָ (veheshivkha)

- Root: שׁוּב (shuv) – "to return"

- Stem: Hiphil (causative)

- Form: Imperfect, 3ms + 2ms suffix

- Literal meaning: "He will cause you to return"

- Significance: The absence of the lamed prefix (ל) before Mitzrayim (מצרים) shows this is not "to Egypt" geographically, but "Egypt" as a symbolic return to bondage.

2. בָּאֳנִיּוֹת (ba'oniot)

- Bet with pataḥ + definite article = "in the ships"

- Definite article marks specificity — "the ships" alludes prophetically to transatlantic slave ships

- Supported by: Rabbi Samson Raphael Hirsch, who interprets this not as a literal return but as symbolic of humiliating exile

3. וְהִתְמַכַּרְתֶּם (ve-hitmakartem)

- Root: מ-כ-ר (makar) = "to sell"

- Stem: Hitpael (reflexive / causative)

- Meaning: "You will sell yourselves"

- Not literal, but figurative for divine consequence — sin reflexively leads to bondage

- Parallels:

- 1 Kings 21:20, 25

- 2 Kings 17:17

- Isaiah 52:3 — "sold for nothing," "redeemed without money"

III. Additional Verses for Context

Deuteronomy 28:36 — "A nation you nor your fathers have known" = not Egypt

Deuteronomy 28:49 — "A nation... whose language you do not understand"

- Aramaic was the lingua franca under Zedekiah (597–586 BCE)

- Israelites clearly understood Aramaic (Isaiah 36:11)

- Also had exposure to Greek by 3rd century BCE

- Therefore, this must refer to truly unknown tongues — English, French, Spanish

- Confirmed by linguistic scholars (John Baugh, Michel DeGraff) on Afro-diasporic linguistic rupture

IV. Lexical Triad Summary

Root	Meaning	Role in v. 68
שׁ-ו-ב	return	veheshivkha – God causes return to bondage
מ-כ-ר	sell	ve-hitmakartem – self-sell into captivity
ק-נ-ה	buy/redeem	ein koneh – no one redeems

V. Theological Conclusion

This passage is a prophetic covenantal reckoning. The Hitpael verb reveals a reflexive judgment, not voluntary slavery. The definite marker "in the ships" (ba'oniot) signals a specific prophetic target — the transatlantic passage. Rabbinic, linguistic, and historical frameworks converge to affirm that this is not a record of an ancient exile, but a divine forecast of a future, foreign captivity.

VI. Visual Reference Notes

- Include a Hitpael binyanim chart (e.g., Jouon-Muraoka §53)

- Include a marked Hebrew version of Deuteronomy 28:68

Sources Cited

- Rabbi Samson Raphael Hirsch, Commentary on Devarim 28:68, trans. Isaac Levy (London: Judaica Press, 1969)

- Isaiah 52:3; 1 Kings 21:20, 25; 2 Kings 17:17

- John Mbiti, African Religions and Philosophy

- Jan Assmann, Cultural Memory and Early Civilization

active			reflexive	passive		
פָּעַל	פִּיעֵל	הִפְעִיל	הִתְפַּעֵל	הוּפְעַל	פּוּעַל	נִפְעַל
paál	piél	hifíl	hitpaél	hufál	puál	nifál
			causative			
		intensive				
		simple				

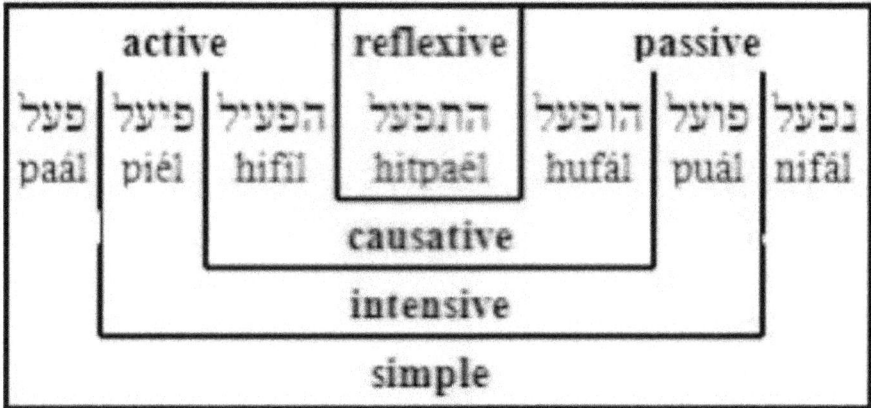

Hithpaʿel *Perfect* 1 הִתְמַכֵּר Kings 21:25; וְהִתְמַכַּרְתֶּם consecutive Deuteronomy 28:68; 2 וַיִּתְמַכְּרוּ Kings 17:17; *Infinitive* 1 הִתְמַכֶּרְךָ Kings 21:20; *sell oneself* as slave Deuteronomy 28:68; figurative 1 Kings 21:20,25; 2 Kings 17:17, **all followed by** לַעֲשׂוֹת הָרַע.

7 Major Hebrew Verb Stems

- Emanuel Tov, Textual Criticism of the Hebrew Bible

- John Baugh; Michel DeGraff (on linguistic loss in the African diaspora)

- Jouon-Muraoka, A Grammar of Biblical Hebrew §53

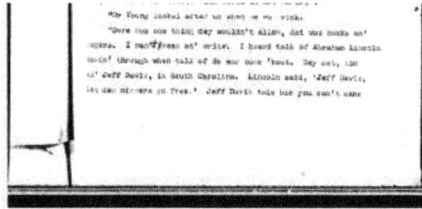

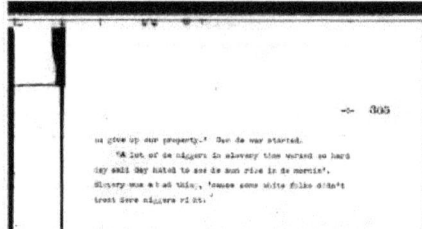

United States Slave Recollections

The transatlantic slave trade, as prophesied in Deuteronomy 28:68, finds direct historical echoes not only in ship registries but also in **state-level cohabitation, manumission, and ownership documentation**. In North Carolina alone, official records affirm this captivity through:

- **North Carolina Cohabitation Records (1866):** Legalized the marriages of formerly enslaved persons post-emancipation, often marking family separations and genealogical erasures stemming from centuries of bondage.

- **The 1748–1856 North Carolina Slave Collection**: Comprising bills of sale, runaway notices, deeds, and estate valuations, these documents affirm the commodification of African bodies consistent with ve-hitmakartem ("you shall sell yourselves") in Deut. 28:68.

- **Sampson County Slave Sale Records (1896)** and **Caswell County Registers**: Archival data confirms generational bondage and sale well after Emancipation.

These institutional archives, now digitized by the North Carolina Digital Collections and UNC's Slave Deeds Project, represent not just social history but covenantal interruption—evidence of an entire people forcibly sold "on ships" to serve foreign masters, as Deuteronomy foretold.

Formal Citation Footnotes

1. North Carolina Digital Collections, *Slave Collection, 1748–1856*, State Archives of North Carolina. https://digital.ncdcr.gov/Documents/Detail/slave-collection-1748-1856

2. State Library of North Carolina, *Records of Enslaved People*. https://statelibrary.ncdcr.gov/genealogy-and-family-history/family-records/records-enslaved-people

3. Cohabitation Records, 1866, NC Freedmen's Bureau Archives.

4. UNC Slave Deeds Project. https://lib.unc.edu/slavedeeds

Hebrew Names Under Bondage — Diaspora Covenant Memory and Afro-Semitic Identity

"And these are the names of the sons of Israel who came into Egypt..." (Exodus 1:1) — *Naming was memory. Naming was resistance.*

The enduring presence of biblical Hebrew names—such as Moses, Jacob, Aaron, and Israel—among enslaved Africans in the Americas constitutes a striking testament to covenantal memory in exile. The historical record confirms that these names were not isolated or incidental, but recurring across plantations, shipping manifests, court records, and personal testimonies.

Ronald Sanders, in *Lost Tribes and Promised Lands*, suggests that enslaved Africans retained a lingering consciousness of their Hebraic past. Though his thesis is framed in a mythic and cultural lens rather than as primary archival history, it raises a powerful interpretive possibility: that African captives preserved remnants of spiritual identity through names aligned with the biblical tradition of Shem, rather than Ham. This possibility is echoed by real archival evidence.

Court records from colonial Delmarva (1727 and 1806) document slaves named Moses and Jacob in legal proceedings, revealing not only the naming pattern but its use within white legal frameworks. In Charles City County, Virginia, enslaved individuals bearing names like Jacob appear on 19th-century plantation inventories. Even broader are the Port of Savannah slave manifests (1790–1860), which preserve thousands of entries, many listing names such as Moses, Aaron, Abraham, and Jeremiah. These names, found in the mouths of the enslaved, reveal a sustained invocation of biblical heritage.

In *Narrative of the Life of Moses Grandy*, the author retains his full Hebrew name, aligning his own story with the deliverance arc of Torah. These instances of naming go beyond Christian acculturation—they reflect a defiant theological remembrance. Hebrew names functioned as more than identity; they were signals of origin, markers of the exile, and quiet declarations of the covenant.

Ronald Sanders, *Lost Tribes and Promised Lands: The Origins of American Racism* (New York: HarperCollins, 1978), 364–367.

"Slave Records in Delmarva," Salisbury University, https://enduringconnections.salisbury.edu/free_black_fa milies_colonial_delmarva_heinegg/records.

"Charles City County Plantation Inventories," Charles City Historical Database, https://charlescity.org/learn/genealogical-databases/enslaved-ancestor-file/enslaved-ancestor-database.

Slave Manifests of Savannah, Georgia, 1790–1860, U.S. National Archives and LexisNexis Academic Collection, https://www.lexisnexis.com/documents/academic/upa_cis/100539_AmSlaveTradeSerDPt1.pdf.

Moses Grandy, *Narrative of the Life of Moses Grandy, Late a Slave in the United States of America* (London: Gilpin, 1843), https://docsouth.unc.edu/neh/grandy/menu.html.

320050

217

BEFORE AND AFTER DE WAR

An interview with Lottie Curtis, 98 years old, of Raleigh, North Carolina, Route # 4.

"I was borned on de plantation of Mr. John Hayes in Orange County, ninety-eight years ago. Several of de chilluns had been sold 'fore de speculator come an' buyed mammy, pappy an' we three chilluns. De speculator was named Bebus an' he lived in Henderson, but he meant to sell us in de tobacco country.

"We come through Raleigh an' de fust thing dat I 'members good wus goin' through de paper mill on Crabtree. We traveled on ter Granville County on de Granville Tobacco path till a preacher named Whitfield buyed us. He lived near de Granville an' Franklin County line, on de Granville side.

"Preacher Whitfield, bein' a preacher, wus supposed to be good, but he ain't half fed ner clothed his slaves an' he whupped 'em bad. I'se seen him whup my mammy wid all de clothes offen her back. He'd buck her down on a barrel an' beat de blood outen her. Dar wus some difference in his beatin' from de neighbors. De folks round dar 'ud whup in de back yard, but Marse Whitfield 'ud have de barrel carried in his

Appendix M: Linguistic and Typological Insights from Zechariah 1–4

Abstract:

This appendix presents a linguistic and typological analysis of Zechariah chapters 1 through 4, with a focus on Hebrew etymology, syntactic structure, and lexical patterns that inform deeper theological meaning. Through a critical examination of prophetic vision, verbal morphology, and literary asymmetry, the text reveals embedded theological architecture supporting a Judah-centered redemptive framework. The findings advance the monograph's thesis that the Tanakh communicates not only through narrative content but also through encoded linguistic and typological devices.

I. Uneven Object Markers and Syntactic Disruption (Zechariah 2:2)

"אֵלֶּה הַקְּרָנוֹת אֲשֶׁר זֵרוּ אֶת־יְהוּדָה אֶת־יִשְׂרָאֵל וִירוּשָׁלָם"

The Hebrew text exhibits a rare triple-object construction in which the direct object marker (אֶת) is applied to both "Judah" and "Israel," but not to "Jerusalem." This structural irregularity draws attention to Jerusalem's distinct narrative role. The omission of the object marker before "Jerusalem" suggests a grammatical reorientation—whereas Judah and Israel are scattered objects of aggression, Jerusalem becomes the unstated object of divine action and restoration.

This syntactic disruption may serve as a literary hinge between the consequences of scattering and the forthcoming comfort and rebuilding themes introduced in Zechariah 1:14–17.

II. The Semantic Field of חרשׁ (Charash): Beyond Craftsmanship

Term: חָרָשִׁים (charashim)

Root: חרשׁ — "to engrave, to craft, to be silent."

The lexeme חרשׁ has a semantic range encompassing engraving, devising, building, and silence. It appears in both literal contexts (e.g., temple construction) and metaphorical ones (e.g., strategic silence or divine contemplation). In Exodus 31:3–5, Bezalel and Oholiab are filled with divine spirit for craftsmanship—an association that reemerges here.

The craftsmen in Zechariah 1:20–21 function not as military agents but as corrective forces with precision and divine intent. Their mission to "terrify and cast down" the horns is best understood as theological counter-inscription—repairing covenantal distortion through skilled restoration. The typological link to scribal authority and messianic roles is further supported by this verb root.

III. Lexical Narrowing: Judah Supplants Israel

Following Zechariah 1:19(Tanakh 2:2), the terms "Israel" and "Judah" both appear as objects of scattering. However, subsequent chapters repeatedly mention only "Judah," "Jerusalem," and "Zion." The removal of "Israel" from the prophetic register indicates a thematic narrowing. This aligns with exilic and post-exilic remnant theology, in which Judah alone returns as the custodial tribe of temple, kingship, and priesthood.

Such lexical narrowing is not accidental but embedded in prophetic literary design. The absence of "Israel" reflects covenantal silence concerning the northern tribes while elevating Judah as the locus of restoration and messianic fulfillment.

IV. Sons of Oil: שְׁנֵי בְנֵי־הַיִּצְהָר (Zechariah 4:14)

Messiah ben Golah—the redeemer from exile—is the prophetic inversion of Messiah ben David. This is the figure who gathers fragments, not crowns kings. Yeshua's post-resurrection exile patterns (e.g., Emmaus Road) align with this lesser-known type, rooted in Isaiah 49:5–6.

Phrase: שְׁנֵי בְנֵי־הַיִּצְהָר — "the two sons of fresh oil."

Root: יצהר (Y-Tz-H-R) — derived from the verbal base יצק, meaning "to pour," and from יצהר, meaning "pressed or refined oil."

The reference to "sons of oil" denotes anointing but is also semantically linked to pressure, refining, and separation. This aligns with typological duality: one messianic figure as the suffering servant (cf. Zech. 12:10), the other as reigning monarch (cf. Zech. 9:9).

This verse encapsulates the dual messianic motif (e.g., Messiah ben Yosef and Messiah ben David), a concept reinforced in later rabbinic tradition (e.g., Sukkah 52a). The phrase implies that both are consecrated through "refined" oil—under pressure, through affliction, or divine appointment.

V. The Genealogy of Zechariah as Literary Foreshadowing (Zechariah 1:1)

Names:

- Zechariah (זְכַרְיָה) — "YHWH remembers"

- Berechiah (בֶּרֶכְיָה) — "YHWH blesses"

- Iddo (עִדּוֹ) — likely derived from עדה, meaning "to assemble" or "appointed time"

This triad of names forms a theologically loaded chain: divine remembrance (זכר), blessing (ברך), and timed assembly or testimony (עד). It serves as a literary microcosm of the book's structure—remembrance of covenant, blessing of return, and restoration of prophetic order.

VI. Etymological Table of Key Terms

Hebrew Term	Shoresh (Root)	Core Meaning	Functional Role
קֶרֶן (qeren)	ק־ר־ן	Horn, authority, power projection	Symbol of geopolitical or theological force
חָרָשׁ (charash)	ח־ר־שׁ	Engraver, builder, silent deviser	Prophetic corrector/restorer of covenant memory
יִצְהָר (yitzhar)	י־צ־ר / י־צ־ק	Pressed oil	Symbol of dual messianic anointing
נָבִיא (navi)	נ־ב־א	To declare or speak forth	Legitimate prophetic agent in Hebrew tradition

VII. Conclusion

Typological Clarification: The Dual Legacy of the Gospels as Horn and Healing

The identification of the Four Horns in Zechariah as typologically mirrored by the Four Gospels does not indict the message of the Gospel itself but critiques its imperial redaction. The horns "that scattered Judah" (Zech. 1:19) refer to oppressive forces; when the Gospel narrative was divorced from Torah, reworded in Latin-Greek frameworks, and weaponized by Rome, it echoed that same scattering—this time, not by sword, but by doctrine.

However, the typology is not condemning Matthew, Mark, Luke, or John in origin, but what became of them under ecclesiastical authority. As patristic redactors aligned gospel expression with empire (e.g., Constantine's Nicene reforms), the original Torah-honoring testimony of Yeshua was submerged beneath theological imperialism. Thus, the Four Gospels in their *distorted form* function as "horns," while their *restored Hebraic witness* operates as the smiths in Zechariah 1:20—those sent to terrify the horns and break their hold.

Torah-observant followers of Yeshua, especially in the first century, did not contribute to this scattering. On the contrary, they embodied resistance and covenantal fidelity. Their legacy must not be conflated with the later horned form of Christendom that canonized through power instead of prophetic fidelity. This typology, therefore, reveals a dual legacy: *restoration when Hebrew grammar is retained, destruction when empire reauthors it.*

This allows the Gospels to remain sacred when reconnected to Lašôn ha-qōḏeš, and indicting only when they function as theological colonialism.

The Hebrew text of Zechariah 1–4 demonstrates a complex and theologically charged interplay of lexical selection, root structuring, and syntactic variation. These linguistic mechanisms function as encoded commentary, reinforcing key themes of covenantal continuity, messianic duality, and Judahite centrality. The patterns identified are not merely stylistic but carry substantial theological weight—affirming that the Hebrew Bible embeds prophecy not only in narrative but also in grammar, morphology, and etymology. This confirms the presence of intentional, layered design meant for decoding by readers literate in covenantal language and prophetic memory.

Appendix N: Linguistic and Etymological Breakdown of the Torah Canon

Abstract: This appendix demonstrates how the Hebrew titles of the Five Books of Moses are not arbitrary but are divinely and linguistically encoded summaries of Israel's covenantal journey. Each title draws from a Hebrew root that reflects profound spiritual, theological, and historical significance.

I. Linguistic Blueprint of the Torah (תּוֹרָה)

Revealing Israel's Covenant Through Sacred Language

Book	Hebrew Title	Transliteration	Literal Meaning	Root (Shoresh)	Covenant Message
Genesis	בְּרֵאשִׁית	B'reishit	In the beginning	ר-א-שׁ (R-'-Sh)	God initiates creation and covenant
Exodus	שְׁמוֹת	Shemot	Names	שׁ-ם (Sh-M)	Israel's identity and remembrance in exile
Leviticus	וַיִּקְרָא	Vayikra	And He called	ק-ר-א (Q-R-')	God calls His people to holiness and proximity

				Root	
Numbers	בְּמִדְבַּר	Bamidbar	In the wilderness	ד-ב-ר (D-B-R)	God speaks and refines in the wilderness
Deuteronomy	דְּבָרִים	Devarim	Words / Matters	ד-ב-ר (D-B-R)	Moses reaffirms covenant through divine speech

II. In-Depth Etymological Notes:

בְּרֵאשִׁית (B'reishit)

- **Root:** רֹ-א-שׁ (rosh) = "head, chief, beginning."
- **Prefix:** בְּ (be) = "in."
- **Form:** Construct state implying "in the beginning of…"
- **Message:** The covenant begins with *intentional creation*, not cosmic accident. It denotes order and purpose.

שְׁמוֹת (Shemot)

- **Root:** שׁ-ם (shem) = "name."
- **Plural Form:** shemot = "names."
- **Message:** Hebrew emphasizes memory and identity. These are not just sons of Jacob; they are named, remembered covenant carriers.

וַיִּקְרָא (Vayikra)

- **Root:** ק-ר-א (qara) = "to call."
- **Prefix:** וַ (va) = narrative "and."

- **Form:** Imperfect, 3ms = "He will call" → with *va* = "And He called."

- **Message:** God's call to holiness and instruction opens the book. Leviticus is about divine proximity through ritual and law.

בְּמִדְבַּר (Bamidbar)

- **Root:** ד-ב-ר (*davar*) = "word, speech."

- **Form:** *midbar* = wilderness → literally "place of word."

- **Prefix:** בְּ = "in."

- **Message:** Wilderness is not silent—it's where God *speaks* and reveals, even amid hardship.

דְּבָרִים (Devarim)

- **Root:** ד-ב-ר (*davar*) = "word, matter."

- **Form:** Plural = "words"

- **Message:** Moses recites *the words*—divinely inspired covenantal summaries. Language is not abstract, but performative and legal.

Final Reflection:

From Genesis to Deuteronomy, the Hebrew titles encode the journey of Israel—not only geographically, but spiritually. The language of Torah was designed to carry memory, mission, and meaning through root structures (shorashim) that speak across time. This appendix restores visibility to the architecture of divine communication embedded within Lašon ha-Qodesh (the Holy Tongue).

Appendix O: Canonical and Prophetic Typology Chart

This appendix presents a comprehensive typological map used throughout the manuscript, integrating Tanakh typologies, New Testament reinterpretations, Dead Sea Scroll parallels, and diasporic prophetic frameworks. Each typology reflects a layered pattern: original covenantal function, prophetic fulfillment, imperial distortion (where applicable), and postcolonial significance for diasporic identity, especially within Black and Afro-Semitic contexts.

Typology	Source(s)	Canonical/Prophetic Function	Diasporic/Theological Application
Bronze Serpent	Num. 21; John 3:14	Symbol of divine healing lifted up	Diasporic uplift as memory of covenant pain made sacred
Dual Messiah (ben Yosef / ben David)	Zech. 12; Rev. 19; Bar Kokhba	Twofold redemptive roles: suffering & reigning	Diaspora as messianic endurance, not failure
Four Horns / Four Gospels	Zech. 1; Rev. 17; Matt.–John	Instruments of scattering vs. covenantal restoration	Gospels distorted by empire = horns; restored Hebraic gospel = smiths
Paul / Joseph	Gen. 37–50; Acts 9	Rejected redeemer later elevated	Covenantal contradiction turned to preservation; Paul as conflicted deliverer
Temple / Structure	1 Kings 6–9; Rev. 21	Center of worship & failure	Imperial theology idolizes structure over movement

Shekhinah / Exile	Ezek. 10; Rev. 21	Glory departs in judgment	Diaspora reflects divine presence carried in exile
Babylon / Beast	Dan. 7; Rev. 17	Political-theological oppression	Typology of ecclesial empire (Rome, Vatican) obscuring covenant
YHWH vs. Caesar	Exod. 3:14; Phil. 2	Divine name vs. imperial naming	Canonization erased divine Name; recovering it is covenantal return
Almah / Parthenos	Isa. 7:14; Matt. 1:23	Virgin birth as sign	Typological theft when mistranslated to fit Greek messianism
Shofar	Lev. 25; 1 Thess. 4	Call to covenant restoration	Sonic memory of scattered tribes and justice rhythms
Scrolls Sealed / Unsealed	Dan. 12; Rev. 5	Prophecy hidden until remnant arrives	Diaspora unseals memory and grammar through remnant literacy
Jeremiah's Fire	Jer. 20:9	Prophetic pain uncontainable	Diasporic grief as sacred voice—

			prophecy through trauma
The Lost Tribes	Isa. 11:11; Ezek. 37	Scattered covenantal identities	Black diaspora as remnant awakening, not theological invention
New Jerusalem / Bride	Rev. 21; Isa. 62	Covenant fulfilled in community	Diasporic inheritance reframed through feminine divine imagery
Ark & Daughter of Golah	Exod. 25; Ezra 9	Ch. XVII	Ark typology extended to female priesthood; Bat Golah identity
Naḥāsh / Tannīn (Serpent/Dragon)	Gen. 3; Rev. 12	Ch. VI	Curse theology reframed through Pauline typology
Seh Lamb (fem.) / Azazel Goat	Lev. 4:32; Lev. 16	App. S	Suppressed feminine messiah typology; gematria anchors

Appendix P

Feminist Notes on Hebrew Prophecy, Grammar, & Canonical Suppression

I. Introduction

This appendix gathers and clarifies the suppressed linguistic and prophetic presence of women in the Hebrew Bible, evaluating how grammatical gender, mistranslation, and canon formation have historically marginalized the feminine voice. Drawing from feminist theologians such as Phyllis Trible, Judith Plaskow, Musa Dube, and Renita Weems, this summary places grammatical erasure alongside theological silence—offering a recovery-oriented lens.

II. Feminine Grammatical Markers in Hebrew

Term	Hebrew	Type	Traditional Role	Common Suppression
almah	עַלְמָה	Noun	Young woman of age; undefined virginity	Misrendered as "virgin" in LXX and Christian Bibles
betulah	בְּתוּלָה	Noun	Virgin (legal/ritual term)	Rarely differentiated from *almah* in English
nəvi'ah	נְבִיאָה	Noun (fem.)	Prophetess (Miriam, Huldah, Deborah)	Translated as "prophet," gender-neutralized

| shofetet | שׁוֹפֶטֶת | Noun (fem.) | Female judge (Deborah) | Often translated as masculine "judge" |
| qehillah | קְהִלָּה | Noun (fem.) | Assembly/congregation (feminine form) | Translations often mask feminine syntax |

III. Notable Feminist Interventions in Hebrew Scripture

Scholar	Key Work	Focus Area	Relevance
Phyllis Trible	Texts of Terror	Narrative violence, feminine absence	Argues Hebrew Bible rewrites or deletes women
Judith Plaskow	Standing Again at Sinai	Canon & exclusion in Judaism	Canon formation overlooked female voices and leadership
Musa Dube	Postcolonial Feminist Interpretation	Colonization of gender and language	Reveals how empire theologies erased both native and feminine speech
Renita Weems	Battered Love	Prophetic marriage metaphors	Unmasks abusive gender imagery in

prophetic
texts

IV. Visual Table: Suppressed Women in Canon vs. Historical Record

Figure	Role	Mentioned in Canon	Attributed Speech	Grammatical Gender Preserved?
Miriam	Prophetess	Yes (Exod. 15:20)	Song of the Sea (Exod. 15:21)	Yes, but minimalized
Deborah	Judge & Prophetess	Yes (Judg. 4–5)	Entire battle prophecy & poem	Somewhat preserved
Huldah	Prophetess	Yes (2 Kings 22)	Confirms Torah found by Josiah	Partially erased in Christian summaries
Anna	Prophetess (NT)	Yes (Luke 2:36–38)	Public praise & prophecy	Often spiritualized, not theologically elevated
Unnamed Prophetesses	Various	No	Lost	Entirely excluded

V. Linguistic Reflection

"The grammar of God's voice was once feminine — until translation made it safe."
– Appendix P Tovi Mickel

Canonical structures are not neutral. When female verbs were masculinized, and when names like nəvī'āh were translated to generic "prophet," the theology shifted. A God who once spoke through both sons and daughters (Joel 2:28) became a God filtered through the masculine plural alone.

VI. Closing Exhortation

This monograph recognizes that the prophetic voice is not just lost—it was taken. Feminist theology, particularly in its Semitic linguistic form, restores what was removed not by omission, but by design. It is not enough to include women in theology—we must recover the very verbs, suffixes, and names through which they once spoke.

VII. Visual Supplements

Figure 1: Canon Timeline – Feminine Prophetic Voice & Canon Suppression

Timeline: Feminine Prophetic Voice & Canon Suppression

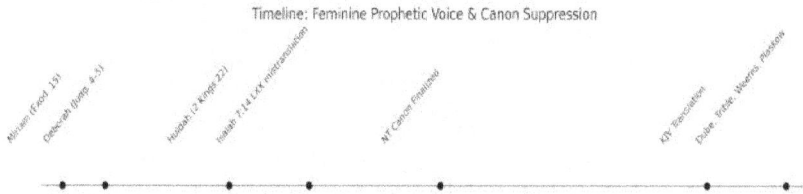

Translation Suppression Flowchart:
The Loss of Feminine Theology in Biblical Transmission

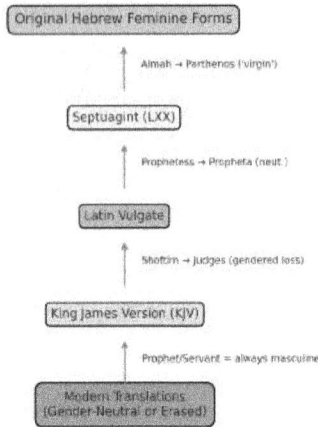

Original Hebrew Feminine Forms

Almah → Parthenos ('virgin')

Septuagint (LXX)

Prophetess → Propheta (neut.)

Latin Vulgate

Shoftim → Judges (gendered loss)

King James Version (KJV)

Prophet/Servant = always masculine

Modern Translations
(Gender-Neutral or Erased)

Figure 2: Translation Suppression Flowchart – The Loss of
Feminine Theology

Feminist Suppression Table

This table illustrates how original feminine elements in
Scripture are often mistranslated, neutralized, or minimized
in modern biblical translations, resulting in suppressed or
erased theological roles for women.

Biblical Reference	Original Feminine Element	Modern Translation Trend	Canonical Impact
Deuteronomy 32:18	חֹלֶלְךָ (bore you) – feminine form	Neutralized as 'who gave you birth'	Feminine depiction of YHWH muted
Isaiah 42:14	כְּמוֹ יוֹלֵדָה (like a woman in labor)	Rendered metaphorically or omitted	Feminine birth imagery stripped

Joel 2:28	וְנִבְּאוּ בְּנוֹתֵיכֶם (your daughters shall prophesy)	Downplayed or spiritualized	Prophetic authority re-centered on males
Exodus 15:20	Miriam as נְבִיאָה (female prophet)	Minimized to singer/dancer	Erasure of female prophetic leadership
2 Kings 22:14	Huldah titled הַנְּבִיאָה	Often omitted in Christian lectionaries	Loss of female exegesis during Josiah's reign
Luke 2:36	Anna the Prophetess (προφῆτις)	Rarely taught or cited as theological authority	Example of temple-era female prophet lost

Grammatical Gender Comparison

This chart compares the grammatical gender systems of Hebrew, Greek, Latin, and English, highlighting especially why Hebrew integrates gender more deeply into its verbal system.

Feature	Hebrew	Greek	Latin	English
Number of Genders	2 (Masculine, Feminine)	3 (Masculine, Feminine, Neuter)	3 (Masculine, Feminine, Neuter)	Natural gender only (he/she/it)

	Marked masc./fem.: *melek* (king), *malkâ* (queen)	Marked masc./fem./neut.: *anthrōpos*, *gunē*, *dōron*	Marked masc./fem./neut.: *rex*, *regina*, *templum*	Not grammatically gendered: king, queen, temple
Nouns	Marked masc./fem.: *melek* (king), *malkâ* (queen)	Marked masc./fem./neut.: *anthrōpos*, *gunē*, *dōron*	Marked masc./fem./neut.: *rex*, *regina*, *templum*	Not grammatically gendered: king, queen, temple
Articles	None (ha- definite prefix, no gender)	ó (masc.), ή (fem.), τό (neut.)	No separate article; gender in pronouns/adjectives	The (no gender distinction)
Adjectives	Must agree in gender & number	Must agree in gender & number	Must agree in gender & number	No gender agreement
Pronouns	Gendered: hu (he), hi (she)	Gendered: autos (he), autē (she), auto (it)	Gendered: ille (he), illa (she), illud (it/that)	Gendered only in 3rd person singular: he/she/it
Verbs – Present/Past	Gender-marked	Not gender-marked	Not gender-marked	No gender

d in 2nd & 3rd person (katav / katvah)		(except participles)	(except participles)	marking in verbs
Participles	Gendered: kotēv (masc.), kotévet (fem.)	Gendered: grapsas (masc.), grapsasa (fem.), grapsan (neut.)	Gendered: scribens (m/f), scribentia (neut. pl.)	Not gendered: writing
Depth of Gender in Verbal System	Deep – verbs change for gender	Shallow – verbs neutral, participles gendered	Shallow – verbs neutral, participles gendered	Minimal /None – no gender marking

Conclusion: Hebrew integrates gender directly into finite verb forms (especially in 2nd/3rd person), while Greek and Latin restrict gender to nouns/adjectives/pronouns, and English has almost entirely lost grammatical gender.

Genesis as Binary Grammar: Feminine, Masculine, and Plurality in Creation

The opening verse of the Torah (Gen 1:1) resists the flattening imposed by later translation and theological simplification. A close grammatical reading shows that the text encodes a binary and even triadic register:

בְּרֵאשִׁית (bərē'šît, "beginning") is a feminine noun, marking the first word of Torah with a feminine register. The verb בָּרָא (bārā', "he created") is a masculine singular perfect, foregrounding masculine action. The subject, אֱלֹהִים

(ʾĕlōhîm), is morphologically masculine plural, yet governs a singular verb, often explained as the "plural of majesty."[1] This construction destabilizes attempts at a rigid, univocal grammar of divinity: unity is carried in plurality. The object pair "heavens and earth" closes the verse with הַשָּׁמַיִם (haššāmayim, dual/plural) and הָאָרֶץ (hāʾāreṣ, feminine), returning the verse to the feminine frame.

Thus, the Torah begins not with a monolithic masculine singular, but with binary grammar: feminine, masculine, plural, feminine. To erase the feminine dimension here is not fidelity to the text, but fidelity to later theological impositions.

Genesis 1:27 confirms this duality explicitly: "male and female he created them" (זָכָר וּנְקֵבָה בָּרָא אֹתָם, zākār û-nəqēvāh bārāʾ ʾōtām). The image of God is not reducible to one gender, nor is divine action reducible to one mode of grammar.[2] The plurality of אֱלֹהִים and the femininity of רוּחַ (rûaḥ, Gen 1:2) reinforce that creation is not born of a masculine God alone, but from a God whose grammar itself contains both registers.[3]

Prophetic tradition, too, knows this language: "Like a woman in labor I cry out, I gasp and pant" (Isa 42:14). To deny the feminine divine is to deny Scripture's own grammar. To reclaim it is to restore what empire erased.[4]

Footnotes

1. Gesenius, Wilhelm. *Gesenius' Hebrew Grammar*. Edited by Emil Kautzsch. 2nd English ed. Revised by A. E. Cowley. Oxford: Clarendon Press, 1910; see also Ludwig Koehler, Walter Baumgartner, and Johann Jakob Stamm, *The Hebrew and Aramaic Lexicon of the Old Testament* (Leiden: Brill, 1994–2000).

2. James Barr, *The Semantics of Biblical Language* (London: Oxford University Press, 1961).

3. Emanuel Tov, *Textual Criticism of the Hebrew Bible*, 3rd ed. (Minneapolis: Fortress Press, 2012).

4. Phyllis Trible, *God and the Rhetoric of Sexuality* (Philadelphia: Fortress Press, 1978); Tikva Frymer-Kensky, *In the Wake of the Goddesses: Women, Culture, and the Biblical Transformation of Pagan Myth* (New York: Fawcett Columbine, 1992).

Appendix Q: Origins of Major Christian Denominations

Roman Catholic Church & The Roman Empire

Formalized: 4th century AD
Key Moments:
- Council of Nicaea (325 AD), called by Emperor Constantine.
- Bishop of Rome (Pope) recognized as supreme authority.
Sources: Jaroslav Pelikan, The Christian Tradition; Henry Chadwick, The Early Church.

Eastern Orthodox Church

Separated: 1054 AD (Great Schism)
Cause: Doctrinal disagreements, papal supremacy.
Sources: John Meyendorff, Byzantine Theology; Steven Runciman, The Eastern Schism.

Lutheranism

Founder: Martin Luther
Year: 1517
Place: Wittenberg, Germany
Core Belief: Justification by faith alone.
Sources: Luther's 95 Theses; Heiko Oberman.

Reformed / Presbyterian

Founder: John Calvin
Year: 1536
Place: Geneva
Core Belief: Predestination.

Sources: Institutes of the Christian Religion; Alister McGrath.

Anglicanism / Church of England

Founder: Henry VIII
Year: 1534
Place: England
Belief: Catholic in theology, Anglican in polity.
Source: Diarmaid MacCulloch, The Reformation.

Baptist Movement

Founder: John Smyth
Year: 1609
Place: Amsterdam
Belief: Believer's baptism.
Source: William Brackney.

Methodist Movement

Founders: John and Charles Wesley
Year: 1738
Place: England
Belief: Holiness, Arminianism.
Source: Richard Heitzenrater.

Pentecostalism

Founder: Charles Fox Parham
Year: 1901
Expanded by: William Seymour (1906)
Belief: Speaking in tongues, Spirit baptism.
Source: Vinson Synan.

Seventh-day Adventist Church

Founders: Joseph Bates, James & Ellen White
Formalized: 1863
Influenced by: William Miller
Belief: Sabbath, Second Coming.
Source: George Knight.

Jehovah's Witnesses

Founder: Charles Taze Russell
Year: 1870 (movement), 1931 (name)
Belief: Non-Trinitarian, Kingdom-focused.
Source: M. James Penton.

Mormonism (LDS)

Founder: Joseph Smith
Year: 1830
Place: New York
Belief: Book of Mormon, Restorationism.
Source: Richard Bushman.

Rome vs. the Nations: Military and Religious Response

People / Region	Date(s) of Conflict	Key Event(s)	Roman Religious Response / Syncretism	Sources
Gauls (Celts)	390 BCE; 3rd–1st c. BCE	Sack of Rome (390); Caesar's Gallic Wars (58–50 BCE)	Interpreted Celtic gods through interpretatio Romana (e.g., Mercury = Lugus)	Livy, Ab Urbe Condita 5.35–55; Caesar, Gallic War 6.16–18
Carthaginians (Phoenicians)	264–146 BCE	Punic Wars; Hannibal invades Italy	After 146 BCE destruction, Punic cults	Polybius, Histories 3; Livy, Ab Urbe Condita 21–30

	(218–202 BCE)		(Baal Hammon, Tanit) absorbed; Roman accusations of child sacrifice reframed them as 'foreign demons'	
Greeks (Macedon, Athens)	2nd c. BCE (168 BCE Battle of Pydna)	Conquest of Greece, annexation of Macedon	Wholesale absorption: Zeus → Jupiter, Hermes → Mercury; Greek philosophy and literature adopted	Plutarch, Life of Aemilius Paullus; Polybius, Histories 30
Parthians (Persians)	53 BCE (Carrhae); 66–217 CE wars	Romans crushed at Carrhae (53 BCE); repeated	Zoroastrian dualism and Mithras cult influenc	Plutarch, Crassus 23–32; Cassius Dio, Roman History 40

		eastern wars	e → Mithraism spreads in Rome	
Germans (Teutons, Cherusci)	9 CE; ongoing 1st–3rd c. CE	Varus disaster (3 legions lost in Teutoburg Forest)	Germanic gods equated with Roman deities (Odin = Mercury, Thor = Jupiter)	Tacitus, Annals 1.55–71; Germania 9
Egyptians	30 BCE (Actium & annexation)	Cleopatra defeated, Egypt annexed	Cult of Isis imported into Rome (by late 2nd c. BCE, massive by 2nd c. CE)	Apuleius, Metamorphoses 11; Plutarch, Isis and Osiris
Jews (Judea)	63 BCE (Pompey enters Jerusalem); 66–70 CE revolt; 132–135 CE Bar	Temple desecrations, destruction (70 CE), expulsion after 135 CE	Attempts at syncretism: sacrifices for Caesar, Caligula's statue of Jupiter	Josephus, War 2.409–417, 6.1–6; Philo, Legatio ad Gaium; Cassius Dio 69.12–14

Kokhba   in
revolt   Temple
                      (40 CE);
                      total ban
                      on Torah
                      practices
                      after Bar
                      Kokhba

Rome's clashes with Israel were not unique; they were part of a long imperial pattern. From the Gauls in the west to the Parthians in the east, Rome faced nations whose identity was inseparable from religion. The Roman method was consistent: conquer militarily, hybridize the local gods through interpretation Romana, and require loyalty through the imperial cult. The Gauls' Mercury, the Egyptians' Isis, and the Persians' Mithras all became Romanized deities. When Judea resisted, Rome tried the same formula—demanding sacrifices for Caesar, even ordering Caligula's statue to stand in the Jerusalem Temple. Josephus identifies the refusal of imperial sacrifices in 66 CE as "the true beginning of our war" (War 2.409). Unlike other nations, however, Israel's Torah-centered resistance refused syncretism, forcing Rome into destruction and dispersal. Thus the rise of Christianity under Rome should be understood not as a unique revelation of canon, but as the empire's final syncretic project: absorbing Jewish messianism into the same system that had already Romanized Gaul, Carthage, Greece, Egypt, and Persia.

References

Caesar, Julius. *The Gallic War*. Translated by H. J. Edwards. Loeb Classical Library. Cambridge: Harvard University Press, 1917.

Josephus. *The Jewish War*. Translated by H. St. J. Thackeray. Loeb Classical Library. Cambridge: Harvard University Press, 1927.

Livy. *History of Rome*. Translated by B. O. Foster. Loeb Classical Library. Cambridge: Harvard University Press, 1922.

Philo of Alexandria. *On the Embassy to Gaius (Legatio ad Gaium)*. Translated by F. H. Colson. Loeb Classical Library. Cambridge: Harvard University Press, 1941.

Plutarch. *Lives*. Translated by Bernadotte Perrin. Loeb Classical Library. Cambridge: Harvard University Press, 1914–1926.

Tacitus. *Annals*. Translated by John Jackson. Loeb Classical Library. Cambridge: Harvard University Press, 1931.

Tacitus. *Germania*. Translated by J. B. Rives. Oxford: Oxford University Press, 1999.

Cassius Dio. *Roman History*. Translated by Earnest Cary. Loeb Classical Library. Cambridge: Harvard University Press, 1914–1927.

Apuleius. *Metamorphoses (The Golden Ass)*. Translated by J. Arthur Hanson. Loeb Classical Library. Cambridge: Harvard University Press, 1989.

Roman-Era Suppressed Voices: Scholarly Chart

This document presents a scholarly overview of major suppressed voices in early Christianity and the Roman-era church, with a chart of figures, their teachings, suppression, and surviving materials. It also includes analytical inserts on Tertullian, Marcion, female prophecy, and practical Marcionism in modern church life. Prepared for integration into Chapter 14.

Suppressed Voices Chart (2nd–5th Century CE)

Figure / Movement	Core Teachings	Dates / Locale	Church Response	What Survives	Primary Witnesses

Ebionites	Torah-observant disciples of Jesus; rejected Paul; Jesus as human prophet.	2nd–4th c.; Palestine /Syria	Branded heretical; excluded from communion; gospels suppressed.	Fragments (e.g. Gospel of Ebionites).	Irenaeus, Adv. Haer. 1.26; Epiphanius, Panarion 30.
Nazarenes	Torah-observant Christ followers; Hebrew /Aramaic Matthew.	2nd–4th c.; Syria/Palestine	Marginalized; absorbed under catholic consensus.	Brief descriptions; Jerome quotes.	Epiphanius, Panarion 29; Jerome, On Matthew.
Marcion & Marcionites	Two gods scheme; OT god = demiurge; canon = edited Luke + 10 Paulines.	c. 140+; Rome → Mediterranean	Excommunicated; communities suppressed; writings destroyed.	Fragments reconstructed from refutations.	Tertullian, Adv. Marcionem; Epiphanius, Panarion 42.

Valentinians	Pleroma myth; Christ as revealer; sacramental exegesis.	mid-2nd c.; Rome, Alexandria	Condemned; texts suppressed.	Nag Hammadi codices (e.g. Gospel of Truth).	Irenaeus, Adv. Haer. I; Tertullian, Adv. Valent.
Basilides	Esoteric exegesis; cosmic archons; docetic Christology.	c. 120–140; Alexandria	Condemned; writings lost.	Fragments in hostile summaries.	Irenaeus 1.24; Hippolytus, Refutation 7.
Montanists	Prophecy via Montanus, Priscilla, Maximilla; rigorous ethics; eschaton.	late-2nd c.; Phrygia → N. Africa	Condemned in synods; clergy disciplined.	Oracles in fragments; Tertullian's Montanist writings.	Eusebius HE 5.16–18; Epiphanius, Panarion 48.
Arius	Son created, not co-eternal; anti-Nicene	256–336; Alexandria → empire	Nicaea condemned; writings burned.	Fragments; opponents' quotations.	Athanasius, Orationes; Socrates, Sozo

	Christology.				men, Theodoret.
Mani & Manichaeans	Dualism; Christ as revealer; asceticism.	216–c.276; Persia → Rome	Suppressed; executions; books burned.	Texts in Coptic, Persian, Chinese; Augustine's polemics.	Hegemonius, Acta Archelai; Augustine, Contra Faustum.
Donatists	Clergy purity essential; rigorist ecclesiology.	4th–5th c.; Numidia /Africa	Condemned by councils; suppressed by force.	Known through Augustine's rebuttals.	Augustine, Contra Ep. Parmeniani; Optatus.
Origen	Pre-existence; universal restoration speculations.	c.185–254; Alexandria/Caesarea	Later anathematized (5th–6th c.); selective survival.	Some Greek, many Latin translations.	Eusebius HE 6; Council edicts.
Pelagius	Human freedom; grace	c.360–420; Rome → Britain	Condemned at Carthag	Few letters, some	Augustine, De

as aid, not ontologi cal change.	e (418) & Ephesus (431).	comm entarie s.	gratia Christ i; Coun cil canon s.

Tertullian, Marcion, and Female Prophecy

Tertullian's arc (Carthage, c. 160–225). The first great Latin theologian forged much of the West's vocabulary (*trinitas; substantia/persona*), aggressively prosecuting heresy (e.g., *Adversus Marcionem, Adversus Praxean*). Yet ca. 207 he aligned with the **Montanist** "New Prophecy," defending stringent morality and the ongoing voice of the **Spirit through women**—notably the prophetesses **Priscilla** and **Maximilla**. His later treatises (e.g., *De Monogamia; De Exhortatione Castitatis; De Virginibus Velandis*) assume a pneumatology in which prophetic utterance continues and can correct communal laxity. Ecclesially, he and his circle (the "Tertullianists") were marginalized; Augustine later reports their eventual absorption back into the Catholic fold. *Primary loci:* Eusebius, *HE* 5.16–18 (on Montanists); Jerome, *Vir. Ill.* 53; Augustine, *De Haeresibus* 86; Tertullian, passim.

Marcion's provocation (Rome, 140s). Marcion's **edited Luke** and **ten-letter "Apostolikon"** (Gal, 1–2 Cor, Rom, 1–2 Thess, Laod. [= Eph?], Col, Phil, Phlm) aggressively severed Gospel and Paul from Israel's Scriptures. The great-church's rejoinder (Irenaeus' "fourfold Gospel," broader Pauline corpus, Acts, Catholic Epistles) and polemical anatomies (Tertullian V; Epiphanius 42) let us reconstruct his text in detail. *Primary loci:* Tertullian, *Adv. Marc.* I–V; Epiphanius, *Panarion* 42.

Female prophecy in contention. Montanism's most scandalous feature to bishops was not ecstatic style alone but **women as authoritative prophets**. The same catholic networks that crushed Marcion also silenced or cordoned the female-prophetic charisma that Tertullian defended in principle. From a feminist-prophetic trajectory, this becomes a crucial data point: **textual control and gendered silencing rise together** in late 2nd-century ecclesiology. *Primary loci:*Eusebius, *HE* 5.16–18; Epiphanius, *Panarion* 48.

"Practical Marcionism" in Modern Church Habits

Even where Marcion is repudiated doctrinally, many modern churches enact **Marcion-like patterns** in practice:

1. **Functional abrogation of the Tanakh.** Sermonic and catechetical cycles center the NT; the OT appears episodically for moral examples or prophecy "proof-texts," not as **ongoing covenantal authority**. This enacts Marcion's severance pragmatically (even when denied confessorily).

2. **Pauline primacy as hermeneutical governor.** Paul's letters—read in a Hellenistic, anti-nomian key—become the lens for Jesus and Torah, rather than the reverse. This is the modern form of what you critique in Chapter 14 as the "Law vs. Grace" dichotomy created by Greco-Roman reception rather than Hebrew covenant categories.

3. **Supersessionist soteriology.** Sinai is treated as preparatory or obsolete; Israel's covenantal grammar (Torah as **instruction**, not punitive "law") is overwritten by Latinized legal metaphors. Result: a practical "Old Testament is done/fulfilled" stance, which Marcion would recognize—albeit with better christological rhetoric.

Citations

- **Marcion:** Tertullian, *Adversus Marcionem* I–V (esp. IV on the Gospel); Epiphanius, *Panarion* 42; Adamantius, *Dialogue* (Pseudo-Origen).

- **Montanists & female prophecy:** Eusebius, *HE* 5.16–18; Epiphanius, *Panarion* 48; Tertullian, *De Monogamia, De Exhortatione Castitatis, De Ecstasi* (fr.).

- **Ebionites/Nazarenes:** Irenaeus, *Adv. Haer.* 1.26; Epiphanius, *Panarion* 29–30; Jerome on Hebrew Matthew traditions.

- **Valentinus/Basilides:** Irenaeus, *Adv. Haer.* I; Hippolytus, *Refutation of All Heresies* 6–7; Clement, *Stromata*.

- **Arius:** Athanasius, *Orationes contra Arianos*; Socrates, *HE* 1; Sozomen, *HE* 1; Theodoret, *HE* 1; imperial rescripts ordering book burnings post-Nicaea referenced in later church historians.

- **Manichaeans:** Hegemonius, *Acta Archelai*; Augustine, *Contra Faustum, De utilitate credendi*.

- **Donatists:** Augustine, *Contra Epist. Parmeniani*; *Letter 93*; Optatus, *Against the Donatists*; acts of the Conference of Carthage (411).

- **Origen/"Origenism":** Eusebius, *HE* 6; anathemas attached to the 5th Council's dossiers (Constantinople II, 553) as received in later collections.

Archeology

- **Jericho strata:** Neolithic tower/fortifications (Tell es-Sultan).

- **Mesha Stele (Moabite Stone):** Mentions Israel, Chemosh; contested *bt dwd*.

- **Tel Dan Stele:** "House of David."

- **Merneptah Stele:** Earliest extrabiblical mention of Israel (c. 1208 BCE).

- **Lachish reliefs (Sennacherib, 701 BCE).**

- **Kurkh Monoliths (Shalmaneser III, battle of Qarqar, mentions Ahab).**

- **Deir ʿAlla inscription (Balaam).**

- **Khirbet Qeiyafa ostracon (early Hebrew justice lexicon).**

Appendix R – Research Bibliography

Herodian Identity, Edomite Origins, and Theo-political Substitution

Josephus, Flavius. *Antiquities of the Jews*. Translated by William Whiston. Peabody, MA: Hendrickson Publishers, 1987.

Brueggemann, Walter. *The Prophetic Imagination*. 2nd ed. Minneapolis: Fortress Press, 2001.

Sugirtharajah, R. S. *The Bible and the Third World: Precolonial, Colonial and Postcolonial Encounters*. Cambridge: Cambridge University Press, 2001.

MacMullen, Ramsay. *Christianizing the Roman Empire: A.D. 100–400*. New Haven: Yale University Press, 1984.

Hirsch, Samson Raphael. *The Pentateuch: Translation and Commentary*. Translated by Isaac Levy. Jerusalem: Feldheim Publishers, 1990.

Talmud Bavli, *Avodah Zarah* 10a.

Midrash Tanchuma, *Toldot* 5.

Bereshit Rabbah 65:21.

Lee Martin McDonald. *The Biblical Canon: Its Origin, Transmission, and Authority*. 3rd ed. Peabody, MA: Hendrickson, 2007.

Dio Cassius. *Roman History*. Translated by Earnest Cary. Loeb Classical Library. Cambridge, MA: Harvard University Press, 1914.

Tacitus. *The Annals of Imperial Rome*. Translated by Michael Grant. London: Penguin Classics, 1996.

Herman, Judith. *Trauma and Recovery: The Aftermath of Violence—from Domestic Abuse to Political Terror*. New York: Basic Books, 1992.

Rambo, Shelly. *Spirit and Trauma: A Theology of Remaining*. Louisville: Westminster John Knox Press, 2010.

Davis, Ellen. *Getting Involved with God: Rediscovering the Old Testament*. Lanham, MD: Cowley Publications, 2001.

Cooper-White, Pamela. *The Cry of Tamar: Violence Against Women and the Church's Response*. Minneapolis: Fortress Press, 2012.

van der Kolk, Bessel. *The Body Keeps the Score: Brain, Mind, and Body in the Healing of Trauma*. New York: Viking, 2014.

Katongole, Emmanuel. *The Sacrifice of Africa: A Political Theology for Africa*. Grand Rapids: Eerdmans, 2011.

Eusebius of Caesarea. *Life of Constantine*. Translated by Averil Cameron and Stuart G. Hall. Oxford: Clarendon Press, 1999.

Jerome. *Prologus Galeatus*. In *Biblia Sacra Vulgata*, edited by Robert Weber. Stuttgart: Deutsche Bibelgesellschaft, 1994.

Pelikan, Jaroslav. *The Christian Tradition: A History of the Development of Doctrine, Volume 1: The Emergence of the Catholic Tradition (100–600)*. Chicago: University of Chicago Press, 1971.

Chadwick, Henry. *The Early Church*. Rev. ed. London: Penguin Books, 1993.

Appendix S: The Sacrificial Lamb and the Silenced Feminine: A Linguistic, Theological, and Numerical Exegesis

I. The Misuse of Seh (שֶׂה): Gender Erasure in Sacrificial Language

In Biblical Hebrew, seh (שֶׂה) is typically rendered 'lamb' or 'young of the flock,' covering both sheep and goats. Unlike keves (כֶּבֶשׂ), which denotes a male lamb, seh functions as a generic category that in when a **lamb** is brought as a ḥaṭṭā't (Lev 4:32), **it must be female**; likewise, Lev 5:6 prescribes a **female** lamb or **female** goat for commoners. Here lies the first rupture: the New Testament applies the title seh ha-Elohim ('Lamb of God') to Yeshua. Yet the Torah requires that in the commoner ḥaṭṭā't prescriptions the **animal is female**. Either the Evangelists misapplied the type or the true fulfillment remains hidden.

II. Lexical Taxonomy of Sacrificial Terminology

Term	Hebrew	Gender	Semantic Range & Notes
Seh	שֶׂה	Neutral (often feminine)	Generic flock animal
Keves	כֶּבֶשׂ	Masculine	Male lamb; Passover and elevation offerings
Kivsah	כִּבְשָׂה	Feminine	Female lamb; Nathan's parable (2 Sam 12:3); personal offering; specified as female for sin-

			offerings (Lev 4:32, 5:6)
Taleh	טָלֶה	Masculine	Suckling lamb; poetic, prophetic usage
Ayil	אַיִל	Masculine	Ram; substitutionary sacrifice (Gen 22)

Excursus: Adam and the Collective Human. The very name adam (אָדָם) encodes duality: Genesis 5:2 affirms, "Male and female He created them, and He blessed them and called their name Adam." Humanity is not fully "adam" until woman is present. To reduce "Adam" to a male-only archetype (as in some readings of 1 Cor 15:45, "the last Adam") is to erase the lexical tension in Torah itself.

III. Encoded Dualities in the Torah

The sacrificial system reflects divine polarity: male and female, sacrifice and exile, blood and bearing.

• Noah (Gen 7:2): Seven pairs of clean animals preserved for renewal.
• Levitical tiers (Lev 4–5): Leaders atone with male goats/bulls; commoners with female lambs/goats.
• Jacob and Esau (Gen 27): Esau as sa'ir ('hairy goat') versus Jacob as 'smooth.'
• Red Heifer (Num 19): A female removed 'outside the camp,' cleansing through ashes.

Excursus: Miriam's Death and Atonement. Torah conspicuously places the Red Heifer ordinance (Num 19) immediately before Miriam's death (Num 20:1). Rabbinic midrash reads this juxtaposition to mean, 'The death of the righteous atones.' Thus, the Torah's very sequence links feminine agency (Red Heifer, Miriam) to the logic of atonement.

• Jeremiah 31:22: 'A woman shall encompass a man.' This eschatological riddle signals reversal: the feminine taking covenantal lead.

IV. Yeshua and Bat Golah: The Two-Goat Polarity

Traditional Christology fixates on Yeshua as the slain lamb. Torah's witness is broader and deliberately dyadic: **two goats**—one "for YHWH," sacrificed for blood-purification (**Lev 16:15**), and one "for Azazel," **kept alive** to **bear** transgression **outside the camp** into the wilderness (**Lev 16:21–22**). In this polarity:

1) Yeshua = the Goat "for YHWH" (the priestly blood). He is the covenantal blood that purges and re-consecrates the sanctuary (cf. **Heb 9:11–14**), the "blood of the covenant" echoing Sinai (cf. **Exod 24:6–8; Matt 26:28**). His death functions as the cultic remedy that addresses **God's side** of the breach—defilement of the holy sphere by Israel's sins (**Lev 16:16–19**).

2) Bat Golah (Israel-in-exile) = the Goat "for Azazel" (the bearer in wilderness). The **second goat is not slain**; it **carries** the people's iniquities away, **alive**, into the **wilderness**. This maps onto **Israel's diaspora**—the **Bat Golah**—who bears the weight of covenant violation and the violent overflow of the nations' iniquity (cf. **Deut 28; Lam 1–5; Zech 1:15**). This is where the corporate Servant reading of **Isa 53** (often interpreted as Israel) becomes a legitimate lens: the nations look on and confess that the Servant's sufferings were borne **for** "many" (**Isa 53:4–6, 11–12**). In this sense, **Bat Golah embodies the Azazel function**—not as a sacrifice to a demon, but as the **exilic bearer** who carries sin-consequence out of the holy camp until reconciliation is complete.

3) The Bronze Serpent clarifies the polarity, not identity. When Yeshua identifies himself with the **serpent lifted**

up (**Num 21; John 3:14**), he signals **paradox as method**: that which appears cursed becomes the instrument of healing (**cf. Deut 21:23**). The sign is **dual**—judgment and cure—just as the Yom Kippur rite is dual—**blood and bearing**. The serpent image explains **how** one figure can embody paradox without collapsing the **two-goat** logic into a single role.

4) The two goats as a broken ketubah awaiting renewal. Israel's covenant is cast as **marriage** (ketubah): "though I was **a husband** to them" (**Jer 31:32**); see also **Hos 1–3; Ezek 16; 23**. YHWH's house (sanctuary) requires **blood** to cleanse the marital home (goat for YHWH), while the **bride** bears the shame into **exile** (goat for Azazel). But the story is not divorce's end; it is **betrothal renewed**: "I will **allure her**... in the **wilderness**... and **betroth** you to me forever" (**Hos 2:14–20**). The **wilderness**, Azazel's terrain, becomes the very place of **re-covenanting**. Thus, the two goats are a **marital tableau**: breach and remedy, separation and wooing, judgment and restoration.

5) Ben David + Bat Golah: the numeric seal of the rite. Gematria tables show that **Ben David (66) + Bat Golah (49) = 115**, precisely the value of **Azazel (115)**. This does **not** identify Yeshua as Azazel; it marks the **pair**—**Davidic sacrifice + exilic bearing**—as the **single Azazel sum**, i.e., the **whole rite** of atonement seen from both sides. The math ratifies the theology: **the redemption requires two**—the **priestly blood** of the bridegroom (goat for YHWH) and the **exilic bearing** of the Bride (goat for Azazel). Together they resolve the broken ketubah.

6) Anticipating the obvious objections.

- **"But Lev 16 says both goats are male."** Correct. The animals are **ritually male**; the **functions** they carry are theologically **gendered** (active/purging vs. receptive/bearing). Torah elsewhere pairs these poles explicitly across male/female rites (e.g., **female** *kivsah* for individual ḥaṭṭā't in **Lev 4:32; female** Red Heifer for "outside-the-camp" cleansing in **Num 19**)—showing the logic, even when Yom Kippur uses two males.

- **"Does Yeshua 'go outside the camp'?"** Yes (**Heb 13:12–13**), but that movement illustrates the **paradox** of his work; it does not require identifying him **as** the Azazel goat. Yeshua provides the **blood; Bat Golah** bears the **exilic** consequence.

- **"Is Israel really bearing the nations' sins?"** Exilic literature persistently depicts Israel suffering under the nations' amplified injustice (**Zech 1:15**), and many Jewish exegetes read **Isa 53** corporately (Israel as Servant). In that reading, the **nations** confess the Servant bore **their** transgression. This is precisely the **Azazel logic** at scale.

Summary.
Yeshua is the **goat for YHWH**—the priestly blood that purges the sanctuary and renews the house. **Bat Golah** is the **goat for Azazel**—Israel-in-exile bearing away the covenant's defilement and the nations' violence, destined to be wooed in the wilderness and brought home. The **two goats** are a **marriage drama**—a **broken ketubah** awaiting re-betrothal—and the **gematria** confirms the unity: **Ben David + Bat Golah = Azazel**. One covenant, two roles, **one atonement made whole**.

V. The Suppressed Feminine and the Bat Golah

Canonical redaction masculinized sacrifice and suppressed the feminine dimension of God: Shekhinah detached, Chokhmah abstracted, Miriam/Magdalene excised. Yet Torah encoded her: kivsah for sin, Red Heifer's ashes, Jeremiah's reversal. This culminates in the Bat Golah (Daughter of Exile), the feminine messianic archetype paired with Ben David.

VI. Gematria-Encoded Prophetic Paradigm

Methods. Standard (Mispar Hechrechi): 400=ת... 1=א; final letters use their base values (90=ץ, 80=ף, 50=ן, 40=ם, 20=ך). Ordinal (Mispar Siduri): 22=ת... 1=א. Reduced (Mispar

Katan): letters map to a 1–9 cycle (e.g., 4→ת, 1→ק, 1→י).
Digit Sum = sum of digits of the Standard total once; Digital
Root = repeated digit-sum to one digit. Kolel: a traditional
±1 adjustment used homiletically by kabbalists to denote the
unity of a word or concept; we label all uses explicitly.

Table A — Standard, Reduced (Katan), and Kolel Notes

Term	Hebrew	Standard	Reduced (Katan)	Digit Sum / Root	Kolel Note
Azazel	עזאזל	115	25	7 / 7	
Golah (Exile)	גולה	44	17	8 / 8	Standard 44 equals Dam 44 and Av(3)+Em(41)=44
Elil (Idol)	אליל	71	8	8 / 8	
Ben David	בן דוד	66	21	12 / 3	
Bat Golah	בת גולה	446	23	14 / 5	Ordinal 50 → 49 (kolel −1) used in homiletic seal with Ben David → Azazel 115
Mashiach	משיח	358	16	16 / 7	Standard 358 = Nachash 358; Katan 16→7

Term	Hebrew				
Nachash	נחש	358	16	16 / 7	Standard 358 = Mashiach 358; Katan 16→7
Notzri	נוצרי	356	23	14 / 5	Katan match: Notzri 23 = Bat Golah 23
Dam (Blood)	דם	44	8	8 / 8	Standard 44 equals Golah 44 and Av(3)+Em(41)=44
Av (Father)	אב	3	3	3 / 3	
Em (Mother)	אם	41	5	5 / 5	

Table B — Ordinal Totals (Base for Kolel Adjustments)

Term	Hebrew	Ordinal
Azazel	עזאזל	43
Golah (Exile)	גולה	26
Elil (Idol)	אליל	35
Ben David	בן דוד	30
Bat Golah	בת גולה	50
Mashiach	משיח	52
Nachash	נחש	43
Notzri	נוצרי	68
Dam (Blood)	דם	17
Av (Father)	אב	3

Em (Mother)   אם   14

Homiletic Seals (Explicit Kolel Usage)

1) Ben David (בן דוד) Standard 66 + Bat Golah (בת גולה) Ordinal 50 with kolel −1 → 49 = Azazel (עזאזל) Standard 115.
Presented as a poetic seal; the lexical–ritual argument stands independently.
2) Golah (גולה) 44 = Dam (דם) 44 = Av (אב) 3 + Em (אם) 41.
3) Mashiach (משיח) Standard 358 = Nachash (נחש) Standard 358; both reduce (Katan) to 16 → 7.
4) Notzri (נוצרי) Katan 23 = Bat Golah (בת גולה) Katan 23.

Rabbinic precedent for numerically grounded exegesis is found across early midrash:
– b. Sanhedrin 38b (Adam created at the sixth hour = 6)
– Genesis Rabbah 44:1 (Abraham's 318 servants = Eliezer via gematria)
– Pesikta de-Rav Kahana 12.25 (gematria for Sabbath as 702 = completeness).
These examples establish that numeric typology is not novel but deeply rabbinic. The present analysis of seh and Azazel continues this trajectory with feminist implications.

VII. Conclusion: The Restoration of Polarity

[48]Appendix S demonstrates: the seh for sin is female, erased in Christological dogma. The two goats encode complementary roles: sacrifice and exile, masculine and feminine. Yeshua embodies the priestly blood; Bat Golah bears the exile. Adam's duality is restored; ha-mashiach's priestly office is recognized; Miriam and the Red Heifer witness to feminine atonement. Jeremiah 31:22 seals the prophetic horizon: 'a woman shall encompass a man.' Thus Torah itself points toward dual messianism: Ben David and Bat Golah, sacrifice and exile, blood and bearing, man and woman—one covering, one redemption.

---

[48] Resurrection typology reinforces seh/GOAT distinction: vindicated by YHWH, not equal to YHWH.

Claimed Divinity Verse	Greek / Syriac Text	Critical Notes (Textual / Typological)	Counter Prepared
John 1:1 — 'the Word was God'	Gk: Ἐν ἀρχῇ ... Θεὸς ἦν ὁ λόγος Syr: ܐܠܗܐ ܗܘܐ ܘܡܠܬܐ	Logos = Memra (agent, not God's essence). Syriac Alaha = divine/authority.	Why is Word personified when Memra = agent?
John 8:58 — 'Before Abraham was, I am'	Gk: πρὶν Ἀβραὰμ ... ἐγώ εἰμι Syr: ܐܢܐ ܐܝܬܝ (I exist)	Egō eimi ≠ Exod 3:14 LXX. Aramaic = existence, not divine self-name.	Exod 3:14 ehyeh ≠ egō eimi.
1 Tim 3:16 — 'God manifest in flesh'	Earliest MSS: ὃς ἐφανερώθη Later: θεός	Proven textual corruption (Metzger, NA28).	If scribes changed it, divinity not original.
John 5:19 — 'Son can do nothing'	Gk: οὐ δύναται ὁ υἱὸς ποιεῖν ... Syr: ܠܐ ܡܫܟܚ ܒܪܐ ܕܢܥܒܕ	Explicit subordination: cannot act apart from Father.	If 'God,' why 'cannot'?
John 3:14 — Bronze Serpent	Gk: καθὼς Μωϋσῆς ὕψωσεν τὸν ὄφιν Syr: ܐܝܟ ܕܐܪܝܡ ܡܘܫܐ ܚܘܝܐ	Yeshua = typology of healing object. Instrumental, not ontological.	If serpent not God, why Yeshua?
Lev 16 — Goat of YHWH	Heb: וְשָׁחַט אֶת־שְׂעִיר ...לַיהוָה	Goat = 'for YHWH,' distinct from YHWH. Yeshua = offering, not deity.	If Azazel goat = exile, offering goat = for YHWH.

Bibliography

Geza Vermes, The Dead Sea Scrolls in English (New York: Penguin, 2004).

Lawrence H. Schiffman, Reclaiming the Dead Sea Scrolls (New York: Doubleday, 1995).

Jacob Milgrom, Leviticus 1–16, Anchor Bible 3 (New York: Doubleday, 1991).

Jacob Neusner, The Mishnah: A New Translation (New Haven: Yale University Press, 1988).

C. T. R. Hayward, Targums and the Transmission of Scripture into Judaism and Christianity (Leiden: Brill, 2010).

Yeshua as the שֶׂה (Seh) of YHWH, Not YHWH

Purpose: To integrate the philology, typology, and diaspora method of this monograph into a single conclusion: Yeshua did not claim to be YHWH; rather, he operated as the Torah-anchored שֶׂה of YHWH and the shaliah (sent agent) whose speech and actions derive authority from the Sender

(YHWH). This explains both the charges of blasphemy and the patterns of 'I am' and 'sent' sayings, without requiring ontological identity with YHWH.

Linguistic Core

1) Exodus 3:14 — Hebrew vs. Greek

Hebrew: אֶהְיֶה אֲשֶׁר אֶהְיֶה ('Ehyeh asher 'ehyeh) = "I will be what I will be" (imperfect, covenantal becoming).

LXX/Greek: ἐγώ εἰμι ὁ ὤν (ego eimi ho ōn) = "I am the One who is" (ontological Being).

Johannine lift: ἐγώ εἰμι (ego eimi) statements reflect Hellenistic framing; they need not imply Jesus claimed YHWH-identity.

2) Agency (שליח / shaliaḥ) Principle

In Second Temple/Jewish law, the emissary carries the authority of the sender without being ontologically identical. Yeshua's repeated 'the Father sent me' sayings align with shaliaḥ agency.

Master Chart — 'I AM' / 'Oneness' / 'Sent' Sayings, with Tanakh Counter-Read

Passage	Apologist Claim	Tanakh-First Reading (Seh/Agency)	Linguistic Note	Citations
John 8:58	Jesus claims to be YHWH ('I Am').	Typology claim: before Abraham's covenantal role, the Torah-sacrificial role (seh/GOA	'Ehyeh (Heb) = 'I will be'; John uses Greek ego eimi from LXX metaphysics.	Exod 3:14 (Heb/LXX); Lev 16; Lev 4:32; Appendix S.

T of YHWH) stands; Yeshua embodies that role, not YHWH Himself.

Passage	Trinitarian Claim	Agency Reading	Key Marker	References
John 10:30–36	"I and the Father are one" = ontological equality.	Oneness of will/mission (agency), not essence. Jesus appeals to Ps 82:6 to de-escalate blasphemy charge.	Hen (one) used for unity; citation strategy deflects divinity claim.	Ps 82:6; John 10:34–36; agency law.
John 5:19–30	Equality in power and judgment proves deity.	Delegated judgment (agency). The Son can do nothing 'of himself' — classic shaliah formula.	Repeated 'not of myself' idiom marks dependence.	Deut 18:18–19; John 5:19, 30.
John 7:16	Divine teacher therefore divine being.	"My teaching is not mine, but His who sent me." Teacher-as-agent, not	Ownership language → sender/agent relation.	Isa 50:4; John 7:16.

		ontological YHWH.		
John 12:49 –50	Divine words = divinity.	He speaks commandments given by the Father → agency transmission.	Given-command vs. innate-identity distinction.	Deut 18:18; John 12:49– 50.
John 14:28	Trinitarian economy only.	"The Father is greater than I" — hierarchical relation contradicts co-equality claim.	Comparative adjective 'greater' undermines ontological equality.	John 14:28.
Mark 10:18	Rhetorical device only.	"Why do you call me good? None is good but God alone." Clear distancing from being called God.	Goodness predicate reserved for God.	Mark 10:18; Ps 118:1.
Matt 24:36	Incarnation limits knowledge but not deity.	"No one knows… nor the Son, but the Father only."	Epistemic limitation inconsistent with ontological	Matt 24:36.

Reference	Claim	Quote / Explanation	Analysis	Citation
		Knowledge asymmetry contradicts co-equality.	al identity.	
John 20:17	Post-resurrection worship proves deity.	"I ascend to my Father and your Father, to my God and your God." Yeshua identifies YHWH as his God.	Possessive 'my God' vs. 'I am God' distinction.	John 20:17; Ps 22:10.
1 Cor 8:6	Paul teaches Jesus is God.	Paul distinguishes 'one God, the Father' and 'one Lord, Jesus Messiah' — functional lordship under the One God.	Elohim/Lord roles divided; not collapsed.	1 Cor 8:6; Deut 6:4 (Shema).
Acts 2:22	Miracles imply deity.	"A man attested by God" — God works through him; agency language.	Passive divine attestation.	Acts 2:22; Isa 42:1.

Stoning Contexts — Why Charges of Blasphemy Arose

Scene	Trigger	Defense / Reframe	Reading
John 8:58–59	Ego eimi + pre-Abraham claim.	No explicit 'I am YHWH'; crowd interprets via LXX lens.	Misread metaphysically; typology/agency better fits Semitic context.
John 10:31–39	"One with the Father."	Jesus cites Ps 82:6 ("you are gods") to reduce claim scope.	If Scripture calls agents 'gods', how more the consecrated shaliaḥ?

Torah Sacrificial Typology: שֶׂה (Seh) and the Two Goats

Torah Element	Text	Function	Messianic Mapping	Notes
שֶׂה (Seh) — female lamb	Lev 4:32	Sin offering (individual/poor).	Feminine messianic typology → Appendix S thesis.	Lexical feminine; suppressed in tradition.
Two goats	Lev 16	One 'for YHWH'; one 'for Azazel' (scapegoat).	Yeshua aligned with GOAT of YHWH (sacred), not Azazel (banishment).	Ritual distinction crucial.

| Passover lamb | Exod 12 | Deliverance sign; blood on doors. | Secondary linkage; not primary to Day of Atonement logic. | Do not collapse categories. |

Quick Citational Ladder

Exod 3:14 (Hebrew vs. LXX); John 8:58; John 10:30–36; John 5:19, 30; John 7:16; John 12:49–50; John 14:28; Mark 10:18; Matt 24:36; John 20:17; 1 Cor 8:6; Acts 2:22; Lev 4:32; Lev 16; Exod 12; Ps 82:6; Deut 18:18–19.

Linguistic anchors: אֶהְיֶה (imperfect "I will be"), ἐγώ εἰμι (Greek present), shaliaḥ (agency), שֶׂה feminine lexeme. Gematria motifs (Appendix S): 305 (seh), 115 (Azazel), 358 (Messiah) — optional visual embeds.

Conclusion: The 'I am' and 'oneness' statements read coherently as shaliaḥ agency and Torah typology of the שֶׂה/GOAT of YHWH. This preserves YHWH's uniqueness while explaining both the charges of blasphemy and Yeshua's authority.

Appendix T — Resurrection Discrepancies & Hebraic Hope

Purpose: To expose contradictions in the resurrection narratives, highlight the role of textual criticism, and reframe resurrection as covenantal vindication within Hebraic categories rather than proof of divinity.

Contradiction Chart: Empty Tomb & Appearances

Source	Who Came First?	Angel(s)/ Messenger(s)	Where Was the Message?	First Appearance	Geographic Location	Theological Spin
Mark 16:1–8 (earliest)	Mary Magdalene, Mary mother of James, Salome	1 young man in white	"He is risen …tell disciples"	Jesus does not appear (original ending)	Galilee promised	Fear, silence
Matthew 28:1–10	Mary Magdalene + other Mary	1 angel, earthquake	Angel speaks, Jesus meets women	Jesus appears to women	Galilee	Authority, worship

Luke 24:1–53	Women (unnamed group)	2 men in dazzling apparel	Angels rebuke disbelief	Jesus appears to disciples on road, in Jerusalem	Jerusalem	Scriptural fulfillment emphasis
John 20–21	Mary Magdalene (alone)	2 angels in tomb	Mary speaks with Jesus directly	Jesus appears to Mary, later disciples	Jerusalem + Galilee (ch. 21 add-on)	Personal intimacy ('My Lord and my God')
1 Cor 15:3–8 (Paul, earliest written)	No tomb scene, no women	None	Jesus appeared to Cephas, Twelve, 500	Collective appearances	No geography	Vindication proof for resurrection hope

Hebraic Categories of Resurrection

• Daniel 12:2 — 'Many who sleep in the dust shall awake' → covenantal vindication, not deity.
• 2 Maccabees 7 — Martyrs expect God to raise them because of Torah faithfulness.
• Ezekiel 37 — Dry bones vision = Israel's corporate restoration, not metaphysical immortality.

• Hosea 6:2 — 'After two days He will revive us; on the third day He will raise us up.'

Conclusion: Resurrection = vindication of the righteous sufferer or nation → Yeshua fits this model as the seh of YHWH, not as YHWH.

Why the Discrepancies Matter

• Inconsistent witnesses undermine 'historical proof' claims.
• The earliest Gospel (Mark) doesn't even narrate an appearance — it leaves resurrection as promise, not sight.
• Paul's account (earliest in writing) has no empty tomb and skips women witnesses → showing theological reframing.
• John 20:28 ('My Lord and my God') is an interpretive climax, not an actual self-claim by Yeshua.

Diaspora Lens

Imperial Rome co-opted resurrection into proof of divinity, but in Hebraic thought, resurrection = YHWH vindicates His servant. Diaspora reclaims resurrection as hope for oppressed peoples, not theology of empire.

Timeline of Resurrection Accounts

Date of Writing	Source	Resurrection Description	Key Features	Textual Notes
~50–55 CE	1 Corinthians 15:3–8 (Paul)	No tomb. Sequence of appearances to Peter, Twelve, 500,	No women, no Galilee/Jerusalem details.	Earliest written witness. Reflects theological kerygma, not narrative.

		James, Paul.		
~70 CE	Mark 16:1–8 (Codex Sinaiticus/Vaticanus)	Women flee tomb in fear; no appearances.	Abrupt ending at 16:8.	'Longer Ending' (16:9–20) absent in earliest MSS; later addition.
~80–85 CE	Matthew 28	Earthquake, angel, women see Jesus, Galilee meeting.	Stronger apologetic: guards at tomb, worship.	Reflects Jewish-polemic context.
~85–90 CE	Luke 24	2 men in dazzling clothes; Jerusalem appearances; Emmaus.	Resurrection tied to Scriptures.	Codex Sinaiticus: Ascension verse (24:51 'carried up') missing; later addition.
~90–100 CE	John 20–21	Mary Magdalene	Personalized encounters,	Later Johannine high

| alone; Doubting Thomas; Galilee fishing. | climax: 'My Lord and my God.' | Christology. |

Textual Criticism Contrast

- Codex Sinaiticus (330–360 CE): Ends Mark at 16:8 (no resurrection appearances). Luke 24:51 lacks explicit Ascension ('was parted from them' only). No 'longer ending' of Mark; no Luke ascension clarity.
- Codex Vaticanus (300–325 CE): Similar to Sinaiticus: Mark ends at 16:8; Luke 24:51 ambiguous. High textual accuracy, but matches early tradition of silence/ambiguity.
- Papyrus P45 (200–250 CE): Earliest, fragmentary; lacks most of Luke's final chapter. Supports absence of fully developed resurrection narratives.
- Byzantine/Later Manuscripts: Add Mark 16:9–20 (appearances, snake-handling, Ascension). Add Luke 24:51 phrase 'and was carried up into heaven.' Reflect theological smoothing → standardizing the doctrine.

Charts of Contradictions

Who Found the Tomb? — Mark: 3 women (fear, silence). Matthew: 2 women. Luke: Group of women. John: Mary Magdalene alone.

Where Did Jesus Appear? — Mark: No appearance. Matthew: Galilee. Luke: Jerusalem. John: Both Jerusalem & Galilee. Paul: No geography.

Angels/Messengers? — Mark: 1 young man. Matthew: 1 angel. Luke: 2 men. John: 2 angels.

Resurrection & Ascension Narratives Across Manuscripts

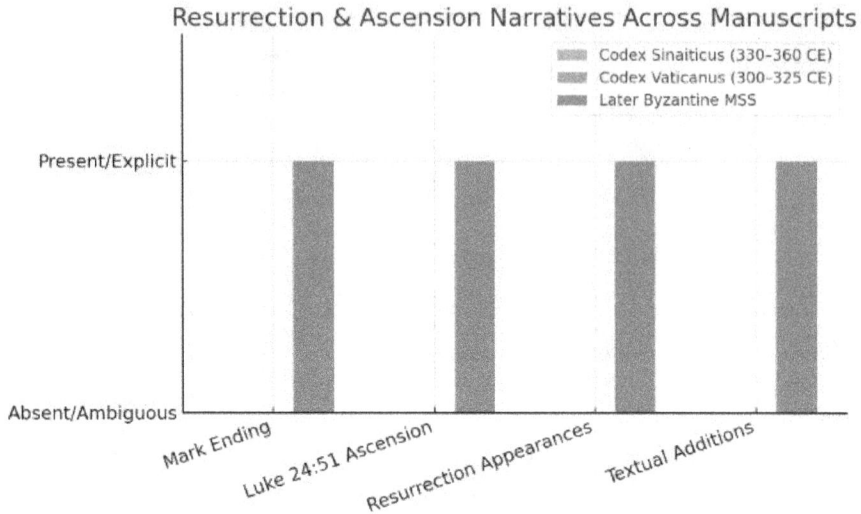

Legend:
- Codex Sinaiticus (330-360 CE)
- Codex Vaticanus (300-325 CE)
- Later Byzantine MSS

Y-axis: Present/Explicit ... Absent/Ambiguous

X-axis: Mark Ending | Luke 24:51 Ascension | Resurrection Appearances | Textual Additions

Scholarly Implications

• Textual Development: The resurrection narratives grow in detail from Paul → Mark → Matthew/Luke → John.
• Theological Motive: Fearful silence (Mark) becomes worship (Matthew), Scripture fulfillment (Luke), and divine identity climax (John).
• Codex Evidence: Earliest manuscripts (Sinaiticus/Vaticanus) show no resurrection appearances in Mark and no clear ascension in Luke — meaning the central 'proofs' apologists use were later textual expansions.
• Diaspora Reading: Resurrection = God vindicates His servant (Daniel 12; 2 Macc 7; Ezek 37). Not identity with YHWH, but confirmation of His election.

Appendix U — Misused Messianic Prooftexts

Purpose: This appendix catalogs the most common Christian 'messianic prophecies' cited by apologists and contrasts them with their original Tanakh contexts. The goal is not merely rebuttal, but reclamation — restoring these passages to their covenantal, Hebraic, and diasporic meaning.

Comparative Prooftext Chart

Passage (Christian Use)	Christian Claim	Original Tanakh Context	Hebraic/Diaspora Re-reading	Scholarly Note
Isaiah 7:14 ('Virgin shall conceive...')	Virgin birth prophecy of Jesus	Immediate sign to King Ahaz: young woman (*almah*) already pregnant; deliverance from Syro-Ephraimite war	Prophecy fulfilled in 8th century BCE; not predictive messianism	BDB, HALOT confirm *almah ≠ betulah*
Isaiah 53 ('Suffering Servant')	Jesus' substitutionary atonement	Servant = collective Israel ('my servant Israel' Isa 49:3); suffering exile, vindicated by YHWH	Diaspora suffering = redemptive testimony, not vicarious atonement	Majority Jewish exegesis, echoed by Childs, Goldingay

Hosea 11:1 ('Out of Egypt I called my son')	Jesus' flight to Egypt	Recollection of Exodus — YHWH calling Israel 'my son'	Collective memory, not messianic prediction	Matthew re-appropriates midrashically
Psalm 22:16 ('They pierced my hands and feet')	Crucifixion prophecy	Hebrew *ka'ari* = 'like a lion' (not 'pierced'); context = David's lament	David's suffering, rhetorical metaphor	DSS + MT support 'lion' reading; LXX misrendered
Micah 5:2 ('Bethlehem prophecy')	Predicts Jesus' birthplace	Ruler from Bethlehem = Davidic continuation	Historical Davidic hope, not 1st-century prediction	Messianic hope re-appropriated later

Hermeneutical Insight

1.   Midrash   vs.   Prophecy:
 – NT authors applied *midrashic re-reading*, not literal predictive prophecy.
 – Diaspora audiences must recognize the difference between re-appropriation and original meaning.

2.   Hebrew   Categories   of   Fulfillment:
 – *Peshat* (plain sense) → historical context (Ahaz, exile, lament).

Misused Messianic Prooftexts: Christian Claim vs. Tanakh Context

	Tanakh Context	Christian Claim
Micah 5:2	Davidic continuation; historical ruler	Predicts Jesus' birthplace
Psalm 22:16	"Ka'ari" = "like a lion"; Davidic lament	Crucifixion prophecy
Hosea 11:1	Exodus memory; Israel = "my son"	Jesus' flight to Egypt
Isaiah 53	Servant = collective Israel; exile & vindication	Jesus' substitutionary atonement
Isaiah 7:14	Immediate sign to Ahaz; young woman ("almah"), 8th c. BCE	Virgin birth prophecy of Jesus

– *Derash* (interpretive reuse) → NT writers adapting old texts.

– Monographs stance: apologists collapse *derash* into *peshat*, which distorts both.

Diaspora Lens

Misuse of prophecy was a key mechanism of imperial theology: Rome absorbed Israel's trauma texts into a Greco-Roman savior narrative. Reclaiming Isaiah 53 as Diaspora Servant Israel turns the charge of 'replacement' back on empire.

Visual Comparison Chart

The chart below contrasts the Christian prooftext claims with their original Tanakh contexts, highlighting how imperial theology re-appropriated Hebraic texts into Greco-Roman Christology.

Appendix V — Patristic Diversity on Jesus' Nature

Purpose: To demonstrate that the earliest centuries of Christianity contained multiple competing views of Jesus' identity. Only later did the Roman Church suppress diversity and impose the Trinity as orthodoxy.

Comparative Chart: Early Christological Views

Group / Writer	View of Jesus	Key Writings / Evidence	Fate / Church Response	Scholarly Note
Ebionites (Jewish followers of Jesus)	Human prophet, Torah-keeper, not divine	Irenaeus *Against Heresies* 1.26	Declared heretical; writings destroyed	Show continuity with Torah-observant Jesus
Adoptionists	Jesus adopted as 'Son of God' at baptism/resurrection	Theodotus of Byzantium, *Shepherd of Hermas*	Condemned, suppressed	Reflects earliest Synoptic themes
Docetists	Jesus only appeared human; divine spirit without flesh	Ignatius combats them (c. 110 CE)	Rejected, resurfaces in Gnosticism	Reveals discomfort with incarnation
Arians	Jesus divine but not eternal; created being subordinate to Father	Arius, c. 318 CE	Condemned at Nicaea (325 CE)	Persisted centuries; evidence of contested orthodoxy
Trinitarians	Jesus fully divine,	Athanasius,	Triumphed at	Dependent on imperial

| (Proto-Orthodox) | consubstantial with Father | Tertullian | councils | enforcement |
| Montanists | Prophetic movement; emphasized Spirit, prophecy, female voices | Tertullian later joins | Declared heretical | Suppression shows erasure of prophetic/feminine roles |

Key Witnesses

• Ignatius of Antioch (d. 110 CE): Stresses obedience to bishops, hints at high Christology, but reveals the fight against docetists and Jewish believers.
• Irenaeus (c. 180 CE): First to push a four-Gospel canon; labels Ebionites heretics; *Against Heresies* exposes diversity.
• Tertullian (c. 200 CE): Coined 'Trinitas,' but also wavered (joined Montanists).
• Origen (c. 250 CE): Subordinationist (Son less than Father). Later condemned.
• Arius (c. 318 CE): Sparked Arian controversy — Jesus divine but not eternal; opposed Athanasius.

Scholarly Insight

• Bart Ehrman: Early Christianity was 'orthodox corruption of scripture.'
• Larry Hurtado: Devotion to Jesus was real, but varied in meaning — not uniform Trinitarianism.
• Geoffrey Dunn & Frances Young: Evidence of 'multiple Christianities' in the 2nd–3rd centuries.

Diaspora Lens

Diversity among early Christians proves that empire, not faith, dictated the Trinity. Ebionites' Torah fidelity resonates with diasporic reclamation of Jesus as Hebrew prophet, not Greco-Roman deity.

Addendum: Worship of YHWH and the King —
Philological and Textual Analysis of 1 Chronicles 29:20

Methodology: Hebrew-first textual criticism; MT-LXX-
Syriac-Vulgate comparison; agency-hermeneutic (שליח);
comparative philology across Hebrew, Greek, and Arabic;
analysis of ANE sociopolitical homage structures. Goal: to
distinguish reverential gestures from ontological worship
and to locate the semantic boundaries apologists often blur
between divine and delegated honor.

1) Primary Text (Masoretic Text and Versions)

Masoretic Text — 1 Chronicles 29:20:

וַיֹּאמֶר דָּוִיד לְכָל־הַקָּהָל בָּרְכוּ־נָא אֶת־יְהוָה אֱלֹהֵיכֶם וַיְבָרְכוּ כָל־הַקָּהָל לַיהוָה אֱלֹהֵי
אֲבֹתֵיהֶם וַיִּקְּדוּ וַיִּשְׁתַּחֲווּ לַיהוָה וְלַמֶּלֶךְ:

Translation: 'And David said to all the congregation, "Bless
now YHWH your God." And all the congregation blessed
YHWH, the God of their fathers, and bowed their heads and
prostrated themselves before YHWH and the king.'

LXX: καὶ προσεκύνησαν τῷ κυρίῳ καὶ τῷ βασιλεῖ — 'they
bowed down to the Lord and to the king.'

Peshitta: ܣܓܕܘ ܠܡܪܝܐ ܘܠܡܠܟܐ — same dual-object structure.

Vulgate: adoraverunt Dominum et regem — later Latin
'adoraverunt' shifted from physical prostration to
theological worship.

2) Morphological Analysis of Verbs

Verb	Root / Binyan	Semantic Range (MT)	Greek / Latin Equivalents
וַיִּקְּדוּ (wayyiqdəû)	קדד (Qal)	To bow the head, physical homage	κάμπτω / incurvo

וַיִּשְׁתַּחֲווּ (wayyištaḥăwû)	שחה (Hishtaphel)	To prostrate oneself (physical, not inherently cultic)	προσκυνέω / adorare
עָבַד ('āvad)	עבד (Qal)	To serve, perform cultic service (divine only)	λατρεύω / servire

Note: קדד and שחה express physical honor; only עבד connotes ritual or divine worship.

3) Syntax and Textual Criticism

The phrase לַיהוָה וְלַמֶּלֶךְ employs the preposition לְ before each noun, distinguishing YHWH and the king as discrete objects. This grammatical separation negates hendiadys (one concept expressed by two words). All textual witnesses support this syntax. Later Greek and Latin theology, however, collapsed physical homage into metaphysical worship.

4) Philological Distinction: Homage ≠ Worship

In the Tanakh, הִשְׁתַּחֲוָה is polyvalent—used for civic submission (Gen 33:3; 1 Sam 25:23) and divine reverence (Exod 24:1). Context dictates interpretation. The Chronicler situates this act in a coronation narrative, marking covenantal hierarchy, not theological equality.

5) Comparative Linguistics: Hebrew, Greek, Arabic

Language	Term	Meaning	Cultic / Non-Cultic Usage

Hebrew	הִשְׁתַּחֲוָה (hishtachavah)	To bow, prostrate	Both (Gen 23:7; Exod 24:1)
Greek	προσκυνέω (proskyneō)	To bow, kiss toward	Both (Gen 33:3; Matt 2:11)
Greek	λατρεύω (latreuō)	To serve ritually	Divine only (Exod 3:12 LXX)
Latin	adorare	To bow, pray (later 'worship')	Originally civic; later divine
Arabic	سجد (sajada)	To prostrate, submit	Both: Q 12:100; 41:37

6) Theological and Hermeneutical Implications

The Chronicler's dual object construction affirms divine kingship (YHWH) and vassal kingship (David/Solomon). Israel's bowing is covenantal allegiance within monotheism, not dual worship. This reflects ancient Near Eastern suzerainty models where homage to the vassal honors the suzerain.

7) Qur'anic Parallels

Qur'anic language distinguishes between **sujūd** (physical prostration) and **ʿibādah** (worship). Joseph's brothers' prostration (Q 12:100) parallels biblical civic honor (Gen 37:9–10), while Q 41:37 restricts sujūd to Allah alone. Thus, Islam preserves the Hebraic semantic monotheism that Christianity later blurred.

8) Summary Chart — Semantic and Theological Differentiation

Action	Hebrew Term	Object	Meaning	Theological Status
Prostration before YHWH	הִשְׁתַּחֲוָה	Divine	Worship (cultic)	Legitimate
Prostration before king	הִשְׁתַּחֲוָה	Human	Reverence/submission	Civic
Service in temple	עָבַד	Divine	Cultic service	Worship
Bowing to idols	הִשְׁתַּחֲוָה	False gods	Idolatry	Prohibited
Sujūd before prophet	سجد	Human	Respect	Permissible (contextual)

9) Conclusion

Linguistically, 1 Chronicles 29:20 encodes reverence and submission under monotheism, not shared worship. Morphological, syntactic, and comparative analysis confirms that the Chronicler's community understood the act as acknowledgment of divine and royal hierarchy. Apologetic readings equating this with co-worship are philologically untenable and result from Greek-Latin semantic compression. The Hebrew lexicon maintains strict lines between service (עבד), prostration (שחה), and worship proper (cultic avodah).

Side Note Addendum — Moshi'im vs. Mashiaḥ in Tanakh (with Implications for the Bronze Serpent Typology)

Method: Hebrew-first exegesis; intertextual control via MT/LXX; socio-legal hermeneutic (shaliach/agency); Second Temple literature for reception history; cautious NT comparison limited to typology (not ontology).

1) Lexical-Morphological Map

ישע (y-š-ʿ) — מושיעים /מושיע (moshiáʿ / moshi'im) = deliverer(s), savior(s). Often charismatic, episodic agents raised in crises.

משח (m-š-ḥ) — משיח (māshîaḥ) = anointed one (priests, kings, selected foreign rulers). Office-bearing, institutional leadership.

גאל (g-ʾ-l) — גֹּאֵל (goʾel) = kinsman-redeemer; family-legal redemption.

פדה (p-d-h) — פֹּדֶה (podeh) = to ransom/redeem (cultic/economic).

שלח (sh-l-ḥ) — שָׁלִיַח (shaliaḥ) = agent; legal principle: "שלוחו של אדם כמותו" (b. Kiddushin 41b).

2) Primary Text Grid (Hebrew Bible)

Category	Key Hebrew Term(s)	Representative Texts (MT)	Function in Context	Notes / LXX
Plural deliverers (moshi'im)	מושיעים	Judg 2:16; 3:9,15; Neh 9:27; Obad 21; Isa 19:20	Charismatic/episodic salvation in crises; eschatological plurality in Obad 21	LXX: σωτῆρες (sōtēres) in Obad 21

Anointed office (mashiaḥ)	משיח	Lev 4:3 (הַכֹּהֵן 1); הַמָּשִׁיחַ Sam 10:1; 16:13; Ps 132:10–17; Isa 45:1 (Cyrus)	Institutional consecration (priestly/royal); instrument of order and governance	LXX: χριστός (christos)
Kinsman-redeemer (goʾel)	גֹּאֵל	Lev 25; Num 35; Ruth 2–4; Isa 41:14; 43:14; 44:6	Family-legal redemption; divine redeemer metaphor in Isaiah	LXX: λυτρωτής / ῥυόμενος
Agent / Messenger of YHWH	מַלְאָךְ; יְהוָה; שְׁלִיחַ	Gen 16; Exod 3; Judg 6; 13; Zech 3	Agency: speaks in first person for YHWH without identity collapse	LXX: ἄγγελος κυρίου

3) Wilderness–Crisis vs. Order–Monarchy Patterning

• Wilderness/crisis epochs → moshiʿim plurality (Judges; Neh 9:27; Obad 21; Isa 19:20).

• Order/monarchy/temple → mashiaḥ as consecrated office (Lev 4:3; 1 Sam 16:13; Ps 132).

• Exile/imperial mediation → mashiaḥ can be a foreign ruler (Isa 45:1, Cyrus).

4) Zechariah & Dual Leadership

• Zech 3:8; 4:14; 6:11–13 — priestly and royal figures ("two anointed ones") function in tandem; anticipates dual leadership motif.

• Aligns with Obad 21 ('moshiʿim shall ascend Mount Zion') — plural agents culminating in YHWH's kingship.

5) The Bronze Serpent Trajectory

• Num 21:4–9 — נחש נחשת = instrumental sign for life upon looking;

• 2 Kgs 18:4 — 'Nehushtan': Hezekiah destroys it as an idol — Torah's own internal critique of object-divinization.

• John 3:14–15 — typological reuse: 'lifted up' (ὑψωθῆναι) parallels function (means of life), not ontology (deity).

6) Methodological Controls (per monograph)

1) Hebrew-first semantics (MT), with LXX for reception and textual nuance (e.g., Ps 118:27 'bind the feast' vs. 'bind the sacrifice').

2) Legal-agency hermeneutic (shaliach): agent speaks/acts for sender without identity collapse (b. Kiddushin 41b; Nedarim 72b).

3) Distinguish roles: moshi'im (episodic deliverers) vs. mashiaḥ (anointed office) vs. go'el (family/legal redeemer).

4) Second Temple patterns: dual-messiah expectation (Qumran: 1QS 9; 1QSa 2; CD 12; 11QMelchizedek), resisting later singular-collapse.

5) NT engagement limited to typology and literary reuse; no retrojection of ontology into MT contexts.

7) Citations — Primary Texts

• Exod 3; 12:48–49; Num 9:14; 15:14–16; 21:4–9; 27; 35; Deut 10:18–19; 14:21; 23:2–9; Lev 4:3; 19:33–34; 24:22; Ruth 2–4; 1 Sam 10–16; Ps 118 (esp. vv. 22–27); 132:10–17; 2 Kgs 18:4; 1 Chr 2–4; 3; Neh 9:27; Isa 19:20; 41:14; 43:11; 44:6; 45:1; Zech 3; 4; 6; Obad 21.

• LXX variants: Ps 117(118):27; Obad 1:21; usage of χριστός for משיח; σωτήρ/σωτῆρες for מושיע/מושיעים.

8) Citations — Second Temple & Rabbinic

• Qumran: 1QS IX; 1QSa II; CD XII; 11Q13 (11QMelchizedek).

• Mishnah/Talmud: m. Kiddushin 2:1; b. Kiddushin 41b; b. Nedarim 72b (agency/shaliach).

• Targumic/Midrashic: Tg. Psalms on 118; Midr. Tehillim 118 (stone as David/Israel).

9) Select Secondary Scholarship

• Milgrom, Jacob. Leviticus (AB 1–3).

• Levine, Baruch. Numbers (JPS; AB).

• Tigay, Jeffrey. Deuteronomy (JPS).

• Collins, John J. The Scepter and the Star (2nd ed.).

• Sommer, Benjamin D. The Bodies of God and the World of Ancient Israel.

• Boyarin, Daniel. Border Lines; and studies on the Memra/Logos.

• Fitzmyer, Joseph A. The Dead Sea Scrolls and Christian Origins.

• Levin, Christoph. The Chronicler's History.

10) One-Page Thesis

Tanakh distinguishes episodic, plural deliverers (מושיעים) from institutional anointed office (משיח), with additional familial/legal redemption (גאל). Obad 21 and Zech 4:14 preserve multiplicity at the eschaton (two/collective agents). Cyrus (Isa 45:1) proves mashiaḥ is a functional, not ontological, category open even to a Gentile king. The Bronze Serpent is a paradigmatic instrumental sign: efficacious when used as commanded (Num 21) and condemned when idolized (2 Kgs 18:4). Therefore, NT typology (John 3:14) aligns Yeshua's role with instrumental elevation (means of life) without requiring ontological identity as 'the only Savior-God,' consistent with Isa 43:11's polemic against idols rather than against human agents.

Addendum II: The Shibboleth Principle — Linguistic
Purity and Sectarian Identity in the Tanakh

This addendum investigates linguistic and phonological
divisions within the Hebrew Bible, centering on the
Shibboleth   incident
(Judges 12:5–6) as the earliest documented case of speech-
based identity policing. It expands on the sociolinguistic,
theological,
and sectarian implications of pronunciation, dialect, and
phonetic accuracy as determinants of covenantal
legitimacy.   The   findings
demonstrate that language functioned not merely as
communication but as covenantal authentication within
Israel's   sacred   corpus.

I. Primary Case: The Shibboleth Tribunal (Judges 12:5–6)

"Then said they unto him, Say now Shibboleth: and he said
Sibboleth; for he could not frame to pronounce it right.
Then they took him, and slew him at the passages of Jordan:
and there fell at that time of the Ephraimites forty
and   two   thousand."   (Judg.   12:6)

The term *šibbōleṯ* (שִׁבֹּלֶת) meaning "ear of grain" or
"stream" contrasted with the Ephraimite pronunciation
sibbōleṯ   (סִבֹּלֶת),
demonstrating a phonological dialect divide between
Gilead and Ephraim. The mispronunciation marked tribal
and   linguistic   identity,
making phonetics a criterion for survival. This represents
the only explicit phonological civil war in the Hebrew
canon.

II. Comparative Cases of Linguistic or Dialectal Markers

Text Reference	Scenario	Linguistic Function	Interpretation
Judg 18:3	Danites recognize Micah's Levite 'by his voice.'	Accent recognition or dialectal difference.	Regional phonology marking tribal identity.
Lev 24:10–16	Blasphemer 'pronounces the Name' (*naqav ha-shem*).	Pronunciation as legal boundary.	Speech act punishable by death.
Exod 3:15; Lev 24:16	Prohibition against misuse of the Divine Name.	Priestly control of pronunciation.	Name as sacred linguistic jurisdiction.
Song of Deborah (Judg 5)	Distinct Northern syntax and morphology.	Dialect variation in poetic Hebrew.	Early linguistic layer reflecting Israelite regionalism.
Neh 8:8	Levites translate Torah aloud for people.	Loss of Hebrew fluency.	Shift to translation as theology of language.

III. Thematic Analysis

1. **Language as Covenant Marker** — From Judges 12 to Nehemiah 8, linguistic correctness equates to covenantal belonging.

To   speak   rightly   is   to   belong   rightly.

2. **Dialectal Divergence as Theological Divergence** —
Northern Israelite versus Southern Judahite speech patterns mirror
theological schisms, marking not just tribal but ideological borders.

3. **From Shibboleth to Masorah** — The Shibboleth principle anticipates Masoretic vowelization, where orthophony became orthodoxy: divine truth preserved through precise articulation.

IV. Secondary Instances with Phonological or Speech Testing

Text	Scenario	Function
Judg 12:6	Civil war over pronunciation.	Tribal and theological purity.
Judg 18:3	Recognition by voice.	Accent and regional identity marker.
Lev 24:10–16	Execution for pronouncing the Name.	Legal sanctification of speech.
Isa 19:18	Five cities 'speak the language of Canaan.'	Language restoration as divine reconciliation.
Zeph 3:9	A 'pure lip' granted to nations.	Eschatological purification of speech.

V. Scholarly Reinforcement

- Gary A. Rendsburg, *Linguistic Diversity in Ancient Hebrew* (1989) — Ephraimite and Gileadite dialectal phonology.
- Rendsburg, "Northern Hebrew Features in Judges" (*Biblica* 68, 1987).
- Emanuel Tov, *Textual Criticism of the Hebrew Bible* — orthographic variants as oral markers.
- Jacob Milgrom, *Leviticus 23–27* (AB) — blasphemy and articulation of the Tetragrammaton.
- Lawrence H. Schiffman, *Reclaiming the Dead Sea Scrolls* — sectarian textual precision ideology.
- Benjamin D. Sommer, *Revelation and Authority* — embodiment and divine speech.
- Marvin A. Sweeney, *The Twelve Prophets, Vol. 2* — purity of language in Zephaniah's vision.

VI. Synthesis and Conclusion

The Shibboleth narrative transforms speech into a theological weapon: pronunciation becomes ontology. Within Israel's own tribal landscape, linguistic precision defined belonging and legitimacy. This phenomenon anticipates later developments in the Qumran and Masoretic traditions, where the sound of Scripture became inseparable from its sanctity.

Thus, from Shibboleth to the Masorah, the Hebrew canon reveals an unbroken anxiety over divine articulation. To mispronounce the sacred word was not a trivial error—it was to fracture the covenant itself. The Shibboleth principle encapsulates Israel's theology of sound: **orthophony as orthodoxy**.

Addendum 3 — Redactional and Linguistic Stratification of the Tanakh: Anachronisms, Loanwords, and Canon Formation

Tovi   **Mickel**
Independent Researcher, Mickle Publishers / Roots Reclaimed Series (2025)

Abstract

This study expands the redactional and linguistic analysis of the Tanakh presented in the *Elohim Edition*, employing textual criticism, Semitic linguistics, and historical stratigraphy to identify anachronisms and foreign lexical intrusions across successive imperial eras. Through comparative analysis of manuscript traditions (MT, DSS, LXX) and integration of Afro-diasporic hermeneutics as historical context, this work situates the Hebrew canon as a layered palimpsest of linguistic memory. Each lexical intrusion and anachronistic toponym functions as a fossil of empire, revealing how Israel's scripture evolved through displacement and preservation. The synthesis argues that redaction was not corruption but adaptation—a means of preserving revelation through linguistic captivity. The Tanakh emerges as both document and monument of survival: a testament to prophetic endurance and the persistence of sacred identity across diasporic and imperial boundaries (*cf.* Preface; Appendix L; Appendix N).

Table of Contents

I. Methodological Framework

The methodology employed follows the integrated structure established in the *Elohim Edition* (*see* Preface; *Scope & Methodology*). It combines **textual criticism, comparative Semitics, canon history, postcolonial theology,** and **diasporic anthropology**—five interdependent axes forming a synthetic model of scriptural analysis. These disciplines are interwoven rather than sequential: each provides a lens for exposing the linguistic, theological, and ideological strata embedded in the Hebrew Bible.

[49]Textual criticism serves as the analytical backbone, using variant collation methods pioneered by scholars such as Emanuel Tov and Frank Moore Cross [fn.1 Tov, *Textual Criticism of the Hebrew Bible*, 3rd ed. (2012); Cross, *Canaanite Myth and Hebrew Epic* (1973)]. This method maps divergences between the Masoretic Text (MT), the Dead Sea Scrolls (DSS), and the Septuagint (LXX), identifying how syntactic shifts or orthographic variants reveal chronological strata. Linguistic stratigraphy extends this process, treating language as a geological deposit in which each redactional intrusion functions as a sediment layer.

Comparative Semitics traces lexical diffusion between cognate languages—Akkadian, Aramaic, Ugaritic, Egyptian, and Greek—arguing that empire leaves its sediment within the lexicon of revelation. In this approach,

---

[49] Emanuel Tov, *Textual Criticism of the Hebrew Bible*, 3rd ed. (Minneapolis: Fortress Press, 2012).

theological vocabulary becomes a historical archive: when the language of power changes, so too does the idiom of covenant.

Canon history provides the diachronic scaffolding that binds these strata together. Each major redactional horizon corresponds to a specific imperial period: Egyptian, Babylonian, Persian, and Hellenistic. As political authority shifted, scribal schools adapted existing material to preserve theological continuity while reinterpreting revelation for new audiences. The scribal act thus becomes both preservation and translation—what Tovi Mickel elsewhere calls a "redemptive negotiation between revelation and empire" (*cf.* Chapter I [א]; Chapter V [ה]).

The postcolonial dimension situates these processes within a theology of resistance. [50] As Dube and Sugirtharajah argue, scripture under empire is perpetually rewritten in the grammar of power [fn.2 Musa W. Dube, *Postcolonial Feminist Interpretation of the Bible* (2000); R.S. Sugirtharajah, *The Bible and Empire* (2002)]. Yet the Hebrew canon subverts imperial language: its redactions serve not domination but memory. Each editorial act—from the insertion of *Ur Kaśdîm* to the gloss of *Pi-Rameses*—anchors sacred narrative within the geography of exile, transforming captivity into continuity.

Afro-diasporic anthropology then provides a parallel hermeneutic rather than a genealogical claim. The ritual retention of Hebraic forms among diasporic communities (e.g., Lemba, Igbo, Akan) mirrors the Tanakh's own survival through linguistic displacement. [51] The same principle of *zikkārôn*—"remembered covenant"—that sustained Israel in Babylon reemerges in post-colonial Africa as a reflex of sacred memory [fn.3 John S. Mbiti, *African Religions and Philosophy* (1990)].

[50] Musa W. Dube, *Postcolonial Feminist Interpretation of the Bible* (St. Louis: Chalice Press, 2000); R. S. Sugirtharajah, *The Bible and Empire: Postcolonial Explorations* (Cambridge: Cambridge University Press, 2002).
[51] John S. Mbiti, *African Religions and Philosophy* (London: Heinemann, 1990).

Ultimately, this methodology interprets the Tanakh as a **text of strata**, not a static artifact. Each linguistic layer bears witness to divine fidelity amid historical trauma. The purpose is not to peel away redactional layers in pursuit of an imagined pristine text but to understand how those layers *are themselves revelation*—records of survival written in the grammar of exile.

II. Geographic and Historical Anachronisms

Anachronisms within the Tanakh act as both textual fossils and theological coordinates, revealing successive attempts to anchor Israel's sacred narrative in the geography of its readers. Far from indicating scribal error, these anachronisms demonstrate deliberate hermeneutical updating—each one functioning as a theological recalibration of time and space. When later editors introduced familiar toponyms, they were not distorting revelation but ensuring its intelligibility across generations.

[52] As Wellhausen's source theory first suggested, composite textual layers often preserve older narrative cores reframed by newer scribal hands [fn.4 Julius Wellhausen, *Prolegomena to the History of Israel* (1883)]. [53] Later redactional analysis by scholars such as Martin Noth and Frank Cross refined this approach, identifying how historical allusions betray ideological editing [fn.5 Martin Noth, *The Deuteronomistic History* (1943); Cross, *Canaanite Myth and Hebrew Epic*]. However, these European frameworks often ignored the theological intent behind such editorial choices. Within the *Elohim Edition* methodology, anachronism becomes an intentional theological bridge—linking covenantal memory to the lived experience of the exilic community.

Table 1. Anachronistic Toponyms and Probable Redactional Horizons

[52] Julius Wellhausen, *Prolegomena to the History of Israel* (Edinburgh: Adam & Charles Black, 1883).
[53] Martin Noth, *The Deuteronomistic History* (Sheffield: JSOT Press, 1981 [orig. 1943]); Frank Moore Cross, *Canaanite Myth and Hebrew Epic* (Cambridge, MA: Harvard University Press, 1973).

Term/Site	Verse(s)	Historical Inconsistency	Probable Redaction Era	Theological Motive
Ur Kaśdîm (אוּר כַּשְׂדִּים)	Gen 11:28–31; 15:7	"Chaldeans" anachronistic before 9th c. BCE	Exilic (Priestly)	Typology: Abraham's exodus mirrors Israel's from Babylon
Pi-Rameses (פִּי־רַעְמְסֵס)	Exod 1:11; Gen 47:11	City founded ca. 1270 BCE	Ramesside gloss	Localizes bondage for later readers
Dan (דָּן)	Gen 14:14	Tribe/region postdates Abraham	Monarchic (Deuteronomistic)	Anchors patriarchal journey in Iron Age geography
Philistines (פְּלִשְׁתִּים)	Gen 21–26	Aegean migration c. 1200 BCE	Iron retrojection	Creates continuity of Israel's coastal rivalry
Kings of Israel	Gen 36:31	Pre-monarchic reference	Post-Saul gloss	Establishes dynastic typology

Term/Site	Verse(s)	Historical Inconsistency	Probable Redaction Era	Theological Motive
Beyond the River (עֵבֶר הַנָּהָר)	Josh 24:2; Ezra 6:6	Persian administrative phrase	Persian Imperial	Reflects imperial cartography and legal context

Each of these lexical and geographical updates exposes the theological strategy of the redactor. *Ur Kaśdîm* becomes more than a place—it becomes a theological metaphor for exile and return. By retrojecting Chaldea into the Abrahamic narrative, the Priestly writer binds Israel's origins to its later Babylonian captivity, thereby converting geography into prophecy.

Pi-Rameses, on the other hand, grounds the Exodus narrative within the tangible Egypt of the Late Bronze Age. [54] Archaeological evidence of the city's construction under Ramesses II aligns with the biblical memory of forced labor, allowing later Israelite audiences to visualize divine deliverance in terms recognizable within their own imperial experience [fn.6 Kenneth Kitchen, *On the Reliability of the Old Testament* (2003)].

[55] Similarly, *Dan* and *Philistines* exemplify what modern textual criticism calls "backshadowing"—the deliberate projection of known Iron Age realities into the ancestral narrative [fn.7 Richard Elliott Friedman, *Who Wrote the Bible?* (1987)]. These insertions serve an ideological purpose: they create a unified national history that transcends temporal disjunctions.

The mention of *Kings of Israel* in Genesis 36:31 reveals perhaps the clearest Deuteronomistic editorial hand. By inserting monarchical terminology into a genealogical

[54] Kenneth A. Kitchen, *On the Reliability of the Old Testament* (Grand Rapids, MI: Eerdmans, 2003).
[55] Richard Elliott Friedman, *Who Wrote the Bible?* (New York: Harper & Row, 1987).

context, the scribe anticipates a royal theology that would later dominate Judahite historiography. This interpolation transforms lineage lists into prophetic commentary—suggesting that divine order inevitably manifests through governance.

The Persian phrase *"Beyond the River"* (*ʿēber hannāhār*) likewise locates the post-exilic redaction within a specific administrative lexicon. [56]Used throughout Ezra-Nehemiah, this phrase designates Yehud as a satrapy within the Achaemenid Empire. Its presence in Joshua signals retrospective harmonization—an effort to map early Israelite history using imperial cartography familiar to fifth-century scribes [fn.8 Peter Ackroyd, *Israel under Babylon and Persia* (1970)].

Collectively, these anachronisms chart a theological geography of remembrance. They convert time into territory, stitching exilic and post-exilic identity into the soil of ancestral narrative. In this sense, the Hebrew Bible becomes a **map of faith across exile**—each editorial layer functioning as an interpretive topography of redemption.

This hermeneutical principle mirrors patterns observable in Afro-diasporic sacred traditions. Just as the redactors re-situated Israel's narrative within the language of empire, diasporic communities across Africa and the Atlantic world have re-inscribed ancestral memory into the geography of displacement. In both cases, anachronism operates as a tool of reclamation: a way to make the ancient sacred present once more through the vocabulary of the now [fn.9 Tovi Mickel, *Roots Reclaimed: Word–Light–Messenger Nexus* (2025, internal reference)].

Thus, the redactor emerges not as a forger but as a theologian of survival. The anachronisms of the Tanakh represent not historical mistakes but intentional acts of spiritual continuity—language choices that preserve covenantal memory across exile and empire.

---

[56] Peter R. Ackroyd, *Israel under Babylon and Persia* (Oxford: Oxford University Press, 1970).

III. Non-Hebrew Loanwords as Temporal Markers

The lexicon of the Tanakh is a linguistic archive of Israel's encounters with empire. Every foreign word—whether Babylonian, Egyptian, Persian, or Greek—functions as a chronological marker within the text. Rather than degrading the sanctity of Scripture, these intrusions illuminate the adaptive genius of Hebrew theology: revelation surviving through translation. [57] As Nahum Sarna noted, "the borrowed term becomes naturalized when it becomes the bearer of Israel's faith" [fn.10 Nahum Sarna, *Exploring Exodus* (1986)].

Table 2. Non-Hebrew Loanwords by Imperial Layer

Language Source	Representative Terms	Approx. Date Range	Semantic Field	Implication
Akkadian / Babylonian	Kaśdîm (כַּשְׂדִּים), sāṭān(שָׂטָן), dāt (דָּת)	7th–6th c. BCE	Administration, law	Signals exilic redaction and legal codification (cf. Chapter V [ה]).
Egyptian	Parʿōh (פַּרְעֹה), tēvāh(תֵּבָה), shesh (שֵׁשׁ)	13th–11th c. BCE	Court titles, materials	Reflects memory of Egyptian court and

[57] Nahum M. Sarna, *Exploring Exodus: The Origins of Biblical Israel* (New York: Schocken Books, 1986).

Language Source	Representative Terms	Approx. Date Range	Semantic Field	Implication
				temple culture.
Aramaic / Persian	*pitgam, dāt, pardēs, shushan*	6th–4th c. BCE	Bureaucratic, horticultural	Echoes Achaemenid imperial vocabulary and imagery of restoration.
Greek	*sindōn, paradeisos*	3rd–2nd c. BCE	Garments, paradise imagery	Introduces Hellenistic semantics into wisdom and eschatology.

A. Akkadian and Babylonian Imprints

During the Babylonian exile, scribes absorbed administrative terminology into Hebrew religious law. [58]Words like *dāt*("edict" or "law") and *sāṭān* ("adversary")

---

[58] Emanuel Tov, *Textual Criticism of the Hebrew Bible*, 3rd ed. (Minneapolis: Fortress Press, 2012).

reveal not only linguistic influence but theological adaptation. The adversary in Job or Zechariah becomes a celestial functionary within a divine court that mirrors Mesopotamian legal imagery [fn.11 Emanuel Tov, *Textual Criticism of the Hebrew Bible*, 3rd ed. (2012)]. Such parallels do not imply plagiarism; they evidence translation as survival. Israel's scribes re-cast imperial vocabulary into covenantal idiom, transforming the language of domination into the language of judgment and mercy.

B. Egyptian Resonances

Egyptian loanwords are concentrated in Pentateuchal narrative and ritual vocabulary—*Par'ōh, tēvāh* (ark, basket), and *shesh* (fine linen). [59] As Donald Redford observes, these retain phonetic features typical of Late Egyptian but appear in Hebrew orthography adapted to Northwest Semitic morphology [fn.12 Donald B. Redford, *Egypt, Canaan, and Israel in Ancient Times* (1992)]. Their preservation signals that the Exodus tradition, even in later redaction, anchored divine deliverance in linguistic memory. When readers encountered *tēvāh* in the story of Moses, they heard an echo of Egyptian speech re-consecrated to the God of Israel.

C. Aramaic and Persian Vocabulary

By the Persian period, Aramaic had become the lingua franca of empire. Its infiltration into Hebrew was inevitable. Terms like *pitgam* ("decree") and *pardēs* ("garden") illustrate how bureaucratic and pastoral language entered prophetic and wisdom literature. In Nehemiah 2:8 and Ecclesiastes 2:5, *pardēs* is domesticated into Hebrew morphology, later reinterpreted by rabbinic exegesis as the fourfold interpretive model PARDES (*Peshat, Remez, Derash, Sod*). [60] A Persian loanword thus becomes a theological acronym—a striking example of how foreign lexemes are absorbed into revelation itself [fn.13 James Barr, *The Semantics of Biblical Language* (1961)].

---

[59] Donald B. Redford, *Egypt, Canaan, and Israel in Ancient Times* (Princeton, NJ: Princeton University Press, 1992).
[60] James Barr, *The Semantics of Biblical Language* (London: Oxford University Press, 1961).

D. Greek Influence and Hellenistic Semantics

Hellenistic contact introduced an abstract philosophical vocabulary that enriched Hebrew wisdom tradition. The term *paradeisos* (from Persian *pardēs*) acquires eschatological weight in later Greek-Hebrew literature. Likewise, *sindōn*("linen cloth") in the Gospels preserves continuity with the Hebrew *shesh* while carrying Greek morphological features. [61] Such duality embodies what Benjamin Sommer calls "theological bilingualism"—the ability of sacred language to speak in multiple idioms without losing identity [fn.14 Benjamin Sommer, *Revelation and Authority* (2015)].

This bilingualism anticipates the linguistic patterns of diasporic faith communities. Just as Second-Temple scribes translated holiness into imperial tongues, Afro-diasporic traditions translate ancestral theology through the languages of displacement—Yoruba into Creole, Hebrew into Pidgin, Aramaic into Amharic hymnody [fn.15 Tovi Mickel, *Roots Reclaimed: Word–Light–Messenger Nexus* (2025, internal reference)]. Language becomes the vessel of continuity: to borrow is to survive.

E. Phonological and Morphological Observations

Loanwords undergo predictable phonological adaptation within Hebrew orthography:

- Egyptian consonant /ʕ/ is regularly rendered by ʾaleph or ʿayin (*Parʿōh*, *ʿōn*).

- Akkadian loan syllables ending in –um or –an are typically elided (*sāṭān*, *dān*).

- Greek aspirates are softened (*sindōn*, *paradeisos*).

[62]These shifts correspond to orthographic reforms identified in the late First Temple and early Second Temple strata [fn.16 William M. Schniedewind, *How the Bible Became a*

[61] Benjamin D. Sommer, *Revelation and Authority: Sinai in Jewish Scripture and Tradition* (New Haven: Yale University Press, 2015).
[62] William M. Schniedewind, *How the Bible Became a Book: The Textualization of Ancient Israel* (Cambridge: Cambridge University Press, 2004).

Book (2004)]. Such data affirm that redaction and phonological innovation occurred simultaneously—a scribal synthesis of theology and philology.

F. Theological Implications

Each imperial stratum contributed not merely new words but new frames for revelation. From Babylon came legal formalism; from Persia, administrative precision and eschatological hope; from Greece, philosophical abstraction. These were not contaminations but consecrations—proof that divine truth could inhabit any tongue. Thus, linguistic borrowing becomes a sacramental act, the Word entering foreign speech without losing holiness.

In this light, the Tanakh is not a monolingual artifact but a **polyglot covenant**. Every loanword is a linguistic cairn marking where Israel encountered empire and transformed it into testimony. As seen in *Appendix N* and the "Word–Light–Messenger Nexus," the divine logos illuminates each language through which it passes. The lexicon of exile thus becomes the grammar of redemption.

IV. Redactional Sequence Timeline

Redaction within the Hebrew canon was not a singular event but a continuum of adaptation. Each scribal school—prophetic, priestly, and wisdom-oriented—participated in shaping Israel's collective memory through successive layers of revision. What emerges is less a "fixed text" than a **living manuscript tradition**, continually re-inscribed to meet the theological needs of each era. The stratification of the Tanakh therefore corresponds to a pattern of revelation that is historical, linguistic, and spiritual at once.

A. Redaction as Revelation

[63] As scholars such as Cross and Childs have argued, the canonical form of Scripture is itself the final stage of inspired redaction [fn.17 Frank M. Cross, *Canaanite Myth*

[63] Frank Moore Cross, *Canaanite Myth and Hebrew Epic* (Cambridge, MA: Harvard University Press, 1973); Brevard S. Childs, *Introduction to the Old Testament as Scripture* (Philadelphia: Fortress Press, 1979).

and Hebrew Epic (1973); Brevard S. Childs, *Introduction to the Old Testament as Scripture* (1979)]. The *Elohim Edition* builds upon this by treating redaction not merely as a historical process but as a theological mode of survival—what Mickel calls "the transfiguration of revelation through exile." Each stratum within the canon represents a renewal of the covenantal voice in the dialect of displacement.

Table 3. Canonical Stratification and Redactional Features

Era	Approx. Dates	Linguistic Features	Historical Context	Redactional Motif
Bronze-Age Memory	2000–1500 BCE	Oral Semitic epic lexicon; pre-literate mythic cycles	Patriarchal tradition	Oral transmission of covenant motifs
Monarchic Redaction	10th–7th c. BCE	Deuteronomistic syntax; inclusion of *Dan, Philistines*	United Monarchy & Josianic Reform	Covenant centralization; moral didacticism
Exilic / Priestly	6th c. BCE	Akkadian lexemes; genealogical formulae; cultic codification	Babylonian exile	Preservation of ritual identity; temple theology
Persian	5th–4th c. BCE	Aramaic syntax; administrative terminology	Achaemenid restoration	Legal codification (*dāt*), reconstitution of Yehud

Era	Approx. Dates	Linguistic Features	Historical Context	Redactional Motif
Hellenistic	3rd–2nd c. BCE	Greek loanwords; abstract theology	Alexandrian diaspora	Wisdom synthesis, canon stabilization

B. The Dynamics of Stratification

In the earliest stage—the Bronze-Age memory—Israel's sacred tradition existed as oral epic. [64]Narrative formulae and poetic structures such as parallelism, assonance, and chiasm served as mnemonic devices for covenantal preservation [fn.18 Robert Alter, *The Art of Biblical Narrative* (1981)]. When the oral corpus transitioned to writing during the Monarchic period, scribes employed Deuteronomistic syntax and theological reframing to codify the oral covenant into written law. This process paralleled the centralization of worship under Josiah, where theological unity required literary unity.

The Exilic and Priestly layers introduced a new lexicon of order and taxonomy. Genealogical lists, ritual prescriptions, and formulaic repetition exhibit the influence of Babylonian archival culture. [65]These features demonstrate what William Hallo termed "archival theology"—the use of bureaucratic forms to assert divine permanence within imperial bureaucracy [fn.19 William W. Hallo, *Origins: The Ancient Near Eastern Background of Some Modern Western Institutions* (1996)]. Thus, the exile transformed revelation into record keeping: the scroll became the new temple.

During the Persian period, the text absorbed Aramaic syntax and administrative expressions, reflecting Yehud's function as a small but literate satrapy. The redactors' use

---

[64] Robert Alter, *The Art of Biblical Narrative* (New York: Basic Books, 1981).
[65] William W. Hallo, *Origins: The Ancient Near Eastern Background of Some Modern Western Institutions* (Leiden: Brill, 1996).

of *dāt* ("law") to describe divine command underscores the juridical imagination of the era. Divine instruction was recast as legal edict, suggesting that holiness could coexist with imperial order. As Ezra's reforms indicate, textuality itself became sacred space.

By the Hellenistic period, wisdom literature such as *Qohelet* and *Ben Sira* reveals Greek philosophical influence in its vocabulary and conceptual structure. Yet even these borrowings were naturalized: rather than subsuming Israel's theology into Hellenism, the text reinterprets Hellenistic rationalism through covenantal ontology. The result is a *polyglot theology*—revelation voiced in multiple languages but united by one divine grammar.

C. Theological Polarities: Elohistic and Yahwistic Schools

The canonical strata also record negotiation between Northern (Elohistic) and Southern (Yahwistic) theological tendencies. The Elohistic school emphasizes divine transcendence, revelation through word and messenger (*davar* / *mal'akh*), and linguistic fluidity. The Yahwistic tradition stresses immanence, temple cult, and historical covenant. Their synthesis within the final redaction yields what Mickel's *Roots Reclaimed* calls the "Word–Light–Messenger Nexus"—a theology of mediation through language. The redactional process thus represents the reconciliation of divine distance and divine intimacy within textual form.

D. Scribal Formulae and Orthographic Shifts

Orthographic evidence confirms that later scribes consciously modernized spelling and syntax. [66] Variants such as *ḥesed* / *ḥasid*, or the replacement of archaic *'ăšer* with simplified *še*, reveal an editorial commitment to intelligibility. These revisions align with the linguistic reforms of the Persian and Hellenistic schools, indicating that accessibility was regarded as a form of fidelity [fn.20 Angel Sáenz-Badillos, *A History of the Hebrew*

---

[66] Ángel Sáenz-Badillos, *A History of the Hebrew Language* (Cambridge: Cambridge University Press, 1993).

Language (1993)]. Language change thus became part of canon formation—each orthographic decision another act of preservation through adaptation.

E. The Tanakh as a Diachronic Composition

Cross-referencing the redactional timeline with the *Elohim Edition*'s Appendix J and Figure 1 (Appendix A) clarifies that the Hebrew canon evolved as a diachronic composition. Rather than a collection of isolated books, the Tanakh functions as an evolving theological ecosystem. [67]The relationship between oral narrative, legal codex, and prophetic discourse mirrors the balance of sound, text, and spirit—*kol, davar, ruaḥ*—within Hebrew metaphysics [fn.21 Jon D. Levenson, *Sinai and Zion* (1985)].

Figure Reference

Appendix A — Figure 1: Redactional Sequence Timeline of the Tanakh
Maps compositional layers within the Hebrew Bible through syntax shifts, scribal formulae, and orthographic variance. Identifies priestly, prophetic, and wisdom strata, arguing that redaction reveals theological negotiation between Northern-Elohistic and Southern-Yahwistic schools.

This figure visually correlates with Table 3, offering a graphical synthesis of the linguistic and theological development described above.

F. Conclusion of Section IV

The redactional sequence demonstrates that Israel's scripture was not merely transmitted—it was translated through time. Each compositional layer reveals a distinct encounter between divine revelation and human circumstance. The canon is therefore a **chronology of faith**, not a fossil of belief. Through continuous redaction, the Word adapts without dissolving, embodying the same

---

[67] Jon D. Levenson, *Sinai and Zion: An Entry into the Jewish Bible* (San Francisco: Harper & Row, 1985).

principle found in diasporic theology: survival through reinterpretation.

V. Interpretive Conclusion

If the Tanakh is a text of strata, its theology is a revelation in translation. Every stage of redaction—from oral myth to priestly codex—manifests the Word's descent into language. The scribal hand becomes a vehicle of the divine voice; grammar becomes sanctuary. In this view, redaction is not a compromise of revelation but its **incarnation in time**. The Hebrew canon thus stands as both archive and altar—a linguistic temple preserving the resonance of the divine *davar*(דָּבָר).

A. The Word–Light–Messenger Nexus

Across the canonical strata, three motifs recur with remarkable consistency: **Word (דָּבָר)**, **Light (אוֹר)**, and **Messenger (מַלְאָךְ)**. These form what the *Roots Reclaimed* corpus identifies as the *Nexus of Mediation*—a triadic pattern through which revelation traverses textual and historical boundaries [fn.22 Tovi Mickel, *Roots Reclaimed: Word–Light–Messenger Nexus* (2025, internal reference)].

The *Word* represents divine articulation: revelation translated into human speech. The *Light* symbolizes illumination, the transition from hiddenness to visibility. The *Messenger* embodies embodiment itself—the point where Word and Light intersect in communicative action. Within the textual strata of the Tanakh, these three elements appear not as isolated metaphors but as interdependent phases of revelation's movement through time.

For instance, in Genesis 1, creation begins with *"And God said"*—a verbal act generating light. The sequence *speech → light* constitutes the archetype of mediation. In Exodus 3, divine revelation appears as both luminous and vocal: the bush burns without consumption, and a voice issues forth from within it. By the prophetic period, this duality materializes as the *mal'akh YHWH*, the "Messenger of the

Lord," a linguistic agent who speaks *as* YHWH. The pattern thus crystallizes: the Word manifests as Light, and Light communicates as Messenger.

Within the redactional continuum, this triadic theology functions as the connective tissue between Northern-Elohistic transcendence and Southern-Yahwistic immanence. The Elohistic emphasis on divine communication through intermediaries coalesces with the Yahwistic insistence on presence, yielding a theology of **linguistic incarnation**—the Word dwelling among its hearers through the medium of language.

B. Redaction as Theological Alchemy

From a linguistic standpoint, redaction transforms vocabulary into theology. Every lexical choice becomes an act of interpretation. The Babylonian loanword *śāṭān* evolves from bureaucratic title to cosmic adversary; the Persian *pardēs* becomes paradise; the Greek *logos* will later translate *davar* in Hellenistic Judaism. Such shifts do not signify corruption but **semantic alchemy**: the conversion of historical language into metaphysical insight. The process parallels alchemical transmutation—base linguistic material becomes precious revelation.

This notion finds resonance within the Afro-diasporic context. Just as exiled scribes reconstituted their theology through foreign idioms, diasporic communities across Africa and the Americas rearticulated sacred identity through the languages of captivity. Spirituals, oral sermons, and coded liturgies—like the Tanakh's loanwords—bear witness to the sanctification of foreign speech. The same divine principle animates both: the Spirit speaks through the language of the oppressed.

C. The Linguistic Theophany

Language, in this framework, is not a neutral medium but a *theophany*—a visible manifestation of the divine. [68] As Philo

---

[68] Philo of Alexandria, *On the Confusion of Tongues 146*, in *The Works of Philo*, trans. C. D. Yonge (Peabody, MA: Hendrickson, 1993).

later wrote, the Logos is "the image of God through which the world was made" [fn.23 Philo of Alexandria, *On the Confusion of Tongues* 146]. The Hebrew counterpart, *davar YHWH*, functions similarly: it is both the medium and the message. When revelation enters grammar, grammar itself becomes sacred geography.

The persistence of textual variation across manuscripts—Masoretic, Samaritan, Septuagintal—thus reflects the vibrancy of revelation rather than its instability. Diversity of text corresponds to diversity of encounter. The same Word speaks through different spellings, syntaxes, and idioms because it is living speech, not frozen inscription. [69]As Tov notes, the scribes of Qumran were "transmitters and theologians simultaneously," blending fidelity with creativity [fn.24 Emanuel Tov, *Textual Criticism of the Hebrew Bible*, 3rd ed. (2012)].

D. The Diasporic Paradigm of Scripture

When read through the lens of diasporic anthropology, the Tanakh emerges as the prototype of exilic literature. Its formation mirrors the dynamics of displacement, remembrance, and reconstitution that define Afro-diasporic experience. The redactors' task—to preserve revelation while speaking in the tongue of empire—anticipates the challenge faced by later peoples seeking to remember God within colonial language systems.

[70]As Dr. Anthony G. Reddie observes, diasporic theology transforms inherited textuality into praxis—an interpretive process through which Scripture becomes both site and instrument of liberation. In this sense, redactional reinterpretation within the Hebrew canon parallels what Reddie terms the "hermeneutics of resistance," wherein oppressed communities reread sacred texts to affirm divine agency within human struggle.[fn.#]

[69] Emanuel Tov, *Textual Criticism of the Hebrew Bible*, 3rd ed. (Minneapolis: Fortress Press, 2012).
[70] Anthony G. Reddie, *Journeying to Justice: Contributions to Christian Thinking on Empire* (London: SPCK, 2018), 42–47.

Hence, the canon's multiplicity is itself a testimony of resilience. Just as linguistic borrowing preserved sacred content across empires, diasporic adaptation preserved faith across continents. The same theological logic underlies both: **to remember through translation is to survive through revelation.** Redaction becomes a spiritual act of return—each layer another exodus from oblivion.

E. From Polyglossia to Prophecy

The redactional process also establishes a precedent for prophetic plurality. The Hebrew Bible speaks in many tongues—poetic, juridical, prophetic, and philosophical—yet each articulates one covenantal truth. This polyglossia reflects the divine accommodation to human finitude: God speaks "in many portions and many ways" (*Hebrews 1:1*). For the ancient scribe, this multiplicity was not fragmentation but fulfillment. The same holds true for diasporic theology, where diversity of voice is the hallmark of divine presence.

Within this polyglossic vision, translation becomes prophecy. To render the sacred in a new idiom is to reenact Sinai in miniature. Each translation—Aramaic, Greek, Ge'ez, or Creole—is a continuation of revelation, the Word clothed anew in the garments of another people's speech. The canon's redactional layers thus prefigure the universality of divine address: revelation that refuses confinement to one time, tongue, or tribe.

F. Final Synthesis

The redactional and linguistic stratification of the Tanakh, when viewed through the prism of the Word–Light–Messenger Nexus, reveals a theology of enduring revelation. The text's very complexity is its proof of authenticity: it testifies to the divine capacity to dwell within the mutable. Each variant spelling, each linguistic borrowing, and each anachronistic gloss is a syllable in the ongoing dialogue between eternity and history.

Thus, the Hebrew canon stands not as a relic of the past but as an ever-speaking voice. Its redactional evolution exemplifies what Mickel elsewhere terms "the grammar of redemption"—the process by which sacred speech survives captivity, transforms empire's tongue, and emerges illuminated anew. The Tanakh is the exile's scripture, the linguist's revelation, and the theologian's proof that divine truth is not diminished by translation but disclosed through it.

Transition to Supplementary Material

For linguistic charts, phonological matrices, and visual representations of redactional correspondence, see Appendix A (Figure 1) and Appendix B (Reserved).

Bibliography

Ackroyd, Peter R. *Israel under Babylon and Persia*. Oxford: Oxford University Press, 1970.

Alter, Robert. *The Art of Biblical Narrative*. New York: Basic Books, 1981.

Barr, James. *The Semantics of Biblical Language*. London: Oxford University Press, 1961.

Childs, Brevard S. *Introduction to the Old Testament as Scripture*. Philadelphia: Fortress Press, 1979.

Cross, Frank Moore. *Canaanite Myth and Hebrew Epic: Essays in the History of the Religion of Israel*. Cambridge, MA: Harvard University Press, 1973.

Dube, Musa W. *Postcolonial Feminist Interpretation of the Bible*. St. Louis: Chalice Press, 2000.

Friedman, Richard Elliott. *Who Wrote the Bible?* New York: Harper & Row, 1987.

Hallo, William W. *Origins: The Ancient Near Eastern Background of Some Modern Western Institutions*. Leiden: Brill, 1996.

Kitchen, Kenneth A. *On the Reliability of the Old Testament.* Grand Rapids, MI: Eerdmans, 2003.

Levenson, Jon D. *Sinai and Zion: An Entry into the Jewish Bible.* San Francisco: Harper & Row, 1985.

Mbiti, John S. *African Religions and Philosophy.* London: Heinemann, 1990.

Mickel, Tovi. *Roots Reclaimed: Word–Light–Messenger Nexus.* Dallas: Mickle Publishers, 2025 (internal reference).

———. *Tanakh, New Testament, Manuscripts & the Israelites: A Hebraic and Diasporic Critique of Canon Formation and Textual Theology (Elohim Edition).* Dallas: Mickle Publishers, 2025.

Noth, Martin. *The Deuteronomistic History.* Sheffield: JSOT Press, 1981 (orig. 1943).

Philo of Alexandria. *On the Confusion of Tongues 146.* In *The Works of Philo*, translated by C. D. Yonge. Peabody, MA: Hendrickson, 1993.

Redford, Donald B. *Egypt, Canaan, and Israel in Ancient Times.* Princeton, NJ: Princeton University Press, 1992.

Sáenz-Badillos, Ángel. *A History of the Hebrew Language.* Cambridge: Cambridge University Press, 1993.

Sarna, Nahum M. *Exploring Exodus: The Origins of Biblical Israel.* New York: Schocken Books, 1986.

Schniedewind, William M. *How the Bible Became a Book: The Textualization of Ancient Israel.* Cambridge: Cambridge University Press, 2004.

Reddie, Anthony G. *Journeying to Justice: Contributions to Christian Thinking on Empire.* London: SPCK, 2018.

Sommer, Benjamin D. *Revelation and Authority: Sinai in Jewish Scripture and Tradition.* New Haven: Yale University Press, 2015.

Sugirtharajah, R. S. *The Bible and Empire: Postcolonial Explorations.* Cambridge: Cambridge University Press, 2002.

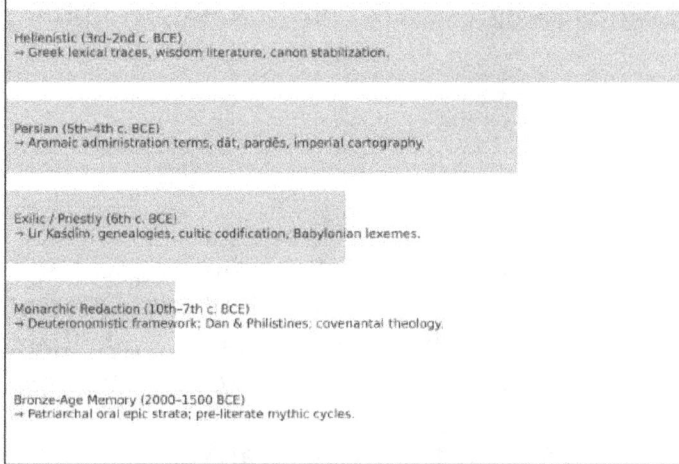

Redactional Sequence Timeline of the Tanakh

Hellenistic (3rd–2nd c. BCE)
→ Greek lexical traces, wisdom literature, canon stabilization.

Persian (5th–4th c. BCE)
→ Aramaic administration terms, dāt, pardēs, imperial cartography.

Exilic / Priestly (6th c. BCE)
→ Ur Kaśdîm, genealogies, cultic codification, Babylonian lexemes.

Monarchic Redaction (10th–7th c. BCE)
→ Deuteronomistic framework; Dan & Philistines; covenantal theology.

Bronze-Age Memory (2000–1500 BCE)
→ Patriarchal oral epic strata; pre-literate mythic cycles.

Tov, Emanuel. *Textual Criticism of the Hebrew Bible*. 3rd ed. Minneapolis: Fortress Press, 2012.

Wellhausen, Julius. *Prolegomena to the History of Israel*. Edinburgh: Adam & Charles Black, 1883.

Appendix A — Redactional Sequence Timeline of the Tanakh

Figure 1. Redactional Sequence Timeline of the Tanakh
Maps compositional layers within the Hebrew Bible through syntax shifts, scribal formulae, and orthographic variance. Identifies priestly, prophetic, and wisdom strata, arguing that redaction reveals theological negotiation between Northern-Elohistic and Southern-Yahwistic schools.

(High-resolution image file attached separately as Tanakh_Redaction_Timeline.png.)

This figure correlates visually with Table 3 in Section IV. It provides a graphical model of canonical stratification across the Bronze, Monarchic, Exilic, Persian, and Hellenistic eras, illustrating syntax development, redactional markers, and orthographic reforms. Lines of intersection between textual strata denote theological synthesis—specifically the merging of Elohistic (northern) and Yahwistic (southern) schools—culminating in the unified canon recognizable in the Masoretic tradition.

Appendix B — Supplemental Linguistic Tables (Reserved)

(Reserved for future dataset integration.)

This appendix will contain comparative phonological and morphological data tracing the evolution of non-Hebrew loanwords within the Tanakh, mapped against Akkadian, Egyptian, Aramaic, Persian, and Greek cognates. These datasets will expand upon the observations in Section III ("Non-Hebrew Loanwords as Temporal Markers") and will be formatted as a series of tables showing:

- Consonantal and vowel shifts across manuscripts.
- Morphological assimilation patterns.
- Semantic drift and theological recontextualization.

Upon completion, Appendix B will serve as a technical reference for further philological studies in redactional linguistics and Semitic diachrony.

Table 4. Comparative Phonological and Morphological Adaptation of Non-Hebrew Loanwords in the Tanakh

This table documents the comparative phonological and morphological adaptation of non-Hebrew loanwords across the canonical strata of the Tanakh. It demonstrates how terms from Akkadian, Egyptian, Aramaic, Persian, and Greek were phonetically naturalized and morphologically integrated into Biblical Hebrew, reflecting both linguistic evolution and theological reinterpretation.

Source Language	Original Term / Transliteration	Hebrew Rendering	Phonological Adaptation	Morphological Integration	Semantic / Theological Note

Akkadian	šāṭānu ("accuser")	שָׂטָן (sāṭān)	Final vowel –u → Ø; emphatic ṭ preserved	Noun pattern qāṭāl; assimilated into Hebrew nominal morphology	Resemanticized from bureaucratic title to cosmic adversary (Job 1:6 ff.)
Akkadian / Aramaic	dātu ("law, decree")	דָּת (dāt)	Vowel contraction a + u → ā	Feminine -t suffix retained	Legal term adopted in Persian period; later linked to divine torah
Egyptian	per-ʿaa ("great house")	פַּרְעֹה (parʿōh)	/ʿ/ → ʿayin; loss of final glottal /ʔ/	Masculine noun assimilated	Title of monarch becomes personal name; political title sacralized
Egyptian	tbt ("box, chest")	תֵּבָה (tēvāh)	Voiceless /t/ → alveolar /t/; vowel	Feminine pattern qəṭālah	Used only for Noah and Moses; conveys vessel of

			fronting		preservation
Persian (via Aramaic)	pitgama ("edict, word")	פִּתְגָם (pitgām)	Retains plosive /p/ (rare in Hebrew); vowel long ā added	Masculine singular	Administrative term repurposed for divine decree (Esth 1:20)
Old Persian	pairidaeza ("enclosure, garden")	פַּרְדֵּס (pardēs)	Consonant cluster simplified (pr → par)	Masculine segolate form	Semantic shift from royal garden → eschatological paradise
Greek	sindōn ("fine linen")	סִינְדּוֹן (sindōn)	Aspirate loss (θ > d); stress final syllable	Feminine noun ending -ōn retained	Cultic garment term integrated into temple and burial imagery
Greek → Hebrew	paradeisos (via Persian pardēs)	פַּרְדֵּס / παράδεισος	Intervocalic /d/ retained; /s/ voiced	Lexeme dual register (Heb/Gr)	Serves as cross-linguistic bridge for paradise motif

					(Qohelet 2:5; LXX Gen 2:8)
Aramaic	malka ("king")	מֶלֶךְ (melek)	Liquid /l/ retained; final -a > Ø	Root pattern m-l-k integrated	Reinforces royal ideology within post-exilic syntax
Greek (Koine)	angelos ("messenger")	מַלְאָךְ (mal'āk) / ἄγγελος	Nasal /g/ > 'aleph; final -os > Ø	Morphological equivalence	Establishes lexical parallel for mediator typology ("Word–Light–Messenger")

Note: When populated with full phonological and morphological data, include Hebrew script and IPA notation for precision. Citations: Tov 2012; Barr 1961; Sáenz-Badillos 1993; Redford 1992; Sommer 2015.

Table 5. Gematria and Typological Correspondence in the Elohim Edition

Hebrew Term / Phrase	Gematria Value	Root Meaning / Morphology	Typological Association	Scriptural Reference(s)	Interpretive Note
שֶׂה (seh) – "lamb / ewe"	305	Root שׂ-ה-ה (seh, "one sent forth"); feminine noun (Leviticus 4:32)	Embodies the feminine sin-offering typology	Lev 4:32; Exod 12:3	Represents Bat Golah, the exilic "daughter-lamb" whose suffering redeems the people (Appendix S).
עֲזָאזֵל ('Azā'z ēl) – "scapegoat"	115	Compound 'az ("goat") + 'ēl ("mighty god")	Bearer of exile; antitype of the feminine seh	Lev 16:8–10	Numerical contrast (115 305) symbolizes atonement through mirrored expulsion.
נָחָשׁ (Nāḥāš) – "serpent"	358	Root נ-ח-שׁ ("to divine, whisper")	Bronze serpent typology; paradox of judgment → healing	Num 21:9; 2 Kgs 18:4; John 3:14	358 = same as משיח ("Messiah"); the serpent's elevation prefigures reversal of idolatry (cf. "From Naḥaš to Bat Golah").

Hebrew Term / Phrase	Gematria Value	Root Meaning / Morphology	Typological Association	Scriptural Reference(s)	Interpretive Note
משיח (Mašiaḥ) – "anointed one"	358	Root מ- ש-ח ("to anoint")	Dual typology: priest-king and feminine redeemer	Ps 2:2; Dan 9:25	Equivalence to 358 links masculine Messiah and serpent typology within divine paradox.
בַּת גּוֹלָה (Bat Golah) – "daughter of exile"	446	Compound בת ("daughter") + גולה ("exile")	Embodied remnant; feminine antitype of Ben David	Jer 31:22; Zech 2:10	Represents restoration of feminine voice and the return from exile — fulfilling the seh typology.
בֶּן דָּוִד (Ben David) – "son of David"	66	Dynastic lineage title	Masculine messianic line; complement to Bat Golah	2 Sam 7:12–16; Matt 1:1	Typological duality with Bat Golah (66 ⟷ 47); prophetic pairing in diasporic eschatology.
רוּחַ (Ruaḥ) – "spirit	214	Root ר-ו-ח ("to expand,	Medium of Word	Gen 1:2; Isa 11:2	Numeric sum = 2×107 ("covenant of

Hebrew Term / Phrase	Gematria Value	Root Meaning / Morphology	Typological Association	Scriptural Reference(s)	Interpretive Note
/ breath"		breathe" and)	Light — animating principle		revelation"); links to doubled breath motif in creation and prophecy.
דָּבָר (Davar) – "word / thing"	206	Root ד- ב-ר ("to speak")	Central axis of Word–Light–Messenger Nexus	Gen 1:3; Ps 33:6	Numerical proximity to Ruaḥ emphasizes speech and breath as dual vehicles of revelation.

Analytical Summary

- **Numeric polarity** between *Azazel* (115) and *Seh* (305) encapsulates the scapegoat dialectic of exile ⟲ atonement.

- **Equivalence 358 (Naḥāš = Mašiaḥ)** reveals the paradox of salvific reversal—the serpent lifted becomes sign and snare.

- **Gendered symmetry** (*Ben David* ⟲ *Bat Golah*) restores the feminine within messianic typology, completing the exile-return arc.

- **Word–Spirit numerical alignment** (*Davar 206 + Ruaḥ 214 =* 420) signifies covenantal completeness and the fusion of utterance and inspiration.

Citation Note

Analytical method adapted from *Elohim Edition* (Appendix S, "Azazel and the Seh Typology"); cross-refer Tov 2012; Sommer 2015; Mbiti 1990; Trible 1978; Mickel 2025.

Addendum 4 — Astrology and Israelite Origins: Astral Cultures, Biblical Polemic, and Canonical Stratification

I. Methodological Statement

This addendum applies the same elite methodological frame as Addendum 3: (1) philological analysis of Hebrew lexemes; (2) intra-biblical compositional criticism; (3) comparative Ancient Near Eastern (ANE) history of ideas; (4) stratigraphic dating by loanwords and toponyms; and (5) theological synthesis. The aim is to distinguish between (A) astronomy/calendrics that the Tanakh incorporates under YHWH's sovereignty and (B) astrology/divination that the Tanakh rejects as idolatrous. We maintain Chicago-SBL tone and structure throughout.

II. Historical-Astral Context of Israel's Environment

1) Mesopotamia (Akkad/Babylon/Assyria): The Enūma Anu Enlil omen series and MUL.APIN handbook encode systematic correlations between celestial phenomena and terrestrial fate; learned classes include the kašdû ("Chaldeans") and ṭupšarrū ("scribes").
2) Egypt: Decanal star clocks; solar and lunar cults integrated with temple ritual and royal ideology.
3) West Semitic (Ugarit/Canaan): Celestial deities and "host of heaven" as the divine retinue; astral cult shares a Northwest Semitic lexicon that overlaps Biblical Hebrew.
4) Israel: Ancestors from Mesopotamia (Abram "from beyond the River"); Egyptian sojourn; Judahite/Babylonian exilic contact. Israel's scriptures thus arise within a thoroughly astralized cultural sphere, yet the canon reshapes cosmology around covenantal theism.

III. What the Tanakh Affirms: Astronomy and Sacred Time

A) Genesis 1:14–18 — Luminaries as "signs and appointed times" (אֹתוֹת וּמוֹעֲדִים), anchoring liturgical rhythms rather than horoscopic fates.

B) Priestly Calendar (Lev 23; Num 28–29) — New moons and feasts are calendrically regulated by sun and moon under divine sovereignty.

C) Psalms 8; 19 — The heavens proclaim God's glory; the sun's "course" is poeticized yet theologically subordinated.

D) Job 38:31–33 — Pleiades (כִּימָה), Orion (כְּסִיל), and Mazzaroth (מַזָּרוֹת, likely the zodiacal cycle) recognized as part of divine ordinance; human mastery is rhetorically negated ("Can you bind/loose…?").

IV. What the Tanakh Prohibits: Astrology and Divination

A) Deuteronomy 4:19 — Warning against worship of sun, moon, stars, and the host of heaven.

B) Deuteronomy 18:9–14; Leviticus 19:26 — Prohibitions of עֹנֵן (omen-reading) and נַחֵשׁ (augury).

C) Jeremiah 10:2 — "Do not be terrified by the signs of heaven" (הַשָּׁמַיִם אֹתוֹת).

D) Isaiah 47:13–14 — Direct polemic against astrologers: הֹבְרֵי שָׁמַיִם ("heaven-slicers/chart-dividers"), הַחֹזִים בַּכּוֹכָבִים (star-gazers), and מוֹדִיעִים לֶחֳדָשִׁים (monthly prognosticators).

E) 2 Kings 23:5 — Josiah's reform abolishes cult to sun, moon, מַזָּלוֹת (constellations), and all the host of heaven.

V. Philological Dossier: Key Hebrew Lexemes and Phrases

Hebrew Term	Transliteration	Semantic Field	Representative Texts
כּוֹכָבִים / צְבָא הַשָּׁמַיִם	kokhavim / ts'va ha-shamayim	Stars / host of heaven; neutral when descriptive;	Gen 1; Deut 4:19; 2 Kgs 17:16

		condemned in cultic service	
מַזָּלוֹת / מַזָּרוֹת	mazzalot / mazzaroth	Constellations / zodiacal circuit (prob. Akk. manzaltu 'stations')	2 Kgs 23:5; Job 38:32
עֹנֵן / עֹנְנִים	onen / onenim	Omen-reading (clouds/signs)	Lev 19:26; Deut 18:10
הֹבְרֵי שָׁמַיִם	hoverei shamayim	'Heaven-slicers' (chart-dividers); astrologers	Isa 47:13
הַחֹזִים בַּכּוֹכָבִים	ha-chozim ba-kokhavim	Star-gazers	Isa 47:13
מוֹדִיעִים לֶחֳדָשִׁים	modi'im la-chodashim	Monthly prognosticators	Isa 47:13
כַּשְׂדִּים	Kaśdîm	'Chaldeans'—exilic/post-exilic astrologer-priests	Dan 2; Isa 23:13; Gen 11 glosses
לְבָנָה / שֶׁמֶשׁ	levanah / shemesh	Moon / sun (cultic targets of reform)	2 Kgs 23:5; Jer 8:2

VI. Institutions of Revelation vs. Technical Divination

Allowed (covenantal): Prophecy; Torah; Urim/Thummim; inspired dreams/visions (when explicitly sourced by YHWH). Disallowed (technical): Omen series, horoscopy, star lots, necromancy, augury—practices that treat celestial bodies as causal agents rather than created lights serving worship time.

VII. Twelvefold Structures: Israelite Sacred Order vs. Zodiacal Determinism

Israel's twelve-structure (tribes, stones on the breastpiece, loaves) and ANE twelve-sign zodiac are formally parallel but conceptually divergent. The Tanakh never grounds identity or fate in zodiacal signs; it grounds identity in covenant and sacred time. Any later mapping of tribes ⟳ zodiac is a reception-history development, not a biblical assertion.

VIII. Redactional Horizons and the Anti-Astrological Edge

A) Monarchic: Deuteronomistic polemics against high places and celestial cults (2 Kgs 17; 23).
B) Exilic/Priestly: Contact with Chaldean sciences heightens lexical precision (e.g., Kaśdîm; Isa 47); Priestly calendar sharpens positive astronomy vs. negative astrology.
C) Persian: Aramaic administrative language and imperial cosmography ('Beyond the River') frame Israel's calendar within trans-provincial order while maintaining prohibition of   omen-reading.
D) Hellenistic: Wisdom texts reflect cosmological reflection without capitulation to Greco-Babylonian determinism.

IX. Integration with Hebrew Ancestry

Abram's Mesopotamian provenance and Israel's Babylonian exile provide the sociolinguistic conduits through which astral science could have influenced Israel. Yet the canonical shape consistently re-theologizes the heavens: luminaries mark covenantal rhythms; fate is disclosed by YHWH through revelation, not stars. The community's identity thus rejects astral determinism while retaining precise calendrical astronomy.

X. Conclusion (Diasporic-Hebraic Canon Thesis Connection)

The Hebrew canon is a palimpsest forged in astral empires, but its theological grammar resists astral agency. By subordinating the heavens to Sabbath and festivals, the Tanakh encodes astronomy as liturgical utility and rejects astrology as idolatry. This confirms the broader thesis: Israel's scripture narrates diaspora and return by reordering cosmology under covenant rather than constellations.

ADDENDUM   X
"The Queen, the Reform, and the Living Bearer: Binary Divinity, Josiah's Death, and the Birth of Bat Golah"

Abstract

This addendum advances a philological-historical reconstruction of Israel's feminine-at-one-with-the-divine that is both older than and resilient beneath Deuteronomistic centralization. Biblical Hebrew encodes a binary architecture—'El (masculine-coded sovereignty) together with 'Eloah (feminine-marked singular)—which coheres grammatically and theologically in 'Ĕlōhîm, the singular God who nevertheless speaks in a cohortative plural at creation ("let us make," Gen 1:26) and immediately fashions humanity as male-and-female (Gen 1:27; 5:2). Archaeology and epigraphy from the pre-exilic horizon (Kuntillet ʿAjrūd; Khirbet el-Qōm) attest that many Israelites in practice paired YHWH with a feminine referent (goddess or symbol), while literary polemic (e.g., Hezekiah, Josiah) sought to excise that feminine presence from the cult.

Ritually, Leviticus 16 grounds atonement in a purposeful dyad: one goat "for YHWH" is slain and its blood purifies the sanctuary; the second, sent alive "for ʿAzazel," bears the people's iniquities away into the wilderness. The Torah likewise pairs the Red Heifer statute (Num 19)—female, outside the camp—with Miriam's death (Num 20:1), which classical midrash reads as encoding the axiom "the death of the righteous atones." Within that canonical logic, Josiah's shocking death (609 BCE) after his anti-Asherah reform functions as an atoning hinge that delays—but does not ultimately avert—exile. Post-reform/post-catastrophe, the feminine does not vanish; rather, it migrates from cultic consort to communal vocation in history: Bat Golah, the dispersed Daughter of Israel, becomes the living bearer who carries the collective burden among the nations, completing the Levitical dyad without divinizing Israel or collapsing signs into identity.

This addendum distinguishes Asherah (a pre-exilic cultic/queenly referent beside YHWH) from Bat Golah (the human feminine collective in exile), reframes the Bronze Serpent as paradoxical sign (healing when beheld; later a snare), and situates pre-/post-exilic shifts in light of ANE kinship, queen-mother institutions, and diaspora religion. The argument relies on grammar, ritual structure, epigraphy, and canonical sequencing; numerical seals (gematria) elsewhere in the Elohim Edition remain homiletic adornments, not evidentiary pillars.

I. Method and Claims

Methodologically, the addendum proceeds on four rails: (1) philology (binary grammar; cohortatives; gendered morphology); (2) textual criticism and redactional horizons (MT/LXX/DSS echoes; Deuteronomistic centralization); (3) archaeology and epigraphy (Kuntillet ʿAjrūd; Khirbet el-Qōm; Elephantine); and (4) ritual typology controlled by the primary texts (Lev 16; Num 19–20), with rabbinic articulation of already-embedded Torah patterns ("the death of the righteous atones"). The terms "Yahwist/Elohist/Deuteronomist" (J/E/D) are used heuristically to map shifts in diction and theology across monarchic, exilic, and post-exilic horizons. These designations are employed here purely as descriptive shorthand for stylistic and theological strata within the received text, not as fixed documentary hypotheses. Their function is analytic, not polemical signposts for variation in diction and emphasis rather than partitions of inspiration. The aim is to illuminate redactional rhythm, not to re-inscribe outdated source-critical binaries.

The claims are six: (a) biblical Hebrew preserves a binary divine grammar ('El + 'Eloah cohering in 'Ĕlōhîm); (b) pre-exilic inscriptions demonstrate YHWH paired with a feminine referent ("his asherah"), whether goddess or cultic symbol; (c) Hezekiah and Josiah represent intensifying attempts to suppress that feminine cultic presence; (d) Josiah's unexpected death stands within a Torah-encoded axiom linking righteous death with atoning effect; (e) the living bearer of communal iniquity migrates—after reform and catastrophe—from a cultic feminine pole to the feminine peoplehood, Bat Golah; and (f) the result completes the Levitical dyad without collapsing it into a single masculine atonement or into goddess worship.

II. Binary Grammar: 'El, 'Eloah, 'Elohim

The lexeme 'El (אֵל) pervades Northwest Semitic with connotations of strength, lordship, and seniority; within the Hebrew Bible it appears in theophoric compounds ('El 'Elyon; 'El Shaddai). The morphologically feminine singular 'Eloah (אֱלוֹהַּ), concentrated in the poetic diction of Job (≈41 times), preserves the feminine-marked singular form within canonical discourse. Regardless of whether one posits 'Eloah as a back-formation from 'Ĕlōhîm or as a conserving archaism, the fact remains that biblical Hebrew keeps a robust feminine-marked divine singular in active theological use. In concert, 'Ĕlōhîm (אֱלֹהִים) regularly takes singular verbs for Israel's God, a grammatical intensification that permits plurality in morphology while insisting upon unity in reference.

Genesis 1:26–27 makes the logic visible: the cohortative plural נַעֲשֶׂה ("let us make") functions as divine self-deliberation within a binary unity; the very next verse codifies the image as male-and-female, and Genesis 5:2 canonically names both together "adam." As grammar, not numerics, this binary frames all subsequent claims: Israel's God is one—yet the canonical speech and anthropological mirror insist upon a duet rather than a solitary masculine.

III. Pre-Exilic Evidence: "YHWH ... and his Asherah"

Two sites dominate the discussion. First, at Kuntillet ʿAjrūd (late 9th–early 8th c. BCE), inscriptions on pithoi and plaster invoke "YHWH of Samaria and his asherah" and "YHWH of Teman and his asherah." Whether "asherah" denotes the goddess Asherah or her cultic symbol/pole is debated in detail, but functionally the pairing of the Tetragrammaton with a feminine referent stands. Second, Khirbet el-Qōm (late 8th–7th c. BCE) preserves a funerary blessing "by YHWH and his asherah," corroborating that the formula was neither unique nor accidental. These finds cohere with West-Semitic religion in which Asherah/Athirat appears as El's consort and a queen-mother figure.

Biblical texts mirror and oppose this reality: popular religion flourished "under every green tree," and Asherah had institutional presence even in the Temple (2 Kgs 23:6–7) until reforms intervened. Jeremiah's polemics ("Queen of Heaven," Jer 7; 44) attest the tenacity of female cult among Judahites both in the land and in diaspora. The Elephantine papyri, though a century later and outside Jerusalem's authority, document Judeans swearing by YHW and, in some texts, invoking Anat-Yahu, a pairing likely incomprehensible to Deuteronomistic reformers but intelligible as diaspora continuity of older patterns.

This dossier establishes the pre-exilic ground on which reformers stood: they did not invent the feminine presence; they targeted it.

IV. Hezekiah, Josiah, and the Bronze Serpent Paradox

Hezekiah (late 8th c. BCE) inaugurated a recognizable iconoclasm: he "broke in pieces the bronze serpent that

Moses had made" (2 Kgs 18:4), calling it *nehushtan*, and cut down *asherah* worship alongside the eradication of high places. The paradox is hard-wired: a sign once divinely authorized (Num 21) had become a snare; reform required its removal.

Josiah's reform (622 BCE) radicalized centralization. A discovered scroll catalyzed a thorough purge: the *asherah* in the Temple removed and burned; vessels for Baal destroyed; high-place priests decommissioned; Passover centralized (2 Kgs 22–23). Thirteen years later, Josiah fell to Pharaoh Neco at Megiddo (609 BCE). Chronicler records national lament and Jeremiah's dirge (2 Chr 35:25), while Zechariah recalls a great mourning "as at Hadad-Rimmon in the plain of Megiddo" (Zech 12:11), traditionally linked to Josiah's death. Theologically, the sequence is disorienting: the king who purified the cult died without miraculous rescue.

The serpent's paradox interprets the moment: signs that heal can become snares; purges that protect can amputate. Josiah's reform eliminated idolatrous feminization; it also removed the cultic feminine pole through which bearing functions had resided. In the wake of his death, the burden to "carry away" migrates from symbol to people.

V. Torah's Template: Red Heifer → Miriam → Atonement

Numbers 19 legislates the Red Heifer—female, without blemish, slaughtered and burned **outside the camp**, with ashes preserved for purification from corpse impurity. Immediately thereafter, "Miriam died there and was buried there" (Num 20:1). The classical midrashic axiom "the death of the righteous atones" arises from just such canonical juxtapositions: when the righteous depart, communal atonement is effected in a manner analogous to sacrificial service. The Talmud (Mo'ed Katan 28a) makes the principle explicit and aligns it with the Temple's cultic efficacy.

Against that backdrop, Josiah's death can be read typologically as a righteous-atoning hinge that **delays** but cannot forestall the Babylonian juggernaut. The analogy is not positivist history; it is covenantal logic: the slain righteous enables the living to bear what blood cannot remove.

VI. Leviticus 16 and the Living Bearer

The Day of Atonement's scaffold is a dyad by design. The goat "for YHWH" is slain; its blood purifies sanctuary, priesthood, and people. The second goat, "for ʿAzazel," remains alive, receives the people's iniquities by confession, and is sent into the wilderness. Debates about ʿAzazel (demonological being; wilderness crag; or "the goat that goes away") do not unsettle the textual contrast: **slain blood** vs. **living removal**. Second-Temple halakhah develops the removal to a cliff to ensure non-return (Mishnah Yoma 6), dramatizing separation and finality.

In the addendum's framework, the living pole migrates to history after the feminine's cultic excision. **Bat Golah**— the dispersed daughter—names Israel's feminine collective vocation: to **bear** the communal weight among the nations until regathering. She is **not** Asherah; she is Israel. The Levitical dyad thus resists replacement: slain purification does not erase living bearing, and neither renders the other redundant.

The Levitical dyad does not end at the wilderness; it opens toward the world. What was once a choreography of two goats becomes, across centuries, a language of divine rhythm—slain and sent, covered and revealed, purged and preserved. In that rhythm, the *Bat Golah* inheres as the living continuation of the rite: she walks where the sanctuary once stood, carrying the tension of blood and breath into history. Yet to understand the depth of that inheritance, one must trace how *kippur* itself—*the act of covering*—moved through time and across nations, from the temples of Hatti and Mari to the fasts of Judah and the prayers of the diaspora. **For Israel, now dispersed, has become a living Torah scroll— words of covenant inscribed not on stone or hide but upon** the flesh of a people—fulfilling the vision that Jerusalem shall be "a town without walls," surrounded not by ramparts but by the fiery presence of YHWH (Zech 2:4–5). The next section situates this sacred grammar within its ancient and evolving landscape, revealing how Israel transformed the shared Near-Eastern language of purification into the covenantal theology of mercy.

VI-B. Yom Kippur in Comparative and Diachronic Frame

The *Day of Atonement* stands as Israel's annual re-articulation of the binary rhythm already embedded in the Levitical dyad. The root כִּפֶּר (*kippēr*)—from the verbal stem meaning *"to cover, to wipe, to purge"*—shares linguistic ancestry with Akkadian *kapāru* and *kuppuru*, both denoting the act of smearing or wiping away impurity from persons or sacred objects.[1] In Mesopotamian usage, the act was mechanical and apotropaic: a wipe that removed contagion from the king's body or the temple precinct. In Israel, the same verb becomes moral and covenantal; *kippēr* no longer only "wipes off," it *mediates*. The nations cleanse by gesture; Israel reconciles by confession. Thus the motion of the verb shifts from **detergent to dialogue**, from cultic appeasement to relational restoration—the essence of what Jacob Milgrom called Israel's "moralization of purity." The covering becomes conversation.

Ancient Near Eastern Parallels

Across the Late Bronze and Iron Age world, cultures performed homologous rites of removal in which guilt or misfortune was physically displaced into a substitute. The Hittite ḫuḫḫana and kuppar ceremonies directed priests to touch the body of the king with an animal or figurine, absorb his impurity, and cast the object into wilderness or water.[2] These *kuppar* texts even use the cognate of Hebrew *kippur*, indicating a shared Semitic root and conceptual field. At **Mari** and **Emar**, royal archives describe an *"ūm kapri,"* a "day of wiping," when twin animals were presented—one slain before the deity, one sent beyond the city gate as an embodied curse.[3] Babylonian *namburbi* rituals and Amorite incantations likewise released a *ṣīhru* ("substitute kid") or *šēp ēli* ("creature of the god"), carrying away the pollution of omen or offense. In all these parallels, atonement is spatial: evil must be exported so the center may remain inviolate. A further window into this semantic and ritual world emerges from the **Akkadian *Ritual Series KAR 298***, in which a goat designated *šā'ilu* is touched to the patient's body while priests recite the formula *ana dannūti šarri lu ušērib ṭēmu*— "may I transfer the king's evil." The animal is then driven into steppe-land, echoing Israel's *'azāzel* procedure both in structure and in the language of transference. As Thorkild Jacobsen noted, the gesture reflects a Mesopotamian conviction that impurity is *real substance* capable of relocation rather than abstraction.[10] Israel's priestly writers inherit this cosmology yet re-interpret its physics of evil into **covenantal ethics**: the substance of sin becomes relational breach, the removal becomes reconciliation.

Israel's priestly legislation neither denies nor imitates this cosmological instinct; it **transposes** it. The Levitical priest does not act as magician but as **covenant proxy**. His manipulation of blood and confession dramatizes that impurity is not autonomous matter but moral fracture. The blood *covers* the sanctum, restoring relationship between heaven and earth; the living goat carries away transgression into *'ereṣ gĕzērâ*, the "cut-off land." Where Hittite kings purchased safety by substitution, Israel rehearses mercy by representation. The ritual structure is recognizable to its ANE neighbors, yet its theology is wholly other: *kapāru* becomes covenant.

Etymology and Theology of "Covering"

The semantic field of *kippēr* reveals a theological paradox. To *cover* (*kpr*) is at once to **conceal** and to **protect**—a shield that hides the object yet affirms its worth. In Genesis 6:14, Noah "covers" the ark with pitch (*kōper*), sealing it against waters of chaos; in Exodus 25, the golden *kappōret* "covering" becomes the throne of divine presence. Thus, every act of covering marks both **separation** and **communion**. Yom Kippur re-enacts this double movement: impurity is concealed from sight so holiness may again dwell in the midst. The rite's genius lies in its *simultaneity*: hiding does not deny, it redeems by deferral until restoration is complete.

Pre-Exilic Praxis and Local *Kippurim*

Before Josiah's centralizing reform (622 BCE), local shrines likely held seasonal *kippur* observances aligned with autumn harvest and new-year renewal.[4] These may have combined agricultural thanksgiving with communal purification, echoing Canaanite *tḥn w npš* offerings where the "soul" of the field was revived. Textual residues—such as 1 Samuel 3:14, which warns that certain sins "shall not be atoned with sacrifice or offering forever"—assume a **plurality of atonement sites**. [71] As Ron Shields has observed, Leviticus 10–16 arose from the priestly crisis of Nadab and Abihu, defining atonement initially as a sanctuary-bound rite of containment rather than a national observance. Archaeological parallels from Arad, Lachish, and Beersheba, each yielding twin-altar remains, suggest regional experimentation with dual-victim expiation. Even Hosea's critique—"they sacrifice upon the tops of mountains and burn incense upon the hills" (Hos 4:13)—presupposes that purification rites once proliferated among Israel's clans. Josiah's Deuteronomistic centralization collapsed that geography into a single Jerusalemite sanctuary. Yet the **memory of multiplicity** persisted in prophetic speech, where atonement was re-imagined as moral return rather than cultic repetition (cf. Isa 1:16–18; Mic 6:6–8). The reform thus refined form but not meaning: *kippur* survived exile by migrating into language.

---

[71] Ron Shields, *From Priestly Crisis to National Atonement: The Redactional Composition of Leviticus 16 and the Silence of Yom Kippur, Jerusalem Theological Review* 52 (1) (2025): 1–25. Shields, *From Priestly Crisis to National Atonement*, 19–23.

With the Temple destroyed and blood unavailable, *kippur* underwent an **anthropological translation**. Whereas Shields interprets this priestly-to-national development as a late editorial expansion of holiness theology, the present study reads the same transition as a *prophetic transference*—the rite leaving the sanctuary to inhabit the exilic body, the *Bat Golah*, as living atonement. What had been spatial became spiritual; what had been ritual became ethical. The verb that once marked blood on altar-horns now described contrition of heart and confession of lips. The **Qumran Community Rule** (1QS vii 3-6) declares that "atonement shall be made by the humble spirit and by walking in perfect way." The **Mishnah** (Yoma 8:9) codifies the shift: "The day itself atones for those who repent." Philo of Alexandria, writing from the diaspora, calls the festival "the soul's purification from passions" (*Spec. Laws* 1.188–190).[5] In Babylonian and Alexandrian communities, fasting and confession supplanted animal blood. The people themselves became the offering—"the calves of our lips" (Hos 14:3).

Second-Temple sources also expand the day's cosmic dimension. Jubilees 34 portrays angels ministering on high as Israel fasts below, while 11QMelchizedek reads Yom Kippur eschatologically: the final Jubilee when *"atonement shall be made for all sons of light."* The rite thus grows from **annual ritual** into **apocalyptic horizon**, anticipating a final cleansing not of sanctuary alone but of creation itself. Post-exilic Israel becomes the theatre in which the Levitical polarity—slain and sent—plays out historically.

Anthropological and Theological Reading

Mary Douglas' structural insight—that purity systems guard **boundaries rather than objects**—illuminates the transformation.[6] When the Temple fell, the physical boundary dissolved; the human body and community became the new sanctuary. Jonathan Klawans extends this reading: impurity moved from *spatial* to *moral*, atonement from priestly hands to communal conscience.[7] In exile, the wilderness that once received the goat now receives the nation itself. The *Bat Golah*—the Daughter of Exile—embodies this substitution: she is Israel's living scapegoat, not annihilated but dispersed, carrying the residual impurity of sacred history until the appointed restoration. Her dispersion is not punishment alone; it is vocation. She bears, as the goat once bore, the sins of the sanctuary into lands of the uncircumcised, transforming geography into pedagogy.

This reading accords with Bernard Janowski's seminal analysis of *Sühne als Heilsgeschehen*—atonement as salvific event rather than mere expiation. Janowski demonstrates that Israel's cultic language encodes a movement from alienation to renewed nearness, a **Heilsgeschehen**, in which divine presence re-enters communal life. The *Bat Golah* embodies this very motion: her dispersion becomes the liminal phase through which the Presence redefines proximity.

Comparative Anthropology: From Royal Substitution to Communal Bearing

Where Hittite and Akkadian rituals focused on the **king** as cosmic center, Israel democratized substitution. Every Israelite participates through fasting and confession; atonement ceases to be royal privilege and becomes **collective priesthood**(cf. Exod 19:6). This theological democratization has no clear ANE parallel. Egypt knew "washing the Pharaoh's heart"; Mesopotamia had the "substitute king" (a temporary stand-in executed to avert omen), yet only Israel turned that logic into *communal ethics*. In the Levitical system, substitution is not scapegoated *onto another person* but distributed across sacred and social spheres: the priest mediates, the goat departs, and the people remain to live differently. Yom Kippur thus redefines power: atonement is responsibility, not privilege.

Linguistic Continuities and Symbolic Evolution

[72]Philologically, the noun *kippūrîm* appears only in Leviticus 23:27–32 and Numbers 29:7–11, always in plural, "Day of Atonements." The plural marks its dual motion—toward heaven and toward earth, inward and outward. Later Hebrew retains this polarity: the *kippah* covers the head, symbol of submission; the *kaporet* covers the ark, seat of revelation. Both gestures veil the sacred to preserve intimacy. Rabbinic commentators later interpret *kaporet* as the place where mercy conquers judgment, implying that *covering* is not suppression but synthesis. The linguistic thread from *kapāru* to *kippah* traces an unbroken theology of protection through humility.

Socio-Diasporic Reverberations

Anthropologically, post-exilic *kippur* reshaped Israel's calendar around repentance rather than agriculture. In diaspora, the fast became the **axis of identity**, the one day every Jew, whether in Elephantine, Babylon, or Alexandria, could enact temple memory without altar. Greek inscriptions from Asia Minor record synagogues closing for the "Great Fast," and Josephus notes that even Hellenized Jews "abstain from labor and food for one day, calling it the Fast." The ritual of removal thus becomes ritual of remembrance: an internal altar carried in the heart. The *Bat Golah*'s fast replaces the priest's blood; endurance itself becomes offering. In her, the atonement rite survives

---

[72] Jacob Milgrom, *Leviticus 1–16* (AB 3; New York: Doubleday, 1991), 1020-1071. Nobuyoshi Kiuchi, *The Purification Offering in the Priestly Literature* (JSOTSup 56; Sheffield, 1987), 17-23. Martha T. Roth, *Law Collections from Mesopotamia and the Levant*, 2nd ed. (Atlanta: Scholars Press, 1997), 288-292. Roland de Vaux, *Ancient Israel*, vol. 2 (New York: McGraw-Hill, 1965), 220-225. Philo, *Special Laws* 1.188-190. Mary Douglas, *Leviticus as Literature* (Oxford: Oxford University Press, 1999), 182-187. Jonathan Klawans, *Impurity and Sin in Ancient Judaism* (Oxford: Oxford University Press, 2000), 143-151. ⬚ Thorkild Jacobsen, *The Treasures of Darkness: A History of Mesopotamian Religion* (New Haven: Yale University Press, 1976), 137-143. Bernard Janowski, *Sühne als Heilsgeschehen: Studien zur Sühnetheologie der Priesterschrift und zum Heilsverständnis des Alten Testaments* (Göttingen: Vandenhoeck & Ruprecht, 1982).

imperial dislocation—the living covering among the nations.

Integrative Implications

Etymology and anthropology converge on a single paradox. To *cover* is simultaneously to hide and to heal. Pre-exilic Israel covered impurity by sending it away; post-exilic Israel covers the nations by enduring among them. Both acts are covenantal gestures of mercy, each stage preserving the binary grammar of **slain and sent**. Yom Kippur is therefore not an isolated cultic memory but the theological prototype of exile itself—the annual rehearsal of what the *Bat Golah* lives continually. When she prays in foreign tongues and faces unseen altars, she extends the ancient rite into history: the living bearer still walks, the covering still holds. The covenant that once purified a sanctuary now sustains a people scattered yet sanctified.

VII. Pre- vs. Post-Exilic Horizons: Feminine Migration

Pre-exilic Israel lived with a felt, often physical, feminine adjacency to YHWH in symbols, inscriptions, and royal/queen-mother institutions (e.g., Bathsheba enthroned at the king's right, 1 Kgs 2:19). Deuteronomistic centralization polemicized against that adjacency as idolatrous. The exile and its aftermath did not annihilate the feminine; it **translated** it. In prophetic poetics, Zion is Daughter; in diaspora praxis, Judeans at Elephantine invoke Anat-Yahu; in post-biblical mysticism, Shekhinah descends into exile with the people. The cultic feminine becomes, in effect, the **communal feminine**.

This migration is not equivalence (Bat Golah ≠ Asherah); it is transposition. What stood **beside** YHWH in pre-exilic practice now stands **as** Israel in exile. The logic of atonement thereby moves from precinct to peoplehood without deifying the latter.

Later mystical and philosophical traditions preserved this same binary presence under new names. Rabbinic and Kabbalistic writings describe the **Shekhinah**—the indwelling feminine aspect of divinity—as descending with Israel into exile (Zohar I:203a), while Hellenistic Judaism re-articulated the mediating principle through **Philo's Logos**, the rational image by which the ineffable God engages creation. Early Christian theology, drawing from both, framed atonement language in Hebrews 9 as the heavenly priest entering not the earthly sanctuary but the eternal one "not made with hands." These developments testify that the **Levitical dyad of slain and sent** continued to shape metaphysical imagination long after the Temple's stones cooled.

VIII. Objections and Replies

(1) "Asherah" denotes a wooden pole, not a goddess. Scholarly debate is substantial. Yet the epigraphic formula "YHWH … and his asherah" is personal/possessive and is difficult to reduce to lumber alone; even where a cultic object is intended, it functions as a queenly referent beside YHWH in popular devotion. Our argument therefore proceeds **functionally**: goddess or symbol, the pair stands.

(2) ʾEloah is merely a late back-formation. Even if one adopts that view, the canonical distribution—especially Job's concentration—demonstrates that biblical Hebrew intentionally **retains** a feminine-marked divine singular in living theology; the binary is grammatical, not speculative numerics.

(3) "Death of the righteous atones" is late rabbinic. The axiom is rabbinic in form but Torah-encoded in sequence (Red Heifer → Miriam). Employing rabbinic diction to name a canonical pattern is standard method.

(4) Azazel's identity is uncertain. The identity is not the lynchpin; the **contrast** (slain vs. sent alive) grounds the typology.

(5) This collapses into goddess worship. On the contrary: Bat Golah is explicitly **not** a deity; she is the **people** in exile as feminine collective bearer. The argument

refuses divinization while protecting the feminine function erased by reform.

IX. Synthesis in Six Moves

(1) **Binary Origin**: ʾEl + ʾEloah → ʾĔlōhîm; *adam* named male-and-female.
(2) **Cultic Pairing**: YHWH and "his asherah" in pre-exilic inscriptions; Queen-Mother institutions.
(3) **Erasure**: Hezekiah and Josiah purge serpent/idols/*asherah*; centralization.
(4) **Atoning Death**: Red Heifer → Miriam encodes the axiom; Josiah's lamented death stands in that logic.
(5) **Living Bearer**: the feminine pole migrates from cult to people—Bat Golah bears sin in the wilderness of the nations.
(6) **Paradoxical Signs**: the bronze serpent heals when beheld and is later destroyed; signs bless and ensnare— purge the idol, preserve the polarity.

X. Conclusion

The Elohim Edition's theological grammar, now reinforced by archaeology and ritual law, guards against two opposite errors: a masculinized atonement that dissolves the living bearer, and a re-divinized feminine that revives goddess cult. Canon offers a third way. The one God who speaks as "us" creates humanity as duet; Israel's history demonstrates how the feminine's cultic sign can be cut down while the feminine's covenantal vocation lives on in the people. Josiah's death, read through Torah's own pattern, marks the hinge: the slain righteous precedes the season in which the Daughter must carry. Naming her **Bat Golah** neither replaces the slain nor enthrones the goddess. It simply lets Scripture finish its dyad—so that, in the promised regathering, the duet with which creation began might be heard again in the assembly of the restored.

Notes (Chicago/SBL Style)

1. On the cohortative plural and singular verbs with ʾĔlōhîm, see Bruce K. Waltke and M. O'Connor, *An

Introduction to Biblical Hebrew Syntax* (Winona Lake: Eisenbrauns, 1990), §§10.2, 12.2; Emanuel Tov, *Textual Criticism of the Hebrew Bible*, 3rd ed. (Minneapolis: Fortress, 2012), 257–60.

2. On the distribution of 'Eloah in Job (~41 occurrences) and its theological freight, see entries in HALOT and DCH; for orientation to Job's diction and dating debates, see John H. Walton, *Job* (Grand Rapids: Zondervan, 2012), 25–31.

3. Kuntillet ʿAjrūd inscriptions: see Zeʾev Meshel et al., "Kuntillet ʿAjrud (Horvat Teman): An Iron Age II Religious Site on the Judah–Sinai Border," *Israel Exploration Journal* 34 (1984): 36–58; for recent synthesis and imagery, see also Othmar Keel and Christoph Uehlinger, *Gods, Goddesses, and Images of God in Ancient Israel* (Minneapolis: Fortress, 1998), 204–12.

4. Khirbet el-Qōm: see P. K. McCarter, "The Khirbet el-Qom Inscription," *BASOR* 238 (1980): 49–61; William G. Dever, *Did God Have a Wife?* (Grand Rapids: Eerdmans, 2005), 176–84.

5. Macro-synthesis on Asherah: Mark S. Smith, *The Early History of God*, 2nd ed. (Grand Rapids: Eerdmans, 2002); John Day, *Yahweh and the Gods and Goddesses of Canaan* (Sheffield: Sheffield Academic, 2002).

6. Popular religion and women's cult: Susan Ackerman, *Under Every Green Tree: Popular Religion in Sixth-Century Judah* (Atlanta: Scholars Press, 1992).

7. Queen of Heaven in Jeremiah: for a clear academic discussion, see Steven Fassberg, "The Queen of Heaven," *Jewish Bible Quarterly* 24.2 (1996): 73–80.

8. Elephantine and Anat-Yahu: Bezalel Porten, *Archives from Elephantine* (Berkeley: University of California Press, 1968), 103–12; also Karel van der Toorn, *Family Religion in Babylonia, Syria, and Israel* (Leiden: Brill, 1996), 267–73.

9. Bronze Serpent: Num 21; 2 Kgs 18:4. For ANE serpent iconography and Israel, see Keel–Uehlinger, *Gods, Goddesses, and Images*, 258–66.

10. Josiah's reform and death: 2 Kgs 22–23; 2 Chr 34–35. For historical synthesis, see Richard D. Nelson, *The Double Redaction of the Deuteronomistic History* (JSOTSup 18; Sheffield: JSOT Press, 1981), 108–16.

11. Zech 12:11 as allusion to Josiah: see Mark J. Boda, *The Book of Zechariah* (NICOT; Grand Rapids: Eerdmans, 2016), 496–500.

12. Leviticus 16: on the two-goat rite and ʿAzazel options, see Jacob Milgrom, *Leviticus 1–16* (AB 3; New York: Doubleday, 1991), 1020–1071; Jonathan Klawans, *Purity, Sacrifice, and the Temple* (Oxford: Oxford University Press, 2006), 143–51.

13. Second-Temple practice: *m.* Yoma 6; see Herbert Danby, *The Mishnah* (Oxford: Oxford University Press, 1933), 170–77.

14. Red Heifer statute and Miriam: Num 19–20; Sifrei Num. 123; *b.* Moʿed Katan 28a (death of the righteous atones).

15. For queen-mother institutions in monarchic Judah, see Carol Meyers, *Discovering Eve: Ancient Israelite Women in Context* (New York: Oxford University Press, 1988), 189–95; and Athalya Brenner, ed., *A Feminist Companion to Samuel and Kings* (Sheffield: Sheffield Academic, 1994), 286–300.

Bibliography

Ackerman, Susan. *Under Every Green Tree: Popular Religion in Sixth-Century Judah*. Atlanta: Scholars Press, 1992.

Boda, Mark J. *The Book of Zechariah*. NICOT. Grand Rapids: Eerdmans, 2016.

Brenner, Athalya, ed. *A Feminist Companion to Samuel and Kings*. Sheffield: Sheffield Academic, 1994.

Danby, Herbert. *The Mishnah*. Oxford: Oxford University Press, 1933.

Day, John. *Yahweh and the Gods and Goddesses of Canaan*. Sheffield: Sheffield Academic, 2002.

Dever, William G. *Did God Have a Wife?* Grand Rapids: Eerdmans, 2005.

Keel, Othmar, and Christoph Uehlinger. *Gods, Goddesses, and Images of God in Ancient Israel*. Minneapolis: Fortress, 1998.

Klawans, Jonathan. *Purity, Sacrifice, and the Temple: Symbolism and Supersessionism in the Study of Ancient Judaism*. Oxford: Oxford University Press, 2006.

McCarter, P. Kyle. "The Khirbet el-Qom Inscription." *Bulletin of the American Schools of Oriental Research* 238 (1980): 49–61.

Meshel, Ze'ev, et al. "Kuntillet ʿAjrud (Horvat Teman): An Iron Age II Religious Site on the Judah–Sinai Border." *Israel Exploration Journal* 34 (1984): 36–58.

Meyers, Carol. *Discovering Eve: Ancient Israelite Women in Context*. New York: Oxford University Press, 1988.

Milgrom, Jacob. *Leviticus 1–16*. Anchor Bible 3. New York: Doubleday, 1991.

Nelson, Richard D. *The Double Redaction of the Deuteronomistic History*. JSOTSup 18. Sheffield: JSOT Press, 1981.

Porten, Bezalel. *Archives from Elephantine: The Life of an Ancient Jewish Military Colony*. Berkeley: University of California Press, 1968.

Smith, Mark S. *The Early History of God: Yahweh and the Other Deities in Ancient Israel*. 2nd ed. Grand Rapids: Eerdmans, 2002.

Tov, Emanuel. *Textual Criticism of the Hebrew Bible*. 3rd ed. Minneapolis: Fortress, 2012.

Waltke, Bruce K., and M. O'Connor. *An Introduction to Biblical Hebrew Syntax*. Winona Lake: Eisenbrauns, 1990.

Walton, John H. *Job*. NIV Application Commentary. Grand Rapids: Zondervan, 2012.

Ron Shields, *From Priestly Crisis to National Atonement: The Redactional Composition of Leviticus 16 and the Silence of Yom Kippur, Jerusalem Theological Review* 52 (1) (2025): 1–25.

Glossary of Key Hebrew Terms

Divine Attributes

Tôrāh (תּוֹרָה) – Instruction or divine teaching, not merely law. Core to covenant theology.

YHWH (יהוה) – The sacred Tetragrammaton; the covenantal Name of the Most High.

ʾĔlōhîm (אֱלֹהִים) – Grammatically plural but often singular in use; denotes majesty or divine assembly.

Šadday (שַׁדַּי) – Usually translated 'Almighty'; conveys nurturing power.

ʾĂdōnāy (אֲדֹנָי) – A reverential term for YHWH; used in prayer.

ʾĒl ʿElyôn (אֵל עֶלְיוֹן) – God Most High; emphasizes divine authority and transcendence.

ʾĒl Roʾî (אֵל רֳאִי) – God Who Sees Me; name given by Hagar, emphasizing divine perception.

Grammar & Linguistics

Šōreš (שׁוֹרֶשׁ) – The three-letter root forming the basis of most Hebrew words.

Cohortative – Verb form indicating volition or exhortation (e.g., 'Let us go').

Hiphil – A causative stem in the binyan system; denotes cause of action.

Piel – An intensive or repeated action stem in Hebrew grammar.

Lašôn ha-qōdeš (לְשׁוֹן הַקֹּדֶשׁ) – Holy Language; refers to sacred Hebrew in scripture.

ʿĒzer kĕnegdô (עֵזֶר כְּנֶגְדּוֹ) – 'Strength opposite him'; traditional term for Eve retranslated with mutuality.

Niqqud (נִקּוּד) – Vowel points added to Hebrew text by Masoretes to preserve pronunciation.

Prophetic & Eschatological Terms

Rûaḥ (רוּחַ) – Spirit, breath, or wind; represents divine presence or power.

Malʾāk (מַלְאָךְ) – Angel or messenger delivering divine revelation.

Ṣedeq (צֶדֶק) – Righteousness; the ethical and covenantal order of justice.

Šālôm (שָׁלוֹם) – Wholeness and peace; connotes completion and restoration.

Sôd (סוֹד) – Hidden knowledge; esoteric layer of Torah study, linked to Kabbalah.

Bat Qôl (בַּת קוֹל) – A divine echo or 'daughter of the voice'; late prophetic signal.

ʾAspaklaryāh (אַסְפַּקְלַרְיָה) – Rabbinic 'lens' or mirror, indicating prophetic vision clarity.

Feminine Theology & Wisdom

Ḥokmâ (חָכְמָה) – Wisdom, often personified as a feminine divine agent.

Dĕbôrāh (דְּבוֹרָה) – Judge and prophetess; female leadership in Israel.

Phoebē (Φοίβη) – Female deacon cited by Paul; early ecclesial authority.

Miryām (מִרְיָם) – Sister of Moses; her name means 'bitterness' and signifies redemptive struggle.

Ḥuldāh (חֻלְדָּה) – Prophetess during Josiah's reform; verified canonical text.

almah (עַלְמָה) – A young woman of marriageable age; often mistranslated as "virgin" in Christian tradition. Carries no explicit virginity marker in Hebrew grammar.

betulah (בְּתוּלָה) – A technical term for virgin. Clearer in legal and ritual contexts.

nəvī'āh (נְבִיאָה) – Female prophet. See Miriam (Exod. 15), Huldah (2 Kings 22), Deborah (Judg. 4). Rarely translated with gender emphasis in most English versions.

shofetet (שֹׁפֶטֶת) – Female judge (e.g., Deborah). The feminine form of *shofet* is often generalized or neutralized in English translations.

Manuscript & Canonical Transmission

Pěšīṭtā – Syriac translation of the Hebrew Bible; used in Eastern churches.

Pěšīṭtā 'Ārāmā'īṭā – Aramaic version of the New Testament; shows Semitic continuity in gospel tradition.

Geo-Historical Terms

Yehûdāh (יְהוּדָה) – Judea; southern province under Roman rule, Second Temple center.

Pāras (פָּרַס) – Persia; empire that allowed Jewish exiles to return and rebuild.

'Afrīqē (Ἀφρική) – Africa; theological and genealogical root of diaspora identity.

Diaspora (διασπορά) – Scattering of Israel; central to Afro-diasporic theology.

Nāḥāš (נָחָשׁ) – Serpent; a complex symbol of rebellion and deception in scripture.

Tiqqunîm (תִּקּוּנִים) – Mystical 'rectifications'; part of covenantal and cosmic repair.

Yēšûaʿ (יֵשׁוּעַ) – Original Hebrew name of Jesus; restores Semitic accuracy.

ʿEzrā (עֶזְרָא) – Scribe central to canon formation and Torah restoration.

Běrît Ḥădašāh (בְּרִית חֲדָשָׁה) – New Covenant; Hebraic root of New Testament identity.

Canon & Structural Terms

Tanakh (תַּנַ"ךְ) – Acronym for Torah, Nevi'im, and Ketuvim—the full Hebrew Bible.

Něvî'îm (נְבִיאִים) – 'Prophets'; the second division of the Tanakh.

Kětûvîm (כְּתוּבִים) – 'Writings'; poetic, wisdom, and historical books of the Tanakh.

Hermeneutics & Prophetic Vision

Midrāš (מִדְרָשׁ) – Rabbinic interpretive tradition using homiletics and parables to explore Torah meaning.

Aspaklaryāh Me'îrāh (אַסְפַּקְלַרְיָה מְאִירָה) – 'The clear lens'; prophetic clarity ascribed to Moses alone.

Hitpaʿēl (הִתְפַּעֵל) – Reflexive stem indicating 'to cause oneself to...'; used in Deut. 28:68.

Něvû'āh (נְבוּאָה) – Formal prophetic revelation distinct from Bat Qôl.

Diaspora, Apostolic, and NT Hebrew Terminology

Šelîaḥ (שָׁלִיחַ) – One sent with authority; Hebraic basis for the term 'apostle'.

Bereshit (בְּרֵאשִׁית) – 'In the beginning'; the first word of Genesis and cosmological anchor.

ʾErev Rav (עֵרֶב רַב) – 'Mixed multitude' that exited Egypt with Israel; a symbol of hybridity and challenge.

Tiqqun ha-ʿOlam (תִּקּוּן הָעוֹלָם) – 'Repair of the world'; ethical and mystical concept of covenantal restoration.

Philosophical & Rabbinic Counter-Terms

Pardes (פַּרְדֵּס) – Four-layer interpretive method: Peshat, Remez, Derash, Sod.

ʾAggādāh (אַגָּדָה) – The narrative and non-legal aspect of rabbinic tradition.

Hēnōch (חֲנוֹךְ) – Enoch; early biblical prophet linked with divine mystery and eschatological ascent.

Bibliography

Primary Textual Sources

Biblia Hebraica Stuttgartensia (BHS), Deutsche Bibelgesellschaft.
The Dead Sea Scrolls, Translations by Geza Vermes, Penguin Classics, 2004.
The Septuagint with Apocrypha: Greek and English, Brenton Translation, Hendrickson, 2005.
Talmud Bavli, Tractates Sukkah and Megillah, Artscroll Schottenstein Edition.
The Peshitta: Eastern Aramaic Text, Syriac Orthodox Edition.

Textual Criticism and Canon Studies

Emanuel Tov, *Textual Criticism of the Hebrew Bible*, Fortress Press, 2012. [Emanuel Tov, *Textual Criticism of the Hebrew Bible*, 3rd ed. (Minneapolis: Fortress Press, 2012), 135.]
Lee Martin McDonald, *The Biblical Canon: Its Origin, Transmission, and Authority*, Hendrickson, 2007.

James C. VanderKam, *From Revelation to Canon: Studies in the Hebrew Bible and Second Temple Literature*, Brill, 2002.

Rabbinic and Patristic Commentaries

Jacob Neusner, *The Mishnah: A New Translation*, Yale University Press, 1988.
Epiphanius, *Panarion*, trans. Frank Williams, Brill, 1987. [Epiphanius, *Panarion*, trans. Frank Williams (Leiden: Brill, 1987).]
Jerome, *Letter to Pope Damasus*, in *Nicene and Post-Nicene Fathers*, vol. 6. [Jerome, *Prologus Galeatus*, in *Biblia Sacra Vulgata*, ed. Robert Weber (Stuttgart: Deutsche Bibelgesellschaft, 1994).]
Neusner, Jacob. *The Theology of the Oral Torah: Revealing the Justice of God*. Albany: SUNY Press, 1999.
Cohen, A. *Everyman's Talmud: The Major Teachings of the Rabbinic Sages*. New York: Schocken Books, 1995.
Talmud Bavli, Tractates Yoma 9b, Sanhedrin 11a.

Afro-Semitic Identity and Diaspora Theology

Tudor Parfitt, *Black Jews in Africa and the Americas*, Harvard University Press, 2013.
John L. Jackson, *Thin Description: Ethnography and the African Hebrew Israelites of Jerusalem*, Harvard University Press, 2013.
Columbus, Christopher. *The Book of Prophecies*. Edited by Delno C. West and August Kling. Gainesville: University of Florida Press, 1991.
Columbus, Ferdinand. *The Life of the Admiral Christopher Columbus by His Son Ferdinand*. Edited and translated by Benjamin Keen. New Brunswick, NJ: Rutgers University Press, 1959.
Vespucci, Amerigo. *Letters from a New World: Amerigo Vespucci's Discovery of America*. Translated by Clements R. Markham. London: Hakluyt Society, 1894.

Feminist Theological Sources

Phyllis Trible, *God and the Rhetoric of Sexuality*, Fortress Press, 1978.

Tikva Frymer-Kensky, *In the Wake of the Goddesses: Women, Culture and the Biblical Transformation of Pagan Myth*, Ballantine Books, 1992.

Delores S. Williams, Sisters in the Wilderness: The Challenge of Womanist God-Talk. Maryknoll, NY: Orbis Books, 1993.

Musa W. Dube, *Postcolonial Feminist Interpretation of the Bible*. St. Louis: Chalice Press, 2000.

Kwok Pui-lan, *Postcolonial Imagination and Feminist Theology*. Louisville: Westminster John Knox Press, 2005.

R.S. Sugirtharajah, *The Bible and the Third World: Precolonial, Colonial, and Postcolonial Encounters*. Cambridge: Cambridge University Press, 2001.

Ani, Marimba. *Yurugu: An African-Centered Critique of European Cultural Thought and Behavior*. Trenton: Africa World Press, 1994.

Gafney, Wilda C. *Womanist Midrash: A Reintroduction to the Women of the Torah and the Throne*. Louisville: Westminster John Knox Press, 2017.

New Testament and Pauline Critique

E.P. Sanders, *Paul and Palestinian Judaism*, Fortress Press, 1977.

Bart D. Ehrman, *Misquoting Jesus: The Story Behind Who Changed the Bible and Why*, HarperOne, 2005.

Codex Bezae. Early Greek-Latin diglot New Testament manuscript, 5th century.

Codex Sinaiticus. Greek manuscript containing most of the Christian Bible, c. 325–360 CE.

Talmud Sanhedrin 90a–93a. Criteria for discerning true and false prophets.

Targum Onkelos. Aramaic translation of the Torah, Babylonian period.

Sefer Yetzirah. The Book of Formation, traditional Kabbalistic text ascribed to Abraham.

Masoretic Text. Hebrew Bible standardized by the Masoretes, 7th–10th century CE.

General Reference

Ben-Jochannan, Yosef A.A. *African Origins of Major Western Religions*. Black Classic Press, 1970.

Finkelstein, Israel, and Neil Asher Silberman. *The Bible Unearthed*. Free Press, 2001.

James L. Kugel, *How to Read the Bible: A Guide to Scripture, Then and Now*. Free Press, 2007.

Bruce M. Metzger, *The Canon of the New Testament: Its Origin, Development, and Significance*. Oxford University Press, 1987. [Bruce M. Metzger, *The Text of the New Testament: Its Transmission, Corruption, and Restoration*, 4th ed. (Oxford: Oxford University Press, 2005), 45–47.]

Claude Tresmontant, *The Hebrew Christ*. Sheed and Ward, 1989.

Florentino García Martínez and Eibert J.C. Tigchelaar, *The Dead Sea Scrolls Study Edition*. 2 vols. Brill, 1997–98.

Dr. Matt Baker, "Biblical Genealogy

Patristic and Canonical Opponents

Origen. *On First Principles*. Translated by G.W. Butterworth. Princeton: Princeton University Press, 1966.

Origen. *Contra Celsum*. Translated by Henry Chadwick. Cambridge: Cambridge University Press, 1953.

Calvin, John. *Commentaries on the Epistles of Paul to the Romans and Thessalonians*. Edinburgh: Calvin Translation Society.

Erasmus, Desiderius. *Annotations on the New Testament*. Edited by Anne Reeve and M.A. Screech. Toronto: University of Toronto Press, 1990.

Dunn, James D.G. *The New Perspective on Paul*. Revised Edition. Grand Rapids: Eerdmans, 2008.

Rabbi Akiva and Messianic Revolt

Schäfer, Peter. *The Bar Kokhba War Reconsidered: New Perspectives on the Second Jewish Revolt against Rome*. Tübingen: Mohr Siebeck, 2003.

Neusner, Jacob. *A Life of Rabbi Akiva*. Leiden: Brill, 1971.

Canon History and Imperial Christianity

Eusebius. *Ecclesiastical History*. Translated by G.A. Williamson. London: Penguin Books, 1989.

Council of Laodicea (c. 363 CE). Canon 59. In: Philip Schaff, *Nicene and Post-Nicene Fathers*, Series 2, Volume 14.

McDonald, Lee Martin. *Formation of the Christian Biblical Canon*. Peabody: Hendrickson Publishers, 1995.

Getatchew Haile, "The Structure and Evolution of the Ethiopian Biblical Canon," in *The Bible in Ethiopia: The Book of Acts*, ed. J. Ross Wagner (Atlanta: Society of Biblical Literature, 2012), 15–28.

R. W. Cowley, "The Biblical Canon of the Ethiopian Orthodox Church Today," *Ostkirchliche Studien* 23, no. 2 (1974): 318–323.

Edward Ullendorff, *The Ethiopians: An Introduction to Country and People*, 2nd ed. (London: Oxford University Press, 1965), esp. 65–87.

Linguistic and Verb Structure Studies

Waltke, Bruce K., and Michael P. O'Connor. *An Introduction to Biblical Hebrew Syntax*. Winona Lake: Eisenbrauns, 1990.

Van Der Merwe, Christo H.J., Jackie A. Naudé, and Jan H. Kroeze. *A Biblical Hebrew Reference Grammar*. Sheffield: Sheffield Academic Press, 1999.

Lexical, Midrashic, and Prophetic Studies

Sifra on Leviticus. Translation by Jacob Neusner.

Paul, Shalom M. *Isaiah 40–66: A Commentary*. Grand Rapids: Eerdmans, 2008.

Rosenberg, Roy A. *The Semantics of Biblical Language*. New York: Ktav Publishing House, 1982.

Kugel, James. *The Bible As It Was*. Cambridge: Harvard University Press, 1997.

Final Citation Index

The following sources were referenced throughout the final manuscript. This includes biblical citations, Dead Sea Scroll evidence, rabbinic commentary, academic research, and linguistic sources.

- Dr. Al Garza: The Hebrew New Testament
- Jeff A. Benner: Ancient Hebrew Lexicon of the Bible
- Rabbi Samson Raphael Hirsch: Commentary on the Pentateuch
- Claude Tresmontant: The Hebrew Christ
- Matthew Black: An Aramaic Approach to the Gospels and Acts
- Figure 4: Dr. Matt Baker: Useful Charts – Biblical Genealogy & Canon Visualization
- Dead Sea Scrolls: Multiple fragments including 4QGenesis-Exodus and 11QMelchizedek highlighting Torah fidelity and messianic expectation
- Codex Sinaiticus: Earliest nearly complete manuscript of the Christian Bible
- Codex Bezae: Early Greek-Latin diglot with unique NT readings
- Codex Vaticanus: 4th century Greek Bible, significant for NT text reliability
- Jerome: Commentaries and references to a Hebrew gospel [Jerome, *Prologus Galeatus*, in *Biblia Sacra Vulgata*, ed. Robert Weber (Stuttgart: Deutsche Bibelgesellschaft, 1994).]
- Papias: Early 2nd-century bishop who attested to Hebrew origin of Matthew
- Epiphanius: Panarion: Refers to Ebionites and a Hebrew Gospel [Epiphanius, *Panarion*, trans. Frank Williams (Leiden: Brill, 1987).]
- Talmud Yevamot 49b: Aspaklaria — prophetic limitation imagery
- Talmud Berakhot 31a: Bat Kol — heavenly voice and prophetic boundaries

- Talmud Sanhedrin 90a–93a: Criteria for true and false prophets
- Isaiah 2:4; 11:12; 42:8: Messianic expectations and divine exclusivity
- Genesis 3:13: Hiphil use of הִשִּׁיאַנִי ('he caused me to be deceived')
- Zechariah 1:20–21; 6:12–13: Four horns, craftsmen, and the messianic branch
- Malachi 4:5: Promise of Elijah before the day of YHWH
- Matthew 13:55: Joseph as 'tekton', craftsman
- John 3:14: Serpent imagery and prophetic parallel
- Deuteronomy 13:1–5: Warning about miracle-working deceivers
- Nehemiah 8: Public Torah reading and explanation in Hebrew
- Revelation: Symbolism of 'Shir' and restored prophetic song
- See Fishbane's analysis of typological recurrence, Tov's treatment of Masoretic authority, and Kugel's work on textual evolution. These voices deepen the manuscript's foundation and embed it within a recognized tradition of textual and covenantal scholarship. Michael Fishbane, *Biblical Interpretation in Ancient Israel* (Oxford: Clarendon Press, 1985), 350–374.

Appendix Figures: Linguistic Origins, Prophetic Timelines, and Script Diagrams

Figure 1: Diagram 1: Evolution of the Alpha-Bet

Flowchart tracing Hebrew script evolution: Proto-Sinaitic → Paleo-Hebrew → Aramaic → Square Hebrew → Latin/Roman → Modern English.

Figure 2: Diagram 2: Hebrew Script Development Chart

Figure 3: Diagram 3: Timeline of Rabbinic Oral Torah transmission

Figure 4: Diagram 4: Zechariah Vision Artwork

Figure 5: Table 1: Messianic Role Comparison – Ben Yosef vs. Ben David

A side-by-side table of traits and scriptural references for Mashiach ben Yosef and Mashiach ben David.

Figure 6: Diagram 6: PARDES TREE

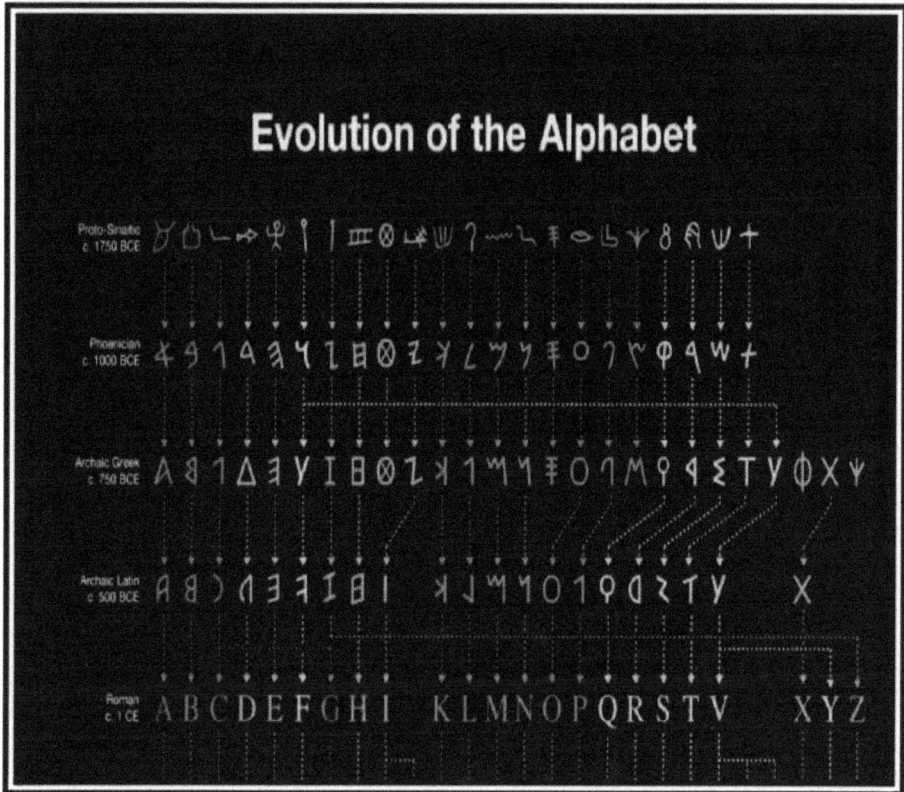

Figure 1. Visual Summary

Abstract: Evolution of the Alpha-Bet (From proto-Hebrew to Roman)

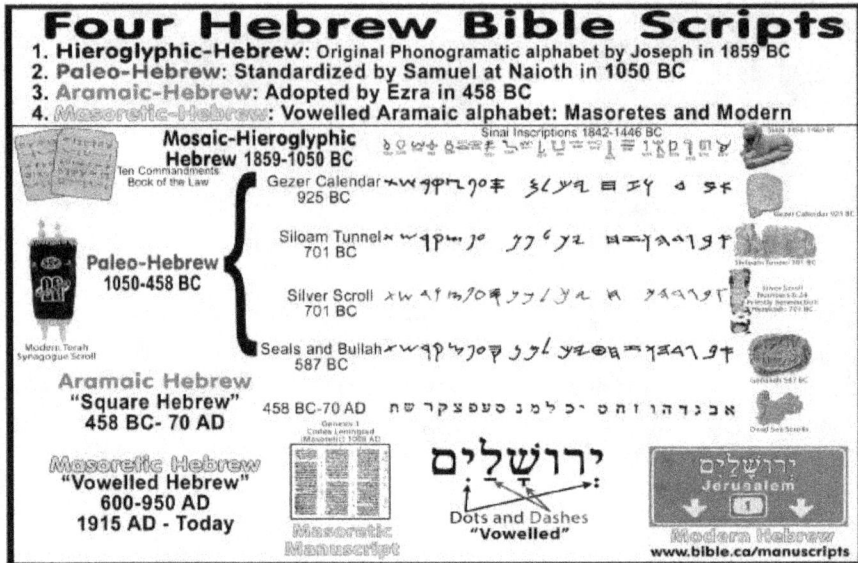

Four Hebrew Bible Scripts

1. **Hieroglyphic-Hebrew**: Original Phonogramatic alphabet by Joseph in 1859 BC
2. **Paleo-Hebrew**: Standardized by Samuel at Naioth in 1050 BC
3. **Aramaic-Hebrew**: Adopted by Ezra in 458 BC
4. **Masoretic-Hebrew**: Vowelled Aramaic alphabet: Masoretes and Modern

Figure 2. Timeline of Script Evolution from ʿIḇrît to ʾAššûrît. (See Sanhedrin 21b)

Abstract:

The inscription in Daniel 5—*Mene Mene Tekel Upharsin*—presents a notable exception in prophetic reception. Unlike Daniel's other visions, which required angelic interpretation (Daniel 8:16), this writing was understood immediately. This suggests the inscription was in an ancestral form of Hebrew—ʿIḇrît **(Paleo-Hebrew)**—rather than the then-dominant ʾAššûrît script.

This phenomenon gains clarity when read alongside **2 Kings 22:8** and **2 Chronicles 34:14**, where the High Priest Hilkiah rediscovers the Torah scroll of Moses, likely written in ʿIḇrît. That rediscovered script predated the Ezra-led script change recorded in **Sanhedrin 21b**. Daniel, having preserved literacy in this earlier form, did not need an interpreter—he recognized the covenantal language that had been forgotten by others. This incident illustrates that prophetic vision can hinge not merely on divine insight, but on **preserved sacred literacy**.

TIMELINE OF THE ORAL TORAH

TEXT	Oral texts only	Oral texts only	Oral texts only	Mishnah	Talmud
TRANSMISSION	Moses, Joshua, Elders	Prophets and scholars	*Zugot* (Pairs)	*Tana'im* (Teachers)	*Amora'im* (Reciters)
TRADITIONAL DATES	1300-1200 BCE (Traditional)	1200-200 BCE	200 BCE - 0 CE	0 - 200 CE	200-500 CE

Figure 3. Zygote to Geonim Timeline – Showing the Oral Tradition's Transition Through Tannaim, Amoraim, Savoraim, and Geonim.

Abstract:

The Oral Law did not arise spontaneously but was a layered process through history, forming what we now know as the Mishnah, Talmud, and Midrashim.

The timeline of transmission is as follows: Tannaim (10–220 CE), Amoraim (220–500 CE), Savoraim (500–650 CE), and Geonim (650–1038 CE).

This development ensured the survival of Torah she-be'al peh—the Oral Torah—as it expanded from memorized rulings to compiled rabbinic code.

Zechariah's Vision: Four Horns vs. Four Carpenters –
Messiah ben David, ben Yosef, Eliyahu, Melchizedek.
A woman shall encompass a man (Jer. 31:22.)

Figure 4. Zechariah's Vision – The Four Horns vs. the Four
Carpenters (Messiah ben David, ben Yosef, Eliyahu,
Melchizedek?).

MESSIANIC ARCHETYPES AND THEIR FUNCTIONS

DIAGRAM OF ROLES ACROSS THE PROPHETS AND WRITINGS

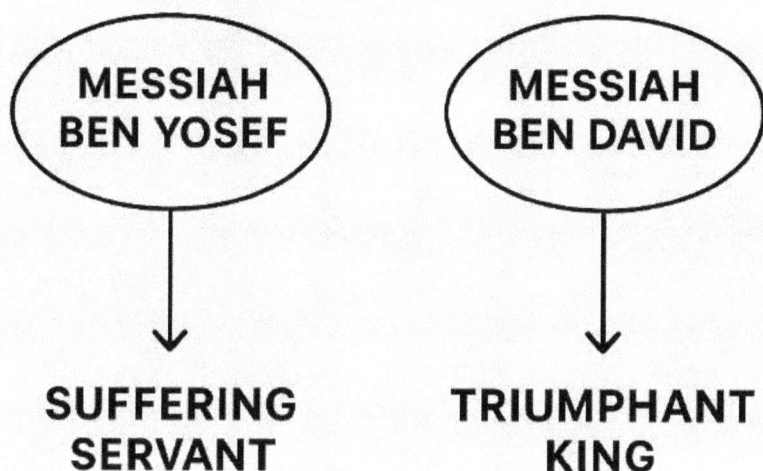

MESSIAH BEN YOSEF

MESSIAH BEN DAVID

SUFFERING SERVANT

TRIUMPHANT KING

Figure 5. Messianic Archetypes and Their Functions

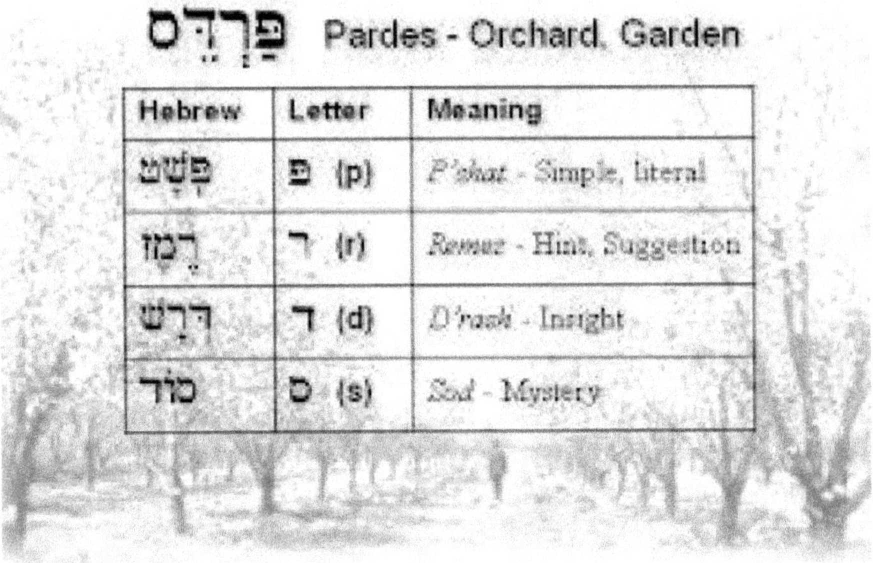

פַּרְדֵּס Pardes - Orchard, Garden

Hebrew	Letter	Meaning
פְּשָׁט	פ (p)	P'shat - Simple, literal
רֶמֶז	ר (r)	Remez - Hint, Suggestion
דְּרַשׁ	ד (d)	D'rash - Insight
סוֹד	ס (s)	Sod - Mystery

Figure 6. PARDES Tree – Four Levels of Hebrew Scriptural Interpretation: P'shat, Remez, D'rash, and Sod.

The PARDES Method

The method of Hebrew scriptural interpretation is traditionally known by the acronym PARDES (פרדס):

- P'shat (פשט) – the simple, literal meaning.
- Remez (רמז) – the hint or allegorical level.
- D'rash (דרש) – the interpretive, homiletical level.
- Sod (סוד) – the secret, mystical insight.

This fourfold paradigm affirms that Torah speaks in layers, to intellect, soul, and spirit alike (cf. Ezra 7:12; 2 Chronicles 24:27; 13:22).

Babylonian Talmud. Sanhedrin 21b, 98b; Sukkah 52b; Menachot 20b.

Kaplan, Aryeh, trans. *Sefer Yetzirah: The Book of Creation*. York Beach: Weiser Books, 1997.

About the Author

Author: *Tovi Mickel* מורה טובי מִיכָאֵל

Parentage: Son of Dr. TeRaze Williams Mickle (Ph.D) and Dr. Toby Lee Mickle (Ph.D)

Hebrew Instructor: Rosh Moreh Avdiel Ben Levi (*Learn Torah Hebrew Academy*)

Affiliated Studies: Grand Canyon University (Theology)

Academic Distinction: Member, *National Society of Collegiate Scholars (NSCS), Class of 2016*

Phrase of Foundation: *Joshua 1:8*

לֹא־יָמוּשׁ סֵפֶר הַתּוֹרָה הַזֶּה מִפִּיךָ וְהָגִיתָ בּוֹ יוֹמָם וָלַיְלָה לְמַעַן תִּשְׁמֹר לַעֲשׂוֹת כְּכָל־הַכָּתוּב בּוֹ כִּי־אָז תַּצְלִיחַ אֶת־דְּרָכֶךָ וְאָז תַּשְׂכִּיל:

"Let not this Book of the Teaching depart from your lips; meditate on it day and night, that you may observe faithfully all that is written in it. Then you shall prosper in your way and have success."

Moreh Tovi Mickel is a Hebraic researcher, theologian, and linguist whose work explores Afro-diasporic prophetic memory, canon formation, and scriptural restoration. He is a **shortlisted finalist for the Society of Biblical Literature's Bernadette J. Brooten Award (2025)** for excellence in gender and feminist theology—recognized for Chapters 7 and 17 and Appendix P of this work. A scholar member of the **Society of Biblical Literature** and an **honored inductee of the National Society of Collegiate Scholars (2016)**, Mickel engages over **500 citations drawn from more than 180 academic sources** across theology, linguistics, and postcolonial studies. His current research is under peer review with editors at **Taylor & Francis** (*African and Black Diaspora: An International Journal*).

He is the founder & creator of *Roots Reclaimed: Voices of the Remnant*, a multimedia platform that bridges academic theology with diasporic heritage and prophetic reclamation for a global audience.